D1715205

The Ethics of Total Confinement

American Psychology-Law Society Series

Series Editor
Ronald Roesch

Editorial Board
Gail S. Goodman
Thomas Grisso
Craig Haney
Kirk Heilbrun
John Monahan
Marlene Moretti
Edward P. Mulvey
J. Don Read
N. Dickon Reppucci
Gary L. Wells
Lawrence S. Wrightsman
Patricia A. Zapf

Books in the Series

Trial Consulting
Amy J. Posey and Lawrence S. Wrightsman

Death by Design
Craig Haney

Psychological Injuries
William J. Koch, Kevin S. Douglas, Tonia L. Nicholls, and Melanie L. O'Neill

Emergency Department Treatment of the Psychiatric Patient
Susan Stefan

The Psychology of the Supreme Court
Lawrence S. Wrightsman

Proving the Unprovable
Christopher Slobogin

Adolescents, Media, and the Law
Roger J.R. Levesque

Oral Arguments Before the Supreme Court
Lawrence S. Wrightsman

God in the Courtroom
Brian H. Bornstein and Monica K. Miller

Expert Testimony on the Psychology of Eyewitness Identification
Edited by Brian L. Cutler

The Psychology of Judicial Decision-Making
Edited by David Klein and Gregory Mitchell

The Miranda Ruling: Its Past, Present, and Future
Lawrence S. Wrightsman and Mary L. Pitman

Juveniles at Risk: A Plea for Preventive Justice
Christopher Slobogin and Mark R. Fondacaro

The Ethics of Total Confinement
Bruce A. Arrigo, Heather Y. Bersot, and Brian G. Sellers

GEORGIAN COLLEGE LIBRARY

GEBL-BK
#83.10

The Ethics of Total Confinement
A Critique of Madness, Citizenship,
and Social Justice

Bruce A. Arrigo

Heather Y. Bersot

Brian G. Sellers

DISCARD

Library Commons
Georgian College
One Georgian Drive
Barrie, ON
L4M 3X9

OXFORD
UNIVERSITY PRESS

OXFORD
UNIVERSITY PRESS

Oxford University Press, Inc., publishes works that further
Oxford University's objective of excellence
in research, scholarship, and education.

Oxford   New York
Auckland   Cape Town   Dar es Salaam   Hong Kong   Karachi
Kuala Lumpur   Madrid   Melbourne   Mexico City   Nairobi
New Delhi   Shanghai   Taipei   Toronto

With offices in
Argentina   Austria   Brazil   Chile   Czech Republic   France   Greece
Guatemala   Hungary   Italy   Japan   Poland   Portugal   Singapore
South Korea   Switzerland   Thailand   Turkey   Ukraine   Vietnam

Copyright © 2011 by Oxford University Press, Inc.

Published by Oxford University Press, Inc.
198 Madison Avenue, New York, New York 10016
www.oup.com

Oxford is a registered trademark of Oxford University Press

All rights reserved. No part of this publication may be reproduced,
stored in a retrieval system, or transmitted, in any form or by any means,
electronic, mechanical, photocopying, recording, or otherwise,
without the prior permission of Oxford University Press.

Library of Congress Cataloging-in-Publication Data

Arrigo, Bruce A.
   The ethics of total confinement : a critique of madness, citizenship,
and social justice / Bruce A. Arrigo, Heather Y. Bersot, Brian G. Sellers.
      p. cm. — (American Psychology-Law Society series)
   Includes bibliographical references.
   ISBN 978-0-19-537221-2
   1. Mentally ill offenders—Legal status, laws, etc. 2. Law—Philosophy.
3. Mental health laws. 4. Solitary confinement. 5. Mentally ill—Care—Moral and ethical aspects.
6. Mentally ill—Commitment and detention. 7. Insanity (Law)—United States. 8. Criminal liability.
9. Punishment—United States. I. Bersot, Heather Y. II. Sellers, Brian G. III. Title.
   K5077.A95 2011
   365'.60874—dc22

                                                          2010048459

XXXXXXXXXXXXXX

Printed in the United States of America
on acid-free paper

For our Critics,
That this book serves as a meditative reminder:
Justice practiced mutually and dynamically is
Citizenship lived virtuously and transformatively.
This is why captivity's release is character's promise.
Its habitual celebration is our praxis invitation
To you, for all, always and already,
Ever more humanely, again and anew.

Series Foreword

This book series is sponsored by the American Psychology-Law Society (APLS). APLS is an interdisciplinary organization devoted to scholarship, practice, and public service in psychology and law. Its goals include advancing the contributions of psychology to the understanding of law and legal institutions through basic and applied research; promoting the education of psychologists in matters of law and the education of legal personnel in matters of psychology; and informing the psychological and legal communities and the general public of current research, educational, and service activities in the field of psychology and law. APLS membership includes psychologists from the academic research and clinical practice communities as well as members of the legal community. Research and practice is represented in both the civil and criminal legal arenas. APLS has chosen Oxford University Press as a strategic partner because of its commitment to scholarship, quality, and the international dissemination of ideas. These strengths will help APLS reach its goal of educating the psychology and legal professions and the general public about important developments in psychology and law. The focus of the book series reflects the diversity of the field of psychology and law, as we continue to publish books on a broad range of topics.

In the latest book in the series, *The Ethics of Total Confinement: A Critique of Madness, Citizenship, and Social Justice*, Bruce Arrigo, Heather Bersot, and Brian Sellers apply a psychological jurisprudence perspective to examine the ethical and legal issues regarding Goffman's notion of total confinement. Drawing on Arrigo's prior writings extending Goffman's work, the authors focus on three key populations in which total confinement is evident: *(1)* adolescents who are waived to adult court, *(2)* prison inmates with mental health problems placed in solitary confinement, and *(3)* sexually violent predators subjected to civil commitment, community notification, and sex offender registration. Their creative analysis focuses on a review of empirical research and case law as it affects all parties involved in the confinement of individuals. Through an analysis of the text of representative court cases, Arrigo and his co-authors seek to understand jurisprudential intent (underlying attitudes, perceptions, and beliefs of the judges) as well at the underlying moral philosophy that is reflected in the court decisions. For example, in the context of waiver cases, they find that court decisions suggest that the interests of state and community are weighed more heavily than the needs of the youth. The authors review the empirical research on the often negative impact on youth that results from waiver to adult court and conclude that the courts fail to consider the consequences that youth face in the adult criminal justice system. They apply the same analysis and come to similar conclusions about how the courts favor perceived public demands over the rights and needs of individuals. Not content to simply identify the impact of total confinement, the authors conclude with their recommendations for legal reform. These reforms are based on the application of policy based on a model of justice that would reflect the concepts of restorative justice, therapeutic jurisprudence, and commonsense justice. As such, this book will be of interest to researchers, legal professionals, and policymakers.

Ronald Roesch
Series Editor

Preface

The ethics of total confinement: A critique of madness, citizenship, and social justice examines the phenomena of captivity and risk management. This examination is based on key insights derived from psychological jurisprudence (PJ) understood as a novel and experimental theory, method, and type of praxis. As theory, PJ indicates that captivity extends not only to the kept but also to their keepers, managers, and watchers. The harm of this captivity is both existential and material in its composition and effects, and it includes harms of reduction (limits on being, on one's humanity) and harms of repression (denials of becoming, of one's transforming potential). Sustaining this captivity is madness for one and all. This is especially the case in an era of total confinement where potential threat is contained or avoided through excessive investments in hypervigilance and panopticism. These disciplinary techniques help to manage the risk that fear of crime and fear of would-be criminals incompletely and inadequately signify. Risk management is maintained through its conditions of control. These conditions include interactive and interconnected symbolic, linguistic, material, and cultural influences. These intensities co-produce captivity and nurture its ubiquity.

As method, PJ considers the question of citizenship, of restoring it and of revolutionizing it, guided by PJ's Aristotelian-derived normative theory. This theory holds that the embodied practice of excellence (or of living virtuously) is dynamic, it evolves. Celebrating human flourishing, then, is about cultivating transformative habits of character. These evolving habits of character— when consumed, spoken, inscribed, and reproduced—have the nearest power to create human/social change, to release us from our captivity, and to insight-fully re-diagnose the madness that presently renders us a mere shadow of who we could be or could become. Advancing this citizenship is a studious pursuit.

As praxis, PJ affirms the interactive link between *thinking about* and *doing* social justice. Theory and action are inseparable and interdependent in this change-oriented and solution-focused endeavor. The possibility of change (i.e., growing individual well-being, communal good, and societal accord) begins as an exercise in critique (i.e., the solution). The critique considers how individual responsibility and institutional accountability co-habitate justice. An assessment of this self–society cohabitation is necessary as it provides a key binary framing from which to explore the possibility of one being and the potential in one becoming more fully human. Undertaking efforts that further actualize this more complete flourishing or mutating self-excellence (the subject-in-process) is a praxis response to captivity, risk management, and the forces that support both. As praxis strategy, cultivating transforming habits of character entails reflexivity or mindfulness. Mindfulness is about dis/re-engaging the images, texts, embodiments, and cultural re-presentations of each that sustain harms of reduction and/or repression for the kept and their keepers, for their managers and their watchers. This praxis strategy is about *overcoming* the forms and forces of captivity that engender harm. This strategy—as an emergent pact for, by, and about the self–society mutuality—awaits additional development; it is the journey for a people yet to come. But this is the journey of thinking about and doing social justice ever more humanely, collectively, virtuously.

To demonstrate the contributions of PJ—particularly in its innovative utility for theory, method, and praxis—three total confinement issues in mental health law are investigated. These issues sourced in prevailing and/or precedent-setting case law include: delinquent juveniles waived to the adult system found competent to stand trial despite developmental maturity problems; psychiatrically disordered offenders placed in long-term disciplin-ary segregation where said isolation is not deemed cruel and unusual punish-ment; and adjudicated sexually violent predators subjected to multiple forms of civil inspection and communal surveillance absent documented or continued evidence that these re-entry correctives work effectively or are even necessary. The judicial endorsement of these practices by way of court decision-making problematically criminalizes, pathologizes, and demonizes citizens. Total confinement's teleology is to reify such constructs. When the legal apparatus legitimizes this reification, it is symptomatic of systemic pathology, of social disease, of risk management gone awry. An investigation of this court-level madness; the citizenship that these legal cases ostensibly promote and neglect; and the justice policy that *could be* for offenders, victims, and the communities that unite them all in each examined instance of total confinement are the subject of detailed analysis and probing commentary.

The book concludes with a series of provocative, yet sensible, recommendations in theory development; methodology and future research; immediate and emergent praxis interventions; pedagogy and (continual) training; and institutional practice, programming, and policy. The relevance of these proposed reforms for the legal, psychiatric, clinical forensic, scholarly academic, bioethical, and human service/social welfare communities is both considerable and varied. Collectively, these change initiatives suggest several vibrant directions by which to activate captivity's release, to re-evaluate the risk management thesis, and to experience character's promise in our lives, in the lives of others, in mental health law, and in all expressions of dynamic human/social cohabitation.

Bruce A. Arrigo
Heather Y. Bersot
Brian G. Sellers
Fall, 2010

Acknowledgments

No book comes to completion without the support, generosity, and counsel of many individuals. This volume is certainly no exception to this long-standing and time honored practice. We thank our anonymous reviewers who, very early on, saw considerable promise in this project. We are indebted to the series editor, Ron Roesch, who patiently allowed our ideas to evolve over time until we found our collective voice. Our families and friends deserve praiseworthy recognition. Collaborative writing can be a selfishly consuming enterprise, especially when work demands trump important obligations to loved ones and other intimates. They willingly provided the requisite space and time that sustained and grew our individual and collective research, reflection, and writing energies. Finally, we thank Northwestern University School of Law and Indiana State University (particularly David Polizzi) for allowing us to reproduce, in verbatim or modified form, portions of our previously published work. Chapter 2 represents a considerably revised version of "Adolescent transfer, developmental maturity, and adjudicative competence: An ethical and justice policy inquiry," that appeared in the *Journal of Criminal Law and Criminology*, *99*, 435–488 (2009). Chapter 3 represents a considerably revised version of "Solitary confinement, inmate mental health, and cruel and unusual punishment: An ethical and justice policy inquiry," that appeared in the *Journal of Theoretical and Philosophical Criminology*, *2(3)*, 1–82 (2010). Finally, we thank Candice Shepard, J.D. for her throughness in preparing the indexes.

Contents

The Ethics of Total Confinement

Introduction

On Madness, Citizenship,
and Social Justice

Total Confinement: Diagnosing Madness

The phenomenon of *total confinement* takes as its origins Goffman's (1961) classic social-psychological critique of *total institutions* and extends through Arrigo and Milovanovic's (2010) probing cultural-philosophical disputation regarding the *society of captives*. Both treatises, in overlapping yet distinct ways, recognized how the exercise of social control—wielded by institutions through their agents—normalizes violence for the kept (prisoners) and their keepers (those who imprison), for their managers (those who administrate imprisonment) and their watchers (the general public). This violence is the power to harm, to deny another person their humanity (Henry & Milovanovic, 1996). This harm as denial can manifest itself through formal or informal mechanisms of restraint/surveillance (e.g., solitary confinement; the underground pariah economy of prisons), as well through conscious or unconscious belief systems (e.g., the mentally ill are diseased, deviant, and dangerous; juveniles who do the "crime" must do the "time;" sexually violent predators [SVPs] are less than human).

In the broader realm of health and social welfare, the scope of total confinement is both gripping and arresting. Its ambit includes such practices as relaxed civil commitment statutes (Saks, 2002); city-wide sweeps of the homeless (Failer, 2002); heightened border patrol efforts targeting illegal immigrants (Andreas, 2009); electronic home monitoring of paroled offenders (MacKenzie, 2006); inspection of non-criminal suspects (Zureik & Salter, 2006); and the legal application of brain imaging technology for trial fitness, criminal responsibility,

3

and competency to execute determinations (Gordon, 2005). These practices are indicative of the ominous *risk society* of which Beck (1992, 2009) and, to a large though varying extent, other commentators (e.g., Hudson, 2003; O'Malley, 1998, 2004; Rhodes, 2004; Simon, 2009) have steadfastly described and perilously warned. This is a society in which threat-avoidance strategies, as potent (and at times insidious) forms of cooptation, presumably promote safety and security for the collective good but often operate at the expense of individual human flourishing (e.g., Arrigo, 2007). Indeed, when the logic of risk management governs choice, action, and progress, policy efforts that support experimentation and innovation are not simply perceived generally with caution, they are interpreted mostly as hazardous. This is the disturbing prism through which total confinement practices are currently enacted, nurtured, and sustained.

However, amidst the burgeoning contemporary landscape of evidenced-based research, the question is whether endorsing the sundry practices of total confinement is, nonetheless, a legitimate enterprise? This question draws attention to the existing social and behavioral science literature regarding the aforementioned (and related) topics. At issue is whether, and to what degree, valid and reliable studies repeatedly demonstrate the empirical sound-ness of such crime and justice policies, absent politics whose intention often advances specialized (and socially stigmatizing/marginalizing) interests consistent with the state's corrosive power to regulate dissent and impose compli-ance (Scranton, 2007). Regrettably to date, scant scientific evidence exists substantiating the need to maintain the previously identified total confine-ment practices. On its face, this statement may seem both problematic and polemical. But the reality is that more (rather than less) human injury and social harm occurs for all those participating in and subjected to such techniques of disciplining and normalization (e.g., Foucault, 1965, 1977). These techniques render the logic of total confinement a kind of panoptic or systemic pathology (Fromm, 1994) whose source is unexamined fear (Simon, 2009) that breeds a spiraling culture of simulated and hypervigilant control *ad infinitum* (Bogard, 1996; Lyon, 2006). Once again, this injury and harm extend from the kept to their keepers, from their managers to their watchers. Clearly, this disabling and all-encompassing logic is nothing short of *madness!*

The present inquiry investigates this madness at the nexus of law, psychology, and crime. The principal and strategic point of access is the ethical reasoning that underscores and informs three longstanding and controversial total confinement practices. In particular, these include: *(1)* developmentally immature juveniles waived to the adult system declared competent to stand trial; *(2)* incarcerates with pre-existing mental health conditions placed in long-term punitive isolation; and *(3)* sex offenders subjected to criminal/civil incarceration followed by communal shaming and public inspection. In each instance, the legal apparatus assumes a promi-nent role in rendering court decisions that sustain such disciplinary and normalizing captivity. These are practices that criminalize, pathologize, and demonize. Not surprising, then, any targeted examination of the judicial decision making that affirms the logic of total confinement is an invitation to rethink the essential ethics by which courts increasingly control some of society's most troubled, vulnerable, and distressed citizens (e.g., juveniles, persons with psychiatric disorders, sex offenders). This regulation represents a type of governmentality that reduces these citizens to the status of docile bodies whose captivity is deemed healthy, natural, and inevitable (Arrigo & Milovanovic, 2010; *see also* Sykes, 1958).

Psychological Jurisprudence: Advancing Citizenship

The nexus that is the law–psychology–crime divide is rich and robust in its interdisciplinarity. Moreover, according to some investigators, three approaches are relevant to the education, training, and study of this subspecialization (Arrigo, 2001; Arrigo & Fox, 2009). These approaches consist of: *(1)* the *clinical* perspective, emphasizing research and practice in *forensic psychology*; *(2)* the *law and social science* orientation, stressing the science of *legal psychology*; and *(3)* the *law, psychology, and justice* framework, promoting social change and action through theory-sensitive *psychological jurisprudence* (Arrigo & Fox, 2009, pp. 161–163; *see also* Arrigo, 2004a). Admittedly, the three identified approaches are somewhat overlapping and intersecting; however, for purposes of this book, the logic of the law, psychology, and justice model will guide the analysis. This is because the other two frameworks do not fundamentally examine core philosophical questions about the nature of ethics (including related matters such as freedom, rights-claiming, dignity, autonomy, equality, and community) in relation to existing or emerging law–psychology–crime controversies (Fox, 1993, 2001).

   Psychological jurisprudence (PJ) is a relatively recent perspective whose intellectual footing continues to evolve, remaining mostly in process and in search of an overarching and integrative conceptual schema (Arrigo & Fox, 2009). This notwithstanding, three conceptual strains of analysis are discernible in the literature that are relevant to our overall project. The first of these is *dignity-focused* PJ. Its premise is that the values and insights of psychology can enable legal institutions and decision makers to undertake actions that advance the aims of human welfare, communal justice, and societal accord (Melton, 1990; Melton & Saks, 1986). It assumes that the law can establish socially desirable outcomes rather than promote citizen control in the furtherance of state authority or governance by elites (Melton, 1992). The second type of PJ that informs our own enterprise is traceable to the *therapeutic jurisprudence* movement. Its premise is that the law can function as a healing agent, pro-socially impacting the lives of those whom it serves, provided the beneficial and harmful effects of relying on legal rules, procedures, policies, and programs are steadfastly evaluated (Winick & Wexler, 2003). It assumes that this infusion of clinical reasoning and acumen into the law can yield a quality of justice in which courts function much like mental health professionals (Wexler & Winick, 1996). The third variation of PJ uniquely suited to the ensuing research is the *critical paradigm*. Its premise is that the exercise of power is not so much an effect of the law as it is a cause, especially because this power is embedded within and conveyed through the very construction of legal language as sourced within legal texts (Arrigo, 2002a). It assumes that the possibility of achieving citizen justice and communal good requires a careful (re)reading of the concealed values, unspoken interests, and hidden assumptions lodged within various legal documents, including those texts affecting vulnerable, troubled, and distressed individuals and/or collectives (Arrigo, 2003a, 2004b). Taken together, these three key variants of PJ inform and chart the trajectory of the following project and serve as a platform for the theory's focus on the mutuality of human/social justice and change.

The principal methodological strategy appropriated by PJ is textual analysis (Arrigo, 1993, 2003b). Specifically in the context of legal inquiry, the precedent-setting and/or prevailing judicial opinions of a law–psychology–crime cognate area become the source of qualitative (and interpretive) scrutiny. Thus, given this book's emphasis on the ethics of total confinement, three distinct data sets will be systematically investigated. These include the precedent-setting and/or prevailing court decisions concerning: *(1)* adolescent waiver, developmental maturity, and adjudicative competence; *(2)* inmate mental health, long-term disciplinary isolation, and cruel and unusual punishment; and *(3)* SVPs, criminal/civil incarceration, and community re-entry.

For purposes of each data set, two levels of textual analysis will be featured. The first level locates the case's *plain meaning* as derived from the legal narrative itself. Once identified as such, the essential jurisprudential intent (e.g., attitudes, perceptions, beliefs) situated within this plain meaning then can be specified. Stated differently, to ascertain the core ethical reasoning that underscores and informs a court's temperament, detailing plain meaning is important. The second level of qualitative inquiry examines the moral philosophy (i.e., ethical formalism, consequentialism, or Aristotelian virtue) embedded in and conveyed through the plain meaning (i.e., the judicial intention and temperament) of a case. This additional stage of textual scrutiny then makes it possible to carefully interpret the overall ethics on which courts rely when sustaining the practices of total confinement. This interpretive process includes an assessment of the fundamental moral philosophy for: *(1)* each case; *(2)* all cases within each of the three data sets; and *(3)* all cases across the three data sets.[1]

Because this book seeks to translate worthwhile theory into meaningful policy, its attention to PJ must be assessed within this necessary rubric. Consistent with this view, we acknowledge that PJ encompasses "theories that describe, explain, and predict law by reference to human behavior" (Small, 1993, p. 11). However, as a practical matter, the theory possesses the capacity to assist judges and legislators, explaining how they *should* make decisions guided by sensible values and pertinent data. These values and data emphasize not merely what law *is* but what law *ought to be* (e.g., Darley Fulero, Haney, & Tyler, 2002; Melton, 1992). The core assumption underlying this rationale is that the legal, mental health, and justice systems are, in effect, "totalizing apparatuses" that can engender harm (Arrigo, 2004a, p. vii). Thus, PJ's theory-to-policy transformative agenda attempts to pragmatically undertake this effort, mindful of the distinct needs of offenders, victims, and the larger society to which both are bound (Arrigo, 2002a; Fox, 1993; Ogloff, 2002). Clearly, then, reliance on PJ implies a kind of deliberate movement from sound theory to rigorous research, whose aim is to identify meaningful reform and practical change tempered by the values of justice, humanism, and well-being.

Strategies of Reform: Seeking Social Justice

Within the domain of PJ, several dominant practices (with corresponding principles) have emerged that attempt to grow the law–psychology–justice agenda, especially in an effort to secure what is best for victims, offenders, and the public more generally. Chief among these practices are: *(1)* commonsense justice, *(2)* therapeutic jurisprudence, and *(3)* restorative justice. Each of these notions is summarily discussed below.

Finkel's (1995) notion of commonsense justice evolved from an understanding that although the law has specified an "objective" path for society to follow in deciding guilt or innocence, this path does not always take into account the ordinary citizen's notion of what is just and fair. Thus, commonsense justice attempts to include community sentiment (the judgment of the people at large) so that the law's more "subjective" character can be honored (Huss, Tomkins, Garbin, Schopp, & Killian, 2006; Finkel, 1997). Incorporating the legal, moral, and psychological reasoning adopted by everyday people enables them to displace the (misguided) direction the law sets forth so that more equitable decision making can be pursued. This is decision making that endeavors to perfect and complete the law (Finkel, 1995 p. 3).

Building on our previous observations concerning therapeutic jurisprudence, others have defined it as "the use of social science to study [where and how] a legal rule or practice promotes the psychological and physical well-being of the people it affects" (Slobogin, 1995, p. 196; *see also*, Schma, Kjervik, & Petrucci, 2005). In other words, therapeutic jurisprudence seeks to understand the potential for law to act as a healing agent (e.g., Wexler & Winick, 1996; Winick & Wexler, 2003). The point of this practice is to address both civil disputes (Perlin, Gould, & Dorfman, 1995; McGuire, 2000) and criminal concerns (Birgden, 2007; Glaser, 2003) in mental health law, wherein salubrious and efficacious outcomes are based on psychological values and insights (Winick, 1997).

Restorative justice is a form of mediated reconciliation (Van Ness & Heetderks Strong, 2007; Zehr & Toews, 2004). Its goal is to repair the harm and suffering that follows in the wake of interpersonal, organizational, or even global violence. This is injury that impacts the victim, the offender, and the community to which all opposing parties belong (Sullivan & Tifft, 2005). Candid disclosures and humanistic dialogue guide the healing process in which genuine, meaningful, and, ideally, transformative resolutions are sought (e.g., Bazemore & Boba, 2007; Coker, 2006; Levine, 2000; Umbreit, Coates, & Armour, 2006).

Interestingly, although not identified as such, these collective practices are consistent with virtue-based ethics. Articulated most explicitly and systematically in Aristotle's treatise, *Nichomachean Ethics* (2000), this version of moral philosophy seeks to promote a type of human excellence that is rooted in reason whereby one's character is not determined so much by what one does (e.g., weighing competing interests; endorsing rights, duties, and obligations) but, instead, is more an expression of living virtuously (Williams & Arrigo, 2008, pp. 247–262). The highest purpose of this existence is to embody *eudaimonia* (a flourishing or excellence in being), happiness, or a fulfilled life. Aristotle's inquiry led him to explore those virtues that most profoundly facilitate such human flourishing. These are *habits* of character learned through practice; these are qualities that become a part of the person through regularly exercising their use.[2] Indeed, as Aristotle (1976) noted:

> Anything that we have to learn to do we learn by the actual doing of
> it. People become builders by building and instrumentalists by
> playing instruments. Similarly, we become just by performing just
> acts, temperate by performing temperate ones, brave by performing
> braves ones (pp. 91–92).

At the core of commonsense justice, therapeutic jurisprudence, and restorative justice is the goal of growing the character of all parties concerned, while simultaneously repairing the harm and reducing the non-therapeutic effects that negatively impact those involved in a civil or criminal conflict. Indeed, rather than emphasizing the infliction of punishment for retributive ends, these three law, psychology, and justice notions endorse, mostly unknowingly although certainly implicitly, Aristotelian moral philosophy. In short, they help to seed and encourage the development of personal character and moral virtue among offenders, victims, and the community to which both are intimately connected. Commonsense justice accomplishes this by promoting the public's reasoned participation in and felt regard for legal decision making. Therapeutic jurisprudence does this by assessing where and how the rule of law can be beneficial or harmful to citizens. Restorative justice achieves this by fostering a culture of forgiveness and compassion among warring individuals or groups. The collective effect of these three practices, then, is the cultivation of an integrity-based society. This is a society in which the moral fiber of individuals is more fully embraced and the flourishing prospects for human justice are more completely pursued. These three reformist strategies, then, constitute habits of ethical engagement in PJ whose aim is to grow a deeper, more fully affirming quality of social justice for the kept and their keepers, for their managers and their watchers.

Organization of the Book

The Ethics of Total Confinement: A Critique of Madness, Citizenship, and Social Justice is divided into three substantive sections. Section 1 focuses on relevant theory, Section 2 focuses on targeted applications, and Section 3 focuses on policy implications. Section 1 consists of one substantive chapter, Section 2 includes three substantive chapters, and Section 3 is composed of two substantive chapters. Some brief background information for each chapter is supplied below.

Chapter 1: The Ethics of Psychological Jurisprudence

This chapter examines prevailing ethical theory, including: *(1)* ethical formalism and deontological *prima facie* duties; *(2)* consequentialism (consisting of ethical egoism, contractualism, and utilitarianism); and *(3)* Aristotelian virtue philosophy (featuring feminist care ethics). The limits of each ethical school of thought and its variants are presented. The relevance of turning to moral philosophy for the purpose of psychological jurisprudential theorizing and law–psychology–crime research is described. This includes commentary on how existing strategies (restorative justice, therapeutic jurisprudence, and commonsense justice) collectively represent an integrative type of ethic that is consistent with the humanizing intentions of PJ. Several important observations on methodological details (i.e., textual legal analysis) conclude the chapter.

Chapter 2: Juvenile Transfer, Developmental Maturity, and Competency to Stand Trial

This chapter provides background on the transfer process, reviews the social and behavioral science literature on developmental maturity, and describes the concept of mental health trial fitness. The prevailing case law in this law–psychology–crime cognate area is identified ($n = 6$)—including how these court opinions were selected—and the two-phase textual analysis of these decisions is delineated consistent with the methodological objectives of PJ.

Although the existing scientific literature repeatedly demonstrates that delinquent youth experience significant cognitive/affective deficits rendering them developmentally immature, they are nonetheless found competent to stand trial and subsequently adjudicated in adult criminal court. Consistent with this rationale, the first level of textual analysis will reveal the courts' preference for promoting the interests of "tough on crime" retributive logic that regards wayward youth as dangerous offenders likely to recidivate. The second level of textual analysis will indicate how this jurisprudential reasoning is informed principally by utilitarian moral philosophy that positions the needs of an organized society and the welfare of those victimized (or potentially harmed) against the adolescent's amenability to treatment, rehabilitation, and recovery. When contrasted with the philosophical underpinnings of PJ, it will be shown that the courts' jurisprudential ethic on the matter of adolescent transfer, developmental maturity, and adjudicative competence does not grow excellence in character for all parties concerned. Indeed, it is not as fully responsive as it could (and should) be to the needs of victims, offenders, and the community that unites both. The implications of these findings are assessed in relation to the dynamics of madness, citizenship, and social justice.

Chapter 3: Inmate Mental Health, Solitary Confinement, and Cruel and Unusual Punishment

This chapter provides background on the types of solitary confinement (administrative/disciplinary; short/long-term), reviews the social and behavioral science literature on inmate mental health and segregation, and describes the concept of isolation for incarcerates with pre-existing mental health conditions in relation to cruel and unusual punishment. The prevailing case law in this law–psychology–crime cognate area is identified ($n = 6$)—including how these court opinions were selected—and the two-phase textual analysis of these decisions is outlined consistent with the methodological aims of PJ.

Although the extant empirical research consistently documents that incarcerates with pre-existing psychiatric conditions are likely to experience considerable health/mental health consequences from sustained exposure to solitary confinement, these penal conditions are not always deemed cruel and unusual punishment by the courts. Consistent with this rationale, the first level of textual analysis will reveal the courts' preference for promoting the interests of staff and other inmates' safety, as well as prison security, given the risk of harm that mentally ill offenders potentially represent to themselves and/or others. The second level of textual analysis will indicate how this jurisprudential reasoning (understood as risk avoidance logic through incapacitation) is principally informed by utilitarian moral philosophy that positions the needs of some groups (correctional personnel, other prisoners) against the liberty rights of other groups (mentally ill offenders), wherein the latter are deemed dangerous and therefore less than fully deserving of said constitutional protections. The second level of textual analysis will also specify how the courts' jurisprudential reasoning is informed by deontological moral philosophy (i.e., duty/obligation to protect prison staff/inmates and to promote institutional security). When the second level of textual analysis is contrasted with the philosophical underpinnings of PJ, it will be shown that the courts' jurisprudential ethic on the matter of inmate mental health, solitary confinement, and cruel and unusual punishment does not grow excellence in character for all parties concerned. Indeed, it is not as fully responsive as it could (and should) be to the needs of all those who live/work within correctional environs. The implications of these findings are reviewed in relation to the dynamics of madness, citizenship, and social justice.

Chapter 4: Sexually Violent Predators, Criminal and Civil Confinement, and Community Re-Entry

This chapter provides background on SVPs, reviews the social and behavioral science literature documenting the recidivism effects of confinement, and describes the concept of community re-entry (i.e., notification and offender registries). The precedent-setting case law in this law–psychology–crime cognate area is identified ($n = 5$)—including how these court opinions were selected—and the two-phase textual analysis of these decisions is explained consistent with the purposes of PJ.

Although social and behavioral science research routinely indicates that the rate of recidivism and relapse for the majority of formerly adjudicated SVPs is essentially no greater than the rate for non-SVP criminal offenders, civil commitment, community notification, and sex offender registration are all sustained by way of judicial decision-making. Consistent with this rationale, the first level of textual analysis will reveal the courts' preference for promoting the demands of an organized society (e.g., public welfare, community safety, citizen protection) given the risk of harm that convicted sex offenders ostensibly represent. The second level of textual analysis will indicate how this jurisprudential reasoning (understood as risk avoidance logic through detainment, inspection, and monitoring) is principally informed by utilitarian moral philosophy. This ethic positions the needs of the many (i.e., the public) against the needs of the few (convicted sex offenders), wherein the latter are deemed dangerous (less than human) warranting hypervigilant surveillance and panoptic disciplining. When the second level of textual analysis is contrasted with the philosophical underpinnings of PJ, it will be demonstrated that the courts' jurisprudential ethic on the matter of SVPs, criminal and civil confinement, and community re-entry does not grow excellence in character for all parties concerned. Indeed, it is not as responsive as it could (and should) be to the needs of victims, offenders, and the communities that tether and interconnect them. The implications of these findings are considered in relation to the dynamics of madness, citizenship, and social justice.

Chapter 5: Rethinking Total Confinement: Translating Social Theory into Justice Policy

This chapter explores the relevance of PJ as policy. Specifically, several provisional, although concrete, recommendations for legal reform are presented. These proposals for progressive change demonstrate how the law's approach to the three total confinement practices systematically reviewed in Chapters 2, 3, and 4 could (and should) be more in keeping with principles emanating from restorative justice, therapeutic jurisprudence, and commonsense justice. As such, these recommendations explain how dignity, healing, and critique could be advanced by way of the practice of PJ. This includes changes that further more humane judicial decision making, as well as reforms that foster more pro-social dispute resolution by and among other legal actors. Several tentative observations also are enumerated that draw attention to the current barriers that impede the possibility of achieving these well-intentioned policy initiatives.

Conclusions

In recognition of the volume's overall theoretical, methodological, and analytical work, a number of suggestive remarks are outlined that signal a next direction (the "awaiting revolution") in PJ. This direction principally consists of four underdeveloped transformations that warrant additional reflection and commentary. The first of these entails re-diagnosing madness. The second involves re-advancing citizenship. The third consists of revisiting social justice. In each instance, the conditions that control or undermine greater prospects for flourishing and change (from the symbolic to the linguistic, from the material to the cultural) are examined in relation to how they influence and are shaped by the human agency—social structural duality. This is a reference to the experience of total confinement for the kept and their keepers, for their managers and their watchers, and how this captivity can be overcome dynamically. Mindful of these observations, the fourth metamorphosis proposes immediate and practical reforms in the realm legal education, clinical/mental health training and practice, future research, as well as human/social welfare programming and policy.

Appendixes

Given the comprehensive textual scrutiny that is so central to this book's assessment of total confinement practices, three distinct appendixes are constructed. This includes one appendix for each of the three data sets. Each appendix documents the comprehensive plain meaning results themselves. Additionally, each application chapter includes two tables. The first of these identifies the jurisprudential intent for the cases constituting the data set as derived from the plain meaning results. The second of these specifies the underlying ethical reasoning or logic by which judicial temperament is conveyed through the cases forming the data set.

1

The Ethics of Psychological Jurisprudence

Introduction

In the traditional sense, justice refers to promoting laws, policies, and practices that sustain basic human dignity and grow universal human rights. In the pursuit of *social* justice, we hold not only the criminal accountable for violations of established rules but also the system itself, especially when its transgressions cause injury. The twin dynamics of individual responsibility and institutional accountability promote a quality of justice that suggests the possibility of developing an ethical framework for assessing and resolving wrongdoing seldom advanced or achieved among various democratic cultures or civilizations.[1]

Complicating the establishment of this potential ethical framework are the manifold citizenship needs that a given public voices. For example, a commitment to liberty, fairness, equality, mutual respect, and individual rights—among others—are the focus of justice studies. The public's resolute pursuit of these principles obligates the state (through its institutions and agents) to establish laws that further their material and existential presence, thereby ensuring that governmental compliance, if not steadfast allegiance, will prevail. Along these lines, John Stuart Mill (1989) argued that liberty (freedom from captivity) is what humans desire most; however, safety of person and security of property are the necessary conditions for liberty to realize its maximal abundance. As he reasoned, this, then, is the point at which the state must appropriately intervene, functioning as the ultimate authority and guarantor on such matters.

This autonomy–protection tension is also found within Rousseau's (1968) social contract theory. A degree of liberty is relinquished to the state so that it can assure a modicum of safeguards to the public. These safeguards protect against predatory acts perpetrated by other citizens (Williams & Arrigo, 2008). In fact, the grotesque crimes committed by some individuals or groups can leave the public in a heightened state of fear and panic, especially when they cannot comprehend the magnitude or severity of such gruesome violence. Often, the problem here is determining how much liberty citizens should forfeit in return for the level of safety/security they seek. However, left mostly unresolved by Mill and Rousseau was the nature of ethics that attaches under such conditions of contractual citizenship, mindful of the *twin dynamics* of criminal harm.

Additionally, the rights of offenders must be considered in the pursuit of social justice. Thus, at what point and under what conditions do the fundamental liberties of the accused or even the offender overshadow the victim's unfettered welfare and society's unimpeded protection? Clearly, a delicate balance is warranted when reaching this determination. But how can it be achieved ethically, and what form would this morality assume? Some argue that equality of liberty is required if this desired equilibrium is to be attained (Hudson, 2003). However, current criminal justice practices—many of which invasively constrain apparent dangerous citizen groups—actually may not be realizing this balance at all (e.g., Simon, 2009). Instead, and often unwittingly, punitive responses can foster more harm than good. Adult and juvenile offenders may lose opportunities to express genuine remorse and undergo meaningful recovery; victims and family members of those injured may experience little to no closure in the wake of their pain and suffering; and the fabric that binds and builds communities may be torn apart absent something more reparative (Strang & Braithwaite, 2001; Sullivan & Tifft, 2005). Here, too, the search for social justice that seeds an ethic steeped in individual responsibility and institutional accountability regrettably remains elusive.

Amid this tumultuous climate, the fear of crime has eroded solidarity, the social contract, so much so recently that the general public hypervigilantly (Baudrillard, 1983a, 1983b) and panoptically (Foucault, 1965, 1977) is receptive to extreme retributive approaches to abating wrongdoing, particularly when committed by vulnerable, troubled, or distressed populations. Three such prominent groups include serious juvenile delinquents, psychologically disordered offenders, and sexually violent predators. These groups present a formidable challenge to criminal justice professionals, treatment and social service agencies, and to a society that does not easily fathom their violence or readily forgive their victimization. These are the logical effects of hypervigilance and panopticism. As such, security through enhanced techniques of punishment takes on a new meaning. Indeed, societal protection is now dominated by the concepts of personal safety and property protection from *perceived* dangerous others (O'Malley, 1998, 2004). In this process of governance through fear (of crime and would-be criminals), the meaning of "justice" becomes synonymous with punishment (Hudson, 2003, p. 203). Moreover, "cosmopolitan" accountability for cultivating a risk-focused and threat-avoidance society (Beck, 1992, 2009) that relentlessly criminalizes, pathologizes, and demonizes remains beyond the purview of targeted scrutiny (Arrigo & Milovanovic, 2009). Given both conditions, prospects for developing an ethic that is sensitive to understanding and addressing individual and organizational forces of harm is largely deferred. This, then, is the point at which total confinement practices are normalized, especially for vulnerable, troubled, or distressed populations. These practices and the system-based mechanisms that sustain them are deemed healthy, natural, and inevitable. As this volume proposes, psychological jurisprudence is a novel and instructive response to dramatically reconceiving—from theory construction to policy formation—such normalization.

To more fully appreciate how total confinement practices obtain for threatening, although disturbed, offender groups, some review of ethical theory is in order. Accordingly, this chapter briefly examines three prevailing schools of normative thought. This cursory assessment considers: *(1)* ethical formalism and deontological *prima facie* duties; *(2)* consequentialism (consisting of ethical egoism, contractualism, and utilitarianism); and *(3)* Aristotelian virtue philosophy (including feminist care ethics). The limitations of each normative theory and their variants are presented. The relevance of turning to moral philosophy for the purpose of psychological jurisprudential theorizing and law–psychology–crime research is described. This involves some commentary on how existing strategies (e.g., common-sense justice, therapeutic jurisprudence, and restorative justice) collectively represent a synthetic type of ethic that is consistent with the humanizing aims of psychological jurisprudence. The chapter concludes with an overview of the methodology used to conduct the qualitative analyses entertained in the subsequent application chapters.

Ethical Schools of Thought: An Overview

Three basic approaches to ethics are discernible in the literature. These include formalism, consequentialism, and virtue-based reasoning. In what follows, the principles embodied by these moral philosophies are summarily recounted. Additionally, applications in relevant research contexts are briefly discussed, particularly where useful to and appropriate for this book's overall law–psychology–crime focus.

Formalism

Formalism is a school of ethical thought wherein the motive or intent of the person determines whether an act is moral or not (Bielefeldt, 2003; Pollock, 2007). Thus, this moral philosophy "shifts attention away from the effects of our actions, placing the focus squarely on the *actions themselves*" (Williams & Arrigo, 2008, p. 216). Formalism is often referred to as deontology or Kantian ethics. Deontology is the practice of behaving out of moral duty because it is deemed "right" rather than because one fears potential or adverse consequences (Albanese, 2006, p. 27; Kant, 2002). Thus, under this moral theory, an act is deemed morally "good" if the agent acts from duty or from what ought to be done because such action is morally good (Dreisbach, 2008, p. 69). In support of this notion, Immanuel Kant identified what he termed the *categorical imperative* (Kant, 2002, p. 216). Categorical imperatives are maxims that are good and morally justified unconditionally. They demand obligatory adherence regardless of personal or unique circumstances. Furthermore, Kant described these categorical maxims—generated from good will and embodied reasoned— as judgments about what constituted absolute moral laws (Dreisbach, 2008; Kant, 2002). Thus, categorical imperatives (e.g., "Never commit murder;" "Never lie, cheat, or steal") are not defined or shaped by any context, and Kant held these "universal laws" to be impervious to the criticisms of ethical relativists and subjectivists (Dreisbach, 2008).

However, Ross (1930) argued that it is possible for an individual to confront a moral dilemma where a choice between two categorical imperatives must be made. In response to this situation, Ross presented the concept of *prima facie* responsibilities. These are "conditional duties" that may be superseded by other obligations because these other obligations possess greater moral importance (Ross, 1930, pp. 19–21). Examples of such conditional duties include, among others, fidelity, prevention of harm, reparation, non-injury, and justice. Above all, Kant deemed human dignity to have the most moral significance; thus, he argued that people should never be used "as a means to some end" (Williams & Arrigo, 2008, pp. 224 & 239). Because Kant postulated that a maxim should always be viewed as a universal law, one's observance of it at all times was considered sacrosanct. However, if the maxim did not attain the status of a universal law, it should be rejected altogether (Kant, 2002; Williams & Arrigo, 2008).

Kant's assertion that one may not justify using another individual as a means to an end (Cahn, 2009; Kant, 2002; Mossman, 2006) emphasizes the moral concept that "*all* human beings have *intrinsic worth* or *dignity*" (Williams & Arrigo, 2008, p. 223). In regard to punishment, Kant believed that it "can never be administered merely as a means for promoting another good either with regard to the criminal . . . or to civil society, but must in all cases be imposed only because the individual on whom it is inflicted has committed a crime" (Shichor, 2006, p. 26). However, Kantian logic holds that violators of the law deserve punishment, thereby making criminal transgressors, like all citizens, responsible for their conduct. This is punishment equaling the severity of one's offensive actions. As he reasoned, justice is sufficiently served through such a retributive approach. Indeed, punishment maintains a legal order that ensures freedom for and autonomy to all yet disciplines those who choose to harm others (Bielefeldt, 2003; Corlett, 2008). However, if and when individuals adopt the perspective that law violators deserve sanctioning (e.g., just deserts) and they interpret their role as agents of a system that morally binds them to administer said punishment for the security of society and/or the welfare of other citizens, then these agents may actually be violating the highest of moral maxims: "using a person as a means to an end" (Williams & Arrigo, 2008, pp. 224 & 239). Here, too, we see how even the intention of administering said punishment could very well be a Kantian ethical concern.

As a duty-based approach to ethical decision making, deontology makes the assumption that the acting agent is rational and aware of his or her obligations. If individuals are in fact rational agents, then the categorical imperatives prescribed by Kant prepare them in advance to anticipate moral dilemmas. This rationally based predictive capacity requires a person to identify the relevant duty necessary to address the ethical problem at hand so that the person can then act accordingly (Dreisbach, 2008). However, the flaw in this logic is that it assumes individuals will act from a common moral duty. Moreover, it assumes that individuals will not justify or endorse ostensibly false duties that might be self-serving or otherwise detrimental to the good will of others. For example, a suicide bomber may feel obligated to blow up a bus of Israeli citizens, although such an act is considered immoral. A major criticism of deontology is that it reinforces the notion of acting out of good intent (i.e., coming from good will) as synonymous with a good act even when the intention may result in negative consequences (Corlett, 2008; Pollock, 2007). Additionally, critics charge that Kant was unsuccessful in precisely defining what morally "good" and "bad" meant, rendering Kantian deontology as nothing more than ambiguously interpretive ethical decision making (Leighton & Reiman, 2001).

In defense of deontology, Ross (1930) argued that *prima facie* duties become intuitively obvious for well-intentioned people (*see also* Dreisbach, 2008, p. 75). However, these duties may not be as apparent as Ross conjectured. For example, one's perceived obligation to protect society at large may be interpreted as a *prima facie* duty, whereby the human rights of the individual are violated because one maxim is superseded by the other. Here, too, the intention/act distinction is relevant ethically. Thus, as Kant acknowledged, we must grapple with the fact that not everyone will abide by categorical moral maxims (Mossman, 2006).

As is apparent, the complexities of human nature can confound the principles set forth by deontology. Hence, the concept of acting always and only from duty presents a host of potential quandaries that may not only be unreasonable but may also be destructive. To be sure, it is not always so clear where one's duty lies, notwithstanding the moral intentions of one's actions (Pollock, 2007, p. 39).

Consequentialism

Following a more strict interpretation of the doctrine, consequentialism asserts that individuals should act in their best interest to ensure optimal effects (i.e., gains) for those actions (Slote, 1985, p. 12). Therefore, unlike deontology, consequentialism focuses on the positive and negative outcomes stemming from behavior instead of the behavior or action itself. Three forms of consequentialist thought exist, and each offers a somewhat modified assessment of this fundamental position. The forms of consequentialism consist of ethical egoism, contractualism, and utilitarianism.

Ethical egoism claims that people are intrinsically motivated by self-interest; thus, they pursue actions and seek outcomes that will benefit themselves over others (Williams & Arrigo, 2008, p. 184). This is an inherent mechanism of self-preservation. Consistent with this view, Thomas Hobbes, a psychological and ethical egoist, wrote in *Leviathan*:

> Every man is enemy to every man . . . wherein men live without other
> security, than what their own strength, and their own invention shall
> furnish . . . there is no place for industry . . . no culture of the earth . . .
> no navigation . . . no knowledge . . . no account of time . . . no
> arts . . . no letters . . . no society; and which is worst of all, continual
> fear, and danger of violent death; and the life of man, solitary,
> poor, nasty, brutish, and short. (Hobbes, 1996, p. 89)

Hobbes' view of the state of nature, or what humankind would be like without formal government, suggests that individuals in pursuit of their own self-interest create an environment of ruthless competitiveness, fear, and insecurity. Hampton (2001, pp. 70–71) appropriated the Hobbesian perspective on self-interest and, by extension, ethical egoism, to explain possible motivations for one's opposition to the law. Specifically, she noted that identifying moral agendas in the furtherance of personal desires helps to account for how the law is or can be egoistically displaced. Such displacement advances laws or legal prescriptions that serve self-regarding, rather than collectivist, interests.

Following the logic of ethical egoism means that the pursuit of one's own greater good leads to moral choice and conduct. As such, individuals have no intrinsic obligation to ensure that the interests and needs of others are met (Banks, 2008; Cahn, 2009). Ayn Rand (1964), Russian immigrant and American philosopher, vehemently defended the egoist perspective based on her objectivist ethics. She acknowledged the possibility of self-sacrifice but critiqued altruism in favor of the self-serving motivation of minimizing relevant consequences affecting one's self (Dreisbach, 2008; Pollock, 2007). Similarly, Hobbes (1996) believed that in the pursuit of self-interest, one obtains the security and comfort needed to enjoy a moral life. Thus, the ethical rationale of egoism encourages individuals to divide themselves into two groups: self versus all others. Unsurprisingly, then, when this logic is fully or largely embodied as a standing practice, it holds the potential for segregation based on race, gender, class, mental health status, and the like.

Ethical objectivists argue that individuals always act out of self-interest, and every act of altruism can be explained away for one reason or another (Rand, 1964). For example, assisting an individual absent receipt of a tangible reward may still cause that person to feel better about his or her act of kindness. Interestingly in this example, self-interest is involved but not so overtly that a claim to it can altogether be proved or disproved. To do so would require faith because the claim cannot be empirically tested. Admittedly, it may be impossible to completely dismiss one's motivation for self-sacrifice as serving some self-satisfying end; however, it is equally difficult to thoroughly rationalize such an act as inherently and altogether self-regarding. Furthermore, as Williams & Arrigo (2008) noted, most people possess an intrinsic positive attitude toward helping others and, as such, it is only through the achievement of goals perceived to be valuable and worthwhile that we experience a pleasant sensation (pp. 109–110). In other words, people do not engage in altruistic activity unless they already have a constructive affinity to it in the first place, wherein their primary motivation is to assist others rather than to promote self-serving ends.

The ethical egoist position that self-preservation and self-interest are instinctual neglects to account for the conflict to which these tenets inevitably would lead. If everyone pursued unbridled personal interests, then exploitative actions by the strong against the weak would quickly materialize and endure (Cahn, 2009; Pollock, 2007). This state of existence is inconsistent with morality. Moreover, evidence of self-centered conduct can be countered by evidence of altruism. Indeed, one's self-interests may easily become irrelevant when accounting for the needs of others, especially because human beings are social creatures often defined by their other-regarding relationships. Thus, to maintain long-term societal welfare, cooperative interactions must follow, and this requires individuals to consider and attend to non-self-interests. Indeed, as Williams & Arrigo (2008) observed, "Morality does not simply entail choices; rather, it involves choices that we make that affect other people" (p. 31).

Contractualism maintains that the establishment of government and its subsequent laws through the notion of a "social pact" or "contract" grants cooperation among individuals and freedom from fear otherwise present in the state of nature (Williams & Arrigo, 2008, p. 193). Jean-Jacques Rousseau (1968), one of the principal architects of this version of consequentialism, noted that "[e]ach of us puts . . . all [our] power in common under the supreme direction of the general will, and, in our capacity, we receive each member as indivisible part of the whole" (p. 192). Thus, contractualism seeks to create the civil nation where moral rules and regulations govern people's actions so that all may co-exist, share in the security the state provides, and engage in unselfishness. The social contract not only legitimizes the need for the state but also the need for nationalized functions such as law enforcement, judicial review, and criminal confinement (Sterba, 2003; Williams & Arrigo, 2008). Indeed, as Rousseau observed, the state's existence permits "us to become fundamentally different types of people" (as cited in Williams & Arrigo, 2008, p. 193). Because the state creates a set of moral rules that provide citizens with the sense of security and welfare that they inherently desire, people are able to genuinely and mutually care about one another (Sterba, 2003).

The contractualist perspective posits the necessity for government to establish laws that ensure the safety and well-being of individuals as a part of its public guarantee. Those who commit crimes against the polis "breach" the social contract and, as a result, must suffer the prescribed punitive course of action. "Under Rousseau's formulation, once . . . the social contract [is broken], the offender is seen as undeserving of its benefits" (Henriques, 2001, p. 194). However, some laws created by the state are unfair to particular segments of the citizenry. As a result, these laws may not provide a sense of security to all and may make it harder for some to peacefully co-exist with others. Under these conditions, said laws would be considered unjust as they lack adequate contemplation of all societal members. In these instances, the state is in breach of the social contract because of its failure to uphold its end of the communal pact. Moreover, establishing policy without considering the willingness of individuals to accept the newly established standard—especially if members are not informed about how these new regulations will affect them—constitutes a violation of the social contract. Thus, a serious shortcoming of social contract theory occurs when a strategy is "forced on the disfavored ones" in society (Leighton & Reiman, 2001, p. 11). Once again, we see the potential for harm affecting racial minorities, women, juveniles, the impoverished, and other vulnerable, troubled, or distressed citizen groups.

Utilitarianism is a unique form of consequentialism in that it is altruistic and fosters the "Principle of Utility." This principle maintains that when faced with a moral situation, one must choose the action that has the best overall outcome for all involved (Bentham & Mill, 1973; Williams & Arrigo, 2008, p. 197). In other words, utilitarianism entails seeking "the greatest amount of happiness altogether" in accordance with the "greatest happiness principle" (Mill, 1957, pp. 15–16). Thus, ethical reasoning, choice, and behavior require that one deliberate over the consequences of one's actions to ensure the greatest good for the greatest number of people. However, in undertaking such an analysis, the individual must be careful to discern whether the ends secured justify the means employed. This is because utilitarian arguments can (and sometimes do) result in the rights of the minority being violated in pursuit of the greater good (i.e., the majority) (Williams & Arrigo, 2008, p. 207). Nevertheless, the prevailing aim of utilitarianism is to make choices and undertake conduct according to that which will promote the most satisfaction for the greatest number of individuals affected by those decisions and behaviors (Cahn, 2009). Interestingly, Steinberg and Schwartz (2000) suggested that researchers should examine the utilitarian perspective with respect to juvenile transfer policies. As they noted, one could "raise questions about fairness and justice and probe whether treating juvenile crime in a particular way strikes an acceptable balance between the rights of the offender, the interests of the victim, and the concerns of the community" (pp. 28–29). Such an investigation will be undertaken in Chapter 2.

The principles of utilitarianism are not without their criticisms, especially in matters concerning justice policy. As Leighton and Reiman argued, "If . . . morality requires that individuals be treated in certain [repressive] ways no matter how many others may profit from their mistreatment, then utilitarianism seems to miss something crucial about morality" (2001, p. 7). For example, if an innocent person's imprisonment serves as an effective deterrent to crime for others in society, then, according to utilitarian logic, this individual injustice is outweighed by the good that results socially (Pollock, 2007, Shichor, 2006). Of course, if such an injustice were ever to be exposed, then the integrity of the legal system would be suspect. Put differently, criminal justice policies fashioned by the utilitarian perspective can, and often do, violate Kant's maxim requiring one to never use another person as a means to an end.

Proponents of utilitarianism rationalize such means/ends practices, declaring them as necessary to preserving the overall condition (i.e., prosperity, health) of the majority. Thus, a significant criticism of utilitarian theory is that it allows for the marginalization of individual rights to the advantage of collectivist ones. Moreover, as a practical matter, utilitarianism can and does ensure that the rights of individuals will be eclipsed by majoritarian "whims." The current plight of crime and justice policy, *ipso facto*, makes this case unmistakably compelling (Reiman, 2007; Walker, 2007). Interestingly, some have even proposed a curious remedy for this malaise, describing it as epidemiological criminology (Ackers & Lanier 2009; Lanier, 2010).[2]

We take the position that determining a person's worth by evaluating one's contribution to the majority's notion of satisfaction is as intellectually disturbing as it is morally problematic. Mill (1957) believed that various "utilities" (e.g., pleasures or benefits in life) could be assigned different weights and values, thereby enabling a person to engage in interest-balancing tests to determine those outcomes most beneficial for or conducive to achieving desired ends based on the majority's definition of well-being. Institutional definitions (e.g., medical, legal, scientific, governmental) and those who enforce them (e.g., physicians, judges, legislators, and researchers) have a stake in equilibrium or status quo dynamics. Therefore, it can be assumed that these interest-balancing tests are seldom, if ever, derived from an unbiased or disinterested majority. This is the "whimsy" to which we refer.[3]

Perhaps the greatest flaw in utilitarian logic is the presumption that one can accurately predict the consequences of one's actions. The annals of social science research stand as evidence that the precise prediction of human outcomes are mostly inconceivable and almost always entail some form of measurement, including resultant statistical error. Thus, one can never be certain that one's conduct benefits society. This is because it is unrealistic to presume that we can ever fully know how a person's actions affect the future. What appears to serve the greater good today may actually result in disastrous harm for the greatest number in the future. Additionally, the Principle of Utility often constrains or silences minority groups and voices, especially when outnumbered in debates surrounding law formation and policy implementation. As a result, utilitarian approaches to law–psychology–crime controversies can and do reinforce the majority's "tyranny." Regrettably, this consequentialist doctrine does little to grow the good will of people, essentially relegating human progress to a social Darwinist view of "survival of the fittest" or, in this case, survival of those with the most power, influence, and/or standing. Hence, as a normative theory, utilitarianism actually may serve to significantly undermine any effort to repair solidarity in modern society.

Virtue-Based Philosophy

Virtue ethics, or Nichomachean philosophy, is Aristotle's (2000) teleological perspective regarding human purpose and existence. Virtue ethics suggests that individuals can flourish, can excel. To do so, they must actualize their potential moral reasoning by expressing moral character through the decisions they make and the actions they undertake (Williams & Arrigo, 2008, pp. 255–256). According to Aristotle (2000), the highest good that all people seek is a flourishing in being. This state of existence is consistent with happiness (*eudaimonia*) and is achieved through developing one's virtues (Albanese, 2006, p. 14; Williams & Arrigo, 2008, p. 260). Aristotle (2000) noted that people have the ability to engage in higher reasoning. He also recognized that we are social beings and that, as such, we can only thrive as moral agents if we cooperate with others and develop lasting relationships that will foster a sense of connectedness (Williams & Arrigo, 2008, p. 257). Excellence in character, along with virtue, must be learned through experience (Albanese, 2006, p. 16). When we live virtuously as a function of our humanity—and not because of duties or because of consequences—we have the greatest likelihood of obtaining genuine happiness. Building on this notion, Aristotle (2000, p. 31) observed that virtue "is a means between two vices: one of excess; the other of deficiency." For example, courage is the "golden mean" or virtue between the excess vice of foolishness and the deficient vice of cowardice (Aristotle, 2000, p. 32). Practical wisdom, then, must be utilized when making the appropriate ethical decision in relation to the moral situation at hand (Williams & Arrigo, 2008, p. 260).

Corriero (2006, pp. 24–27) applied Aristotle's moral philosophy to the impulsiveness of adolescents. He specified how such impetuousness affects the criminal responsibility of juvenile offenders, especially when considering the issue of waiver to the adult system. In addition, Corriero (2006) explained how Aristotle's ethical precepts and the Aristotelian method of persuasion can be employed by judges. Specifically, he indicated how judges can assist transferred juveniles gain perspective on their behavior by engaging the youthful offender "in a process of remembrance [and] 'empathetic association'" (Corriero, 2006, pp. 87–88).

As noted previously, the aim of virtue ethics is to ensure that all individuals within a society flourish. For this to occur, people must practice (learn) integrity by interacting with others and by cultivating a mutual sense of understanding. Aristotle (2000) argued that our ability to feel genuine compassion for others is compromised if we believe that the individual deserves to suffer. After all, Aristotle emphasized that people are social beings who need to connect with other humans. Unlike Kant (2002), who espoused the notion of just desert, Aristotle asserted that if we are consumed by that which we think is deserved, we diminish our capacity to feel empathy and care toward others. Therefore, character is developed through habituation of virtuous action, whereas practical wisdom is the capacity to succeed through virtuous character (Aristotle, 2000). Indeed, in an interdependent society, we define the good of all as we define the good for ourselves. Because our best opportunity for attaining our own good lies with a concerned involvement with the welfare of others, it is our imperative to engage in empathetic association with others (Huigens, 1995).

Although Aristotelian moral philosophy endeavors to ensure that all individuals excel, it is not without its shortcomings. Leighton and Reiman (2001) intimated that virtue ethics, like the other schools of normative thought, leaves the notion of what is moral open to interpretation. In other words, Aristotelian ethics fails to elucidate any established standards for morality (Leighton & Reiman, 2001, p. 7). Moreover, as MacIntyre (2007) asserted, "where virtues are required ... vices may also flourish" (p. 193). In short, he questioned whether the arguable nature of our humanity (e.g., self-centered, mean-spirited, vicious) undoes any purposeful effort to cultivate integrity. Interestingly, however, perhaps the issue to raise is whether despite our inherent evilness, we should nevertheless seek to embody, to grow, virtue.

A parallel to virtue-based ethics is found in John Rawls' (1971) principles of justice. His distributive theory does not endorse duty nor consequences; rather, it promotes an appropriate balance between the two by equating justice with fairness. In other words, "we do unto others as we would have them do unto us" so that the social cooperation needed to create societal laws and norms that are just for and fair to all regardless of one's station in life can be achieved (*see* discussion, Dreisbach, 2008, p. 79). In other words, Rawls posited that collective welfare/good requires cooperation in the face of self-interest so that all may prosper under mutual advantage. Acknowledging that no one is born into a natural state of equality, Rawls proffered the theoretical view that principles of justice ought to be chosen behind a "veil of ignorance," whereby inequalities of birth are to be ignored so that everyone's well-being depends on cooperation vis-à-vis fair agreement and bargaining (1971, pp. 12 & 15). Rawls' theory hinges on the conviction that individuals can eliminate the inequalities that place them at odds with one another wherein just principles and fair procedures can be established that do not exploit society's disadvantaged.[4]

The way in which auditions for Munich's Philharmonic Orchestra have evolved serves as the perfect metaphor to explain the phenomenon about which Rawls theorized. In the epilogue of *Blink*, Gladwell (2005) explained how the audition by the son of an administrator for the Munich Philharmonic Orchestra in 1890 led to a unique change in the way auditions were conducted. To avoid a biased response from judges who might recognize the administrator's son, screens were used to conceal the identity of the performers. At this time in history, prejudices largely prevented women and minorities from being hired with the same pay male musicians received. This practice of concealing identities ensured that merit-based salaries would prevail over prejudicial considerations, and it led to the diversification of orchestras. Indeed, using screens (i.e., veils of ignorance) to take the focus away from one's gender and race allowed administrators to hire talented musicians based on their abilities rather than their endogenous characteristics. This metaphor suggests, then, that by taking control of a given environment, pro-social changes in decision making can occur (Gladwell, 2005). Therefore, following Rawls, legislators and government officials essentially must step behind the veil when setting law–psychology–crime policies or developing practices relevant to the same so that the system's (and the public's) overall integrity can be maximized.

Consistent with this notion of how we "ought" to develop personal moral fiber or excellence in character, Carol Gilligan (1982) and Nel Noddings (2003) advocated a philosophical approach based on an ethic of care (*see also*, Gilligan, Lyons, & Hanmer, 1990; Sterba, 2003). This ethic "stresses relationships, situational and contextual factors, and the unique needs and interests of affected parties as key considerations in the face of conflicts and dilemmas" (Williams & Arrigo, 2008, p. 262). As Noddings explained:

> . . . ethical caring does have to be summoned. The 'I ought' arises but encounters conflict: An inner voice grumbles, "I ought but I don't want to," or "Why should I respond?" or "This guy deserves to suffer, so why should I help?" On these occasions we need not turn to a principle; more effectively we turn to . . . a picture or ideal of ourselves as carers . . . Ethical caring's great contribution is to guide action long enough for natural caring to be restored and for people once again to interact with mutual and spontaneous regard (2003, p. 187).

In this framework, moral rules and duties cannot be delineated in regard to care; rather, a genuine sense of sympathy, compassion, and tolerance for others must be developed. In this way, "[c]are is thus not a principle that should or must be followed, but a way-of-being or way of perceiving, experiencing, and responding to the world" (Williams & Arrigo, 2008, p. 263). Much like Rawls' theory of justice, then, feminist care ethics as articulated here seeks to rediscover and build habits of character consistent with Aristotle's moral philosophy.

Psychological Jurisprudence as Moral Philosophy

As the introduction to this volume suggested, the collective practices and principles of psychological jurisprudence (PJ) yield a moral philosophy that is strikingly similar to Aristotle's virtue ethics. Steeped in the law, psychology, and justice framework (as opposed to the clinical or law and social science perspectives), PJ first realizes this brand of well-being and excellence by way of sound theory construction. In what follows, then, we elaborate more fully on the meanings of commonsense justice, therapeutic jurisprudence, and restorative justice; revisit their interrelationships for purposes of advancing PJ theory; and further specify how the promotion of Aristotelian human flourishing obtains in the process.

Commonsense Justice

According to Finkel (1995), commonsense justice grows our subjective regard for the law. This is both reasonable and prudent because it takes into account the ordinary citizen's notion of what is just and fair. Thus, by considering the public's perspective on the law, the conscience of the community (i.e., practical judgment and informed opinion on issues of fairness, equity, and honor) is conveyed in justice-related matters (Huss et al., 2006; Finkel, 1995, 1997). Moreover, by incorporating moral and psychological communal sentiment into the law, everyday citizens are empowered to challenge and resist the law when they deem it unjust and then pursue their sense of more equitable choice and action. Among other things, these efforts seek to "perfect and complete" courtroom practices and judicial rulings often personified in the process of jury nullification (Finkel, 1995, p. 3). In other words, when jurors render a verdict that displaces case and statutory law in favor of their own soundly reasoned views, they communicate that the law cannot "be respected and obeyed, [unless it is] grounded closely to the common ground" (Finkel, 1996, p. 13). Clearly, then, commonsense justice, above all else, attempts to promote the public's engaged role in the legal system.

Unlike Rawls' (1971) *Theory of Justice,* which holds that fairness is secondary to justice, Finkel and colleagues (2001) argued that the two constructs overlap and in certain instances fairness is primary. The concept of fairness takes on numerous meanings (e.g., distributive justice, procedural justice, reciprocity, and human dignity); however, it is the presence of "unfairness" that often captures the outrage of ordinary citizens (Finkel, Harre, & Lopez, 2001). With this concern in mind, commonsense justice does not seek to replace existing black-letter law; rather, it endeavors to inform and solidify law's legitimacy (Finkel, 2000b). Jurors embody the everyday citizen's perspective on whether a law and its application are unfair. Not surprisingly, then, commonsense justice attempts to evaluate the veracity of legislative and judicial claims that laws "on the books" serve the public's best interest and uphold humanity's basic dignity. As such, impaneled jury members examine the credibility and authority of the law so that commonsense justice may prevail, positively enhancing law's force and meaning (Finkel, 2000a, 2000b).[5]

Therapeutic Jurisprudence

Therapeutic jurisprudence identifies and utilizes interventions that enable the law to function constructively as a healing agent so that legal outcomes minimize harm for all parties in dispute (Wexler & Winick, 1996; Winick & Wexler, 2003, 2006). This more cooperative model of decision-making entails some sensitivity to the emotional and physical effects that legal processes can have on attorneys and clients when otherwise guided by the traditional adversarial process (Arrigo, 2004b). The values of psychology ground the interventions employed. Examples of such values include mutual respect, dignity, autonomy, non-invasiveness, and community well-being (Wexler, 2008a). The aim is to promote effective and beneficial resolutions, whether as judge, criminal defense attorney, or other courtroom problem-solving official (e.g., Boldt & Singer, 2006).

Given this framework, legal professionals are encouraged to embrace the role of a therapeutic counselor (Winick & Wexler, 2006, pp. 605–606). Consistent with an ethic of care, when jurists embrace a "judge-as-counselor" role, they seek to "know the defendant, consider her or his life circumstances and motives, and take these into consideration when making a ruling" (Williams & Arrigo, 2008, p. 265; see also Braithwaite, 2002; Strang & Braithwaite, 2001; Wexler, 2008a; Winick & Wexler, 2006). Moreover, therapeutic jurisprudence casts judges and lawyers into the "roles of peacemakers and creative problem solvers" (Scott, 2004, p. 388). Extending this logic to penal policymakers and other institutional decision-makers, they, too, are invited to adopt a similar therapeutic position. In this way, adjudicators, counselors, fact-finders, and those who manage the kept have an opportunity to perceive offenders as fellow human beings defined by more than the crimes or harms they have committed.

We take the position that moving beyond the false dichotomy (us vs. them) that the fearful public currently engenders entails the development of an alternative mindset about incarcerates, serious juvenile offenders, the mentally ill, and sexually violent predators. Therapeutic jurisprudence— steeped in a moral philosophy of connectedness, relationships, belonging, and community—posits that those who are confined and incapacitated are no less fully human than those who are not. This more civilizing orientation challenges the watchers of the kept to transcend their perception of offenders as objects to be manipulated or as entities to be demonized (i.e., monsters). They are in and of society, and they return to us (Maruna & LeBel, 2003). Moreover, adopting this more salubrious orientation helps to better appreciate the plight of the vulnerable, troubled, or distressed including racial minorities, children, women, the poor, and the psychiatrically disordered. Thus, when offenders are regarded as citizens as opposed to deviant, diseased, or dangerous predators, their potential for life-alerting growth in personal accountability is more completely seeded.[6]

Restorative Justice

Restorative justice is a form of mediated reconciliation (Van Ness & Heetderks Strong, 2007; Zehr & Toews, 2004) in which a process of conflict resolution is developed through discussion, dialogue, and negotiation among all injured parties (Karp, Sweet, Kirshenbaum, & Bazemore, 2004, p. 199). The conceptual framework of restorative justice is grounded in the theory of reintegrative shaming (*see* Braithwaite, 1989). Reintegrative shaming seeks to repair the harm and suffering that crime engenders without causing the community, the victim, and the offender to feel "alienated, more damaged, disrespected, disempowered, less safe and less cooperative with society" (Braswell et al., 2001, p. 142). Candid disclosures and humanistic dialogue guide the healing process in which genuine, meaningful, and, ideally, transformative resolutions are sought (Bazemore & Boba, 2007; Coker, 2006; Levine, 2000; Umbreit, Coates, & Armour, 2006). Consistent with this healing orientation is the "community conference model" (Dignan & Marsh, 2001, p. 99). It seeks to secure a reparative resolution for both the victim and the offender, while also attempting to "maintain order and social and moral balance in the community" (Braswell, Fuller, & Lozoff, 2001, p. 141).

In recent years, restorative justice practices have been implemented in numerous countries and regions around the globe, including New Zealand, Australia, the United Kingdom, Western Europe, Israel, South Africa, Canada, and the United States among others (McGarrell & Hipple, 2007; Mulligan, 2009). The initial programming for restorative justice was applied to juveniles who committed minor infractions. Contemporary usage extends to both adults and juveniles whose crimes include misdemeanors and serious and/or violent felonies (McGarrell & Hipple, 2007).

Several studies indicate that juvenile offenders who participate in and successfully complete programming such as family group conference (FGC) are less likely to recidivate over a 24-month follow-up period when compared with their control group counterparts (*see* McGarrell 2001; McGarrell & Hipple, 2007; McGarrell, Olivares, Crawford, & Kroovand, 2000; Rodriguez, 2005). Additionally, since 1989, the use of mediation and FGC in New Zealand has resulted in a two-thirds decline in juvenile offending (Mulligan, 2009). Still further, the Resolve to Stop the Violence Project found success through direct and indirect mediation, as well as through conferencing, resulting in an 80% reduction in recidivism for those who spent 16 weeks in the program (Parker, 2005).

Restorative justice reminds us that the state is only secondarily agrieved when crime occurs and that the victim primarily deserves a voice in criminal justice proceedings (O'Hara & Robbins, 2009). Experiments utilizing restorative justice practices (e.g., the Bethlehem Pennsylvania Study; the Reintegrative Shaming Experiments from Canberra, Australia; and the Indianapolis Experiment) offer evidence suggesting that higher rates of victim participation as well as victim satisfaction follow under these reparative conditions (McGarrell & Hipple, 2007). Researchers have also found that offenders are very satisfied when involved in victim–offender mediation (*see* Abrams, Umbreit, & Gordon, 2006).[7] In fact, the addition of the offender in FGCs appears to foster feelings of inclusion, respect, and procedural fairness among participants (McGarrell & Hipple, 2007; Roche, 2006).[8]

Psychological Jurisprudence: Integrating Principles and Cultivating Virtue Ethics

It is our view that the theory of PJ as developed from the collective practices (and corresponding principles) of commonsense justice, therapeutic jurisprudence, and restorative justice, represents a virtue-based approach to justice-rendering (Bersot & Arrigo, 2010, 2011; Sellers & Arrigo, 2009). This is a theory that is resolutely wedded to its trifold conceptual pillars of growing dignity, welcoming the therapeutic and undertaking critique. Moreover, this approach is deeply committed to the twin dynamics of individual responsibility and institutional accountability, especially in its efforts to embrace the fair-minded sentiment of community conscience; to humanize the law through healing reflection, choice, and action; and to reconnect and restore all stakeholders harmed in the aftermath of debilitating violence and victimization. Still further, each of these activities is informed by rigorous and ever-mindful criticism of the very structures such reification practices legitimize, whether symbolic, linguistic, material, and/or cultural in their origin or form.

In its collective an integrative way, then, PJ theory seeks to build *transformative* habits of character. This is an edifice of meaningful reform. The theory's moral philosophical anchoring in excellence and by way of virtue both grounds and guides its logic of decision making. The theory's synthesis of this flourishing and goodness intends to reinstate natural care and compassion as vital dimensions to an emergent process of mutual and spontaneous regard for others. Accordingly, with all of these overarching conceptual nuances in mind—and recognizing that as a nascent system of thought still more elaboration on theoretical particulars is needed—we argue that PJ's philosophical framework makes more completely realizable an ethic of citizen justice, communal well-being and societal accord than any other schematization to date. The law–psychology–crime nexus is one access point by which to explore the theory's explanatory properties.

What remains to be delineated, therefore, is whether PJ theory can soundly facilitate an empirical examination of current-day total confinement practices. This includes the hypervigilance and panopticism presently surrounding serious juvenile delinquents, incarcerates with psychiatric disorders, and sexually violent predators. As we posit, the Aristotelian-derived theory of PJ is quite relevant to qualitatively investigating the precedent-setting and/or prevailing case law on these very contentious and complex matters.

Psychological Jurisprudence and Methodology

Three separate data sets formed the basis of our overall study. The sample of cases selected for each investigation required a criterion-based sampling design. This design endeavored to use specific target terms sourced in

LexisNexis searches. A detailed explanation of terms used for each subject of interest will be supplied in Chapters 2, 3, and 4, respectively. Additionally, at that time, particular accounts of those court cases retained for and excluded from textual analyses will be clarified and justified. All cases of interest were shepardized, and internal cites were scrutinized to ascertain any other important court decisions that should be included in the sample, notwithstanding their lack of identification as derived from initial LexisNexis inquiries. An explanation of all cases obtained for each of the three data sets vis-à-vis these sampling strategies is found in the "case law method" sections of the subsequent application chapters.[9] However, before addressing these specific concerns and their relevance for furthering our assessment of this volume's thesis concerning total confinement practices, some global comments about the methodology of psychological jurisprudence are warranted.

Two levels of textual inquiry inform the qualitative research enterprise of PJ. The first of these identifies the jurisprudential intent found within a legal case. To ascertain jurisprudential intent, the *plain meaning* evident in the judicial opinion is the source of inspection and analysis. Because the plain meaning of a court case is expressed through a jurist's selection of various words and phrases, these data must be carefully reviewed. The meanings detected here reveal the courts' underlying jurisprudential intent.

As noted by Sellers and Arrigo (2009) and Bersot and Arrigo (2010), previous studies have utilized an approach sourcing intent as a basis to conduct *statutory* analyses. For example, to specify legislative intent, investigators have explored the "ordinary usage" of terms and the "textual context" discerned within various legislative provisions (Hall & Wright, 2008; Phillips & Grattet, 2000; Randolph, 1994). To be clear, some researchers have challenged the anecdotal nature of this method, noting its inability to effectively extract the meaning lodged within a statute (Easterbrook, 1994; Posner, 2008). Indeed, those critical of this method assert that meaning is interpreted based on context. Thus, results from an analysis of this kind may differ according to an individual's comprehension of the legislative language employed (Posner, 2008). However, we contend that determining a court's intent through a systematic textual examination of precedent-setting and/or prevailing legal opinions represents a more rigorous—although admittedly heuristic—methodology than if statutorily derived. This is because the use of juridical language is constrained in ways not found within or anticipated by its legislative counterpart.[10]

To undertake the first level of proposed textual legal analysis, a series of questions were compiled and posed in relation to each of the judicial opinions comprising the overall data set. As first delineated by Ritchie and Spencer (2002), the queries represent a robust qualitative strategy intended to provide direction for researchers conducting applied policy analyses (*see also* Sellers & Arrigo, 2009; Bersot & Arrigo, 2010). This initial research step included both contextual (i.e., the state of what is) and diagnostic (i.e., the cause or reasoning for what is) features (p. 307). Accordingly, the following questions were applied to each judicial opinion:

1. What are the dimensions of attitudes or perceptions that are held?
2. What factors underlie particular attitudes or perceptions?
3. Why are decisions or actions taken or not taken?
4. Why do particular needs arise?
5. Why are services or programs not being used?
6. What are the goals, purposes, and concerns of the decisions or actions taken or not taken?
7. What needs of society are represented by the decisions or actions taken or not taken?

Collectively, these queries are designed to elicit plain meaning from which a court's jurisprudential intent can then be extracted. Stated differently, the judicial temperament is the meaning extracted from the plain meaning as guided by the set of contextual/diagnostic queries.

The first two questions intend to discern how courts comprehend and contemplate the complex legal issues and/or controversies presented in the cases constituting a data set and the factors that influence or inform their attitudes regarding the same. For example, do jurists uphold total confinement tactics for serious juvenile delinquents, incarcerates with psychiatric disorders, and sexually violent offenders because they perceive members of these specific groups as incapable of being rehabilitated? Questions 3 through 5 attempt to determine the underlying motivations and rationales lodged within a court's decision making. For example, based on the legal opinions pertaining to sex offenders, what resources are (or should be) made available to them, particularly predatory assailants, as they re-enter their respective communities? Moreover, given the public's acute and chronic disdain for sexual predation and violence, are United States Supreme Court opinions influenced by this widely held sentiment when they assess control and monitoring functions beyond criminal incarceration for this constituency group? Additionally, do the prevailing rulings on the matter of serious juvenile delinquency reflect the perception that violent youths are mature enough to receive adult sanctions rather than rehabilitative alternatives because jurists adhere to a "get tough on crime" retributive logic? Still further, does the court express an awareness of the extant literature indicating the social and financial hardships that these troubled offenders typically face (e.g., maintaining family relationships and obtaining a job)? Finally, by way of illustration, does the public's outrage toward serious crime in relation to the psychiatrically ill affect or influence the courts' opinions about these vulnerable individuals? Questions 6 and 7 draw attention to specific terms and phrases found in the judicial opinions in an effort to reveal the court's values when considering legal challenges raised by serious offenders classified as at-risk youth, the mentally disordered, or sexually violent. For example, does the precedent case law on sexually violent predators communicate the view that these wrongdoers are such a threat to society that their total confinement (i.e., criminal incarceration, civil commitment, sex offender registration, and community notification) is the only way to ensure the public's safety? Moreover, does an expressed interest in society's general welfare supercede the constitutional rights of individuals designated as members of the three specific offender groups investigated in this volume? Data retrieved from the first level of qualitative analysis regarding jurisprudential intent are located within the "discussion" section of each application chapter under the subheading "Level 1 Analysis." These finds are derived from the plain meaning data located in the "results" portion of the book. These results consist of three Appendixes and are organized according to the particular offender group in question.

However, in addition to discerning jurisprudential intent by way of carefully investigating plain meaning, a second level of textual analysis complements and completes the qualitative research enterprise of psychological jurisprudence. This is the realm in which the underlying moral logic that informs juridical intent is made thematic. This second level of inquiry, more interpretive in nature, is designed to "explicate how assumptions about self and society, private and public, and state and society—the essentials that underlie traditional legal thought—are encoded in law" (Mercuro & Medema, 1998, p. 169; see also Arrigo, 1993, 1999, 2003b; Mackin, 2006).[11] The data sources for this second level of analysis are the plain meaning findings themselves gathered on jurisprudential intent. Thus, these findings and the legal language that conveys jurisprudential intent undergo additional review to better ascertain what they mean ethically.

When uncovering or making explicit the courts' ethical reasoning, the legal language that constitutes jurisprudential intent is carefully scrutinized. This process initiates phase two of the proposed methodology. After relying on the seven questions to extrapolate the plain meaning and to discern the underlying jurisprudential intent of that meaning, the textual content itself is the subject of inquiry. Specifically, the terms and/or phrases indicating plain meaning are then filtered through the prism of moral philosophy. Thus, each word or expression is analyzed mindful of the three previously enumerated principal schools of ethics. These moral philosophies comprise consequentialism (consisting of ethical egoism, contractualism, and utilitarianism); formalism (including Kantian deontology and prima facie duties); and virtue ethics (Aristotelian- and feminist care-based).

The purpose of this second level of qualitative analysis is to determine what Holsti described as a text's "manifest content" (1969, p. 12). Essentially, manifest content represents the message conveyed during a court proceeding or within a legal opinion. When manifest content is made explicit, it is then possible to identify the content's underlying ethical import.[12] To illustrate, if a court employs plain meaning rhetoric noting a *duty* to uphold deference to correctional institution administrators, then this constitutes manifest content. This content indicates that the court's opinion is guided by deontological principles. Moreover, if the justices' language features the weighing of competing interests such as *balancing* the mental health needs of an offender against the security needs of society, then this also constitutes manifest content. In this example, that underlying ethic informing this content is utilitarian in scope. In those instances where manifest content (as derived from plain meaning about jurisprudential intent) fails to convey normative import, no moral philosophy can be specified.

The sequencing from jurisprudential intent by way of plain meaning to ethical rationale by way of manifest content represents a data point that helps to specify the core moral philosophy located within a given judicial opinion (Bersot & Arrigo, 2010; Sellers & Arrigo, 2009). However, this analysis is incomplete. To more fully ascertain the predominant ethic of a given legal opinion, it is necessary to engage in a thematic investigation. Thus, as a dimension of the methodology's second level of inquiry, an identification of ethical-philosophical themes derived from the particular instances of manifest content (words/phrases) in each judicial opinion is conducted. This is an *intratextual* analysis. Additionally, as a basis to determine the overall moral philosophy informing the case law for each data set, a similar thematic examination takes place. This is an *intertextual* analysis. When the predominant thematic findings across each data set are reviewed, they yield *comprehensive* results concerning the ethics of total confinement at the law–psychology–crime nexus. Data retrieved from the second level of qualitative exegeses regarding underlying ethics are located within the "discussion" section of each application chapter under the subheading "Level 2 Analysis." These findings are arranged according to the particular legal cases and ethics-derived data in question.

To summarize, then, the method of psychological jurisprudence is qualitative, textual, and interpretive in design. To determine jurisprudential intent, plain meaning is the source of inquiry. This is ascertained by extracting information from those cases constituting each data set as guided by the seven previously specified questions. This undertaking represents the first level of analysis. The second level of investigation is more textual in orientation and it consists of two layers. First, the manifest content is reviewed as derived from those plain meaning passages conveying jurisprudential intent. At issue here are the actual words or phrases communicated by jurists in rendering their opinions. Second, these words and/or phrases are themselves evaluated against the logic of three schools of ethics (and their variants) as a way to determine what moral philosophy informs this manifest content. To more completely specify the underlying ethics of a particular case in the data set, thematic analysis is performed. All instances of manifest content based on an ethical rationale are identified and compared against all others within that judicial opinion (i.e., intratextuality). The same strategy is employed across all cases in a particular data set. This volume considers the prevailing and/or precedent-setting case law for three distinct law–psychology–crime cognate areas; thus, the essential ethic for each of them is specified (i.e., intertextuality). These three independent assessments then make it possible to more inclusively and completely evaluate the moral philosophy governing the identified total confinement practices.

2

Juvenile Transfer, Developmental Maturity, and Competency to Stand Trial

Introduction

One particular law–psychology–crime topic where the logic of psychological jurisprudence and the philosophy of virtue ethics are most germane is the competency to stand trial doctrine. According to some investigators, the issue of trial fitness is "the most significant mental health inquiry pursued in the system of criminal law" (Redding & Frost, 2001, p. 353; *see also* Bardwell & Arrigo, 2002b, p. 3). More specifically, on the issue of *juvenile* competency to stand trial, the matter is even more complicated, especially given the presence of developmental maturity factors. Indeed, "[d]espite the fact that attorneys and judges need guidance to recognize and address these issues in dealing with young defendants, the relationship between immaturity and competence to stand trial has been largely ignored in research and policy circles" (Steinberg, 2003, p. 20). The historical understanding of juvenile fitness for trial neglects to account for the psychological limitations that such youthfulness naturally entails (e.g., Feld, 2003; Grisso, 2006; Grisso et al., 2003). In particular, many juveniles possess similar deficits as those who experience mental illness or mental retardation. However, those deficits affecting adolescent competency are not because of mental illness or mental retardation; rather, they are because of cognitive or emotional immaturity (Grisso, 2003).

In recent years, given the increase in violent juvenile crime, a more punitive response by the criminal justice system has followed (Fagan & Zimring, 2000; Feld, 2001, 2004; Grisso & Schwartz, 2000; Kupchik, 2006). For example, in terms of court adjudication, automatic forms of juvenile transfer to adult court have steadily been appropriated given the current "get tough" policy rationale used to address serious adolescent offending (Feld, 2004; Kurlychek & Johnson, 2004; Steiner, Hemmens, & Bell, 2006). Unsurprisingly, however, the decision to rely on automatic waiver strategies has led to a number of processing, confinement, and recidivism concerns. Along these lines, investigators have empirically shown how developmental immaturity negatively affects a waived juvenile's ability to be fit for trial in the adult system (Bell, 2004; Grisso et al., 2003; Scott & Grisso, 2005; Steinberg, 2003; Viljoen & Grisso, 2007).

Notwithstanding these findings, both the courts and state legislatures have mostly elected to ignore the adverse impact current transfer policies have on juvenile offenders and on society more generally. Although researchers have outlined the need to properly assess transferred youths for trial fitness purposes—with special consideration given to developmental factors—the legal community has regrettably not endorsed these recommendations. Interestingly, no study has undertaken an exploration of the ethical reasoning that informs legal decision making with respect to automatic juvenile transfer practices where issues of developmental maturity and adjudicative competence figure prominently into the analysis. Stated differently, the logic of psychological jurisprudence and the philosophy of ethics communicated through the relevant court cases on the law–psychology–crime subject of adolescent automatic waiver have not been systematically examined. A thoughtful inquiry into both may very well be the basis for translating (assumed) theory into worthwhile public policy.

Accordingly, the present inquiry focuses on these prescient matters. Specifically, the moral philosophy embedded within those court cases that reflect the prevailing judicial perspective on automatic juvenile transfer, developmental maturity, and trial fitness will be made explicit. In so doing, it will then be possible to assess whether, and to what extent, current retributive policies toward serious juvenile offenders promote (or fail to promote) excellence in character for all stakeholders in which the value of living virtuously guides the jurisprudential reasoning.

The first section of the chapter presents the relevant literature on adolescent waiver and the social and behavioral science community's assessment of it. The juvenile transfer commentary explains current practices in court processing and the problems that are correspondingly associated with them. The empirical research examines adolescent waiver, notably when complicated by developmental maturity and competency to stand trial issues. The second section of the chapter describes the qualitative "case law method" utilized for the proceeding inquiry. This includes a review of how the specific court cases were selected for inclusion in the data set. The third section of the chapter discusses the research findings. Of particular interest are the types of ethical principles conveyed through the jurisprudential reasoning of each court case and across all of the decisions. The fourth section of the chapter comments on the findings themselves and briefly considers their implications for the dynamics of madness, citizenship, and social justice.

The Literature on Juvenile Waiver: An Overview

Juvenile Transfer: Current Practices in Court Processing

Approximately 200,000 adolescents under age 18 years in the United States are tried as adults each year, and roughly 12% of these transferred juveniles are under age 16 years (Steinberg, 2003). The legal basis for adjudicating youths to the adult system is the waiver process. Three such forms exist.

During the 1960s and early 1970s, the most common transfer strategy was judicial waiver (Feld, 2004). In this approach, the juvenile court judge uses his or her discretion and determines whether transfer to a criminal court is warranted based on a hearing. At the hearing, the judge reviews the evidence regarding the youth's amenability to treatment and potential threat to society (Feld, 2001, 2004; Poythress, Lexcen, Grisso, & Steinberg, 2006; Rossiter, 2006). Typically, a decision to transfer hinges on the seriousness of the offense and the extent and type of one's prior record.

The second waiver strategy is known as legislative offense exclusion or statutory waiver (Brink, 2004; Feld, 2001; Kupchik, 2006; Rossiter, 2006). This approach is the easiest way for the state legislature to emphasize the seriousness of the crime and to promote a retributive agenda. Legislatures create juvenile courts, and as such, they are responsible for defining the appropriate jurisdictional venue in which a case can be considered. Moreover, they can support transfer based on the presence of offense seriousness and the youth's age. For example, a state may exclude from juvenile court jurisdiction any youth age 16 years or older who is charged with a serious offense such as murder (Feld, 2001, p. 17; Feld, 2004, p. 600).

The third strategy is prosecutorial waiver or direct file (Brink, 2004; Feld, 2004; Kupchik, 2006; Poythress et al., 2006). In this approach, concurrent jurisdiction grants the prosecutor discretion to choose whether a youth can be charged in a juvenile or criminal court, without having to justify the decision through a judicial hearing or a formal record (Brink, 2004; Feld, 2004, p. 600; Kupchik, 2006). Current trends suggest that both statutory and prosecutorial waivers are the primary forms of juvenile transfer (Brink, 2004; Grisso, 2006; Kupchik, 2006, p. 155; Rainville & Smith, 2003), whereas judicial waiver is utilized less frequently (Bishop & Frazier, 2000, p. 231; Feld, 2001; Feld, 2004; Poythress et al., 2006, p. 77). In other words, for example, the focus of a state's juvenile court can easily be altered to fit "get tough" policies demanded by the public in which a maximum age limit (e.g., 14 years) could guarantee that youths who exceed this restriction were automatically waived to the adult system (Brink, 2004; Feld, 2001, 2004).

The various ways by which a juvenile can be transferred to criminal court enables judges, prosecutors, and legislatures to have considerable discretion in exercising their respective waiver decisions. Interestingly, judicial waiver allows for a hearing in which the juvenile's maturity level, amenability to treatment, and danger to society are all evaluated (Corriero, 2006). However, mandatory forms of transfer—specifically statutory and prosecutorial waivers—do not adequately assess psychological maturity and amenability to rehabilitation (Feld, 2004; Oberlander, Goldstein, & Ho, 2001; Rossiter, 2006). A mandatory waiver only requires that the juvenile court find sufficient probable cause, suggesting that the youth committed the crime according to the guidelines of the waiver statute (Rossiter, 2006).

Additionally, in 2003, the Bureau of Justice Statistics reported findings from data collected in 40 different jurisdictions on transferred juveniles during 1998. The data revealed that 41.6% of the adolescents were transferred by statutory exclusion, 34.7% were transferred by prosecutorial direct file, and only 23.7% were transferred by judicial waiver (Rainville & Smith, 2003). Consistent with these figures, new statutory waiver laws enacted in 1994 increased the amount of juveniles automatically transferred to criminal court by 73% as compared with the waiver rate in 1986 (Baerger, Griffin, Lyons, & Simmons, 2003; Katner, 2006). Collectively, these statistics suggest a departure from judicial waiver in favor of automatic forms of transfer whose purpose is to streamline the process of adjudicating youthful offenders. Statutory exclusion laws expose juveniles to adult criminal proceedings and sanctions without assessing for psychological maturity, social history, prior record, and so forth (Dawson, 2000, p. 48; Feld, 2004, p. 601; Oberlander et al., 2001; Rossiter, 2006). Moreover, these laws ensure that adjudication will be based on the offense, that the severity of penalties will increase, and that judicial discretion will greatly diminish (Corriero, 2006, p. 130; Zimring, 2000, p. 214). No formal guidelines govern prosecutorial discretion in direct file waivers, and inadequate access to proper personal and clinical records about youthful offenders may inaccurately lead to false determinations concerning the most dangerous juveniles (Feld, 2004, p. 601). In addition, the lack of formal guidelines means that prosecutorial discretion is based more on subjective factors such as where the youth resides and offense severity rather than more objective measures such as assessing for maturity level, amenability to treatment, and level of risk/threat (Feld, 2004, p. 601).

A primary policy rationale for relying on the newer forms of automatic waiver is the deterrence of future juvenile crime (Bishop & Frazier, 2000, pp. 245–248; Feld, 2004, p. 602; Rossiter, 2006). Regrettably, evidence-based research has yet to support this rationale (Kupchik, 2006, p. 151). For example, employing a quasi-experimental, multiple-interrupted-times series design, investigators concluded that statutory exclusion laws in 22 states had no statistically significant effect on general deterrence (Steiner, Hemmens, & Bell, 2006). Another study utilizing the same research design examined 14 states with direct file statutes. Investigators found that direct file laws had no lasting deterrent effect on juvenile crime (Steiner & Wright, 2006).

Moreover, New York statistics indicate that more than 60% of transferred youth recidivate inside a period of 36 months (Corriero, 2006, p. 47). Conversely, a study of 800 adolescent offenders charged with robbery found that those adjudicated in juvenile court recidivated roughly 20% less than those waived to the adult system (Redding & Howell, 2000, p. 151). A Pennsylvania study revealed that juveniles transferred to criminal court received harsher punishments for similar crimes than young adults (e.g., 18–24 years old) deemed ineligible for juvenile court (Kurlychek & Johnson, 2004). As investigators noted, transferred adolescents received an average of 18 months incarceration, whereas their young adult counterparts were confined for an average of only 6 months (Kurlychek & Johnson, 2004). Thus, youthfulness or young age is used as an aggravating rather than a mitigating factor for transferring juveniles (Tonry, 2004, p. 155 as cited in Feld, 2004, p. 602; *see also* Feld, 2003), despite the absence of empirical evidence supporting juvenile transfer based on deterrence-of-future-crime justification. Complicating this disturbing trend are studies that report the rate of adult incarceration for transferred adolescents. To illustrate, the Bureau of Justice Statistics reported in 2003 that 64% of juveniles convicted in criminal court during 1998 were sentenced to incarceration, with 43% of that total serving terms in adult prisons and the remainder sentenced to confinement in jail settings (Rainville & Smith, 2003).

Empirical Research on Juvenile Transfer: Developmental Maturity and Trial Competency

The extant research on juvenile waiver—including types of transfer, policy justifications for such a practice, and recidivism trends that follow from both— have led to several social and behavioral science questions about the appropriateness of exposing an adolescent to the criminal trial. In particular, investigators have examined six concerns. These include the following: *(1)* Are automatic waivers punitive in nature, and do the courts adequately assess developmental maturity factors when considering competence to stand trial?; *(2)* Can the psychosocial aspects of developmental maturity be specified, and if so, what are they?; *(3)* Is developmental immaturity a sufficient factor to declare a waived juvenile incompetent to stand trial?; *(4)* How does one accurately measure the multiple dimensions of maturity?; *(5)* What have researchers proposed to ensure the inclusion of developmental maturity factors in competency evaluations for purposes of courtroom decision making?; and *(6)* Why is it important to assess developmental maturity in cases where juveniles are waived to the adult system? Each concern is summarily discussed below.

Some researchers note that the principal focus of waivers based on prosecutorial discretion and automatic transfer emphasizes the crime committed to the near exclusion of the juvenile who transgresses (Feld, 2004, p. 602; Zimring, 2000; Steiner & Wright, 2006). As investigators warn, this orientation makes issues such as public safety, retribution, and deterrence so compelling that the courts and legislatures are less inclined to preserve the legal distinctions between adolescents and their adult counterparts (Brink, 2004; Feld, 2001, pp. 12–14; Kupchik, 2006, pp. 18–19; Kurlychek & Johnson, 2004; Steinberg & Cauffman, 2000, p. 380; Steiner & Wright, 2006; Steiner, Hemmens,

& Bell 2006). Critics maintain that the danger with sustaining this "conventional belief" is that it assumes that once a juvenile has been designated for automatic transfer to criminal proceedings, the judgment regarding adult sanctions has also been reached (Corriero, 2006, p. 170). As a practical matter, this means that the youth faces imminent punishment as an adult, without consideration for possible developmental immaturity or related deficits. Further, investigators argue that ignoring the importance of developmental immaturity and offender age in waiver determinations is akin to "ignoring an elephant that has wandered into the courtroom" (Steinberg & Cauffman, 2000, p. 381). Indeed, as the empirical evidence indicates, deficiencies in "psychosocial maturity" among juveniles are caused by their impulsivity (Grisso et al., 2003; Grisso, 2006; Oberlander et al., 2001; Scott & Grisso, 2005), reliance on peer acceptance (Feld, 2003; Katner, 2006; Kupchik, 2006, p. 19; Redding & Frost, 2001; Scott, 2000, p. 304; Scott & Grisso, 2005), lack of autonomy (Katner, 2006), and poor judgment in relation to future consequences (Grisso, 2006; Katner, 2006; Oberlander et al., 2001; Redding & Frost, 2001; Scott & Grisso, 2005, p. 335). Given these findings, researchers conclude that youthful offenders must be evaluated for trial fitness before a transfer decision can be made (Allard & Young, 2002, p. 75; Bell, 2004; Grisso et al., 2003; Redding & Frost, 2001; Scott & Grisso, 2005; Steinberg & Cauffman, 2000, pp. 397 & 404).

As previously mentioned, psychosocial factors affecting a youth's reasoning process and ability to adequately function cognitively during the trial are numerous, varied, and profound (Grisso et al., 2003; Scott, 2000; Scott & Grisso, 2005). For example, with respect to peer influence, impaired adolescents are not fully capable of understanding the long-term consequences of their actions, engage in decision making that typically reflects an absence of independent reasoning, and are highly inclined to pursue risk-taking behaviors symptomatic of their impulsivity (Grisso et al., 2003; Grisso, 2006). Moreover, with respect to autonomy, Corriero (2006, p. 175) asserted that the diminished criminal responsibility of wayward juveniles is "explained in part by the prevailing circumstances [in which they] have less control, or less experience with control, over their own environment . . . [and] lack the freedom that adults have to extricate themselves from a criminogenic setting." Certainly, as researchers endeavor to more clearly define and operationalize developmental maturity factors, their potential use in a legal context (especially for furthering the construct of competence to stand trial) will likely increase as well (Grisso et al., 2003, p. 335). However, to date, no official premise exists in which developmental immaturity represents a basis to declare a juvenile incompetent for adjudicative purposes (Bonnie & Grisso, 2000, p. 88). The lack of such a premise is linked to the significance courts and state legislatures avail to the notion of maturity.

Indeed, one of the more common concerns regarding competency to stand trial among transferred youth is whether developmental immaturity is a sufficient factor when making determinations about a juvenile defendant's mental fitness for trial (Grisso et al., 2003, pp. 335–336; Grisso, 2006; Katner, 2006; Redding & Frost, 2001; Scott & Grisso, 2005). Most courts require that the defendant be diagnosed as suffering from some form of psychiatric illness or mental retardation as a condition of an incompetency determination (Baerger et al., 2003, p. 31; Bardwell & Arrigo, 2002a, p. 163; Oberlander et al., 2001, p. 548; Scott & Grisso, 2005; Viljoen & Grisso, 2007). Research indicates that roughly one-third of juveniles between ages 11 and 13 years and one-fifth of juveniles between ages 14 and 15 years lack the requisite competence to stand trial (Steinberg, 2003). Importantly, the findings reveal that adolescent immaturity affects the juvenile defendant's behavior and ability to make decisions regarding future orientation and risk perception during the legal proceedings (Katner, 2006; Scott & Grisso, 2005; Steinberg, 2003). When one's judgment is impaired or when maturity stemming from sufficient psychosocial development is absent, then the youth's ability to competently function in adult criminal proceedings is compromised.

In contrast to previous research, a Florida study recently found that a sample of 118 direct-filed male youths, between the ages of 16 and 17 years, had few differences in competence-related abilities when compared to a sample of 165 incarcerated adults between ages 18 to 24 years (Poythress et al., 2006). The investigators noted that although their findings supported direct file policies for 16- and 17-year-old juveniles whose immaturity did not impair their competence-related abilities, future research would do well to assess whether the results were peculiar to the sample and jurisdiction (Poythress et al., 2006, pp. 88–90). Moreover, and consistent with the thrust of the ensuing inquiry, the findings did not include a discussion of the jurisprudential basis on which juveniles were direct-filed by prosecutorial discretion. Thus, underlying ethical considerations operating here in support of waiver were not subjected to careful scrutiny or systematic analysis.

Although researchers have found that developmental immaturity is a potentially significant factor affecting the adjudicative competence of juveniles, they have yet to determine how best to measure it. One study investigated the specific abilities psychologists considered pertinent when assessing maturity in juvenile defendants for purposes of adjudicative competence (Ryba, Cooper, & Zapf, 2003). The majority of psychologists focused on cognitive or social skills, whereas only a few clinicians expressed concerns for psycholegal abilities—that is, how a defendant's level of maturity affects his or her functioning in a legal proceeding (Ryba et al., 2003, pp. 40–41). Findings such as these suggest that forensic psychologists lack adequate guidelines to properly assess maturity factors, especially given the variety of testing instruments used to evaluate (juvenile) competency (Ryba et al., 2003, p. 27; *see also* Grisso, 2000, p. 330). Thus, as some experts have concluded, the "judgment-related" factors associated with developmental immaturity are not consistent with adult competency evaluations; as such, it is a difficult task for psychologists, attorneys, and courts to take these factors into consideration (Redding & Frost, 2001, p. 378, as cited in Ryan & Murrie, 2005, p. 92).

Bonnie (1992) proposed a reformulation of the concept of competency. As a multifaceted construct, it would include: *(1)* the ability to assist counsel; *(2)* the ability to reason and understand the legal proceedings and charges against the accused; and *(3)* the ability to make legal decisions. In this reformulation, adjudicative competence requires "maturity of judgment" (Bonnie, 1992; *see also* Grisso et al., 2003, p. 335). Psychosocial factors greatly influence an adolescent's level of maturity and ability to make sound, autonomous judgments (Grisso et al., 2003, p. 335). However, psychosocial immaturity is not clearly defined by the *Dusky v. United States* (1960) standard of adjudicative competency. This case represents the legal criterion most often applied to transferred juveniles facing criminal sanctions (Grisso et al., 2003, pp. 335–336; Scott & Grisso, 2005).

Grisso et al. (2003) addressed the challenges the courts might confront if developmental immaturity were identified as a sufficient basis to find adolescents incompetent to stand trial in criminal court. These investigators proposed a "two-tier standard" for adjudicative competency, arguing that juveniles found incompetent to stand trial in adult adversarial proceedings because of developmental immaturity might still face adjudication in delinquency proceedings, consistent with a new "relaxed competence standard" (Grisso et al., 2003, p. 360). However, some commentators suggest that the two-tier competency standard represents a hopeful remedy developed by researchers who fear that the courts and legislatures will not address developmental immaturity as a basis for incompetence *unless* these decision brokers can be assured that juvenile offenders will not be immune from sanctions precisely because of their "developmental incompetence" (Grisso et al., 2003, p. 360; Scott & Grisso, 2005). This concern is well-founded, especially because maturity cannot be easily restored[1] (Viljoen & Grisso, 2007).

The significance of the incompetency doctrine, as supported by rights protected under the Sixth and Fourteenth Amendments to the U.S. Constitution, guarantees the credibility of the criminal proceedings while upholding the "accuracy, fairness, and dignity of the process" (Bardwell & Arrigo, 2002a, p. 154; Scott & Grisso, 2005). The integrity of the adversarial system requires that courts not adjudicate incompetent defendants; thus, understanding how developmental maturity affects competency to stand trial for transferred juveniles is extremely important.

Grisso (2000; Grisso et al., 2003) identified four areas pertinent to the developmental concerns regarding trial competence for juveniles. These include: *(1)* adolescents' understanding of the legal system; *(2)* their belief that legal circumstances applied to them; *(3)* their capacity for communicating with counsel; and *(4)* the processes underlying their decision making (*see also* Heilbrun et al., 1996, p. 577). Oberlander et al. (2001) outlined various developmental factors that might enhance trial competency deficits. These consisted of motor behavior, emotional functioning, attention span, language development and expressive communication, frame of reference and capacity for role differentiation and group relating, and passage of time. As the investigators observed, improper development in these areas of maturity might adversely affect a juvenile's capacity to function sufficiently and rationally under the *Dusky* standard of trial competence. Moreover, the lack of proper developmental maturity might compel a fact-finder to conclude that a youth with such deficits was too immature to cope with the dynamics of the adversarial system (*see also* Grisso et al., 2003, p. 357; Scott & Grisso, 2005). Thus, following Grisso (2000), "psychosocial immaturity" appears to restrict an adolescent defendant's abilities to understand the four legal areas of trial competence. This is because the youth might not possess the decisional competence necessary for sound "legal decision making" in regard to the long-term consequences of his or her legal judgments (e.g., plea bargaining, confessing guilt, etc.) (Grisso et al., 2003, p. 357). Given this analysis and mindful of the *Dusky* standard, some researchers have concluded that "it should make no difference whether the source of the defendant's incompetency is mental illness or immaturity" (Grisso et al., 2003, pp. 358 & 361).

Case Law Method

The following case law methodology sourced jurisprudential intent as communicated in state supreme court and state appellate court decisions[2] addressing adolescent waiver, developmental maturity, and competency to stand trial where the mechanism of automatic transfer was employed. To identify this judicial temperament, specific criteria were established to determine which court cases would be considered for examination. First, an initial search on LexisNexis was conducted for key terms and phrases. Those words/phrases included *juvenile transfer*, *competency to stand trial*, and *maturity*. *Juvenile transfer* was chosen over *juvenile waiver* because a preliminary search with the latter term yielded cases primarily involving waiver of rights; however, the former term yielded cases specifically regarding juvenile transfer practices. Additionally, *competency to stand trial* was selected over the relatively new usage, *adjudicative competency*, because the latter phrase produced no results; however, the former expression led to the retrieval of several court decisions. *Maturity* was chosen over *immaturity* because the former usage is the root of the developmental question courts consider, thereby making it more likely to ascertain cases that examine aspects of (youth) development. With these criteria in mind, the LexisNexis search yielded seven court cases. These judicial decisions included the following: *Tate v. State* (2003); *M.D. v. State* (1997); *Stanford v. Kentucky* (1989); *Gonzales v. Tafoya* (2001); *Otis v. State* (2004); *People v. Hana*, (1993); and *State v. McCracken* (2000).

An eighth case, *In re Causey* (1978), was also identified. However, it was not included in the analysis for very clear and compelling reasons. Although *Causey* appears to be the only court decision that recognizes that a juvenile may be incompetent to stand trial because of developmental immaturity alone, the case's outcome originated in juvenile court. Because *Causey* assesses competency to stand trial and immaturity *only* in delinquency proceedings, it must be excluded because the present inquiry investigates cases dealing with juvenile waiver—particularly direct file or statutory exclusion—where issues of developmental maturity and competency to stand trial are featured.

The next step in the selection of cases was to determine which of them dealt with direct file or statutory exclusion (automatic transfer) instead of traditional judicial waiver. Both *M.D. v. State* (1997) and *People v. Hana* (1993) are judicial waiver cases; consequently, they were excluded from consideration. *Gonzales v. Tafoya* (2001) is a New Mexico case. It is unique in that this state does not have a typical transfer system and, rather, relies on a blended sentencing provision (*see* N.M. Stat. Ann. § 32A). With this provision, juvenile defendants are classified into three different categories: delinquent offenders, youthful offenders, and serious youthful offenders. Delinquent offenders are charged in children's court, whereas serious youthful offenders may be direct-filed to adult court when older than age 15 years and following the commission of first-degree murder (*Gonzales v. Tafoya*, 2001). Further, youthful offenders who are age 14 years or older and who commit 1 of 12 violent felonies are subject to a judicial hearing to assess amenability to treatment, serious nature of the crime, maturity, prior record, and so forth. This protocol is similar to a judicial waiver hearing (*Gonzales v. Tafoya*, 2001). Gonzales was classified as a youthful offender. Because the New Mexico form of a judicial hearing was held in this instance, the case was excluded from review.

Stanford v. Kentucky (1989) was excluded because the decision was overturned by the subsequent case of *Roper v. Simmons* (2005). In examining *Roper*, it was determined that although the case did in fact discuss juvenile transfer and maturity, it did not adequately address the issue of competency to stand trial and, rather, focused on capital punishment and the Eighth Amendment's prohibition on cruel and unusual punishment.[3] Thus, this court decision was excluded from consideration.

Otis v. State (2004) and *State v. McCracken* (2000) were identified as direct-file cases and, as such, were retained for the analysis. *Tate v. State* (2003) is slightly different than the two cases previously mentioned. As a Florida decision, *Tate* is different in that the state requires that juvenile offenders younger than age 14 years be indicted before they are direct-filed for adult criminal trial purposes. However, because the grand jury hearing to indict *Tate* was not representative of a traditional judicial waiver hearing and only examined whether sufficient clear and convincing evidence existed to proceed to criminal trial, this case was included in the analysis.

Having determined which cases addressed adolescent transfer, developmental maturity, and competency to stand trial in the context of mandated waiver, these decisions were then shepardized. In other words, at issue were those subsequent court decisions that cited *Otis v. State* (2004), *State v. McCracken* (2000), and *Tate v. State* (2003), relying on these respective rulings for jurisprudential guidance. Moreover, each list of cases generated from these three shepardized summaries was then scrutinized. The point of this examination was to ascertain whether juvenile transfer, competency to stand trial, and developmental maturity within the context of automatic waiver were discussed. Given these specific selection parameters, several cases were immediately excluded from consideration. However, the case of *Williams v. State* (2006) was deemed acceptable, especially because it was a direct-file decision exploring the issue of a juvenile's competency to stand trial as an adult in lieu of evidence suggesting developmental immaturity and low I.Q. Accordingly, the *Williams* decision was included in the analysis.

Finally, for purposes of thoroughness, the specific legal cases cited within *Otis v. State* (2004), *State v. McCracken* (2000), and *Tate v. State* (2003) were reviewed to determine whether they met the criteria for inclusion in the analysis. Following this investigation, two additional court decisions were identified. *State v. Nevels* (1990) was cited in *McCracken*. It was chosen for inclusion because the court weighed several arguments made by various mental health professionals regarding the psychosocial factors affecting one's maturity that impacted whether defendant Nevels was competent to stand trial in an adult criminal setting. *Brazill v. State* (2006) cited *Tate*. It was selected for inclusion because the court explored the rationale underlying Florida's indictment and direct-file process of juvenile offenders as well as the extent to which this protocol failed to adequately assess a youth's competency and suitability to stand trial in adult court. Overall, then, the ensuing research analyzed six cases: *Otis v. State* (2004), *State v. McCracken* (2000), *Tate v. State* (2003), *Williams v. State* (2006), *State v. Nevels* (1990), and *Brazill v. State* (2006).

Discussion

The above data set was subjected to two levels of qualitative textual scrutiny. The details of the investigatory approach were delineated in chapter one (*see* the section on "psychological jurisprudence and methodology"). Appendix A includes all plain meaning case law findings relative to adolescent transfer, developmental maturity, and competency to stand trial. Table 2.1 lists key concepts and exact quotes as derived from the plain meaning findings that summarily represent the responses to the seven questions posed to these legal decisions. Collectively, these data represent the various attitudes, perceptions, purposes, and concerns that reflect the courts' jurisprudential intentions on the subject matter at hand.

Level 1 Analysis

The data collected from *Tate v. State* (2003) yielded several clues regarding the court's underlying jurisprudential intent. Specifically, statements made in this opinion conveyed the perception that "there is no absolute right requiring

Table 2.1 Jurisprudential Intent as Derived from Plain Meaning Data

	Tate v. State	Otis v. State	State v. McCracken	Williams v. State	State v. Nevels	Brazill v. State
1	Court obligation to ensure competency; no special treatment for serious juvenile offenders	Violent nature of offense negates mitigating factors and demands societal protection	Balancing test to weigh public protection against the juvenile's rights; extreme risk to society	Williams' offenses were aggressively violent and required criminal prosecution to protect society	"... obliged to consider protection for the public and deterrence;" "balance individual justice with needs of society"	Not unreasonable to treat serious juvenile offenders as adults to protect society
2	"Nothing in the law or constitution requiring children be afforded a special system for juveniles"	Court not required to give equal weight or proof for each statutory factor	No method to weigh factors; offense was extremely violent	Evidence revealing great culpability in a serious crime	No formula required in the court's consideration of statutory factors	Legislature and the prosecutor have discretion in deciding who can be treated as a juvenile
3	Not uncommon for Florida courts to impose life imprisonment on juveniles; substantial evidence of intent	Weight given to each statutory factor is at the discretion of the court	Jurisdiction was retained in adult court because of violent nature of offense	Expert testimony states that Williams had no mental defect and understood his actions	Nevels repeatedly violated the law and engaged in violent antisocial acts	Florida legislature has considered the rise in crimes committed by juveniles

#						
4	Tate was entitled to a pre-trial competency hearing to ensure his ability to stand trial as an adult	No data ascertained	McCracken was 13 years old, had no prior record, and his maturity was unclear	Williams was immature and his IQ was borderline; refusal to transfer to juvenile court was contested	Testimony on defendant's mental health suggests immaturity and several disorders	State is allowed to bypass hearing to decide if adult sanctions are appropriate
5	Life without parole is not considered cruel & unusual for a 12-year-old in Florida	Programs and facilities available are not likely to rehabilitate him	Best interest of juvenile and society to retain jurisdiction	Court failed to consider rehabilitative programs for juvenile	Expert opinions are not binding on the court; future dangerousness is a concern	No data ascertained
6	Treat serious juvenile offenders as adults to protect societal goals	Need for greater protection from serious offenders is not arbitrary	McCracken should be held accountable to deter future misconduct	"Protection of Society"	Balancing individual justice with the needs of society; public protection and deterrence	"... interest in crime deterrence and public safety"
7	Treat serious juvenile offenders as adults to protect societal goals	Society demands greater protection from serious offender	Security of the public; deterrence of future antisocial behavior	"Protection of Society"	Protection for the public; effectively deter future antisocial behavior	"... protect societal goals ... society demands greater protection"

children to be treated in a special system for juvenile offenders" (p. 52) and that "the common law presumption of incapacity of a minor between the ages of seven and fourteen years to commit a crime no longer applies" (p. 53). Thus, the court, in *Tate*, upheld the attitude that the state's "statutory scheme" (p. 53), which "supplanted the common law defense of 'infancy,'" (p. 53) was sufficient to make the assertion that "competency hearings are not, per se, mandated simply because a child is tried as an adult" (p. 50). The court buttressed its perspective with the observation that "it is not unreasonable for the legislature to treat children who commit serious crimes as adults in order to protect societal goals" (p. 54). Moreover, mindful of its articulated perspective, the *Tate* court stated that it possessed the "obligation" (p. 51) to make certain that young juveniles with apparent deficits be competent to stand trial.

Questions 3 through 5 elicited the court's rationale regarding its decision to ensure that the juvenile, Tate, was competent to stand trial. The court's opinion that "Tate was entitled to a complete evaluation and hearing" (p. 50) was motivated by "the argument that the proper inquiry was whether the defendant *may be* incompetent, not whether he *is* incompetent" (p. 51, emphasis added), especially because he was only 12 years old and this was his first offense. Initially the trial court overlooked this argument; thus, the *Tate* court determined that in light of Tate's age, any doubt in fitness to stand trial should be eliminated by a complete competency evaluation. In other words, because of his age, there was a possibility that Tate was incompetent to stand trial.

However, other statements in the decision expressed no objection to current transfer practices and the adult sanctions these youthful offenders therefore face. For example, the *Tate* court communicated its approval of transfer trends and subsequent sanctions with the following observation: "[W]e reject the argument that a life sentence without the possibility of parole is cruel or unusual punishment on a twelve-year-old child" [because] "sentences imposed on juveniles [as adults] of life imprisonment are not uncommon in Florida Courts" (p. 54). Indeed, consistent with the logic of favoring juvenile transfer trends, the *Tate* court opined that "it is not unreasonable for the legislature to treat children who commit serious crime as adults in order to protect societal goals" (p. 54). Thus, previous arguments made by the *Tate* court in which it maintained that "there is no absolute right requiring children to be treated in a special system for juvenile offenders" (p. 52) and "competency hearings are not, per se, mandated simply because a child is tried as an adult" (p. 50), suggest that competing interests are jurisprudentially weighed. These are interests in which "societal goals" take precedence over individual rights. Although the *Tate* court recognized the responsibility to determine a juvenile offender's trial fitness in criminal proceedings when the offender was "less than the age of fourteen" (p. 51), it nonetheless perceived such offenders as a severe threat to society. Thus, the issue of public safety compelled the court to conclude that it was reasonable for serious youthful offenders to be treated as adults.

In *Otis v. State* (2004), the court's jurisprudential intent was similar to the reasoning adopted in *Tate v. State* (2003). This perspective was clearly conveyed in the following statement: "[I]t can be inferred from the serious and violent nature of the offense that the protection of society demands that Otis be tried as an adult" (p. 607). In addition, the *Otis* court held the perception that "while Otis' lack of sophistication and maturity may be mitigating factors, they are not of such a nature to warrant a transfer to juvenile court" (p. 609). When the factors underlying these perceptions are examined more closely, several declarations made by the *Otis* court indicate how it weighed the various criteria that must be assessed to determine if a direct-filed youth should be transferred back to juvenile jurisdiction. For example, as the majority opined, "[T]he trial court [was] not required to give equal weight to each of the statutory factors;" (p. 608) "the State was not required to put on proof of each statutory factor;" (p. 609) and "each factor need not be supported by clear and convincing evidence" (p. 610). Furthermore, in *Otis*, the court reasoned that "the second factor does not require proof of premeditation; rather, the second factor pertains to whether the alleged offense was committed in an aggressive, violent, premeditated, or willful manner" (p. 608). Thus, when considering the rights of the individual versus the goals of society, the *Otis* court endorsed the view (the attitude) that the defendant's "lack of sophistication and maturity" (p. 609) gave sway to the "protection of society" (p. 607), particularly because of the violent nature of the crime.

Hence, the intent of the *Otis* decision seems both plain and clear. In short, "the discretion of the trial court" (p. 608) warrants endorsement so that it can gauge the importance of statutory factors when reviewing those interests that are most important when reaching a decision about whether a youth predisposed to a "lack of sophistication and maturity" (p. 609) should be tried as an adult. Moreover, the emphasis placed on "the serious and violent nature of the offense" (p. 607), as well as the *Otis* court's contention that it "[did] not require proof of premeditation" but only "whether the alleged offense was committed in an aggressive, violent, premeditated, or willful manner" (p. 608), suggested that "the protection of society" (p. 607) was most paramount.

In *State v. McCracken* (2000), the concept of interest-balancing was made most obvious when it delineated the criteria and process used to determine whether criminal trial proceedings should be supplanted by decision making in juvenile court. The *McCracken* court held that "it is a balancing test by which public protection and societal security are weighed against the practical and non-problematical rehabilitation of the juvenile," (p. 247) where "there are no weighted factors and no prescribed method[s] by which more or less weight is assigned to each specific factor" (p. 247). Despite the evidence detailing that "McCracken's age of 13 favored transferring jurisdiction; [that] McCracken had no prior criminal history . . . ; [and that] McCracken's sophistication and maturity was unclear" (p. 247), the court reasoned that "without question the best interests of the juvenile and the security of the public require[d] that the court retain jurisdiction, especially since the crime was so violent and McCracken's psychiatric prognosis was so poor" (p. 248).[4]

Given that the defendant's "crime involved extreme violence" (p. 247), other noteworthy factors (i.e., age and maturity level) were overshadowed in the court's "balancing test" assessment. Indeed, the majority's perception and attitude toward the brutal nature of the offense revealed the court's punitive resolve designed to ensure "public protection and societal security" (p. 247). To illustrate, the *McCracken* court stipulated that "it is not appropriate that [the accused] be treated as a juvenile because of the extreme risk of danger that he presents to himself and society" (p. 248). Moreover, the court expressed its concern for the seriousness of the crime in several instances throughout the opinion. For example, the majority in *McCracken* alternately described the offense as being "of a particularly violent and aggressive nature" (p. 248) and as representative of an "extremely violent nature" (pp. 247–249). Finally, the court's more punitive intention was reinforced when it opined that "the record therefore reveals that the district court's decision to retain jurisdiction rested, to a great extent, upon the nature of the offense with which McCracken was charged" (p. 249).

The unequivocal language the court employed when commenting on the violent nature of the crime made evident its rationale for concluding that public protection was more important than the defendant's age and level of maturity. This perspective was summarily disclosed in the following passage:

> " . . . in spite of McCracken's youthful age at the time of the crime, the extreme violence perpetrated upon the victim and the protection of the public in light of McCracken's poor psychiatric prognosis lead us to conclude that the district court did not abuse its discretion when it denied McCracken's motion to transfer to the juvenile court" (p. 249).

Thus, the *McCracken* court concurred with the district court's opinion that the defendant should "be held accountable through proceedings in the adult criminal justice system for effective deterrence of future antisocial misconduct" (p. 249).

In *Williams v. State* (2006), the court also made several statements that conveyed a concern for the violent nature of those crimes committed by the juvenile defendant and the danger such wrongful acts posed toward the public's safety. To illustrate, the court asserted that "Williams' offenses were serious; that they were committed in an aggressive, violent, and premeditated manner" (p. 161) and that "the protection of society required prosecution in the criminal division of circuit court" (p. 162). Interestingly, Williams was diagnosed with a "borderline" I.Q.—that is, he "function[ed] at a lower-than-average range," (p. 161). However, based on the psychiatric testimony, the court noted that "Williams had no mental disease or defect, was competent to proceed to trial, had no problems understanding the criminality of his actions, and had the ability to conform his conduct to the law" (p. 161). As such, the court perceived the "evidence showing that Williams had great culpability in a serious crime" (pp. 164–165) to be sufficient to prosecute him in an adult court. Consistent with *McCracken*, then, the *Williams* decision hinged on the violent nature of the crimes committed.[5] Absent diagnosed psychiatric illness or disability, the defendant was competent to stand trial in a criminal court, especially because the offenses "were committed in an aggressive, violent, and premeditated manner" (p. 161). Here, too, the underlying rationale for this determination was in the furtherance of societal goals and needs—specifically, the "protection of society" (p. 162).

In *State v. Nevels* (1990), the court communicated its perspective regarding the rehabilitation of juvenile offenders and the maintenance of the public's general welfare. In particular, the court opined that although "rehabilitation has traditionally played a key role in the treatment of young offenders . . . nevertheless, the concept of deterrence and the need to balance individual justice with the needs of society . . . also have a place in the juvenile justice system" (pp. 50–51). This language makes clear that the court intended to adopt a "balancing test" (p. 50) standard in which competing rights and needs were subjected to jurisprudential scrutiny. Moreover, the *Nevels* court stipulated that "there is no arithmetical computation or formula required in a court's consideration of the statutory criteria of factors" (p. 50) and that "the court need not resolve every factor against the juvenile" (p. 50). Thus, the attitude endorsed in *Nevels* was one in which an assessment of those factors that outweigh others rightfully falls under the court's discretion.

Numerous accounts from mental health experts raised concerns for defendant Nevels' ability to stand trial in an adult criminal setting. For example, commenting on his personality difficulties, one forensic specialist indicated that the defendant's problems stemmed from a "lack of identity in that Nevels' engage[d] in negative behavior which [made] him feel more secure about his black, male identity and which secure[d] acceptance in his peer groups" (p. 46). Additional testimony as reported in the case intimated that the accused "suffer[ed] from several disorders and disabilities, including a mixed development disorder involving several speech-and language-base[d] learning disabilities" (p. 44). Moreover, restating the proffered psychiatric evidence, the *Nevels* court indicated that this particular deficit was only compounded by:

"[a] conduct disorder socialized aggressive, which means Nevels is
aggressive during periods of anxiety and has difficulty in
conforming his behavior to the norms of society; a major depressive
disorder; and an adolescent identity disorder which means Nevels is
still . . . in the process of forming his own identity, [and] [is] very
immature" (p. 44).

These diagnoses led one psychiatrist to conclude that the defendant was "treatable because he [did] not yet have a fixed personality" (p. 46). A second forensic expert similarly deduced that "Nevels' disorders [were] treatable as evidenced by his favorable response to treatment" and that "mainstreaming Nevels into an adult prison population 'would probably be [devastating]' " (p. 45).

Despite the varied testimony of medical specialists documenting the bases for defendant Nevels' misconduct, the court rejected it. Indeed, notwithstanding the significant psychosocial factors raised by mental health professionals, the underlying rationale informing the court's perspective was located elsewhere. In short, the *Nevels* majority ruled that "as the trier of fact, the district court was not required to take the opinions of experts as binding upon it" (p. 51). To reinforce this jurisprudential attitude, various arguments were made.

For example, the court held the opinion that "if Nevels' case were to have been transferred to the juvenile court, he might have viewed the transfer as his manipulation of the system and [he might] not [have] taken responsibility for the crime," (p. 52). The court adopted this view, especially because it found "the facilities available to the juvenile court would not provide enough protection to the public" (p. 52). Thus, more consideration was given to the general welfare than to defendant Nevels' developmental immaturity. In support of this logic, the court stipulated that the accused had "repeatedly violated the law and performed other antisocial acts, culminating in [a] very violent and cruel beating" (p. 51).[6] Elsewhere, the court reasoned that "an individual's future dangerousness" could not be predicted by mental health professionals (p. 45). Consequently, the *Nevels* court opined that "in addition to considering the defendant's age, [it was] obliged to consider protection of the public and deterrence," (p. 53) because "dealing with Nevels in the juvenile court system might diminish the seriousness of the offense" (p. 48). Once again, and consistent with prior cases on the matter, an assessment of the plain legal language yielded underlying jurisprudential intent. Defendant Nevels needed to be prosecuted in criminal court for the sake of society's protection and to deter future violent juvenile offenses (p. 51).

A review of the data in *Brazill v. State* (2006) indicates that this ruling mirrors the opinions of the cases previously analyzed. Specifically, the *Brazill* court stated that "the legislature was entitled to conclude that the *parens patriae* function of the juvenile system would not work for certain juveniles, or that society demanded greater protection from these offenders than that provided by that system" (p. 288). Moreover, the decision in *Brazill* reaffirmed prior court holdings when it opined that "there is no absolute right conferred by common law, constitution, or otherwise, requiring children to be treated in a special system for juvenile offenders" (p. 287). The court in *Brazill* conveyed its motivation here when noting that "it is not unreasonable for the legislature to treat children who commit serious crimes as adults in order to protect societal goals" (p. 288). In addition, the *Brazill* court embraced the perspective that "the legislature could reasonably have determined that for some crimes the rehabilitative aspect of juvenile court must give way to punishment" (p. 288). The court's rationale for adopting such perceptions is embedded in several comments. To illustrate, the majority in *Brazill* observed, "The legislature has the power to determine who, if anyone, is entitled to treatment as a juvenile" (p. 287). Elsewhere, the court reasoned, "[T]he discretion of a prosecutor in deciding whether and how to prosecute is absolute in our system of criminal justice" (p. 289). With these two statements, the *Brazill* court summarily approved statutory exclusion and direct-file laws.

Defense counsel in *Brazill* raised numerous concerns about how the transfer practices in Florida did not adequately assess whether a juvenile could stand trial in criminal court. To illustrate, drawing attention to the relevant state statute, counsel argued, "Section 985.225 does not require a court to hold a hearing to decide whether adult sanctions are appropriate" (p. 288). An additional objection was proffered specifying that Section 985.225 failed to permit "the state to bypass a hearing on the suitability of adult sanctions by [first] securing an indictment" (p. 288). Therefore, the automatic waiver practices of Florida provided a statutory loophole in which prosecutors could direct-file juveniles like Brazill (aged 13 years) into criminal proceedings without having to initially undertake a thorough assessment of the child's competency to stand trial as an adult. The legislative rationale in support of automatic transfer is made most evident wherein Section 985.255 stipulates that it "applies to '[a] child of any age who is charged with a violation of state law punishable by death or life imprisonment . . . It does not differentiate between age groups'" (p. 289).

The decision in *Brazill* was motivated by a concern for societal interests over and against the protection of individual rights. This conclusion follows, given that the court emphasized an "interest in crime deterrence and public safety," (p. 288) and acknowledged that "society demanded greater protection from . . . offenders" (p. 288). Thus, the court's jurisprudential intent in *Brazill* was consistent with prior court rulings on adolescent (mandated) waiver, developmental maturity, and competency to stand trial. The societal goals of safety and security were balanced against the rights and interests of the youthful offender.

Level 2 Analysis

The second level of qualitative analysis reconsidered each instance of jurisprudential intent as derived from plain meaning and subjected it to additional textual scrutiny. The aim of this endeavor was to interpret what this legal language (i.e., manifest content) communicated ethically (i.e., deeper meaning embedded in the words/phrases themselves). Stated differently, the goal of this particular inquiry was to determine what moral philosophy was conveyed through judicial temperament, mindful of the three ethical schools of thought under consideration, including their variants and corresponding principles. Table 2.2 identifies the particular phrases in question for each legal case constituting the data set.

When closely re-reading the *Tate* opinion, specific words and phrases were employed signifying a reliance on the consequentialist perspective of utilitarianism. For example, expressions such as "treat children who commit

Table 2.2 Underlying Ethical Reasoning Conveying Jurisprudential Intent

	Consequentialism (Utilitarianism)	Formalism	Virtue Ethics
Tate v. State	"treat children who commit serious crimes as adults in order to protect society goals" "no absolute right requiring children to be treated in a special system"	"obligation to ensure that the juvenile defendant . . . was competent"	
Otis v.State	"not required to give equal weight to each of the statutory factors" "Society demands greater protection from serious offenders"		
State v. McCracken	"balancing test by which public protection and societal security are weighed against . . . rehabilitation" "best interests of the juvenile and security of the public [(factor 8)] without question [weigh] in favor of the Court continuing the court here"	"McCracken should be held accountable through proceedings in the adult criminals justice system for effective deterrence of future antisocial misconduct"	
Williams v. State	"protection of society required prosecution in the criminal division of circuit court"		
State v. Nevels	"the concept of deterrence and the need to balance individual justice with the needs of society . . . also have a place in the juvenile justice system" " balancing test"	"we 'are obliged to consider protection for the public and deterrence'" "responsibility for the crime"	
Brazill v. State	"society demanded greater protection from these offenders than that provided by that system" "interest in crime deterrence and public safety"		

serious crimes as adults in order to protect society goals" (p. 54) and "no absolute right requiring children to be treated in a special system" (p. 52) indicate that two conflicting interests were weighed by the court. In other words, as manifest content, the welfare of the general public was balanced against the rights of the individual. However, upon closer investigation, this concept of interest-balancing is most closely related to the utilitarian principle of ascertaining the greatest good for the greatest number of people.

Conversely, other phrases found in the *Tate* ruling were consistent with ethical formalism, or Kantian moral philosophy. To illustrate, the expression "obligation to ensure that the juvenile defendant . . . was competent" (p. 51) suggests the court had a duty or responsibility to determine the defendant's competency to stand trial. The word "obligation" clearly refers to "duty," which formalism recognizes as a moral maxim or categorical imperative. Thus, the deeper (ethical) meaning located in the jurisprudential intent of the *Tate* decision communicated both the logic of utilitarianism as well as formalism.

Similar to the *Tate* ruling, *Otis v. State* (2004) appropriated legal language that, when re-evaluated for its ethical significance, endorsed utilitarian objectives. For example, phrases such as "not required to give equal weight to each of the statutory factors" (p. 608) and "society demands greater protection from serious offenders" (p. 613) once again signaled an interest-balancing argument. Indeed, the court in *Otis* intended to consider competing factors (e.g., age, maturity, severity of the offense) where determining which of them was more substantive than others was left to the discretion of the court of first instance. Declarations of this sort constituted manifest content. Moreover, the court's opinion that " 'greater protection' for society outweighed the defendant's lack of sophistication and maturity" (p. 609) similarly conveyed jurisprudential intent and functioned as manifest content warranting textual exegeses. Thus, when interpreted ethically, this statement represented an appeal to the greatest happiness principle articulated within the philosophy of utilitarianism.

In *State v. McCracken* (2000) the court's decision embodied utilitarian reasoning, given an assessment of those key phrases that reflected its underlying jurisprudential intent. For example, the *McCracken* court referred to the case as "a balancing test by which public protection and societal security [were] weighed against . . . rehabilitation" (p. 248). As manifest content, this statement amounts to an interest-balancing argument. Moreover, the court agreed with the lower court's finding that the "best interests of the juvenile and security of the public [(factor 8)] without question [weighed] in favor of the court" retaining jurisdiction (p. 248). When interpreted ethically, the deeper meaning lodged within this legal language is that ensuring protection for the collective good was preferred over the rights and interests of the individual.

In addition to the utilitarian underpinnings located within *McCracken's* jurisprudential intent is an instance in support of formalist principles. Specifically, the court argued that "McCracken should be held accountable through proceedings in the adult criminal justice system for effective deterrence of future antisocial misconduct" (p. 249). The manifest content, "should be held accountable," refers to the deeper, ethical signification of responsibility. By logical extension, then, it could be inferred that the court felt a (moral) duty to hold McCracken "accountable," given the serious crime he committed. Additionally, and consistent with this reasoning, the statement could be interpreted to mean that McCracken was viewed by the court as violating a categorical imperative. As such, he was duty-bound to take responsibility for his failure to adhere to an unqualified maxim (i.e., adult accountability for one's serious criminal actions committed as a juvenile).

The *Williams v. State* (2006) opinion similarly employed legal language whose underlying jurisprudential intent ethically communicated a commitment to the philosophy of utilitarianism. To illustrate, the court's declaration that "protection of society required prosecution in the criminal division of circuit court" (p. 162) represented manifest content. However, when interpreting this phrase within the context of ethical thought, the court's meaning is consistent with the view that the greatest good for the greatest number of people was most paramount in the *Williams* decision. Indeed, issues such as "age, I.Q., immaturity, and lack of sophistication" (p. 164) were all eclipsed by a desire to ensure the "protection of society" (p. 162). Here, too, it is noted how legal language can be subjected to additional textual exegeses when filtered through the prism of moral philosophy.

In *State v. Nevels* (1990), the court also conveyed its reliance on utilitarian principles when endorsing a "balancing test" (p. 50) approach. In particular, the *Nevels* court stated that "the concept of deterrence and the need to balance individual justice with the needs of society . . . also have a place in the juvenile justice system" (pp. 50–51). Declarations such as these constituted manifest content. However, when subjected to additional textual exegeses, the ethical rationale operating here is consistent with the greatest happiness principle. Moreover, the court's decision to disregard the developmental immaturity factors raised by defense counsel in favor of pursuing alternative goals that protected society further communicated the notion that utilitarian objectives informed *Nevels'* underlying jurisprudential intent.

On the other hand, the *Nevels* court also appropriated language that, when interpreted ethically, conveyed fidelity to the philosophy of formalism. For example, the statement, "[W]e 'are obliged to consider protection for the public and deterrence'" (p.53), represented underlying jurisprudential intent. Indeed, as manifest content, it indicated a concern for the collective good in which future harm was to be abated. However, the deeper level of signification embedded in this phrase ethically implied that the *Nevels* court also felt a *duty* to seek an outcome in support of the citizenry's general welfare in which future crime prevention was reasonably assured. Additionally, the expression "responsibility for the crime" communicated formalist sensibilities in that the court believed the defendant violated a moral maxim and, as such, ought to be held accountable for it. Moreover, consistent with this logic, the expression's fundamental meaning suggests that the court understood its moral duty to hold Nevels responsible for violating a categorical imperative (i.e., several antisocial acts that culminated in a very violent and cruel beating).

Finally, when reviewing the jurisprudential intent of the decision in *Brazill v. State* (2006), the ethical meaning endorsed by the court was compatible with utilitarian principles. For example, phrases such as "society demanded greater protection from these offenders than that provided by that system" (p. 288) and "interest in crime deterrence and public safety" (p. 288) once again drew attention to an instance in which the court engaged in an interest-balancing test. As manifest content, societal protection was given consider-able emphasis, notwithstanding those concerns raised by defense counsel regarding competency and age-related deficits (p. 288). Moreover, when interpreting this legal language for its ethical significance, the court's focus on "greater protection" (p. 288) for society constituted *the* linchpin factor in its decision to not transfer the case to juvenile court. Hence, textual exegeses of the sort undertaken here affirmed that utilitarian objectives were conveyed through the court's juridical discourse.

When considering the ethical reasoning communicated through the juris-prudential intent for all six court cases, it is overwhelmingly evident that the philosophy of consequentialism and the principles of utilitarianism were prominently featured. The themes of "interest balancing" and "the greatest good for the greatest number" were located throughout each case and, to a lesser extent, were made patently obvious in some of them. Indeed, not only did the utilitarian perspective appear most often in the courts' language usage, but the prestige and reverence afforded this perspective was far greater than what was found in those passages endorsing Kantian formalism. Although *Tate, McCracken,* and *Nevels* clearly appropriated expressions or phrases con-sistent with this latter moral philosophy, the full ethical meaning lodged within these respective instances of manifest content was not easily ascertainable. Consequently, the first and second levels of analyses indicate that with regard to the issue of juvenile (automatic) transfer, developmental maturity, and com-petency to stand trial, the primary ethical rationale embedded within the court's jurisprudential intent is consistent with the logic of utilitarianism. This finding is obtained in each court decision and, correspondingly, across all of them.

Implications: The Dynamics of Madness, Citizenship, and Social Justice

This chapter undertook a qualitative examination of state supreme court and appellate court reasoning on the practice of automatic transfer for juveniles, where issues of developmental maturity and trial fitness were notably fea-tured. The first level of analysis focused on plain meaning as guided by a series of questions that elicited information (key words or expressions), specifying the court's jurisprudential intent. The second level of analysis resituated these terms or phrases within their respective legal contexts and evaluated them against prevailing moral philosophical thought as a basis to ascertain the underlying ethical logic communicated by the court.

Intriguingly, although not surprisingly, the results indicated that juridical decision making principally entails a utilitarian balance of competing interests in which concerns for the majority's (the public's) greater good is esteemed and sought. In other words, it is unremarkable that courts weigh (and value) the interests of the state over and against the needs of youths. This finding is consistent with one main contention of this book. Simply put, legal tribunals fail to take seriously the empirical findings from the social and behavioral science community on the manifold confinement, treatment, and recidivism problems that developmentally immature adolescents face when automatically waived and deemed fit to stand adult criminal trial. The traditional hearing conducted by the judicial transfer process has been supplanted with legislative and (direct-file) prosecutorial waiver. These efforts circumvent any thorough examination of the juvenile's competence to stand trial. Unlike judicial transfer, where developmental immaturity (among other things) is assessed, mandated forms of waiver mostly bypass this critical evaluative step.

Accordingly, we maintain that the total confinement practice at work here wrongly criminalizes troubled youth, and the judicial endorsement that follows—as reflected through an ethically derived assessment of the prevailing case law on the matter—is nothing short of *madness*. This madness stems from a number of interdependent forces, mostly unexamined in the relevant literature. However, the source of these forces is the fear of crime (Simon, 2009) and its governance through hypervigilant and panoptic disciplining and normalization (e.g., Foucault, 1965, 1977). As techniques and strategies of control, this governance includes the prevailing images conjured about the offender, victim, and/or community in which the injury occurred (the Symbolic realm); the privileged story told or constructed about the harm committed or experienced (the Linguistic realm); the body (or bodies) of knowledge produced from both whose lived inscriptions are deployed as preferred treatment/corrective action(s) (the Material realm); and the carnival-like replications of "offender," "victim," "community," "treatment," and "recovery" that are repetitively (and reductionistically) propagated *ad infinitum* by way of this cyclical process (the Cultural realm). Intended or otherwise, this process sanctions an ethic of harm. This harm extends from the kept to their keepers, from their managers to their watchers. We will have more to say about these forces or conditions of control and captivity in the concluding chapter. Suffice it to say, however, that the dynamics of this captivity represent a kind of madness that dangerously undermines the prospect of citizenship and the evolution in social justice.

Although this investigation produced significant findings regarding the court's ethical reasoning on the issue of automatic juvenile transfer, competency to stand trial, and developmental maturity, it also suffered from several limitations. First, this study addressed a very specific law–psychology–crime problem that yielded only six court cases warranting textual scrutiny. The small data set raises serious questions about the generalizability of the overall findings. This matter goes to the selection of case law data, the methodology employed to review them, and the results themselves. Admittedly, our criterion-based sample design was targeted. We focused on a narrow, although contentious, theme in mental health law. This focus produced only those decisions relevant to investigating that theme. Further, our two-phase model of textual legal analysis is experimental and novel. The first stage, qualitative and interpretive, located plain meaning data guided by a series of questions designed to identify connotations of judicial temperament. The second stage, more textual and probabilistic, re-examined this jurisprudential intent (these meanings) and filtered each instance through the prism of prevailing normative theory. These instances of ethically interpreted judicial temperament underwent thematic intra- and inter-textual evaluation. Thus, from our perspective, concerns for the data set seem unwarranted, if not unfounded.

Second, even if these sampling and methodological concerns were reasonably hurdled, the heuristic nature of the study possesses limited evidentiary utility. Its explanatory and predictive properties are problematic. This matter goes to the intention of our overall project on judicial decision making, mental health law, and ethics, and why it even matters. So, let us be clear. We are noting that the manifest content of the legal cases themselves on which jurisprudential intent was derived from plain meaning did not address ethics in any virtue-based way. No mention of Aristotelian habits of character (e.g., courage, magnificence, gentleness, humility, or compassion) served as underlying moral principles by which judicial temperament was communicated in any case or across the data set. Still, objection could be raised: absence of evidence is not the same as evidence of absence. Stated differently, the lack of virtue ethics data does not "prove" that the courts or judicial community place no value in conveying this reasoning through the respective decisions. On this matter, we agree. But here the call is certainly for further and more probing analyses. Along the lines of establishing greater evidence-based depth, we maintain that the question is how, if at all, did (and do) jurists speak of excellence and human flourishing when rendering their court decisions? This is a quality of existence that celebrates or otherwise seeks to spark the transformative possibilities of one and all. This is how virtue is cultivated. This cultivation is the engine of change. Change matters individually, communally, and socially in an era of total confinement practices.

Third, the attention to ethical inquiry and sourcing its presence (or absence) in the data set more generally may be a point of criticism as well. After all, the purpose of judicial decision making is not to advance a particular ethic as much as it is to interpret and settle a dispute in and about the law. This matter challenges the relevance of our qualitative undertaking. We maintain that the pursuit of individual accountability and institutional responsibility for wrongdoing fosters a type of justice that makes ethical examination by way of citizenship standards (i.e., dignity, the therapeutic, and critique) and excellence habits (virtues) both necessary and possible. The idea of dignity we embrace is fair-minded and commonsensical in that it recognizes the moral gravitas of discerning (judging) the self–society mutuality or twin dynamics operating in a given instance. On issues of total confinement, we are all jurors (evaluators and decision makers); otherwise, we *are* captive! This, too, fits our meaning for commonsense justice. Further, the idea of the therapeutic (and the restorative) to which we allude encompasses the individual–institutional spheres, counsels by way of their interconnectedness, and heals and repairs all those within its ambit injured in the process. This includes victim, offender, and the community that tethers both. To be sure, the kept and their keepers, their managers, and their watchers all play a role in this recuperative and regenerative experience. Thus, the standard of citizenship we embrace acknowledges that few are ever "guilty," whereas all are often "responsible." Finally, the critique we have in mind probes the constructed meanings for such notions as dignity, the therapeutic, crime, recovery, responsibility, and even health. These meanings endorse and privilege certain definitions that can be contested by dynamic alternatives. These replacement meanings possess the potential to more fully celebrate and grow human flourishing for one and about all. This reservoir of excellence is an untapped habit whose practice we seek to advance and replicate elsewhere. We will have more to say about these notions in the concluding chapter as well. However, given our reasoning above, we argue that pursuing a systematic normative investigation of the sort undertaken in this chapter is quite relevant in and to law, mental health, and jurisprudential ethics.

Having addressed the concerns for the case law data and findings, the study's evidentiary utility, and the emphasis on ethical inquiry more generally, we are led to the following question: How were virtues such as courage, dignity, and compassion communicated through the jurisprudential intent of the data set? And, if they were, what quality of fair-minded dignity and what version of healing interests were advanced? Further still, were all (or some) restored through this supposed exercise in practiced excellence? To posit the query more plainly still: How does the prevailing case law on juvenile transfer, developmental maturity, and competency to stand trial dignify, heal, and restore by way of excellence? We argue that it does not. And this absence is what helps to sustain the madness that is the total confinement practice issue under critical investigation. This madness is lodged in a dark and foreboding ethic whose interactive symbolic, linguistic, material, and cultural grounding limits possibilities in being and thwarts possibilities in becoming by way of the self–society mutuality. This is how captivity for the kept and their keepers, for their managers, and for their watchers harmfully endures. And, for those who find this thinking naïve or no more than progressive liberal outrage, we take exception to this characterization. The well-being, collective goodness, and social change we seek include *transformative habits of character*. No Justice— regardless of apparent, presumed, or observed political allegiances—communicated anything remotely signifying virtuous reasoning of this sort. This quality of reform is our politics.

We also note that additional analyses could (and likely would) further inform our findings. Specifically, no statutory analysis on the issue at hand was undertaken. Undoubtedly, this legislative inquiry would have resulted in a more complete portrait of the state's (not just the court's) unstated intent and the ethical regard conveyed through that intent. Additionally, the interpretive nature of our investigation could benefit from some form of quantitative elaboration (perhaps corroboration). For example, a survey instrument could be developed in which judges were queried about the moral philosophy they believed informed their decision making. Specifically, it would be noteworthy to evaluate how jurists talk about the ethical reasoning that informs their rule-making on adolescent waiver as contrasted with what their court judgments actually say (i.e., jurisprudential intent via plain meaning, as well as moral philosophical logic communicated through that intent).

These shortcomings notwithstanding, the results delineated drew attention to a number of unambiguous concerns. At their most manifest level, the results demonstrated how inadequately or insufficiently legal tribunals rely on the empirical research for judicial guidance when endorsing automatic juvenile transfer. First, courts excessively focus on the serious nature of the offense in which public safety, deterrence, and retribution mostly override an evaluation of a juvenile's competency-related abilities (Brink, 2004; Feld, 2004, 2001, pp. 12–14; Kupchik, 2006, pp. 18–19; Kurlychek & Johnson, 2004; Steinberg & Cauffman, 2000, p. 380; Steiner & Wright, 2006; Steiner et al., 2006). Second, courts routinely neglect to consider how psychosocial immaturity factors are, to a certain extent, the cause of violent juvenile crime (Corriero, 2006; Feld, 2004) and, correspondingly, how such causes affect the juvenile's legal decision-making abilities (Grisso et al., 2003; Katner, 2006; Scott & Grisso, 2005; Steinberg, 2003). Third, courts generally fail to recognize the significant impact developmental immaturity has on the defendant's adjudicative competence (Oberlander et al., 2001, p. 548; Scott & Grisso, 2005; Viljoen & Grisso, 2007) as well as the psychosocial factors that greatly impair an adolescent's decisional competence when transferred to an adult criminal proceeding (Bonnie, 1992; Grisso et al., 2003; Katner, 2006; Scott & Grisso, 2005; Steinberg, 2003). Fourth, courts typically emphasize a "get tough on juvenile crime" perspective, thereby readying the youth to become a hardened (career) criminal (Bishop & Frazier, 2000, p. 257; Rossiter, 2006, p. 130), eroding prospects for rehabilitative treatment (Rossiter, 2006; Kupchik, 2006, p. 152), and undermining the possibility of successful community reentry (Bishop & Frazier, 2000, p. 260; Corriero, 2006, p. 49).

Collectively, then, the approach adopted by the courts, as repeatedly borne out in this qualitative endeavor, satisfies the needs of an organized society; however, it does little to address the replicated empirical problems raised when waiving adolescents to the adult system. These problems are rooted in "the belief that serious crimes committed by young offenders may reflect developmental deficiencies in autonomy and social judgment, [that if treated could lead to] a reduction in their culpability" (Kupchik, 2006, p. 82). Accordingly, if society is to create meaningful change in the character of (the ethic surrounding) persistent youthful offending, then it must reconsider what is for "the greater good." This deeper level of investigation entails a re-assessment of the moral philosophy through which the court's logic could be communicated, mindful of the more current trends in the law–psychology–crime subfield, and as developed within the integrative praxis of psychological jurisprudence.

3

Inmate Mental Health, Solitary Confinement, and Cruel and Unusual Punishment

Introduction

The imprisonment of mentally ill offenders is another topic within the realm of law–psychology–crime in which the logic of psychological jurisprudence and the philosophy of virtue-based ethics applies. Research overwhelmingly indicates that a significant number of those confined suffer from wide-ranging mental health problems (Baillargeon, Binswanger, Penn, Williams & Murray, 2009; Haney, 2003; James & Glaze, 2006; Kupers, 1999; Lamb & Weinberger, 1998; Rhodes, 2004, 2005). Indeed, as Rhodes poignantly asserted, "increasingly punitive sentences combined with the deinstitutionalization of psychiatric treatment centers have resulted in correctional facilities becoming the 'asylum of last resort' for the psychologically disordered" (2005, p. 1693).

In response to a burgeoning prison population—many of whom are mentally ill and arguably unable to conform their behavior to institutional rules and regulations—correctional administrators increasingly place incarcerates in solitary confinement. Although some prison segregation units vary slightly depending on the jurisdiction, the facilities are typically designed to house inmates 23 hours a day in steel-door-enforced cells measuring approximately 6 by 8 feet in size (Arrigo & Bullock, 2008). One hour of exercise time a day is allowed for most segregated prisoners. Often referred to as the "dog run[s]," the exercise pens in isolation units and facilities are surrounded by concrete walls or are, essentially, a wire cage. Thus, segregated incarcerates have little to no daily exposure to fresh air, natural light, or opportunity for physical health-enhancing activities (Haney, 2003; Shalev, 2009). To limit interaction with others, some facilities employ "tele-psychiatry" and "tele-medicine" procedures in which the prisoner may only be "examined" through video conferencing with medical and mental health professionals and staff (Haney, 2003, p. 126; *see also* Shalev, 2009). In addition to imposed seclusion, mechanical, physical, chemical, and technological restraints are utilized to ensure minimal psychological stimulation and to control nearly every aspect of an inmate's existence (Haney, 2003; Kupers, 2008; Toch, 2003).

Although the mental health of prisoners in isolative confinement is monitored according to policies specified in each penal setting, the extreme solitude to which incarcerates are subjected raises a number of thorny ethical questions. Research, dating back as far as the mid-nineteenth century, delineates the deleterious effects of solitary confinement on prisoners' mental health (Grassian, 1983; Haney, 2003; Kupers, 2008; Mears, 2006; Rhodes, 2004, 2005; Toch, 2003). Indeed, as Haney observed, "there are few if any forms of imprisonment that appear to produce so much psychological trauma and in which so many symptoms of psychopathology are manifested" (2003, p. 126).

According to the extant literature, isolation of varying types and durations negatively impacts the mental health of incarcerates with no known psychiatric disorders. However, the effects of placing inmates with pre-existing mental health conditions in solitary confinement—particularly in extreme isolative conditions and for protracted periods of time—are especially devastating. Moreover, research suggests that mentally ill inmates are significantly more likely to be placed in segregation and supermax facilities (Haney, 2003; Kurki & Morris, 2001; Toch, 2001; *see also* Mears & Watson, 2006). Indeed, psychiatrically disordered offenders "are more likely . . . to break prison rules, engage in arguments with other inmates, and decompensate mentally" (Naday, Freilich, & Mellow, 2008, p. 87; *see also* Haney, 2003; Rhodes, 2004). Thus, given the frequency with which mentally ill inmates are placed in isolation and noting the gravity of the associated risks, the focus of the ensuing inquiry is on psychiatrically disordered inmates in prolonged disciplinary solitary confinement.

Regrettably, the legal community has yet to incorporate the extant social and behavioral science findings on mentally ill incarcerates in protracted punitive segregation into the relevant case law on cruel and unusual punishment matters. Moreover, no study has purposefully explored the essential ethical rationale that informs the courts' decision making. This is obtained especially when Eighth Amendment challenges proffered by prisoners in long-term disciplinary isolation who suffer from pre-existing mental health conditions are the source of inquiry. In other words, the logic of psychological jurisprudence and the philosophy of ethics conveyed through the pertinent case opinions on the subject of punitive segregation and mentally disordered inmates have not been systematically examined.[1] A thorough analysis of both may very well be the basis for converting (tacit) theory into constructive public policy.

This chapter qualitatively focuses on these critical issues. Specifically, what will be made clear is the moral philosophy discernable in the judicial opinions that communicates the courts' perspective on Eighth Amendment challenges raised by inmates with pre-existing mental health conditions placed in long-term disciplinary solitary confinement. Addressing this matter then makes it possible to evaluate whether, and to what extent, current punitive isolation practices impacting psychiatrically disordered incarcerates support (or fail to support) excellence in being for all participants in whom the merits "of living virtuously [inform] the jurisprudential reasoning" (Sellers & Arrigo, 2009, p. 441).

Accordingly, the first section outlines the distinct types of solitary confinement and recounts the relevant literature on inmate mental health in both the general prison population and while in isolation. The second section delineates the "case law method" employed in this study. This includes the procedures followed that led to the selection of those court cases consti- tuting the data set. The third section discusses the results. This portion of the chapter identifies the ethical rationales and/or principles that informed the courts' judicial temperament both intra- and inter-textually. The fourth section comments on the relevance of the findings in relation to the total confinement practice of inmate mental health, long-term disciplinary segre- gation, and cruel and unusual punishment.[2] These observations consider whether the moral philosophy underlying this practice, as appropriated by the legal apparatus, is suspect or flawed, especially given the empirical evidence documenting the deleterious health, mental health, and social welfare effects that follow from said practice's maintenance. Further, these remarks are explored within the dynamic contexts of madness, citizenship, and social justice.

The Literature on Solitary Confinement: an Overview

Types of Solitary Confinement

Although solitary confinement facilities are designed to physically isolate and constructively curtail the violent behavior of disruptive inmates, there are variations in the types and lengths of imprisonment. Segregation facilities and units are known by a number of names, including extended control units and secured housing units (SHUs) (Haney, 2003). Although the names of the units may differ, the facilities share a number of psychological characteristics that often make the conditions within them indistinguishable from one another (Haney, 2003; *see also* Riveland, 1999). Indeed, what constitutes short- and long-term administrative and disciplinary solitary confinement also varies according to individual correctional institutions and their respec- tive jurisdictions. Moreover, the degree of isolation imposed within each unit is not uniformly representative of every solitary confinement facility (Haney, 2003; Rhodes, 2004; Mears & Watson, 2006; Naday et al., 2008). Noting these definitional and generalization concerns, the ensuing discussion focuses on the research findings delineating the conditions of the two types of solitary confinement as they are formally designated by the Federal Bureau of Prisons (BOP) and recognized within the prevailing literature.

Administrative segregation (Ad-Seg) is one type of solitary confinement. As noted, the conditions under which inmates are placed in Ad-Seg vary slightly depending on the jurisdiction; however, many inmates are placed in this type of isolation based on a pending investigation of a rule infraction or a possible transfer to disciplinary segregation. According to Riveland, "inmates who have demonstrated that they are chronically violent or assaultive, who present a serious escape risk, or who have demonstrated a capacity to incite disturbances or otherwise are threatening the orderly operation of the [institution's] general population may become target populations" (1999, p. 6).

Conditions in Ad-Seg are restrictive. However, in addition to basic necessities such as hygiene products and an hour of physical activity time, Ad-Seg incarcerates also may receive literary materials and mail. These and other items are often contingent upon the behavior of the inmate while in Ad-Seg. If the incarcerate is uncooperative or disruptive, these privileges can be removed (Federal BOP Guidelines; 2008; O'Keefe, 2008).

Perhaps one of the greatest concerns regarding Ad-Seg is that an inmate may be placed there indefinitely. In fact, the typical stay of an inmate in Ad-Seg may exceed the average stay of an individual in disciplinary segregation. Placement in this type of solitary confinement relies solely on the discretion of correctional administrators and staff. As such, there is no formally imposed due process procedure that precedes administrative isolation. Consequently, human rights advocates have raised concerns regarding prisoners in Ad-Seg receiving a "punishment disproportionate to the seriousness of the behavior" (O'Keefe, 2008, p. 126).

The second type of solitary confinement is disciplinary or punitive segregation. Unlike its administrative counterpoint, punitive isolation "is a time-limited response to a disciplinary infraction after due process hearings resulting in a finding of guilt" (O'Keefe, 2008, p. 124). According to the Federal BOP, a designated Discipline Hearing Officer (DHO) is required to consider an inmate's violation of prison rules. If the DHO determines that no other "course of action will adequately punish the inmate or deter her or him from violating BOP rules again," then the DHO may order the inmate to be placed in disciplinary segregation (Federal BOP Guidelines, 2008, p.1).

Depending on the jurisdiction in which the correctional facility is operating, incarcerates placed in disciplinary segregation may only spend months in punitive solitude (Arrigo & Bullock, 2008; O'Keefe, 2008). However, if an inmate repeatedly violates BOP rules while in isolation, their period of segregation can extend to years (Kupers, 1999, 2008; Rhodes, 2004). Regardless of the length of confinement, the conditions of punitive isolation are intended to be extremely restrictive. Although disciplinary segregation is considered by some to be excessively harsh, the BOP requires prison administrators and staff to ensure that inmates in said confinement receive "the basic living levels of decency and humane treatment" (Federal BOP Guidelines, 2008, p. 2). Moreover, the guidelines require that inmates' fundamental needs, such as nutritionally adequate meals and access to a toilet, must be met (Federal BOP Guidelines, 2008).

Empirical Research on Imprisonment, Inmate Mental Health, and Solitary Confinement

Before considering the current literature on solitary confinement, it is imperative to examine the prevalence of mental health problems within penal institutions. Reflective of the contemporary trend toward increasingly punitive sentences and overburdened psychiatric care resources, correctional facilities have quickly become a crude haven of sorts for the psychologically disordered (Rhodes, 2005). For example, a study published by the Bureau of Justice Statistics indicated that well over half of all prisoners suffer from a mental illness. In terms of percentages, 56% of state prisoners, 45% of federal prisoners, and 64% of jail incarcerates are estimated to have a psychological health problem (James & Glaze, 2006).

To conduct the study, researchers utilized two measures for determining such problems. These measures included a history of mental health issues within the past 12 months or the presence of symptoms as delineated by the Diagnostic and Statistical Manual of Mental Disorders (DSM-IV). Among the mental health concerns reported, major depression and mania were the most common. Perhaps unsurprising given the often volatile environment of correctional facilities, persistent anger and insomnia or hypersomnia were the most frequently reported symptoms. Only a small percentage of inmates indicated that they had attempted suicide in the last 12 months. Nearly a quarter of all jailed inmates (24%) had symptoms of a psychotic disorder. Among those in prison, 15% of state inmates and 10% of federal inmates indicated that they had experienced at least one psychotic symptom (James & Glaze, 2006). Additional studies exploring various associations between mental illness and incarceration have reported similar findings (Abramsky & Fellner, 1999; Baillargeon et al., 2009; Haney, 2003; Kupers, 1999; Lamb & Weinberger, 1998; Rhodes, 2004, 2005).

At the present time, the approximate number of prisoners serving time in solitary confinement is regrettably imprecise. Definitional concerns coupled with the unwillingness of penal institutions to allow access to isolated prisoners have presented a challenge for researchers attempting to reach an accurate figure. Although published reports estimate that between 5,000 and 100,000 incarcerates are serving time in supermax facilities, "the most frequently cited figure in the past 6 years is 20,000" (Naday et al., 2008, p. 77; *see also* Haney, 2003; Mears & Watson, 2006; Pizarro & Stenius, 2004). Although this number has been mentioned throughout much of the existing literature, the estimate was obtained from two reports compiled in the 1990s using dated findings.

As such, while the estimate fails to provide an accurate account, it nonetheless is an acknolwedged reference point from which other scholarly investigations have proceeded (Naday et al., 2008).

Among segregated inmates, the estimate of those with a pre-existing mental health condition is perhaps slightly more clear. Current findings indicate that nearly one-third (29%) have been diagnosed with a psychiatric disorder (Haney, 2003; Lovell, 2008; Lovell, Cloyes, Allen, & Rhodes, 2000). However, most researchers contend that the number of mentally ill incarcerates may be far greater. According to Kupers, "correctional mental health clinicians, on average, and without thinking about it in precisely this way, respond to the fact [that] there is such a large number of prisoners with mental illness they cannot treat by under-diagnosing mental illness in the prisoners they see" (2008, p. 1008). He claimed that there are significant numbers of segregated incarcerates who either receive no treatment or rotate between being placed in observation and segregation. As a psychiatric expert in litigation, Kupers provided a stark look at the forlorn plight of many mentally ill inmates in segregation:

> Often, after performing a chart review and briefly interviewing a prisoner in a supermaximum unit, I conclude that he suffers from schizophrenia, bipolar disorder, or recurrent major depressive disorder. For example, the individual may have been hospitalized two or three times in the community . . . may have been awarded Social Security Total Disability . . . and he may have been prescribed antipsychotic medications with good effect. Yet when I look further in the chart, I discover that . . . he has been given a diagnosis of "no mental illness" on Axis I. (2008, p.1008)

Errors, from both the well-meaning and the beleaguered correctional psychiatric practitioner, significantly compromise the treatment that segregated prisoners with pre-existing mental health conditions receive (Baillargeon et al., 2009; Kupers, 2008).

Although correctional psychiatric practitioners play a role in how incarcerates cope with solitary confinement, it is crucial to consider how the condition and duration of segregation impacts prisoners. The extant literature on solitary confinement and its deleterious effects is, in part, ambiguous. As previously mentioned, administrative and disciplinary segregation include long and short time-frames. Depending on the jurisdiction of the particular correctional facility, Ad-Seg inmates may spend longer periods in isolation, but those in punitive segregation often live in far more restrictive conditions. Nevertheless, what is consistently borne out in the research is that prisoner isolation—particularly for long periods of time and under harsh conditions—is harmful to the incarcerate's mental well-being (Arrigo & Bullock, 2008; Grassian, 1983; Haney, 2003; Haney & Lynch, 1997; Pizarro & Stenius, 2004; Toch, 2001, 2003).[3] In what follows, the conditions and duration of isolation—as well as their impact on mental health—are discussed.

Mental Health Concerns and Administrative Segregation

Studies involving contemporary data on prolonged solitary confinement support early empirical evidence documenting the debilitating mental health effects of this penal practice (Toch, 2003). However, the current research specifically investigating the psychological consequences of Ad-Seg is scant, particularly in regard to short-term isolation. Although widely used in correctional institutions throughout the United States, the literature exploring this form of isolation and its duration has mostly been conducted internationally. To illustrate, researchers in Canada have undertaken a number of studies with inmates isolated for periods varying from 7 to 60 days, and they have found little to no harmful effects on incarcerates' psychological well-being (Bonta & Gendreau, 1995; Ecclestone, Gendreau, & Knox, 1974; Gendreau, Freedman, Wilde, & Scott, 1972; Gendreau & Bonta, 1984; Zinger, Wichmann, & Andrews, 2001). However, the ability to generalize these findings to all Ad-Seg inmates— particularly those in the United States—is spurious at best (Arrigo & Bullock, 2008; O'Keefe, 2008; Zinger & Wichmann, 1999).

In the early 1980s, Dr. Grassian of Harvard Medical School conducted a study to determine the effects of extended periods of Ad-Seg on incarcerates. Grassian found that inmates in administrative isolation suffered from a notable decline in mental health. Specifically, the inmates exhibited the following symptoms: "massive free-floating anxiety, hyper-responsivity to external stimuli, perceptual disillusions, hallucinations, derealization experiences, difficulties with thinking, concentration, memory, acute confusional states, aggressive fantasies, and paranoia" (Grassian, 1983, pp. 1452–1453).

Mental Health Concerns and Disciplinary Segregation

As noted previously, the psychological impact of short-term isolation remains empirically undetermined. Thus, the deleterious effects of punitive segregation, especially for a brief period, have yet to be adequately examined. However, similar to the research on long-term Ad-Seg, the extant literature on long-term disciplinary segregation overwhelmingly indicates that such isolation affects the mental well-being of prisoners.[4]

Haney's study of 100 prisoners located at California's Pelican Bay supermax facility offers compelling insight into the living conditions of those housed in prolonged punitive isolation. As he explained, inmates in solitary confinement:

> Can live for many years separated from the natural world around
> them and removed from the natural rhythms of social life, are
> denied access to vocational or education training programs or other
> activities in which to engage, get out of their cells no more than a
> few hours a week, are under virtually constant surveillance and
> monitoring, are rarely if ever in the presence of another person
> without being heavily chained and restrained, having no

opportunities for normal conversation or social interaction. (Haney, 2003, p. 127)

Indeed, at a U.S. Department of Health conference, Haney delineated the consequences of protracted solitary conditions as:

An impaired sense of identity; hypersensitivity to stimuli; cognitive dysfunction (confusion, memory loss, ruminations); irritability, anger, aggression and/or rage; other directed violence, such as stabbings, attacks on staff, property destruction, and collective violence; lethargy, helplessness and hopelessness; chronic depression; self-mutilation and/or suicidal ideation, impulses, and control; hallucinations; psychosis and/or paranoia; overall deterioration of mental and physical health. (as cited in Elsner, 2004, pp. 150–151)

These symptoms have been found to be so common that researchers often refer to them collectively as "SHU Syndrome" (Haney, 2003).[5] In Haney's study, he discovered that a number of inmates exhibited patented signs of mental deterioration. The symptoms commonly reported were heightened anxiety (91%), confused thought processes (84%), and hallucinations (41%). To ameliorate the psychological effects of isolation, some inmates develop social pathologies. Some of the behavioral adaptations include difficulties exercising self-control, lack of self-efficacy, and a diminishing capacity to test reality (Haney, 2003).[6]

Although suicide attempts are less common among inmates housed in the general population of jails and prisons than their isolated counterparts, some empirical evidence substantiates the argument that incarcerates subjected to long-term solitary confinement are more inclined to attempt suicide than any other imprisoned group. As previously noted, Kupers cited the rotation of inmates from observation to segregation as the reason for the astonishing suicide rate among convicts placed in extended isolation. Of all the inmates who commit suicide, "approximately half occur among the 6% to 8% of the prison population that is consigned to segregation at any given time" (Kupers, 2008, p. 1009). According to Way, Miraglia, Sawyer, Beer, & Eddy (2005), 76 inmates housed in a New York solitary confinement facility committed suicide within a period of less than 10 years. Similarly, 70% of the inmates in the California correctional system who committed suicide over a 1-year period were those confined to long-term solitary isolation (Mears, 2006).

In addition to suicide attempts, research indicates that a number of inmates placed in long-term solitary confinement engage in self-injurious behavior (Haney, 2003; Kilty, 2006; Thomas, Leaf, Kazmierczak, & Stone, 2006). Providing an account of self-harm among male inmates, Rhodes suggested that, "Cutting, near-hanging, self-mutilation and swallowing sharp objects appear as bodily enactments of emotional pain that teeter at the brink of suicide" (as cited in Thomas et al., 2006, p.196). Although self-harm has typically been considered an individual pathology, some researchers assert that it is a way for prisoners to cope with the unremitting and unbearable conditions of isolated confinement (Kilty, 2006; Thomas et al., 2006). According to Thomas and his colleagues, "In this view, self-injurious behavior becomes symptomatic not only of individual mental health, but of the pathology of prisons as well" (2006, p. 197).

In response to convict social pathology and maladaptive coping, correctional administrators and officers typically seek to control and punish individuals, especially those who exhibit self-destructive behaviors (Kilty, 2006; Thomas et al., 2006). Because the inmate is in state custody, self-injurious behavior is treated as "destruction of state property—to wit, the prisoner's body" (Fellner, 2006, p. 397). Further, because correctional workers fail to recognize that the conditions of the solitary environment may be a causal factor in self-injurious conduct, correctional facilities tend to "retain a myopic thrust that may in fact encourage such behaviors" (Thomas et al., 2006, p. 194). Thus, the segregated incarcerate is once again consumed in a cycle of behavior that ensures and extends their placement in long-term punitive isolation.

While the empirical findings on solitary confinement and their harmful effects are growing, the current research also includes a number of methodological weaknesses. As noted previously, a "lack of consensus" regarding how solitary confinement and supermax facilities are defined and classified presents a number of challenges for investigators seeking to accurately determine the number of inmates in isolation and to systematically examine the conditions of segregation (Naday et al., 2008, p. 73). Indeed, according to Mears and Watson (2006), the very nature of isolation precludes investigators from gaining meaningful access to those whom they seek to study. Interestingly, as Toch noted, the early studies on solitary confinement were unique in that they involved both "formal experimentation and the collection of evaluative data" (2003, p. 221). However, since that time, few inquiries have utilized robust methods to determine the deleterious effects of short- and long-term administrative and disciplinary solitary confinement on incarcerates with pre-existing mental health conditions.

Case Law Method

This chapter examines the underlying ethical thought in the extant case law concerning: *(1)* prisoners placed in long-term, disciplinary solitary confinement[7]; *(2)* with pre-existing mental health conditions; *(3)* where the Eighth Amendment's prohibition on cruel and unusual punishment is at issue. The data set of relevant cases was complied through a LexisNexis search. The search terms included *long-term, disciplinary, solitary confinement, mental illness, Eighth Amendment,* and *cruel and unusual punishment.* The constructs "*long-term*" and "*disciplinary*" were deemed essential. Mindful of the prevailing literature chronicling the harmful effects of solitary confinement and the relevance of this research for the ensuing study, both terms fundamentally signify the worst-case scenario for psychiatrically disordered offenders as delineated by the BOP. Admittedly, the length of time constituting "long-term" varies according to institution-specific standards and practices. However, the phrase was selected to yield only those cases involving prisoners subjected to a protracted period of confinement as defined by the penal facility.

As noted previously, administrative and disciplinary segregation are often indistinct when categorized psychologically. However, the term *disciplinary* was chosen solely based on how this type of solitary confinement is identified by the respective jurisdiction and correctional facility. Moreover, a preliminary exploration undertaken without these specific parameters yielded a substantial number of cases involving both long- and short-term administrative and disciplinary solitary confinement. The attention to short- and long-term Ad-Seg is not pertinent to the present inquiry.

Use of the search term *punitive* rather than or in addition to *disciplinary* was also considered. However, the latter construct more accurately yielded cases involving the specific type of confinement concerns germane to the ensuing exploration. *Solitary confinement* was chosen over *segregation*. The latter construct is not exclusively used by jurisdictions to identify conditions consistent with extreme isolation; thus, it produced a considerable number of cases involving: *(1)* forms of separation (e.g., in housing, education); and *(2)* various types of seclusion tactics employed in correctional facilities (e.g., restrictions on reading material). These issues are not relevant to this study.

Phrases such as *mental health* and *mental health condition* combined with the other established search terms produced too few case law results ($n = 2$); thus, these terms were not considered useful. A search was also executed utilizing the word "pre-existing." However, its inclusion did not increase the number of relevant cases. Mindful of these collective results, the term *mental illness* was included. This ensured that all cases involving individuals with psychological disorders, particularly those with recognized diagnoses, would be incorporated into the analysis. The phrases *Eighth Amendment* and *cruel and unusual punishment* were included, given the present inquiry's obvious focus on solitary confinement conditions that potentially inflict a particularly atypical and harsh penalty on prisoners.[9] Accordingly, based on these search term criteria, the LexisNexis search yielded 20 U.S. District Court and U.S. Appellate Court cases.

The preliminary search regarding the extant case law was undertaken in an effort to identify all precedent-setting decisions. These include court rulings that establish a standard for subsequent judicial deliberations addressing Eighth Amendment challenges involving prolonged punitive segregation and inmates with psychological disorders. Thus, initial focus was directed toward opinions rendered by the United States Supreme Court. The social science and legal literature point to decisions, such as *Farmer v. Brennan* (1994) and *Rhodes v. Chapman* (1981), that have guided the courts' rule-making on issues related to harsh conditions in segregation (Harvard Law Review, 2008; Perlin &

Dlugacz, 2008; Weidman, 2004).[10] However, the United States Supreme Court has yet to hear a case that meets the specific parameters established for the ensuing inquiry.[11] As such, an exploration of the current state of this correctional law entailed a critical examination of district and appellate court cases identified through the previously articulated LexisNexis search.

A cursory review of these 20 cases revealed that a number of them discussed long-term segregation and mental illness. However, in these instances, administrative confinement was at issue. Thus, the second step in the process was to discern which judicial opinions dealt exclusively with disciplinary confinement. Among the court rulings initially identified through the LexisNexis search, four cases were eliminated given their clear focus on Ad-Seg or some other form of nonpunitive confinement. These decisions included: *Adnan v. Santa Clara County Department of Corrections* (2002), *Ruiz v. Estelle* (1980), *Giano v. Kelly* (2000), and *Pearson v. Fair* (1989). *Rennie v. Klein* (1981) was removed from the data set, as the case involved treatment within a civil psychiatric hospital. A sixth case, *Ruiz v. Johnson* (1999), was also excluded. This judicial ruling is often cited in the extant social science and law review literature as a landmark decision in which the court considered the deleterious effects of long-term *administrative* segregation on prisoners with pre-existing mental health conditions (Fellner, 2006; Haney, 2003; Harvard Law Review, 2008; Perlin & Dlugacz, 2008). The inmates in this case sought protection under the Eighth Amendment's prohibition against cruel and unusual punishment based on the conditions of the Ad-Seg unit in which they were confined.[12]

After excluding judicial decisions that did not involve disciplinary solitary confinement, the next step was to determine which of the remaining cases involved prisoners raising Eighth Amendment challenges based on the claim that the confinement itself exacerbated a pre-existing mental health condition. Clearly, several judicial rulings considered mental health issues that relate to long-term punitive segregation. These cases include: *Tillery v. Owens* (1989), *Dawson v. Kindrick* (1981), *Laaman v. Helgemoe* (1977), *Kane v. Winn* (2004), *Davenport v. DeRobertis* (1987), and *Dantzler v. Beard* (2007). However, in each instance, prisoners did not assert that they suffered from a previously diagnosed psychological disorder. As such, these court opinions were removed from the data set.

The next matter was to determine if the remaining eight court cases were appropriate for textual analysis. *Comer v. Stewart* (2002) involved a prisoner exhibiting symptoms of SHU syndrome after being confined in disciplinary segregation. However, in this case, the court considered whether Comer's claim of suffering from SHU syndrome affected his competency to waive his right to *habeas corpus* appeal. Thus, the case was eliminated. *Coleman v. Wilson* (1995) explored the conditions within the solitary confinement unit at Pelican Bay State Prison. However, the court's deliberation chiefly focused on inadequate mental health care throughout the California correctional system. As such, *Coleman v. Wilson* (1995) was excluded.

In *Farmer v. Kavanagh* (2007), an inmate sought protection from cruel and unusual punishment after being placed in solitary confinement at a super-max facility. Farmer, who suffered from a number of physical ailments and psychological disorders, argued that the conditions of his confinement wors-ened his mental health problems. Although the court acknowledged his Eighth Amendment claim, the court focused on Farmer's assertion of a due process violation based on a sudden transfer to the supermax segregation unit. As such, *Farmer* was deemed not suitable for critical examination.

Redden v. Ricci (2008) was considered for review, but it was eventually eliminated. The case met each investigatory parameter, with one exception. Although the Eighth Amendment challenge was raised in part because of the inmate's time in disciplinary segregation, the duration of confinement was only 15 days. Furthermore, the claim that time spent in solitary confinement exacerbated a pre-existing mental health condition was made strictly on a prolonged period in Ad-Seg. Therefore, *Redden v. Ricci* (2008) was removed from consideration.

Having excluded those cases that did not meet the criteria delineated for this study, four judicial decisions remained. These cases included the follow-ing: *Madrid v. Gomez* (1995), *Scarver v. Litscher* (2006), *Jones 'El v. Berge* (2001), and *Goff v. Harper* (1997). Cited by both social science and legal schol-ars as the foremost case addressing long-term disciplinary solitary confine-ment and prisoners with pre-existing mental health conditions, the court in *Madrid v. Gomez* (1995) contemplated the issue of excessive use of force on inmates confined in the SHU (Haney, 2003; Haney & Lynch, 1997; Harvard Law Review, 2008; Lobel, 2008; Perlin & Dlugacz, 2008; Pizarro & Narag, 2008; Weidman, 2004; Wynn & Szatrowski, 2004). More importantly for pur-poses of the present qualitative exploration, the court also considered the "totality of conditions" in the segregation unit and their effect on inmates with psychological disorders. As such, the judicial ruling was included for consideration.

An appellate court case, *Scarver v. Litscher* (2006), is also often identi-fied in the existing social science and legal literature as a significant ruling for mentally ill incarcerates seeking Eighth Amendment protection from seg-regation conditions (Fellner, 2006; Kupers, 2008; McConville & Kelly, 2007; Perlin & Dlugacz, 2008). Scarver was an inmate suffering from severe schizo-phrenia and delusions. He was placed in prolonged punitive solitary confine-ment. As he alleged, the conditions in segregation were so severe that they dramatically aggravated his psychological disorders. Thus, the case was included in the data set.

In *Jones 'El v. Berge* (2001), a group of inmates housed in extended disci-plinary segregation, including six diagnosed with mental illnesses, sought protection from cruel and unusual punishment. Although a consent decree agreement was reached, a judgment was entered. Despite the agreement, the opinion itself is widely referred to in the current literature as particularly use-ful when discerning the court's understanding of matters related to long-term disciplinary segregation and incarcerates with psychological disorders (Arrigo & Bullock, 2008; Harvard Law Review, 2008; Perlin & Dlugacz, 2008; Pizarro & Narag, 2008; Weidman, 2004). Consequently, the case was included in the analysis.

   Goff v. Harper (1997) involved three inmates who sought protection from cruel and unusual punishment after spending a prolonged period in punitive segregation. Although the Eighth Amendment violation claim included time in Ad-Seg, the court focused primarily on the conditions in disciplinary solitary confinement and their effect on prisoners with alleged mental health conditions. Although the case does not appear frequently in the relevant empirical and legal research, it met the criteria delineated for this study. As such, it was included in the data set.

   For the purpose of thoroughness, the judicial opinions cited and subsequently referenced in each of the four aforementioned cases were reviewed to determine if any of them warranted inclusion in the data set. This step in the process produced a significant number of judicial opinions. However, mindful of the extant social science and law review literature, the vast majority of these cases did not meet the specific criteria established for this investigation. Notwithstanding this finding, two cases were appropriate for consideration. Citing *Scarver v. Litscher* (2006), *Vasquez v. Frank* (2006) involved an incarcerate who sought protection from cruel and unusual punishment given his prolonged disciplinary solitary confinement. Vasquez claimed that the conditions in which he was held were so severe that they exacerbated his mental health condition.[13] Citing *Madrid v. Gomez* (1995), the court in *Torres et al. v. Commissioner of Correction et al.* (1998) reviewed an Eighth Amendment violation claim based on prisoners' extended confinement in a disciplinary isolation unit in which some of them alleged deteriorated psychological conditions. Thus, both cases were retained for critical textual examination.[14]

Discussion

Having identified six district court and appellate court cases that met the evaluative criteria, two levels of qualitative analysis were performed.[15] The details of the approach were delineated in Chapter 1 (*see* the section titled, "Psycyhological Jurisprudence and Methodology"). Appendix B includes all plain meaning case law results on the matter of inmate mental health, long-term disciplinary solitary confinement, and cruel and unusual punishment. Table 3.1 chronicles specific words, phrases, and passages that summarily reflect the judicial temperament conveyed by the courts as sourced through the seven questions used to locate this meaning. These meanings communicate judicial attitudes, perceptions, goals, and concerns to which the case is directed and on which the decision is based.

Table 3.1 Jurisprudential Intent as Derived from Plain Meaning Data

	Madrid v. Gomez	Scarver v. Litscher	Jones 'El v. Berge	Goff v. Harper	Vasquez v. Frank	Torres et al. v. Comm'r of Corr. et al.
1	No prison can deprive inmates of a basic human need, even if the conditions promote a penological objective	"Prison authorities must be given considerable latitude in the design of measures for controlling homicidal maniacs without exacerbating their manias. It is a delicate balance"	"Supermax is known to cause psychiatric morbidity, disability, suffering, and mortality"	Court's job is to identify Eighth Amendment violations and show deference to officials in their role as prison managers	Conditions exacerbated Vasquez's mental health condition, but prison officials refused to lessen their impact	Court determines whether conditions are cruel and unusual
2	Prison officials are "entitled to design and operate the SHU consistent with the penal philosophy of their choosing, absent constitutional violations"	Inmates like Scarver, who are already serving a life sentence, are undeterrable	Supermax was built to house recalcitrant inmates; mentally ill prisoners cannot conform their behavior	Court could have taken a "hands-off" position	Prison officials violate the Eighth Amendment when they deliberately ignore an inmate's mental health condition	Conditions must put inmates at a substantial risk of harm and prison officials must be deliberately indifferent to this risk

(Continued)

Table 3.1 Continued

	Madrid v. Gomez	*Scarver v. Litscher*	*Jones 'El v. Berge*	*Goff v. Harper*	*Vasquez v. Frank*	*Torres et al. v. Comm'r of Corr. et al.*
3	Conditions may be harsher than necessary to house mentally ill inmates, but deference must be given to prison officials	Federal courts must not tell a state how to "run its prison system"	The PLRA limits the scope of injunctive relief; conditions can lead to mental deterioration	The conditions are not cruel and unusual, but the prison officials were deliberately indifferent to those with pre-existing mental health conditions	Although Vasquez has been released from segregation, he may still be entitled to damages	Isolation is not unconstitutional
4	Prison officials were aware that a number of inmates were mentally ill and such conditions could exacerbate their pre-existing conditions	The Constitution is unclear on prison conditions; treating a mentally ill inmate is complicated	Many of the conditions serve no penological purpose	The needs of mentally ill inmates are not being met	Prison officials were aware of Vasquez's adverse reactions to the conditions	Dr. Grassian opined that such conditions can cause mental harm and deterioration

5	Current staffing levels are not sufficient to respond to prisoners exhibiting signs of mental deterioration	"Maybe there is some well-known protocol for dealing with the Scarvers of this world, though probably there is not"	"Mentally ill inmates do not have access to the programming because they are not able to control their behavior to reach higher levels"	There is "great demand for a special needs program"	No data ascertained	No data ascertained
6	Conditions may hover above what is humanly tolerable, particularly for mentally ill inmates	Court must seek to protect inmates, guards, and Scarver from himself	"Balancing of harms" in which mentally ill prisoners are protected from being placed in segregation, but prison officials are not overburdened logistically or financially	Mentally ill prisoners have serious health needs that are unlikely to be addressed by officials	Vasquez may proceed on Eighth Amendment claims	No data ascertained
7	Prisoners are "still fellow human beings . . . most of whom will one day return to society . . . [and] have nonetheless, a human dignity"	No data ascertained	". . . the public interest will be served by protecting the Eighth Amendment rights of inmates housed at Supermax"	No data ascertained	No data ascertained	No data ascertained

Level 1 Analysis

In *Madrid v. Gomez* (1995), the court communicated its perceptions regarding prisoners with pre-existing mental health conditions serving time in long-term solitary confinement. For example, the court noted, "By virtue of their conviction, inmates forfeit many of their liberties and rights" (p. 1244). This statement conveys the judicial attitude that under certain delineated circumstances, incarcerates are not guaranteed the same lawful protections that are otherwise afforded to those not criminally confined. As such, the court did not perceive the rights and liberties of prisoners in the same manner as non-prisoners who might bring a complaint before a legal tribunal.

Furthermore, the decision in *Madrid* clearly expressed the court's perception regarding its role in determining how correctional administrators ought to manage prison facilities. As the case opinion explained, "It is not the Court's function to pass judgment on the policy choices of prison officials" (p. 1262). Thus, correctional administrators are "entitled to design and operate the SHU consistent with the penal philosophy of their choosing" (p.1262), which may include punitive responses that "emphasize idleness, deterrence, and deprivation" (p. 1262). In fact, the court acknowledged the challenges prison officials face in maintaining penal institutions designed to confine individuals who cannot conform to society's or the institution's rules and regulations. As such, the attitude expressed by the *Madrid* court maintained that it is "well within defendants' far ranging discretion" (p. 1261) to segregate "inmates for disciplinary or security reasons" as it "is a well established and penologically justified practice" (p. 1261).

Statements made in the *Madrid* decision also offered some clues regarding the degree to which correctional conditions might inflict psychological harm on incarcerates. To illustrate, the court observed, "[T]he very nature of prison confinement may have a deleterious impact on the mental state of prisoners" (p. 1262). In regard to the SHU discussed in this case, the legal opinion acknowledged that such confinement "will likely inflict some degree of psychological trauma upon most inmates confined there for more than brief periods" (p. 1265).

Notwithstanding the court's contention that prison officials must be given deference in managing correctional facilities—including solitary confinement units that may induce or expedite mental deterioration—the *Madrid* decision communicated a fundamental belief that "all humans are composed of more than flesh and bone" (p. 1261). This assertion includes prisoners who are so irascible that they must "be locked away not only from their fellow citizens, but from other inmates as well" (p. 1261). In support of these statements, the court expressed the perception that psychological well-being is as significant as is corporal health. Indeed, the court opined that mental wellness "is a need as essential to a meaningful human existence as other basic physical demands our bodies may make for shelter, warmth or sanitation" (p. 1261). Additional statements emanating from the decision indicated that although conditions of confinement might be "restrictive and even harsh . . . , 'basic human need[s]' and 'life's basic necessities'" (p. 1262) must be met and available to those serving prison time, including those held in long-term disciplinary solitary confinement.

In the *Madrid* case, the conditions that met (or failed to meet) the "basic necessity of human existence" (p. 1263) constituted the core Eighth Amendment challenge. As the court reasoned:

> On the one hand, a condition that is sufficiently harmful to inmates or otherwise reprehensible to civilized society will at some point yield to constitutional constraints, even if the condition has some penological justification. Thus, defendants' insistence that the SHU is "working" as a secure environment for disruptive prisoners does not and cannot determine whether the SHU passes constitutional muster. No prison, for example, can deprive inmates of a basic human need, even though the underlying conditions might otherwise arguably promote some penological objective. On the other hand, a condition or other prison measure that has little or no penological value may offend constitutional values upon a lower showing of injury or harm. (pp. 1262–1263)

However, as the court explained, "psychological pain that results from idleness in segregation is not sufficient to implicate the Eighth Amendment" (p. 1262), nor does the prohibition against cruel and unusual punishment "guarantee that inmates will not suffer some psychological effects from incarceration or segregation" (p. 1263).

Finally, the *Madrid* court articulated a perspective on what it deemed best for society. As a source for communicating jurisprudential intent, the opinion commented on how inmates who serve time in long-term disciplinary solitary confinement might nevertheless thrive once released from prison. As the legal opinion stipulated, "those who have transgressed the law are still fellow human beings–most of whom will one day return to society" (p. 1244). As such, "even those prisoners at the 'bottom' of the social heap . . . have, nonetheless, a human dignity" (p. 1244). Basing its rationale on the view that our nation "aspires to the highest standards of civilization," the court maintained that "there is simply no place for abuse and mistreatment, even in the darkest of jailhouse cells" (p. 1245). These comments disclosed the court's felt obligation to recognize the humanness of incarcerates and responsibility to ensure that they were psychologically equipped to engage with others in a pro-social manner should custodial release and community re-entry follow.

Given these collective assertions, perceptions, and attitudes, the court did not extend the Eighth Amendment's prohibition against cruel and unusual punishment to all prisoners serving time in long-term disciplinary solitary confinement. Although mindful that "the conditions in the SHU [might] press the outer bounds of what most humans can psychologically tolerate" (p. 1267), the court communicated its intentions when stating that "the record does not satisfactorily demonstrate that there is a sufficiently high risk to all inmates of incurring a serious mental illness from exposure to conditions in the SHU to find that the conditions [themselves] constitute a per se deprivation of a basic necessity of life" (p. 1267). Consequently, the *Madrid* court ordered that only those inmates with pre-existing mental health conditions must not be placed in long-term punitive segregation.

Data collected from the *Scarver v. Litscher* (2006) case also provided insight into underlying jurisprudential intent. Similar to the decision in *Madrid*, the *Scarver* court held the perception that "[f]ederal judges must always be circumspect in imposing their ideas about civilized and effective prison administration on state prison officials" (p. 976), especially because judges "know little about the management of prisons" (p. 977). Statements made that affirmed the trial court's decision communicated the attitude that "managerial judgments generally are the province of other branches of government" (p. 977) and, furthermore, that "it is unseemly for federal courts to tell a state . . . how to run its prison system" (p. 977).

Mindful of the lack of judicial authority to determine and/or evaluate penal institutional administration, the court attempted to strike a "delicate balance" (p. 976) by stating, "Prison authorities must be given considerable latitude in the design of measures for controlling homicidal maniacs without exacerbating their manias beyond what is necessary for security" (p. 976). Following the rationale for the use of long-term disciplinary solitary confinement employed in the *Madrid* case, the *Scarver* court affirmed the trial court's view that such custodial placement was necessary, especially in curbing the behavior of extremely volatile inmates who either refuse to follow or are incapable of adhering to prison rules and regulations. Scarver, a diagnosed schizophrenic who murdered two fellow inmates while incarcerated, was perceived by the court as "extremely dangerous" (p. 973) and "undeterrable" (p. 976).

The court acknowledged the dearth of policies and programs designed to address the unique needs of both correctional administrators and inmates, like Scarver, who suffer from psychiatric illness and consistently violate prison rules. Revealing its intent, the court opined, "Maybe there is some well-known protocol for dealing with the Scarvers of this world, though probably there is not (we have found none, and his lawyer has pointed us to none)" (p. 976). Indeed, the *Scarver* case indicated, "[T]he treatment of a mentally ill prisoner who also happens to have murdered two other inmates is much more complicated than the treatment of a harmless lunatic" (p. 976). Thus, although the conditions in a solitary confinement unit "disturb psychotics" (p. 974) like Scarver, the lower court's decision was nonetheless upheld. As the appellate case intimated, "It is a fair inference that conditions at Supermax aggravated the symptoms of his mental illness and by doing so inflicted severe physical and especially mental suffering" (p. 975). Ultimately, the *Scarver* court reasoned that although segregating the petitioner from fellow "inmates and staff . . . [might] unavoidably aggravate his psychosis . . . the measures [did] not violate the Constitution" (p. 976).

In the case of *Jones 'El v. Berge* (2001), the court's commentary regarding the placement of mentally ill incarcerates in long-term disciplinary segregation was based on its knowledge of the supermax prison. The court recognized that the "Supermax was built to respond to a perceived need by wardens" to house "dangerous and recalcitrant inmates" (p. 1103). Although the language of the legal opinion considered the assertion by correctional officials that at times prisoners "manipulate[d] staff" (p. 1118), the court reasoned that "this does not mean that they [incarcerates] are not seriously mentally ill" (p. 1118).

The rhetoric employed in the *Jones 'El* case indicated the court's acute awareness of how prolonged segregation might worsen the mental health conditions of inmates with pre-existing diagnoses. To illustrate, the court stated, "Supermax is known to cause severe psychiatric morbidity, disability, suffering and mortality" (p. 1101). Indeed, the court poignantly expressed concern and a resolute sense of motivation to act regarding the potentially cruel and unusual circumstances surrounding long-term disciplinary segregation. The following description of the correctional facility in the *Jones 'El* case conveys this attitude:

> Several features of Supermax are particularly damaging to inmates
> with serious mental illnesses. The almost total sensory deprivation
> in Levels One and Two is relentless: inmates are kept confined alone
> in their cells for all but four hours a week. The exercise cell is devoid
> of equipment. The constant illumination is disorienting, as is the
> difficulty in knowing the time of day. The vestibule architecture and
> solid boxcar doors prevent any incidental interaction between
> inmates and guards. (p. 1118)

Comparable to the ruling in *Madrid*, the *Jones 'El* court deliberated on whether confining incarcerates in solitary confinement served a "legitimate penological interest" (p. 1117). In determining the reasonableness of prolonged segregation for inmates, the judicial opinion engaged in the weighing of relevant interests—that is, the court sought to ascertain a "balance of harms" in which the interests expressed through the testimony of supermax administrators were balanced against the interests stated by those suffering under the alleged cruel and unusual solitary confinement conditions. With respect to correctional officers, the court communicated a desire to "interfere" (p. 1125) only to a "minimal degree" (p. 1125) in the operation of the supermax facility. However, the court also revealed its unease with confining mentally ill prisoners in prolonged punitive segregation and ultimately elucidated its intent in the following passage:

> Defendants assert that an order from this court requiring the
> transfer of seriously mentally ill inmates is not the least intrusive
> means of alleviating the problems the inmates are experiencing.
> Instead, defendants suggest, increasing the mental health staff
> would be a way to lessen the court's interference with prison

management. I disagree. I am convinced that the staffing ratio is
not the sole factor making up the potentially damaging conditions
for mentally ill inmates; the physical architecture of Supermax
and the customs and policies also contribute to the conditions.
(pp. 1123–1124)

The court's language disclosed a second balancing test. Similar to the
Madrid and *Scarver* decisions, the *Jones 'El* opinion undertook a review of
competing interests to discern what would be of the greatest benefit to
society. As the court noted, "the public interest is not served by housing seriously mentally ill inmates at Supermax under conditions in which they risk
irreparable emotional damage and, in some cases, a risk of death by suicide"
(p. 1125). Affirming the intent revealed in the previous statement, the court
concluded, "[T]he public interest will be served by protecting the Eighth
Amendment rights of inmates housed at Supermax" (p. 1125).

Although the decision in the *Jones 'El* case confirmed that conditions
in the Supermax facility were a factor in the deterioration of psychologically
disordered inmates, the court was also fully aware of its restricted influence on
prison management. Specifically, the "Prison Litigation Reform Act limits
the scope of preliminary injunctive relief available in challenges to prison conditions" (p. 1116). As such, the Act provides no basis for a court to significantly impose correctional policy changes. Mindful of this, the *Jones 'El* court
ordered that only incarcerates suffering from diagnosed mental health conditions were protected under the prohibition of cruel and unusual punishment,
as delineated by the Eighth Amendment. Consistent with this perspective, the
legal opinion stipulated, "Supermax was designed to house especially disruptive and recalcitrant prisoners but not mentally ill ones" (p. 1118). Thus,
although the decision in *Jones 'El* recognized that correctional administrators
"should be afforded due deference," the court concluded that "it does not
overstep these bounds to order that [psychiatrically disordered convicts] not
be housed at Supermax" (p. 1124)

Consistent with previous Eighth Amendment cases involving long-term
disciplinary solitary confinement and mentally ill incarcerates, an evaluation
of the plain meaning of the legal language found in the *Goff* case revealed its
underlying jurisprudential intent. In ascertaining whether Goff was capable of
invoking protection from overtly harsh prison conditions, the court cited the
Eighth Amendment standards set forth in several Supreme Court decisions.
This undertaking conveyed the *Goff* court's perception of what constitutes
cruel and unusual punishment, and how a legal tribunal must act when presented with such circumstances. As the court opined:

Justice Douglas' pronouncement that, "The Eighth Amendment
expresses the revulsion of civilized man against barbarous acts – the
'cry of horror' against man's inhumanity to his fellow man." Along
these same lines, Justice Brennan described a court's duty in Eighth

Amendment cases as the need to determine "whether a challenged punishment comports with human dignity" (pp. 111–112)

The rhetoric employed in the *Goff* ruling articulated a duty to provide "great deference to the expertise of the officials who perform the always difficult and often thankless task of running a prison" (p. 153). Supporting this statement, the legal opinion reasoned, "The Court does not pretend that it knows more than the men and women who run the Penitentiary" (p. 153), and accordingly, "is not attempting to run or micromanage the prisons" (p. 157). Although the court intimated that it "could have easily taken the position that a hands-off position as to these violations [was] the only way to go based on today's law-and-order mentality" (p. 156), it ultimately disagreed with this perspective. Instead, underlying jurisprudential intent was made evident in the assertion that, "the Court's job is only to identify constitutional violations if any exist" (p. 153).

Similar to previous judicial rulings on the subject, the *Goff* court expressed concern for the lack of programs available to mentally ill inmates in solitary confinement. For example, commenting on testimony related to the prison's failure to meet the distinct needs of incarcerates with psychological disorders, the legal opinion observed that:

> . . . there is a great demand for a special needs program at the
> Penitentiary which can handle maximum security inmates. The
> Court also found Dr. Loeffelholz has expressed this professional
> opinion to his bosses (presumably the director of the Iowa
> Department of Corrections) but no action has been taken. Then-
> Warden Acevedo, testified that the Illinois Department of
> Corrections, his immediate past employer, had special needs
> programs such as separate wings of prisons devoted to taking care
> of inmates with mental problems, that were far superior to those
> established by the Iowa Department of Corrections. He said, when a
> facility devotes itself exclusively to taking care of mentally ill
> patients, it can provide much better psychiatric care. (p. 118)

In consideration of this testimony, the court reasoned, "The State has had opportunities to rectify or partially rectify the situation and has done nothing" (p. 156). In addition to the court's attitude conveyed through this statement, the language of the decision communicated an intention to hold correctional administrators responsible for their "deliberate indifference" (p. 113) with respect to the mental health status of prisons. The *Goff* court was "unpersuaded" (p. 153) that the "extraordinary long lockup sentences" (p. 153) and the considerably "small size of the cells in which lockup inmates serve twenty-three or twenty-four hours a day" (p. 153) constituted an Eighth Amendment violation. However, it did indicate that psychologically disordered incarcerates were not suited for confinement in segregation. As such, the *Goff* court concluded that "inmates with mental health disorders at ISP [Illionis Supermax Prison] who are not receiving treatment for their needs, are being held under conditions which violate the Eighth Amendment" (p. 120).

A review of the data extracted from the *Vasquez v. Frank* (2006) case revealed the court's knowledge of the debilitating effects isolation poses for inmates with pre-existing mental health conditions, especially as discussed in those cases previously subjected to textual exegeses. The court's rhetoric communicated a concern for certain conditions in solitary confinement units, such as continuously illuminated cells, that "may inflict severe suffering on mentally ill inmates" (p. 541). In this instance, the appellate court acknowledged that Vasquez "suffers from emotional distress, depression, anxiety, and 'other psychological problems'" (p. 540). While in segregation, Vasquez's cell "was illuminated 24 hours a day. Although he was able to lower the lighting, he could not turn it off completely. [Vasquez] allege[d] that the constant illumination aggravated his mental illness and caused him to suffer from insomnia, migraines, eye pain, and blurry vision" (p. 540).

Citing the lower court's ruling, the *Vasquez* judicial opinion asserted that petitioner's "allegations about the lighting and air quality in his cell [were] not so fantastical that the district court could dismiss them out of hand" (p. 540). Moreover, although "a district court [might] strongly suspect that an inmate's claims lack merit . . . [this] is not a legitimate ground for dismissal" (p. 540). Similar to the previous cases analyzed thus far in the data set, the *Vasquez* decision elucidated the standard by which jurists must determine an Eighth Amendment violation. As the court opined, "prison officials violate the Eighth Amendment when they deliberately ignore a serious medical condition . . . or create 'an unreasonable risk of serious damage' to an inmate's future health" (p. 540).

In determining whether correctional administrators subjected Vasquez to cruel and unusual conditions of confinement, the court considered the extent to which management officials were cognizant of his psychological maladies. As the court noted, Vasquez "filed grievances and told medical personnel about these conditions, but prison personnel did not rectify the problem for over three years" (p. 540). The *Vasquez* court further asserted, "Prison officials were aware of these adverse reactions" (p. 541), but failed to respond appropriately. As such, petitioner's claims that the segregation conditions exacerbated his mental illness were deemed meritorious.

In *Torres et al. v. Commissioner of Correction et al.* (1998), the court affirmed the trial court's decision. The opinion of the court was consistent with previously analyzed cases regarding the perceived role of the judiciary in matters related to Eighth Amendment challenges and mentally ill prisoners in long-term segregation. However, unlike these earlier cases, the *Torres et al.* court limited its scope of analysis to the testimony of mental health professionals. This included witness evidence from Dr. Stuart Grassian, who offered his expert testimony on the deleterious effects of prolonged punitive segregation in the *Madrid* case. Departing from the decisions in *Madrid* and the other prior cases reviewed, the *Torres et al.* court reasoned, "[E]xpert opinion regarding what constitutes cruel and unusual punishment is entitled to little weight" (p. 614). Indeed, the court explicitly delineated its position by stating, "[W]hether prison conditions are sufficiently harmful to establish an Eighth Amendment violation, is a purely legal determination for the court to make" (p. 614).

However, following the *Madrid, Scarver, Jones El, Goff,* and *Vasquez* rulings, the *Torres et al.* court established the standard that must be met to succeed on an Eighth Amendment challenge. Utilizing a two-prong test, the court noted that the "plaintiff-inmate" must demonstrate that the "conditions of confinement presented 'a substantial risk of serious harm' and that correctional officers acted with 'deliberate indifference' to prisoner safety and well-being" (pp. 613–614). Further, the opinion of the *Torres et al.* court was informed by previous decisions made by both the U.S. Court of Appeals and the presiding court on Eighth Amendment challenges raised by incarcerates alleging psychological harm stemming from the conditions of their confinement. Consider the following passage found in the *Torres et al.* opinion:

> As the United States Court of Appeals for the First Circuit has observed, 'federal appellate decisions during the past decade which have focused on the factor of segregated confinement and lack of inmate contact reveals to us a widely shared disinclination to declare even very lengthy periods of segregated confinement beyond the pale of minimally civilized conduct on the part of prison authorities. Similarly, in *Libby v. Commissioner of Correction,* 385 Mass. 421, 431, 432 N.E.2d 486 (1982), we held that a prison isolation unit whose conditions were more restrictive than those in DDU [Department Disciplinary Unit] did not offend the Eighth Amendment because its inmates were provided adequate food, clothing, sanitation, medical care, and communication with others' *Libby,* 385 Mass. at 431-432. The isolation and loneliness of which the plaintiffs complain, we concluded, is not in and of itself unconstitutional. (p. 615)

Thus, by relying primarily on earlier court rulings, the *Torres et al.* court affirmed the lower court's decision. In this instance, the harsh conditions claimed by the plaintiff-inmates were balanced against those asserted in the case of *Libby v. Commissioner of Correction* (1982). This judicial opinion reasoned, "If conditions of confinement [that were] harsher than those posed by DDU did not offend the Eighth Amendment, it follows that DDU's confinement is likewise constitutional" (p. 615). As such, the *Torres et al.* court based its opinion on the fact that the "only arguable dispute" concerns the "extent to which these conditions generally caused inmates' psychological problems" (p. 614). As a result, the court determined, "The judge's findings and the parties' stipulation demonstrate that DDU confinement, while uncomfortable, [was] a far cry from . . . 'barbaric' conditions" (p. 617), and "[The] judge acted properly in allowing the defendants' motion for summary judgment" (p. 615).

Level 2 Analysis

After the data obtained from each of the six cases were examined for purposes of delineating unstated jurisprudential intent, the second level of analysis was the focus of qualitative scrutiny. This second and more textual stage entailed an interpretation of the legal language (manifest content) itself and the underlying ethical meaning communicated through and embedded within the words and/or phrases that constituted the Level-1 data. In other words, "the goal of this [subsequent] inquiry was to determine what moral philosophy was conveyed through jurisprudential intent, mindful of the three ethical schools of thought under consideration as well as their corresponding principles" (Sellers & Arrigo, 2009, p. 471).[17] Table 3.2 presents these Level-2 data.

A review of the phraseology employed in the *Madrid* decision revealed the court's orientation toward consequentialism and its utilitarian variant. The following passage is illustrative of the court's interest-balancing logic: "Conditions may be harsher than necessary to accommodate the needs of the institution with respect to these populations. However, giving defendants the wide-ranging deference they are owed in these matters, we can not say that the conditions overall lack any penological justification" (p. 1263).

Central to the philosophy of utilitarianism is the notion of consequences in choice-making and action that advance the greatest happiness or interests for the greatest number of citizens (e.g., Bank, 2008; Cahn, 2009; Mill, 1957). Consistent with this ethical reasoning, the *Madrid* court expressed concern for the conditions of disciplinary solitary confinement units, especially if excessively severe ("harsher than necessary"), potentially impacting adversely incarcerates suffering from pre-existing psychological disorders. However, the court was also cognizant of the need to afford great discretion to prison administrators ("wide-ranging deference") in determining policies and procedures essential to effectively managing penal institutions. Thus, the manifest content communicated the court's utilitarian ethic of weighing the mental well-being of incarcerates against the rights of prison administrators to promote the greatest happiness for and interests of the majority of individuals affected by the ruling.

The manifest content discernable in the *Madrid* court's rhetoric aligned with a second moral philosophy. Words and phrases employed in the court's decision were consistent with the logic of formalism and, in particular, Kantian ethics. As noted previously, ethical formalism is based on moral duty. Mindful of this dimension of Kantian philosophy, statements such as "duty and responsibility of this Court to ensure that constitutional rights are fully vindicated" (p. 1263) and "duty to assume some responsibility" (p. 1245) explicitly conveyed the *Madrid* court's ethical commitment to uphold both a legal *and* moral obligation. Moreover, other statements such as, "prisoners . . . have, nonetheless, a human dignity" (p. 1244) and "must ensure that prisons . . . do not degenerate into places that violate basic standards of decency and humanity" (p. 1245) were consistent with the Kantian maxim that all individuals are

Table 3.2 Underlying Ethical Reasoning Conveying Jurisprudential Intent

	Consequentialism (Utilitarianism)	Formalism (Kantian Ethics)	Virtue Ethics
Madrid v. Gomez	"Conditions may be harsher than necessary to accommodate the needs of the institution with respect to these populations. However, giving defendants the wide-ranging deference they are owed in these matters, we can not say that the conditions overall lack any penological justification."	"duty and responsibility of this Court to ensure that constitutional rights are fully vindicated" "prisoners . . . have, nonetheless, a human dignity" "duty to assume some responsibility for his safety and general well being" "must ensure that prisons . . . do not degenerate into places that violate basic standards of decency and humanity"	
Scarver v. Litscher	"Prison authorities must be given considerable latitude in the design of measures for controlling homicidal maniacs without exacerbating their manias. It is a delicate balance." "protect other inmates or guards from Scarver or Scarver from himself"		
Jones 'El v. Berge	"balancing of harms" "court interferes in the management of Supermax to a minimal degree yet casts the net wide enough to catch any seriously mentally ill inmates" "public interest is not served by housing seriously mentally ill inmates at Supermax" "public interest will be served by protecting the Eighth Amendment rights" "the potential harm to yet unidentified seriously mentally ill inmates is just as detrimental as to those who have already been identified"	"defendants should be afforded due deference"	

(Continued)

Table 3.2 Continued

	Consequentialism (Utilitarianism)	Formalism (Kantian Ethics)	Virtue Ethics
Goff v. Harper	"serve justice with a minimum of judicial intervention and provide prison officials with the maximum possible discretion"	"court's duty [is] to determine 'whether a challenged punishment comports with human dignity" "courts owe great deference to officials" "Court's job is only to identify constitutional violations"	
Torres et al. v. Comm'r Corr. et al.	"conditions . . . more restrictive than those in DDU did not offend the Eighth Amendment because its inmates were provided adequate food, clothing, sanitation, medical care, and communication with others"	"an Eighth Amendment violation, is a purely legal determination for the court to make"	

deserving of dignity. Accordingly, when subjecting the manifest content located in the *Madrid* decision to Level-2 textual exegeses, both utilitarian and Kantian reasoning informed the court's jurisprudential intent.

Similar to the *Madrid* ruling, the manifest content found in the *Scarver v. Litscher* (2006) decision advanced the consequentialist perspective of utilitarianism. Specifically, the case attempted to strike a "delicate balance" (p. 976) between the competing interests of correctional administrators and incarcerates. As the court declared, "Prison authorities must be given considerable latitude in the design of measures for controlling homicidal maniacs without exacerbating their manias beyond what is necessary for security" (p. 976). Endorsing the utilitarian objective of achieving the greatest good for the largest possible constituency, the court sought to "protect other inmates or guards from Scarver or Scarver from himself" (p. 977). Thus, informing the case's jurisprudential intent was an ethic that endeavored to reach a decision based on an assessment of what was deemed in the best interest of those employed by and serving time in the Supermax prison, including Scarver himself.

The rhetoric utilized by the court in the *Jones 'El v. Berge* (2001) case was also reviewed to determine its underlying moral philosophy. Interestingly, similar to the *Madrid* opinion, the *Jones 'El* court embraced both utilitarian and formalistic ethical principles in its manifest content. To illustrate, the court engaged in a "balancing of harms" (p. 1123). Statements, such as "the court interferes in the management of Supermax to a minimal degree yet casts the net wide enough to catch any seriously mentally ill inmates" (p. 1125) reflected some consideration of competing interests. On the one hand, the court sought to afford deference to Supermax administrators; on the other hand, the court recognized the psychological welfare of inmates. In other instances, the rights of incarcerates were measured against societal protection. Illustrative of this point are the following passages: "The public interest is not served by housing seriously mentally ill inmates at Supermax" (p. 1125) and "[T]he public interest will be served by protecting the Eighth Amendment rights of inmates" (p. 1125). As manifest content, these statements indicated a utilitarian approach that sought to ensure the greatest happiness for the greatest number of people.

Elsewhere, the *Jones'El* court also appropriated legal language consistent with formalist ethics. Consider the following phrase: "Defendants should be afforded due deference" (p. 1124). The notion of availing that which is due to another reflects judicial obligation to honor prison administration rights. This interpretation is consistent with comparable studies involving textual analyses of court opinions (Sellers & Arrigo, 2009).

A textual evaluation of the legal rhetoric expressed in the *Goff* opinion signifies that the case was guided by consequentialist and formalist logic. For example, the court stated that its goal was to "serve justice with a minimum of judicial intervention and provide prison officials with the maximum possible discretion to manage their own institution" (pp. 155–156). This manifest content is indicative of an interest-balancing argument in which the need to remedy a potential Eighth Amendment violation was weighed against the need to respect those who create and implement prison policies. When interpreted ethically, the underlying meaning situated within this legal language is made evident. Although the court wanted to ensure that inmates were lawfully protected from cruel and unusual punishment, it sought to limit its imposition on the rights and interests of correctional administrators.

In addition to utilitarian principles informing the *Goff* court's jurisprudential intent, a formalistic orientation was also apparent. Indeed, the manifest content revealed the court's perceived obligations regarding prisoners with pre-existing mental health conditions placed in long-term disciplinary solitary confinement. As the case opinion stipulated, "[T]he Court's job is only to identify constitutional violations if any exist; it is in the province of the Penitentiary's officials to attend to those violations" (p. 153). Similar to *Madrid, Scarver,* and *Jones'El,* the *Goff* court expressed a duty to demonstrate "great deference to the expertise of the officials . . . running a prison" (p. 153). Consistent with the Kantian maxim of ensuring that all individuals are afforded a sense of dignity, the legal decision stated, "[A] court's duty in Eighth Amendment cases [is] to determine 'whether a challenged punishment comports with human dignity'" (pp. 111–112). As previously noted, textual exegeses of this manifest content endorse Kantian ethics.

In the *Torres et al.* ruling, the court conveyed its reliance on consequentialist thinking. As with the other cases comprising the data set, the *Torres et al.* court focused on whether correctional officers denied inmates their basic necessities of life, including psychological wellness. Once again, the manifest content signified a commitment to interest-balancing in which the rights of incarcerates were assessed in relation to the rights of prison administrators. As the judicial opinion explained, "[C]onditions . . . more restrictive than those in DDU did not offend the Eighth Amendment because its inmates were provided adequate food, clothing, sanitation, medical care, and communication with others" (p. 615).

The *Torres et al.* decision also relied on legal rhetoric that, when interpreted ethically, indicated that an adherence to formalist principles informed the court's underlying jurisprudential intent. Although *Madrid, Scarver, Jones 'El,* and *Goff* discussed a duty to show deference to penal institutional administrators, the *Torres et al.* court expressed its primary obligation differently. Specifically, the case opinion declared, "whether prison conditions are sufficiently harmful to establish an Eighth Amendment violation, is a purely legal determination for the court to make" (p. 614). The conviction in *Torres et al.* that the judiciary bears sole responsibility for such legal determinations is consistent with the notion of duty as found in formalist thought.

Having subjected the six cases that constitute the data set to additional textual exegeses, the results indicate that the courts' underlying jurisprudential intent was informed by the philosophies of consequentialism (including its variant utilitarianism) and ethical formalism (including its variant Kantian moral reasoning). Intratextually, consequentialism and the utilitarian perspective were most prominently featured in the cases of *Jones 'El* and *Scarver.* Multiple examples of interest-balancing or comparable rhetoric were discerned from these legal opinions. In contrast, the *Madrid and Goff* courts intratextually were more closely associated with formalism and Kantian ethics. The courts' language communicated numerous instances of this underlying ethical rationale; conversely, only one instance of utilitarian thinking was found in each of these two cases. The underlying moral philosophy informing the jurisprudential intent of *Torres et al.* endorsed utilitarianism and Kantian ethics. One example of each type of ethical reasoning was detected vis-à-vis the interpretive and heuristic methodology.

Intertextually, each of the legal opinions engaged in interest-balancing arguments intended to promote the greatest good for the greatest number of individuals affected by the courts' decision-making rhetoric. Moreover, in several other notable instances, the manifest content significantly aligned intertextually with formalism and its variant, Kantian ethics. Indeed, underscoring the jurisprudential intent of all the legal opinions but *Scarver* was an obligation to uphold a particular duty to correctional administrators, to inmates, or to both.

Thus, the textual analyses performed within and across the six cases involving: *(1)* Eighth Amendment challenges; *(2)* incarcerates with pre-existing mental health conditions; and *(3)* confinement in long-term disciplinary solitary segregation yielded compelling ethical findings. In short, the predominant moral reasoning situated within the courts' jurisprudential intent advanced philosophical principles emanating from utilitarianism and Kantian formalism.

Implications: the Dynamics of Madness, Citizenship and Social Justice

This chapter qualitatively explored the extant case law regarding Eighth Amendment challenges raised by inmates with pre-existing mental health conditions serving time in prolonged disciplinary solitary confinement. To determine the courts' normative rationale, two levels of analyses were performed. The first level involved an examination of plain meaning that was educible from six judicial opinions. A series of questions was put to each of the cases. These queries allowed for an extraction of data from the legal language itself in the form of key terms and/or phrases that revealed underlying jurisprudential intent. After eliciting this pertinent information, the second level of analysis was performed. This additional stage, more textual in nature, resituated the courts' specific words or phrases within their respective contexts, filtering them through prevailing moral philosophy as a way to ascertain the ethical reasoning embedded in the courts' rhetoric.

The results indicated that principles traceable to utilitarian and Kantian moral philosophy informed the courts' decision-making logic. Specifically, within each case and across the decisions, an ethic of interest-balancing was employed wherein the needs of correctional administrators and the public were weighed against the rights of individual prisoners. In other words, the legal opinions constituting the data set predominantly sought the greater good for the majority (penal officials and society) over the minority (psychiatrically disordered inmates). Additionally, underscoring the courts' jurisprudential intent was a commitment to upholding a duty as delineated by Kantian ethics. In some instances, the bench expressed an obligation to defer to correctional administrators in their respective roles as prison managers. In other instances, the bench endorsed a deontological duty to ensure that incarcerates benefited from the dignity that they deserved as human beings, notwithstanding their segregation from society and/or from others criminally confined.

The qualitative findings also showed that legal tribunals largely disregard the social and behavioral science literature on inmate mental health, solitary confinement, and the potentially cruel and unusual conditions of long-term punitive isolation. Moreover, the preceding analysis revealed that the underlying ethical reasoning that informs judicial decision making concerning mentally ill offenders subjected to protracted disciplinary solitary confinement is inadequate. This is because virtue-based moral philosophy does not underscore—does not anchor—the jurisprudential intent of the court.

Accordingly, we maintain that the total confinement practice operating in this instance wrongly pathologizes citizens who are already vulnerable to their experiences of psychiatric distress. Moreover, the judicial affirmation that sustains the long-term disciplinary segregation of such individuals—as sourced through the ethics-based evaluation of the prevailing case law on the matter—is indicative of juridical *madness*. As previously identified in the discussion portion of Chapter 2, the forces that seed and nurture this madness can be traced to fear of crime (and would-be offenders). To stave off the possibility of future imagined violence and victimization, the public demands governance (institutional responses to such conjured terror), including excessive investments in policing difference (through techniques and technologies of discipline, normalization, and control).

At issue here, however, is the prevailing mental representation that is summoned about the psychiatrically disordered inmate, prison management of the same, and the experience of solitary confinement that correspondingly attaches (the Symbolic realm); the privileged narrative that is told about this criminal transgressor and the offender's status as necessitating isolation (the Linguistic realm); the body (or bodies) of knowledge that follow from both whose lived text inscribes on all a preferred type of corrective intervention embraced as appropriate remedial action (the Material realm); and the incomplete and illusory portrayal of "mental illness," "violence," "prisons," "solitary confinement," "treatment," and "recovery" that is repeatedly disseminated by way of this recurring process (the Cultural realm). Intended or otherwise, these interdependent and interactive forces, or conditions of control, advance a quality of self and society excellence that limits and denies the possibilities inherent (and awaiting recognition) in both. The dynamics of this reductionistic ethic of harm, understood as the madness of captivity, dangerously impacts the prospect of citizenship and the evolution in social justice for one and all. The concluding chapter will revisit these notions in some greater detail.

Although the chapter's research findings are significant, they ostensibly possess several problematic limitations. However, consistent with the previous chapter's examination of juvenile transfer, developmental maturity, and competency to stand trial, these shortcomings are not altogether insurmountable.[18] Specifically, the case law sampling design, two-phase qualitiative methodology, and thematic results; the investigation's overall explanatory and predictive efficacy; and the emphasis on ethical inquiry more globally understandably could be the source of some concern. The first matter challenges the generalizability of the research findings, the second matter questions the intention behind our heuristic evidence, and the third matter takes exception to the likely relevance of the study itself. As we explained in the previous chapter, these criticisms seem to miss the point. So, again, we wish to be clear.

Our qualitative textual analysis concerning the prevailing case law on the matter of inmate mental health, solitary confinement, and cruel and unusual punishment produced a striking normatively sourced result. The manifest content of the legal opinions themselves on which judicial temperament was derived from plain meaning was not informed by an underlying ethic of virtue. No commentary on Aristotelian habits of character (e.g., gentleness, humility, compassion, courage) functioned as moral principles by which jurisprudential intent was conveyed in any case or across the data set. And although the absence of said evidence does not resoundingly make the case for evidence of absence, this realization is, quite fittingly, a recommendation for more detailed (and sophisticated) analysis. As such, we assert that the question to subsequently consider is how, if at all, did (and do) jurists write about excellence and human flourishing throughout the entirety of their legal narratives (decisions)? A response to this query necessitates a type of justice wherein the presence of injury is situated within an examination of individual accountability and institutional (societal) responsibility. Once this condition is in place, a more probing ethical inquiry by way of citizenship standards (i.e., dignity, the therapeutic, and critique) and excellence habits (virtues) naturally follows. This process of investigation would extend from those victimized to those who offend, from the communities that they inhabit to the society that binds them all together.

Thus, we argue that the prevailing case law on the total confinement practice matter under consideration did not dignify, heal, or restore by way of exercised habits of human flourishing for one and about all. This failing is madness. This madness, as linked to the consumption of circumscribed images, the narrative of exclusionary politics, the embodiments of disciplinary technologies and normalizing techniques, and the cultural reproduction and circulation of them all sustains an ethic of harm. This ethic of harm promulgates a society of captives. This captivity erodes the potential in being (the recovering subject) and undoes the possibility in becoming (the transforming subject). The quality of individual, institutional, communal, and societal change we have in mind, however, seeks to instantiate *transformative habits of character*. No Justice articulated anything approximating virtuous reasoning of this sort. This quality of reform is our politics; its images, narratives, embodiments, and reproductions await further elaboration. Here, too, the concluding chapter will provide some additional commentary along these lines.

Despite these shortcomings, the results drew attention to a number of pressing and unambiguous matters regarding mentally ill offenders and prolonged punitive isolation. First, although the manifest content of the courts' opinions indicated, to varying degrees, a concern for the psychological well-being of incarcerates, the findings showed that legal tribunals largely disregard the empirical literature when determining Eighth Amendment violations alleged by psychiatrically disordered prisoners in long-term disciplinary solitary confinement. Second, the court opinions stipulated that incarcerates who sought protection from so-called cruel and unusual isolative conditions were so confined because they were a threat to the correctional milieu as much as to society. Third, the case opinions specified that inmates did not enjoy the same protections and liberties that were afforded to nonprisoners presenting a complaint before the bench. As such, the courts' primary concern focused on the safety of society and the security of penal institutions. Fourth, the respective courts relied on prescribed standards when determining whether confinement conditions should be deemed cruel and unusual. In doing so, their obligation was to adhere to the legal protocol established for Eighth Amendment cases rather than to consider if placement in extreme solitude could reasonably be construed as inhumane. Fifth, overall, the judicial opinions demonstrated a concern for empirical research and expert witness testimony regarding the inability of mentally ill offenders to conform their behavior in such a way that they could, essentially, earn their way out of isolation. However, the case opinions failed to acknowledge the assorted adjustment deficits psychiatrically disordered inmates struggle to overcome. These deficiencies include compliance problems with the rules of isolation units and supermax prisons, as well as transfer difficulties when returned to the general prison population and community re-entry impediments following their release back into society (Fellner, 2006; Haney, 2003; Kupers, 2008; Lovell et al., 2007; Rebman, 1999; Rhodes, 2004; Weidman, 2004).

Thus, as this chapter's qualitative and interpretive analysis demonstrated, the courts endorsed an order-maintenance approach and, as such, advanced the needs of an organized society. However, the case decisions woefully failed to address the concerns raised by the empirical evidence regarding psychiatrically disordered prisoners subsequently placed in prolonged disciplinary solitary confinement. Perhaps this critical finding furthers the position that mentally ill offenders are not suited for isolation or any other type of strictly punitive confinement (e.g., Fellner, 2006; Haney, 2003; Johnson, 2002; King, Steiner, & Breach, 2008), especially when the psychosocial attention they so desperately need is denied to them. This is stimulation that enables incarcerates to retain a sense of autonomy, to improve their mental well-being, and to interact productively with others (Arrigo & Bullock, 2008).[19]

The mental health and justice systems seek to ensure the protection and welfare of citizens. However, the furtherance of this notion must be assessed in relation to how the legal edifice effectively achieves what is needed (dignifying, healing, and caring) for *all* societal members, all citizens. As the foregoing inquiry revealed, the judicial apparatus is not addressing the specific needs of incarcerated offenders with pre-existing mental health conditions placed in long-term disciplinary isolation. As such, policies delineated to ensure that "the greater good" is realized must be re-evaluated. We contend that this reassessment entails another level of engagement with normative theory and the contexts in which judicial decision making could be articulated. These contexts draw attention to the practice of psychological jurisprudence and contemporary reformist-based strategies that advance psychological jurisprudence's collective and integrative commitment to pursuing social justice.

4

Sexually Violent Predators, Criminal and Civil Confinement, and Community Re-Entry

Introduction

A third law–psychology–crime phenomenon in which the theory of psychological jurisprudence and the logic of virtue ethics can be employed to investigate our thesis on total confinement is the criminal/civil detention, inspection, and surveillance of adjudicated sexually violent predators (SVPs). This chapter examines this matter in considerable detail. Specifically, what will be made clear are the moral philosophical principles evident in the precedent-setting judicial opinions that convey the United States Supreme Court's perspective on four total confinement measures impacting sex offenders—particularly SVPs. These measures or sanctions include criminal incarceration, civil commitment, sex offender registration, and community notification. Providing clarity here will then make it possible to assess whether, and to what degree, current judicial decision making impacting convicted sex offenders supports or fails to support excellence in being for all participants (victims, assailants, and the communities that unite them), in which habits of character underscore and inform jurisprudential temperament.

To address the above concerns, this chapter is divided into four parts. Section one reviews the extant empirical literature on sexual violence and SVPs, mindful of findings related to post-incarceration recidivism effects, involuntary civil commitment, and modes of community re-entry supervision. With respect to this latter issue, the research on sex offender registries, community notification, residency restrictions/exclusion zones, and global positioning systems (GPS) tracking will be outlined. The section concludes with a brief assessment regarding the significance of post-incarceration sanctions, especially in relation to potential for re-offense. Section two sequences the steps of our case law methodology. This includes the procedures utilized that led to the selection of those court cases forming the data set. Section three discusses the results. This portion of the chapter identifies the ethical rationales and/or principles that informed the Court's judicial intent both intra- and inter-textually. Section four comments on the findings, and addresses their relevance for the total confinement practice of containing sexually violent predators through criminal and civil confinement and community inspection/surveillance. These observations consider whether the moral philosophy that anchors this practice as communicated by the United States Supreme Court is suspect or flawed, especially given the empirical literature questioning its evidentiary soundness. These remarks are further explored within the dynamic contexts of madness, citizenship, and social justice.

The Literature on Sexual Violence and Sexually Violent Predators: An Overview

Empirical and Legal Background

The number of incarcerated adult sexual offenders has increased dramatically in the past two decades, surpassing all other criminal populations except for drug offenders (LaFond, 2005). Under current laws, sex offenders are typically defined as those who have been convicted of a sexually violent crime (Wright, 2008, p. 23). Interestingly, the existing literature delineates several findings regarding the prevalence of sexual violence that contradict a number of prevailing assumptions on which SVP policies and public sentiment are based. It is important to note that research examining the incidents of sexual assault—particularly when the victim is a child—often goes unreported (Bureau of Justice Statistics, 2005; Janus, 2006). Nevertheless, the empirical evidence suggests that the public's perception of sex offenders is largely unsupported by the existing body of literature. Consider the following data.

Although researchers acknowledge the widely held perception that sex crimes are commonly committed by strangers, the statistical research suggests that the majority of violent sexual assaults are perpetrated by relatives or acquaintances of the victim(s) (Catalano, 2005; Douard, 2007; Janus, 2006). Indeed, studies reveal that among victims who were either raped or sexually assaulted, approximately 60% indicated that the crimes occurred in their own home or at the home of a relative, friend, or neighbor (Janus, 2006; *see also* Snyder & Sickmund, 2006). Moreover, according to the Bureau of Justice Statistics (2000), 93% of child victims were sexually assaulted by someone within their family (34%) or by an acquaintance (59%). Although incidents of sexual homicides are highly publicized, they are, in actuality, rare (Chan & Heide, 2009; Janus, 2006). To illustrate, of the more than 14,000 murders that occurred in the United States in 2004, only 1.1% of those were identified as sexual homicides (Chan & Heide, 2009). Notwithstanding these empirical findings, significant confinement and treatment interventions have been pursued to address the threat posed by the most despised of criminal types in contemporary American society: the adult sex offender.[1]

Within this population of offenders is a subgroup of acutely dangerous individuals seemingly incapable of controlling their sexual proclivities, and they are known as SVPs.[2] Not only are these individuals identified as lawbreakers who committed a sexually violent offense, they are also formally diagnosed with a mental abnormality or personality disorder elevating them to the status of high-risk offenders for likely violent reoffending (Janus, 2006; LaFond, 2008; Prentky, Janus, Barbaree, Schwarts, & Kafka 2006; Sreenivasan et al., 2003). Along with criminals warehoused in supermax security prisons, SVP assailants bear the dubious label: the "worst of the worst" (Janus, 2006, p. 2).

In general, laws aimed at controlling and confining offenders classified as SVPs involve four criteria: "*(1)* past sexually harmful conduct, *(2)* a current clinical condition, *(3)* a substantial risk of future sexual violence, and *(4)* a causal relationship between the mental abnormality and the potential sexual harm" (Sparks, 2008, p. 177; *see also* Williams, 2008). However, making SVP determinations is rather complex, and they present a number of challenges for both legal professionals and forensic evaluators (Prentky et al., 2006; Williams, 2008). For example, the term *SVP* includes both legal and psychological definitions (LaFond, 2008; Sparks, 2008; Sreenivasan et al., 2003). Indeed, although SVP statutes delineate what constitutes mental abnormality, the phrase "does not describe a mental disorder recognized by authoritative medical texts, mental health organizations, or mental health professionals" (LaFond, 2008, p. 161; *see also* Sreenivasan et al., 2003).

Unlike mental abnormality, personality disorder has been medically defined and recognized by psychiatric professionals. Interestingly, some research suggests that when assessing whether a sex offender should be classified as an SVP, evaluators often review the individual's past criminal behavior to identify symptoms of "antisocial personality disorder" and then make determinations based on this diagnosis (LaFond, 2008).[3] Furthermore, determining a sex offender's "likelihood of future violence [or dangerousness]" (e.g., highly likely) is a particularly complicated undertaking because the validity of risk assessments is uncertain (Prentky et al., 2006, p. 359; *see also* Fabian, 2003, 2009; Janus & Prentky, 2003). In fact, some researchers contend, "[S]ocial scientists have yet to prove themselves capable of predicting future violence with even a reasonable degree of accuracy" (Williams, 2008, p. 186; *see also* Williams & Arrigo 2002; Louw, Strydom, & Esterhuyse, 2005).

Although the current academic literature provides some insight into SVPs and sexually violent offending, this research remains incomplete. To illustrate, sanctions applied to SVPs largely fail to address the "psychological roots of sexually aberrant behavior" (Arrigo & Shipley, 2005, p. 468). Moreover, presumptions regarding SVPs and their inability to be rehabilitated have dramatically overshadowed available and relevant social science findings (Janus, 2006; Prentky et al., 2006; Wakefield, 2006). Mindful of these deficiencies, some investigators argue that attempting to obtain an "accurate picture" of SVPs is difficult (Janus, 2006, p. 45; Wright, 2008). Indeed, the variety of measurement instruments used to determine sexual violence and the frequently shifting definition of such behavior have confounded efforts to establish sound and reliable evidence concerning SVPs (Janus, 2006).

Post-Incarceration Recidivism Effects

The principle argument in favor of SVP policies largely entails several questionable assumptions lacking empirical support about sex offenders and their likelihood to re-offend. As Edwards and Hensley (2001) explained, "society itself—and by extension, its lawmakers—has gradually adopted a one-dimensional image of what a sex offender is, and one that is generally limited to his or her deviant behavior" (p. 85). Frequently, both policymakers and the public express the belief that sex offenders—particularly SVPs—*always* recidivate (Turner & Rubin, 2002; Williams, 2008; Wright, 2008). In this way, it is often presumed that these offenders also victimize hundreds of people, particularly those widely considered to be the most vulnerable in society (i.e., women and children). Additionally, the lack of distinction made between the type of sexual offender (e.g., incest offender, pedophile, and/or rapist) and their respective recidivism rates is both routine and considerable (Wright, 2008). Thus, policies intended to control SVPs that are informed by these fixed and false suppositions clearly raise a number of concerns regarding the soundness and efficacy of such laws (Janus, 2006; Wright, 2008).[4]

Interestingly, the empirical evidence on sex offender recidivism demonstrates the flawed and misinformed nature of existing sex offender and SVP policies. Among those previously convicted of a sex crime, the recidivism rate is typically between 5% and 15%, and this figure is significantly lower than the rate of those who commit non-sexual crimes (Durose, Lagan, & Schmitt, 2003; Duwe & Goldman, 2009; Hanson & Morton-Bourgon, 2005). Moreover, although the extant literature documenting the efficacy of sex offender treatment on recidivism rates for those confined is somewhat conflicting, treated sex offenders have low recidivism rates compared to their non-treated counterparts (Alexander, 1999; Gallagher, Wilson, Hirschfield, Coggeshall, & Mackenzie, 1999; Hanson et al., 2002; Losel & Schmucker, 2005; Olver et al., 2009).

However, research indicates that certain sex offenders are significantly more likely to re-offend than others. This subgroup of offenders includes those who exhibit strong signs of sexual deviance in conjunction with elevated levels of psychopathy (Harris & Hanson, 2004), and these indicators are consistent with what some researchers classify as SVP behavior.[5] For these offenders, recidivism rates range from slightly more than 40% (Olver & Wong, 2006) to 82% (Hildebrand et al., 2004). Still, these studies are not entirely conclusive. As noted previously, there are a number of complexities surrounding

SVP classification. Without a sound uniform method for determining whether an offender should be designated an SVP, it is difficult to ascertain if, how quickly, and in what way (e.g., non-sexual crime vs. sexual offense) SVPs re-offend (Janus, 2006). Additionally, the follow-up period in which investigators collect data on these offenders widely varies. Thus, although the current body of literature indicates that sex offenders do not have high or significant recidivism rates, the need for research remains. Specifically, inquiries that yield robust findings about sex offender (especially SVP-specific) treatment and recidivism are essential (Duwe & Goldman, 2009; Grady & Brodersen, 2009).

Involuntary Civil Commitment of Sexually Violent Predators

Unquestionably, public fear of SVP offenders in contemporary society is both chronic and acute. The push for confinement and isolation through "whatever means necessary," including civil commitment, remains strong and unabated (Janus, 2006). Civil commitment is not a novel method for containing those identified as sexually violent (Wright, 2008). Indeed, current laws authorizing the civil commitment of sex offenders are rooted in the sexual psychopath statutes established in the 1930s (Rayburn Yung, 2007; Wright, 2008). As Wright (2008) noted, "these laws [emerged] from the growth of the psychiatric movement that linked sexual deviance [primarily homosexuality] with mental illness during a period of strong moral conservatism" (p. 38). As public sentiment shifted in the 1960s, sexual psychopath laws became less prevalent.

However, several brutal and broadly publicized sexually violent attacks that occurred over the span of two years in Washington re-ignited public and political interest in protecting society from those who commit sexually deviant acts. Consider the following atrocities. In 1988, while on work release, convicted sex offender Gene Raymond Kane stabbed 30-year-old Diane Ballasiotes to death during an attempted rape (Websdale, 1996). In 1989, three young boys (Lee Iseli as well as brothers Cole and William Neer) were sexually assaulted and murdered by Westley Allan Dodd. Dodd was executed in 1993 for these crimes (Steinbock, 1995). In the same year, 7-year-old Ryan Hade (a.k.a. the "Little Tacoma Boy") was raped, sexually mutilated, stabbed, and left for dead by Earl Kenneth Shriner, a convicted sex offender with a history of mental illness (Eldridge, 2009). In response to these shocking attacks, Washington passed the 1990 Community Protection Act. The Act was the first in the "next generation" of a number of SVP civil commitment statutes that largely relied on the notion of future risk of dangerousness for legislative traction (Deming, 2008, p. 355; *see also* Petrila, 2008; Sparks, 2008; Williams, 2008). In other words, these laws endorsed confinement beyond penal incarceration to prevent *potential* harm.

Currently, 20 states and the District of Columbia have laws sanctioning involuntary civil commitment for sex offenders (Deming, 2008; Lave &

McCrary, 2009). These states include: Arizona, California, Florida, Illinois, Iowa, Kansas, Massachusetts, Minnesota, Missouri, Nebraska, New Hampshire, New Jersey, New York, North Dakota, Pennsylvania, South Carolina, Texas, Virginia, Washington, and Wisconsin (Lave & McCrary, 2009; Sparks, 2008). Although the laws within these states share "common elements," the structure of civil commitment programs and the manner in which these respective facilities are operated differ (Schneider, 2008, p. 464). To be clear, civilly committing a repeat sex offender or SVP is a costly proposition for these states. On average, the national annual expense per offender placed in a psychiatric treatment facility is $90,000 (Schneider, 2008). The average length of stay for SVPs varies according to state. For example, offenders in Florida were civilly confined for approximately two years (760 days). The cost per SVP was slightly less than the national average, at $80,000 (OPPAGA, 2008).

At present, the precise number of SVPs civilly committed has yet to be determined. Some contend that "thousands" have been confined under SVP commitment statutes because of future dangerousness (Janus & Logan, 2003). Others cite a more specific estimate of SVPs civilly committed or detained that as of 2006 was 3,646 (2,627 committed and 1,019 detained) (Deming, 2006, 2008). Leading the states in the number of SVPs that are civilly committed or detained is California, with slightly more than 600 offenders (Deming, 2006; Lave & McCrary, 2009).

A study conducted by Vess et al. (2004) offered perhaps the most thorough clinical and demographic profile of SVPs who were civilly committed. On average, SVPs were 10 years older than other patients, and their mean age was 46 years old. Additionally, the investigators found that SVPs were less likely to be diagnosed with a psychotic disorder (e.g., schizophrenia) and were more likely to be psychopathic than any other patient committed to a treatment facility (Vess et al., 2004).

Although SVP statutes vary according to jurisdictions, civil commitment typically follows the completion of a criminal sentence.[6] As the convicted sex offender's release date draws near, the correctional institution from which he or she is scheduled to be released notifies the state attorney general (Janus & Bolin, 2008; Sparks, 2008). The offender's history and *dangerousness* is assessed to ascertain whether a petition for commitment as an SVP should be filed. Risk-assessment software and actuarial guides, such as the STATIC-99 and the Psychopathy Checklist-Revised (PCL-R), are often utilized to determine the likelihood that a SVP will recidivate (Hanson, 2005; Jackson & Hess, 2007; Levenson, 2004; Prentky et al., 2006; Shipley & Arrigo, 2001; Sreenivasan et al., 2003). If a petition is filed, then the state trial court reviews it and makes a decision as to the post-incarceration fate of the sex offender (Janus & Bolin, 2008; LaFond, 2008; Levenson, 2004; Sparks, 2008).[7]

The premise that sustains SVP civil commitment laws is that "patients" will be treated, and once they are "rehabilitated" (i.e., no longer psychiatrically disordered or dangerous), they will be discharged (Janus, 2004; *see also* Prentky et al., 2006; Shipley & Arrigo, 2001; Sparks, 2008; Sreenivasan et al.,

2003; Williams, 2008). However, the extant research indicates that few civilly confined SVPs are ever released (Janus & Bolin, 2008; Wright, 2008). For example, in the approximately 15 years since Minnesota has been civilly committing SVPs, "Just 24 men have met what has proved to be the only acceptable standard for release. They died" (Oakes, 2008, p. A1). Recent legislation in various states across the nation permits the ongoing confinement of sex offenders and SVPs. To illustrate, according to California's civil commitment statutes, a convicted sex offender without any previous criminal history and with a minimum of one victim may be committed indefinitely (Wright, 2008).

Although public sentiment seems to support civilly committing the "worst of the worse," behavioral and social science scholars have joined human rights activists in questioning the ethical rationale and efficacy of sustaining such a practice.[8] According to Janus (2008), "SVP laws provide a secondary pathway for social control, unencumbered by the strict procedural constraints circumscribing the criminal justice system" (p. 27). Some researchers argue that civil commitment laws are decidedly vague and rely on citizens' acceptance of preventive detention, a notion that American society has historically rejected (Janus, 2004, 2006; Palermo, 2009; Williams, 2008). Other commentators assert that the expressed purpose of civil commitment egregiously harms offenders, as these individuals are labeled incurably "sick" amidst a climate in which they must endure proscribed punishment and society's scorn (Douard, 2007; Wright, 2008). Furthermore, the non-therapeutic implications of these conflicting labels (i.e., mentally abnormal, personality disordered, sick) distort and hinder the possibility of positive treatment outcomes, potentially contributing to increased recidivism as well as preventing successful community reintegration (Douard, 2007; Levenson, 2004; Levenson & Cotter, 2005; Shipley & Arrigo, 2001).

In addition to these ethical, diagnostic, and treatment concerns is the absence of any empirical analysis that adequately assesses the process and practice of whether a classified SVP offender should subsequently be civilly committed (Levenson, 2004, 2008; Sreenivasan et al., 2003). Indeed, as Fabian (2009) observed, "Many courts have not translated 'likely' into a statistical probability" (p. 44). Additionally, critics charge that Diagnostic Statistical Manual (DSM) criteria are perhaps too vague and not precise enough to be utilized in the courtroom to inform judicial decision making on the matter of civilly confining a sexually violent offender (Doren, 2002; Levenson, 2008; Reid, Wise, & Sutton, 1992). Some researchers also contend that forensic evaluators often expand their definition of mental abnormality such that it explains criminal sexual behavior and meets the mental disorder criterion for SVP commitment (Janus, 2006; Prentky et al., 2006; see also Shipley & Arrigo, 2001). Moreover, others argue that because the legal standards for determining risk thresholds are especially ambiguous, "it is tempting for legal decision makers to treat mental health testimony as if it had normative, as well as descriptive, import" (Prentky et al., 2006, p. 360; see also Fabian, 2009; Schopp, Scalora, & Pearce, 1999).[9]

Community Re-Entry

Whereas convicted offenders are subjected to some form of post-release community supervision, those who have committed sexually violent crimes are vigilantly watched and intensely controlled unlike any other offender group. Indeed, "the environment for newly released sex offenders is highly stigmatized, isolated, and stressful" (Edwards & Hensley, 2001, p. 89). Laws at the federal, state, and local levels have been created to monitor sex offenders—particularly SVPs—upon their release from a penal institution or treatment facility (Janus, 2006; Wakefield, 2006). The most common examples of this hyper-surveillance include sex offender registries, community notification, residency restrictions/exclusion zones, and GPS tracking.

Sex offender registration

Whether convicted sex offenders are paroled from a penal institution or released following the satisfactory completion of treatment requirements at a psychiatric facility, their reintegration into society entails unrelenting supervision. Consider the following case.

Eleven-year-old Jacob Wetterling and his abductor were never located; however, the crime itself led to another phase in the evolution of legislation intent on monitoring sex offenders (Scott & Gerbasi, 2003; Wright, 2008; see also Frierson, Dwyer, Bell, & Williamson, 2008).[10] During the highly publicized search for Jacob, the local media disclosed the fact that law enforcement authorities had discovered approximately 300 sex offenders residing within the area of his home county in Minnesota. In the aftermath of this revelation, the public expressed outrage and demanded that law enforcement agencies be given more options in preventing and deterring crimes against children (Scott & Gerbasi, 2003; Wakefield, 2006).

Included in the 1994 Violent Crime Control and Law Enforcement Act, the Jacob Wetterling Act was the first piece of federal legislation specifically targeting sex offenders. The law mandated that all 50 states require those convicted of a sex offense to register their residential and employment information with police agencies so that these offenders could be monitored subsequent to prison release or hospital discharge (Appelbaum, 2008; Wakefield, 2006; Wright, 2008). Presently, well over half a million individuals are registered as sex offenders in the United States (Appelbaum, 2008; National Center for Missing and Exploited Children, 2007).

Community notification

Stemming from a series of sexually violent crimes committed by psychologically disordered individuals and sex offenders in the 1990s, Washington became the first state to enact a sex offender community notification statute (Appelbaum, 2008; Veysey, Zgoba, & Dellasandro, 2008). Following the highly publicized sexual molestation and murder of 7-year-old Megan Nicole Kanka by a twice-convicted sex offender neighbor of the Kanka family, public outrage led to the New Jersey legislature's emergency passage of what is now known as Megan's Law (Edwards & Hensley, 2001; Scott & Gerbasi, 2003; Veysey et al., 2008). Megan's Law proved seminal in establishing a federal sex offender community notification requirement for released offenders, particularly those classified as SVPs. In 1996, Congress amended the Wetterling Act by passing Megan's Law (Appelbaum, 2008; Scott & Gerbasi, 2003). The statute mandates that police agencies notify communities of sex offenders in their midst by providing the ex-offender's name and residential address. If a state fails to comply with this mandate, it risks losing 10% of its federal law enforcement funding (Scott & Gerbasi, 2003).

In 2006, after law enforcement authorities lobbied for more effective and efficient means to disseminate sex offender information, the Adam Walsh Child Protection and Safety Act (AWA) was passed (Fabian, 2009). The Bill amended a portion of the Wetterling legislation, wherein the new law was created "in response to vicious attacks by violent sexual predators" (Wright, 2008, p. 32). The Act cited the names of 17 victims, their home states, and the year of their sexual assaults and murders (e.g., Polly Klaas [Cal., 1993], Jetseta Gage [Iowa, 2005]). The AWA requires that all 50 states not only notify communities but also make offenders' information available on the Internet. Among other provisions, the law increases mandatory sentences for federal sex offenders, sanctions their civil commitment, and requires that DNA samples be collected and stored (Fabian, 2009; Freeman & Sandler, 2009, Telsavarra & Arrigo, 2006).

The AWA also established a federal classification tier system for sex offenders with corresponding sanctions. The requirement for classification as a tier I sex offender is exceptionally straightforward. A tier I offender is simply "a sex offender other than a tier II or tier III sex offender" (Wright, 2008, p. 32). As a tier I sex offender, individuals must register for 15 years and allow their respective jurisdiction to confirm their home address and take a current photograph of them each year. According to the system, a tier II sex offender is an individual who has been convicted of committing sex offenses against a minor or "an attempt or conspiracy to commit these crimes including: sex trafficking, coercion and crimes of enticement, transportation with the intent to engage in criminal sexual activity, abusive sexual contact, use of a minor in a sexual performance, solicitation of a minor to practice prostitution, and the production or distribution of child pornography" (Wright, 2008, p. 32). Tier II sex offenders must remain registered for 25 years and have their address verified and their photograph taken every 6 months. Tier III sex offenders are classified according to their conviction of a sex crime or conspiracy to commit such a crime with assaultive or violent behavior. These are persons who have perpetrated aggravated sexual abuse or sexual abuse, abusive sexual contact with a minor younger than aged 13 years, or the non-parental or custodial kidnapping of a minor (Freeman & Sandler, 2009; Wright, 2008). As the most serious offender in the tier system, tier III ex-incarcerates are required to register for life and to have their address and a photograph taken every three months (Freeman & Sandler, 2009; Wright, 2008).

Residency restrictions and exclusion zones

To further control sex offenders and SVPs, residency restriction laws have been created. In recent years, states such as New Jersey and Pennsylvania have created *sex-offender-free* or *predator-free* zones that prohibit released sex offenders from establishing a residence within designated areas of communities (Rayburn Yung, 2007; Tekle-Johnson, 2009; Toutant, 2005).[11] Like other sex offender regulations, the "assumption within these laws is that if sex offenders cannot live near [i.e., prevented from living near] potential victims, they will be less likely to re-offend" (Wright, 2008, p. 42; *see also* Tekle-Johnson, 2009).

Residency restriction laws for sex offenders continue to hold favor with policymakers and the public. Although these exclusion zone laws are typically enacted for the common purpose of physically separating sex offenders and potential victims, the specific conditions applied to sex offenders differ according to jurisdiction (Logan, 2006; Rayburn Yung, 2007). The majority of states that have established residency restrictions for sex offenders require these individuals to abide by these limitations regardless of whether the victim was an adult or child. However, a few states, like Florida, only subject those whose sex crimes involved a minor to residency restrictions (Rayburn Yung, 2007).

Among the states with exclusion zones, Georgia, Iowa, and Louisiana have perhaps the most stringent laws in which these prohibited areas have been established. In Georgia, those convicted of committing a sex crime must stay at least 1,000 feet away from a number of public places (including churches, parks, playgrounds) where children are likely to congregate (Toutant, 2005; Wright, 2008). If an offender is found within the radius of any of these environs, the individual may receive a sentence of up to 30 years in prison (Rayburn Yung, 2007). Iowa established an exclusion zone that prohibits convicted sex offenders from being within 2,000 feet from schools or registered child care facilities. Louisiana has created sex-offender-free zones around locations such as public swimming pools and video arcade facilities. The statute specifically applies to sex offenders classified as SVPs who have victimized both adults and children (Logan, 2006; Rayburn Yung, 2007). Although some specific terms concerning restriction may vary, most exclusion zone statutes do not allow for due process and are rather broad in their scope. Arkansas' exclusion zone law is, perhaps, the one exception. The state employs a tiered risk scheme in which a sex offender's dangerousness is assessed on an individual basis (Logan, 2006; Rayburn Yung, 2007).

Global Positioning System (GPS) monitoring and tracking

Following the horrific sexual molestation and slaying of 9-year-old Jessica Lunsford by repeat sex offender John Couey, Jessica's Law was introduced.

In an effort to manage those deemed uncontrollable, the statute proposed the implementation and expansion of electronic monitoring for sex offenders ranging from those classified as non-violent low risk to SVPs (Padgett, Bales, & Blomberg, 2006; Wright, 2008). It is important to note that at the time, no empirical evidence existed to suggest that electronic surveillance of this kind would effectively deter violent sexual offending (Padgett et al., 2006). Global Positioning System monitoring, which typically involves placing an electronic unit on the ankle of an offender, allows probation and parole officials to track a convicted sex offender or SVP generally within 10 feet of their location (Mortensen, 2006; Rayburn Yung, 2007). Utilized in conjunction with established exclusion zones, GPS monitoring ensures that officials will be able to detect whether or not a registered sex offender has entered one of these zones. If a sex offender is situated within an exclusion zone, it is likely to result in a violation of his or her probation or parole status (Rayburn Yung, 2007).

With federal support consisting of financial assistance to develop GPS infrastructures that monitor and track sex offenders and SVPs, some states have enacted legislation that addresses the specific needs of their respective jurisdictions. For example, California created the Sexual Predator Punishment and Control Act to track high-risk sexual predators (Mortensen, 2006). The Act authorizes GPS monitoring of offenders during parole and over the course of their lifetime (Mortensen, 2006).

Post-Incarceration Sanctions and Recidivism

In theory, the ostensible aim of each of the above laws is to incapacitate and deter sex offenders and SVPs as well as to protect society (Janus, 2006).[12] However, the current body of literature suggests that the efficacy of these post-incarceration sanctions in reducing recidivism—ranging from civil commitment to residency restrictions to GPS tracking—is largely inconclusive (Levenson, 2003). Nevertheless, some studies have examined possible recidivism effects stemming from post-incarceration sanctions, and as such, these findings are worth considering.

Intriguingly, in terms of sex offender registries and community notification, researchers have yet to determine that central registries deter or prevent re-offending (Levenson, 2003; Wakefield, 2006). For example, Lieb (1996) conducted an investigation on recidivism effectiveness following the first few years of Washington State's sex offender registry. The results indicated that there were no statistically significant differences between the percentages of sex offenders who were required to register and were subjected to community notification (19% recidivated) versus those who were not (22% recidivated) (Lieb, 1996).

As noted previously, the premise of exclusion zone statutes seems only rational—prohibit convicted sex offenders from residing or being near locations where potential victims, especially minors, congregate. Moreover, laws delineating these zones find favor with political leaders and the concerned public

(Logan, 2006). Indeed, as Toutant (2005) observed, these laws "are usually passed with little debate and zero opposition, since sex offenders are the pariahs of modern society" (p. 1A). However, the effectiveness of exclusion zone laws is, at best, uncertain. At this time, research suggests that "there is no correlation between residency restrictions and reducing sex offenses against children or improving the safety of children" (Levenson & Cotter, 2005, p. 170).

Preliminary research findings suggest that GPS monitoring is perhaps most effective in reducing recidivism among those deemed high-risk sex offenders (Padgett et al., 2006). However, as with the previously discussed measures designed to control and confine SVPs, future empirical analysis is necessary. Investigators overwhelmingly contend that "research has not kept pace with the rapid implementation of the penal strategy [electronic monitoring]" (Padgett et al., 2006, p. 65; *see also* Gainey, Payne, & O'Tool, 2000; Renzema, 2003; Vollum & Hale, 2002).

Still further, studies indicate that those constrained by post-incarceration sanctions experience a range of interpersonal and social difficulties, particularly as a result of community notification and residency restrictions. Indeed, sex offenders required to register and subjected to community notification indicate that they suffered from diminished self-esteem, fractured relationships with family and friends (Levenson & Cotter, 2005; Tewksbury, 2005; Tewksbury & Lees, 2006, 2007), and an overall feeling of detachment from their community and the greater society (Zevitz & Farkas, 2000).[13-14] A significant number of offenders encountered financial hardships principally based on their inability to acquire and maintain employment (Tewksbury, 2005; Zevitz & Farkas, 2000). Among those sex offenders able to sustain a permanent residence, a number of them reported incidents of harassment and damage to their property (Tewksbury, 2005; Tewksbury & Lees, 2006). In recent years, several citizens suspected of seeking to exact revenge on registered sex offenders have obtained their residential address information on the Internet, tracked them down, and murdered them (Wright, 2008). Although these acts of vigilantism are rare, they are nonetheless an indication of the public's unwavering and unrestrained disdain for sex offenders.[15]

Case Law Method

This chapter explores the underlying ethical rationale discernable in the extant judicial decisions on four total confinement measures that affect sex offenders, particularly sexually violent predators. These measures or sanctions include criminal incarceration, civil commitment, sex offender registration, and community notification. To compile the data set, a LexisNexis search was conducted utilizing specific key words and phrases. The search terms included *sexually violent predator, criminal confinement, civil commitment, sex offender registration,* and *community notification.* The legal construct *sexually violent predator* was chosen over *sexually deviant predator, sexually dangerous person, sexually dangerous individual*, and *sexual psychopathic personality*. These latter terms did not yield any additional or relevant court decisions. The phrase *criminal confinement* was chosen over *criminal incarceration*. Criminal incarceration produced too few results; thus, criminal confinement was utilized. The search phrase, *civil commitment*, was included as this legal construct is used to describe confinement beyond a period of criminal incarceration that is intended to treat SVPs until they have been rehabilitated and are no longer considered a threat to society.

Moreover, given the chapter's supplementary focus on investigating post-confinement sanctions imposed on those who have committed sex offenses, the terms *sex offender registry* and *community notification* were deemed essential. The specific phrase *sex offender registry* was chosen over *sex offender registration* because the latter expression failed to produce any additionally relevant results. *Community notification* was included for one very clear and compelling reason: the phrase describes the statutory sanction aimed at ensuring that the public has access to critical information on sex offenders—especially SVPs—in their community.

Utilizing the aforementioned search words and terms revealed that the existing case law does not consist of a single judicial ruling involving an SVP or high-risk sex offender wherein each of the four total confinement measures is addressed by the court. Thus, to yield precedent-setting decisions on criminal confinement, civil commitment, sex offender registration, and community notification matters, it was necessary to include the connector *[OR]*. As such, the parameters established for the subsequent textual analysis consisted of: *sexually violent predator, criminal confinement, civil commitment [OR] sexually violent predator, sex offender registry*, and *community notification*.

To make explicit the courts' most complete language to date on total confinement sanctions imposed on SVPs and sex offenders, this chapter reviews those opinions rendered by the United States Supreme Court. Based on the aforementioned delineated criteria, the LexisNexis search yielded five Supreme Court cases. These decisions include the following: *Smith v. Doe* (2003), *Connecticut Department of Public Safety v. Doe* (2003), *Kansas v. Hendricks* (1997), *Kansas v. Crane* (2002), and *Seling v. Young* (2001).

In *Smith v. Doe* (2003), the Justices heard arguments regarding Alaska's Sex Offender Registration Act (ASORA). This is the state's version of Megan's Law.[16] The Act, which includes both registration and community notification components, requires those who have been convicted of sex offenses to provide their personal details, including current information on their appearance, location, employment, and the offenses for which they were convicted. This information is then disseminated to the public and placed on the Internet. The offenders involved in the case argued that the ASORA violated the Constitution's *Ex Post Facto* Clause because it was retroactively imposed (i.e., followed a criminal sentence served) registration and notification provisions. Officials countered this claim by asserting that the Act was designed to protect the public; thus, it was consistent with a non-punitive regulatory scheme.

Justice Kennedy delivered the majority opinion and was joined by Chief Justice Rehnquist and Justices O'Connor, Scalia, and Thomas.[17-18] The Court upheld the lower court's ruling, noting that the ASORA was indeed intended only to protect society from high-risk sex offenders. As such, the decision did not violate the Constitution's *Ex Post Facto* Clause. Moreover, offenders claimed that the Act's registration and notification aspects imposed a stigma on them, making them susceptible to adverse reactions from the community. Here, too, the Court rejected this reasoning. The Court contended that most of the information was a matter of public record; therefore, disseminating offenders' personal information to the community in which they resided did not impose significant disability or restraint. Given the Court's clear focus on the Act's sex offender registration and community notification provisions, the case was included in the data set.[19]

Connecticut Department of Public Safety v. Doe (2003) involved a convicted sex offender who challenged the registration and community notification provisions of a similar statute based on Megan's Law.[20-21] Doe asserted that the law violated his procedural due process rights because offenders are not afforded a hearing to determine their level of dangerousness prior to being listed on the registry. Further, he claimed that the registration and notification provisions constituted government actions that both harm and stigmatize sex offenders. On appeal at the U.S. Court of Appeals for the Second Circuit, the jurists ruled that the Connecticut statute did indeed implicate a liberty interest of affected sex offenders. Additionally, the court asserted that before sex offenders could be subjected to being labeled as dangerous and included in a publicly disseminated registry, they must be afforded due process. On *certiorari* at the Supreme Court, the Justices reversed the Court of Appeal's judgment. Chief Justice Rehnquist, joined by Justices O'Connor, Scalia, Kennedy, Souter, Thomas, Ginsburg, and Breyer, delivered the majority opinion. The Court held that the Connecticut statute in question did not violate procedural due process because officials are not required to determine whether a sex offender is "currently dangerous" (*Connecticut Dept. of Public Safety v. Doe* (2003). The Court refused Doe's claim of a liberty interest, noting that the matter of a sex offender's current dangerousness is of no consequence.[22] Although the Justices refused to engage in any considerable deliberation regarding whether a statute authorizing sex offender registration and community notification stigmatizes offenders, the case, nevertheless, further elucidated the Court's position on this matter. As such, the case was retained for textual scrutiny.

Perhaps the most influential decision on post-incarceration sanctions imposed on SVPs, *Kansas v. Hendricks* (1997) involved an inmate who raised a challenge to Kansas' Sexually Violent Predator Act (SVPA).[23] Following a writ of *certiorari* to the U.S. Supreme Court, the Justices considered whether the Act's civil commitment provisions, which are based on its definition of "mental abnormality," violated substantive due process and protection against double jeopardy requirements.[24] The Court reversed the Kansas Supreme Court's decision, holding that the SVPA's definition of "mental abnormality" was not too arbitrary to sustain a civil commitment order. Because the Act required notable evidence of an offender's previous violent sexual behavior and a mental abnormality that made recidivism highly likely, it did not infringe on Hendricks' substantive due process rights. Further, the Court found that the Act did not violate the Constitution's double jeopardy clause because the SVPA authorized civil, rather than criminal, commitments. Moreover, it did not constitute an *ex post facto* violation.[25] The *Hendricks* decision represents the Court's conclusive position on a post-confinement sanction to which SVPs are frequently subjected.[26] Thus, this case was included in the data set.

In *Kansas v. Crane* (2002), the Justices evaluated the merits of the case based on the Court's prior ruling in *Kansas v. Hendricks* (1997).[27] Similar to *Hendricks, Crane* involved a challenge to civilly committing a SVP as delineated by Kansas' SVPA. However, the cases were distinct in that, unlike Hendricks who was diagnosed with a mental abnormality, Crane suffered from exhibitionism and an antisocial personality disorder. Interestingly, the Court held that the SVPA, applied as it was written, was in violation of substantive due process.[28] Although the judgment rendered by the Kansas Supreme Court was ultimately vacated and the case was remanded for further proceedings, *Crane* is widely cited in the extant law review and social science literatures as a precedent-setting decision on the issue of civil commitment for SVPs (Fabian, 2009; Mercado, Schopp, & Bornstein, 2003; Perlin, 2007; Price, 2005; Slobogin, 2006). Thus, mindful of the ensuing inquiry's intention to assess the Courts' most definitive language on matters relating to confinement and post-incarceration sanctions imposed on SVPs, the decision was retained for analysis.

Seling v. Young (2001) involved an offender classified as a sexually violent predator subjected to civil commitment.[29] The plaintiff, Young, raised an "as applied" challenge to the statute, claiming that although the Washington Supreme Court held that the law was not in violation of the Constitution's due process clause, it was punitive as fitted to him.[30] Relying upon the *Hendricks* decision, the Ninth Circuit ruled that although the statute might be facially valid, Young could pursue the case. The State of Washington appealed the court's decision. Before the Supreme Court, Young's attorneys argued that the statute needlessly imposed harsh punishment on him. Specifically, plaintiff argued that the restrictive conditions under which Young was detained and the indefinite timeframe beyond criminal confinement for which he was civilly committed were excessive. In particular, Young asserted that the treatment, which is an essential component that legally distinguishes civil commitment from criminal incarceration, was inadequate. The Supreme Court reversed the U.S. Court of Appeals for the Ninth Circuit's judgment. The majority concurred with the Washington Supreme Court finding that the statute was indeed, on its face, constitutionally valid.[31] As noted in the existing literature, this precedent-setting decision highlights the difficulties that civil committees confront when attempting to establish that a civil statute is punitive in nature based on its effects (Perlin, 2007; Ristroph, 2008; Smith, 2008

Because the case provided further insight into the Court's sentiment regarding this involuntary confinement measure imposed on SVPs, it was included in the data set.

To ensure that all landmark decisions germane to this chapter's focus were accurately identified for case inclusion, a subsequent search was performed. Specifically, each U.S. Supreme Court decision cited in *Smith v. Doe*, *Connecticut Dept. of Public Safety v. Doe*, *Kansas v. Hendricks*, *Kansas v. Crane*, and *Seling v. Young* was reviewed to determine whether these rulings met the aforementioned evaluative criteria. However, having completed this process, no additionally relevant Supreme Court cases were identified for inclusion. Thus, the data set consisted of five precedent-setting decisions.

Discussion

The above data set underwent two levels of qualitative textual scrutiny. The specifics of the investigatory approach were delineated in Chapter 1 (*see* the section on "Psychological Jurisprudence and Methodology"). Appendix C includes all plain meaning case findings relative to the precedent-setting case law on sexually violent predators subjected to criminal confinement, civil commitment, sex offender registration, and community notification. Table 4.1 lists key concepts and exact quotes as derived from the plain meaning results that summarily represent the responses to the seven questions posed to these legal decisions. Collectively, these data represent the various attitudes, perceptions, purposes, and concerns that reflect the Courts' jurisprudential intentions on the total confinement matter in question.

Level 1 Analysis

In *Doe v. Smith*, the Justices acknowledged, "This is the first time we have considered a claim that a sex offender registration and notification law constitutes retroactive punishment forbidden by the *Ex Post Facto* Clause" (p. 92). Although the Court had not previously deliberated on this matter, the Justices noted that the "framework for our inquiry, however, is well established" (p. 92). Citing the *Hendricks* ruling (a precedent-setting decision on civil commitment included in the ensuing inquiry's data set), the Court made explicit that they traditionally "defer to the legislature's intent" and "only the clearest proof will suffice to override legislative intent" (p. 92). In doing so, the Justices expressed a desire to respect the Alaska legislature's right to create statutes that it considers both necessary and civil.

Further, the Court's plain meaning indicated that those who raise *ex post facto* challenges and question the State's underlying intention concerning these laws must overcome an extraordinary high standard of proof. Indeed, the Justices asserted that, "[a] statute is not deemed punitive simply because it lacks a close or perfect fit with the nonpunitive aims it seeks to advance" (p. 103).

Table 4.1 Jurisprudential Intent as Derived from Plain Meaning Data

	Doe v. Smith	Doe v. Smith Concur by Thomas	Doe v. Smith Concur by Souter	CT Dept. of Public Safety v. Doe	CT Dept. of Public Safety v. Doe Concur by Scalia	CT Dept. of Public Safety v. Doe Concur by Souter with whom Ginsburg joins
1	"the intent of the Alaska Legislature was to create a civil, nonpunitive regime"	Whether a law is civil or criminal is determined by examining "the statute on its face"	Dissemination of information informs public, but also humiliates and ostracizes offenders	"Sex offenders are a serious threat"	"... a convicted sex offender has no more right to additional 'process' enabling him to establish that he is not dangerous"	A substantive due process challenge is not the only claim available to sex offenders
2	Availability of information may cause lasting and painful harm; these consequences result from the conviction that is public record	The determination rests on the statute's requirements	No data ascertained	Sex offenders are highly likely to recidivate; the challenge to the law is not "properly before us, [so] we express no opinion"	No data ascertained	Connecticut exempts certain offenders from registration and notification sanctions
3	Although Alaska's Megan's Law may have a deterrent element, it is not punitive	No data ascertained	No data ascertained	Doe's current dangerousness is irrelevant	No data ascertained	No data ascertained

Table 4.1 Continued

	Doe v. Smith	Doe v. Smith Concur by Thomas	Doe v. Smith Concur by Souter	CT Dept. of Public Safety v. Doe	CT Dept. of Public Safety v. Doe Concur by Scalia	CT Dept. of Public Safety v. Doe Concur by Souter with whom Ginsburg joins
4	"Widespread public access is necessary for the efficacy of the scheme, and the attendant humiliation is but a collateral consequence of a valid regulation"	No data ascertained	No data ascertained	No data ascertained	No data ascertained	No data ascertained
5	No data ascertained	No data ascertained	No data ascertained	No data ascertained	No data ascertained	No data ascertained
6	"dissemination of truthful information in furtherance of a legitimate governmental objective [is not] punishment"	No data ascertained	"Selection makes a statement, one that affects common reputation and sometimes carries harsher consequence"	"Sex offenders are a serious threat"	No data ascertained	"This Court's ruling does not mean that offenders cannot raise an equal protection challenge to Connecticut's statute"

7	Risk of recidivism is "frightening and high;" the Act's purpose is to protect the public	No data ascertained	Public safety is a legitimate goal, but the law's use of prior convictions suggests it is more than a civil regulatory scheme	"Sex offenders are a serious threat"	No data ascertained	No data ascertained
	Kansas v. Hendricks	*Kansas v. Hendricks Concur by Kennedy*	*Kansas v. Hendricks Dissent by Breyer with whom Stevens and Souter join and Ginsburg in Parts II & III*	*Kansas v. Crane*	*Kansas v. Crane Dissent by Scalia with whom Thomas joins*	*Seling v. Young*
1	Involuntary civil commitment of a "subclass of dangerous" offenders is consistent with "ordered liberty;" the SVPA is civil	If a civil commitment scheme becomes punitive, it will no longer be supported by our established precedents	The SVPA exacts incapacitation based on past criminal acts, which is consistent with a punitive scheme	SVPs are "unable to control their dangerousness;" Hendricks did not distinguish the "emotional" and the "volitional"	"I would reverse, rather than vacate;" the Court should have clarified "inability to control"	The Act is "strikingly similar" to Kansas' SVPA; the Washington Courts must determine if the facility is operating properly

(Continued)

Table 4.1 Continued

	Kansas v. Hendricks	Kansas v. Hendricks Concur by Kennedy	Kansas v. Hendricks Dissent by Breyer with whom Stevens and Souter join and Ginsburg in Parts II & III	Kansas v. Crane	Kansas v. Crane Dissent by Scalia with whom Thomas joins	Seling v. Young
2	That SVPA is valid because it commits only those diagnosed with a mental abnormality or personality disorder who cannot control their behavior	No data ascertained	If the SVPA is civil in nature, it must ensure adequate treatment is provided to those committed	Although it informs decisions, psychiatry does not determine legal outcomes	Legislators typically determine the definition of medical terms	Conditions are similar to those in *Hendricks*, which were consistent with a non-punitive regulatory goal
3	Hendricks is a pedophile, which qualifies him for civil commitment; the law was created to protect the public	No data ascertained	No data ascertained	We have never distinguished between volitional, emotional, and cognitive impairments	We have not distinguished volitional impairment because it makes no sense	State and federal courts are capable of adjudicating and remedying civil commitment challenges
4	Medical knowledge may be too limited to accurately access treatment and predict future dangerousness	No data ascertained	Dr. Befort testified that Hendricks had not received effective treatment	There must only be proof that an offender has difficulty controlling their behavior	The Court does not adequately elaborate on the inability to control requirement	The Act requires offender treatment but does not delineate the conditions

5	No data ascertained	No data ascertained	Kansas refused to consider "alternative and less harsh methods" for dealing with Hendricks, which fails to support Kansas' assertion that the SVPA has a non-punitive objective	No data ascertained	No data ascertained	No data ascertained
6	Incapacitation is a common civil and criminal system aim; punishment and general deterrence are a criminal goal	No data ascertained	"...it is difficult to see why rational legislators who seek treatment would write the Act in this way"	"...the Constitution's safeguards of human liberty...are not always best enforced through precise bright-line rules"	The Court has an obligation to elaborate on what determines inability to control	Although there may be vagaries in the statute's implementation, it can be civil in nature; challenges to treatment can still be raised

(Continued)

Table 4.1 Continued

	Kansas v. Hendricks	Kansas v. Hendricks Concur by Kennedy	Kansas v. Hendricks Dissent by Breyer with whom Stevens and Souter join and Ginsburg in Parts II & III	Kansas v. Crane	Kansas v. Crane Dissent by Scalia with whom Thomas joins	Seling v. Young
7	Confining Hendricks and others for life may be the only way to protect society	No data ascertained	An individual's liberty should not be infringed upon any more than what is necessary to protect the public	SVPs are known to be unable to control their "dangerousness"	"It is obvious that a person may be able to exercise volition and yet be unfit to turn loose on society"	States have an interest in protecting the public from dangerous offenders.

	Seling v. Young Concur by Scalia with whom Souter joins	Seling v. Young Concur by Thomas	Seling v. Young Dissent by Stevens
1	The Court has determined in the first instance a law's nature	A statute can be civil regardless of its implementation; a "first instance" and subsequent challenge is indistinct	Conditions of confinement should be considered, including in a "first instance" challenge

2	The Court has previously made a "first instance" determination	All factors must be considered equally in determining a sanction's nature	If Young's allegations are true, he and others like him are subjected to prison-like confinement and worse treatment
3	The State's judiciary should make a "first instance" determination, which comports with our reluctance to interpret state law	The conditions are the effect of improper implementation	Whether a statute is civil or criminal in nature is a matter of federal law
4	No data ascertained	No data ascertained	No data ascertained
5	No data ascertained	No data ascertained	No data ascertained
6	No data ascertained	No data ascertained	No data ascertained
7	No data ascertained	No data ascertained	No data ascertained

As such, the Court revealed its perspective that although a law may fail to wholly meet its planned objectives, this is not sufficient evidence to find it punitive in nature.

The *Smith* decision clearly exposed the Court's attitude on the impact that sexually violent predator laws have on an offender's ability to re-integrate into society. Although those convicted of sex offenses are required to notify authorities when "they change their facial features (such as growing a beard), borrow a car, or seek psychiatric treatment," they nevertheless are "free to move where they wish and to live and work as other citizens, with no supervision" (p. 101) and "free to change jobs or residences" (p. 100). Further, the Court opined:

> Landlords and employers could conduct background checks on the
> criminal records of prospective employees or tenants even with the Act
> not in force. The record in this case contains no evidence that the Act
> has led to substantial occupational or housing disadvantages for former
> sex offenders that would not have otherwise occurred through the use
> of routine background checks by employers and landlords. (p. 100)

As such, the Court's rhetoric advanced the perception that although Alaska's statute may create some challenges for offenders in securing a job or a residence, it "imposes no physical restraint, and so does not resemble the punishment of imprisonment" (p. 100).

The language employed in rendering the *Smith* decision revealed insight into the Justices' level of awareness regarding the ASORA's harmful psychological effects (i.e., shame and humiliation) on offenders. The Court stated, "[P]ublic availability of the information may have a lasting and painful impact on the convicted sex offender" (p. 101). In determining whether the ASORA's requirements were a violation of the *Ex Post Facto* Clause, the Justices considered punishments utilized during America's colonial past. As the Court noted, "Punishments such as whipping, pillory, and branding inflicted physical pain and staged a direct confrontation between the offender and the public. Even punishments that lacked the corporal component, such as public shaming, humiliation, and banishment, involved more than the dissemination of information" (pp. 97–98). The majority concluded:

> Our criminal law tradition insists on public indictment, public
> trial, and public imposition of sentence. Transparency is essential to
> maintaining public respect for the criminal justice system, ensuring
> its integrity, and protecting the rights of the accused. The publicity
> may cause adverse consequences for the convicted defendant,
> running from mild personal embarrassment to social ostracism.
> In contrast to the colonial shaming punishments, however, the State
> does not make the publicity and the resulting stigma an integral
> part of the objective of the regulatory scheme. (pp. 98–99)

In addition to evaluating the ASORA's sanctions against the punishments inflicted on offenders in the past, the Justices also noted the role of the Internet in determining the degree of harm associated with the statute's requirements. The Court articulated a perspective, explaining that "notice of a criminal conviction subjects the offender to public shame, the humiliation increasing in proportion to the extent of the publicity. And the geographic reach of the Internet is greater than anything which could have been designed in colonial times" (p. 99). Further, the Court reasoned that when citizens "take the initial step of going to the Department of Public Safety's Web site, proceed to the offender registry, and then look up the desired information," this effort is "more analogous to a visit to an official archive of criminal records than it is to a scheme forcing an offender to appear in public with some visible badge of past criminality" (p. 99). As such, the Justices concluded that "the stigma of Alaska's Megan's Law" (p. 98) and its registration and notification sanctions stem "from the fact of conviction [which] is already a matter of public record" (p. 101) and the Internet simply makes information-finding "more efficient, cost effective, and convenient" (p. 99).

Finally, at the core of the *Smith* decision was the Court's explicit desire to protect society. The language utilized to render the opinion revealed the Justices' familiarity with the extant literature on sex offenders and recidivism. Citing findings used to support previous decisions, the Court observed that the likelihood of those "adjudged to be dangerous" (p. 93) committing future acts of sexual violence is "frightening and high" and that they are "much more likely than any other type of offender to be rearrested for a new rape or sexual assault" (p. 103). Indeed, the majority asserted that Alaska's Megan's Law was enacted to "inform the public for its own safety" (p. 99). Consequently, citizens "can take the precautions they deem necessary before dealing with the registration" (p. 101).

Based on these perceptions and assertions, the Court upheld the lower court's ruling that the ASORA's registration and notification provisions did not violate the *Ex Post Facto* Clause. The Court reasoned that although these sanctions may create a stigma or hinder an offender's efforts to secure a job or place to live, information regarding registrants is readily available to the public, and any "attendant humiliation is but a collateral consequence of a valid regulation" (p. 99). Hence, the *Smith* Court concluded that the "*Ex Post Facto* Clause does not preclude a State from making reasonable categorical judgments that conviction of specified crimes should entail particular regulatory consequences" (p. 103).

Two members of the Court, Justices Thomas and Souter, concurred separately with the *Smith* opinion. Justice Thomas noted that to properly evaluate the nature of a law, "the analysis of the obligations actually created by the statute" must be determined (p. 106). In his concurring opinion, Justice Souter raised a concern regarding "[e]nsuring public safety [which is] a fundamental regulatory goal" without imposing "burdens that outpace the law's stated civil aims" (pp. 108–109). He concluded by remarking that because ASORA requires registration and notification based on previous convictions, it has "probably [swept] in a significant number of people who pose no real threat to the community" and "serves to feed suspicion that something more than regulation of safety is going on" (pp. 108–109).

A review of the plain meaning data collected from the *Connecticut Dept. of Public Safety v. Doe* case revealed the Court's view on the danger posed by convicted sex offenders. Citing a previous ruling, the Justices contended that "[s]ex offenders are a serious threat to this Nation" (p. 4). Adopting a judicial attitude similar to that expressed by the *Smith* Court, the majority poignantly articulated their concern regarding sex offender recidivism rates. Indeed, as noted in an earlier opinion, the Justices stated, "[W]hen sex offenders reenter society, they are much more likely than any other type of offender to be rearrested for a new rape or sex assault" and the "victims . . . are most often juveniles" (p. 4).

In rendering its judgment, the Court indicated a desire to rest its decision making on the fact that the registration and notification provisions of Connecticut's Megan's Law "turn on an offender's conviction alone" (p. 7). Much like in *Smith*, the Court considered the role of the Internet in disseminating offender information. Doe, the respondent in the case, claimed that because he was no longer deemed a dangerous threat, he should not be subjected to the online registration requirement. However, the Court reasoned that although "the disclaimer on the Website explicitly states that respondent's alleged nondangerousness simply doesn't matter," Doe's claim "that he is not currently dangerous–is of no consequence" (p. 7). Indeed, the Court made clear that "even if respondent (Doe) could prove that he [was] not likely to be currently dangerous Connecticut has decided that the registry information of all sex offenders . . . must be publicly disclosed" (p. 7). As such, the Justices concluded that "because the question is not properly before us, we express no opinion as to whether Connecticut's Megan's Law violates principles of substantive due process" (p. 7).

Justices Scalia and Souter offered separate concurring opinions. In his concurrence, Justice Scalia not only agreed with the Court's logic but offered additional judicial temperament on the legal matter at hand. As he opined, "even if the requirements of Connecticut's sex offender registration law implicate a liberty interest of respondent, the categorical abrogation of that liberty interest by a validly enacted statute suffices to provide all the process that is 'due'" (p. 8). From his perspective, "a convicted sex offender has no more right to additional 'process' enabling him to establish that he is not dangerous than . . . a 15-year-old has a right to 'process' enabling him to establish that he is a safe driver" (p. 9).

Justice Souter, with whom Justice Ginsburg joined, offered a separate concurring opinion noting that "a substantive due process claim may not be the only one still open to a test by those in the respondents' situation" (p. 9). He delineated the number of ways in which the State does not require certain offenders convicted of sex offenses to register. These offenses included "unconsented sexual contact" or "sexual intercourse with a minor aged between 13 and 16 while the offender was more than two years older than the minor" (p. 9).

In addition, Justice Souter indicated that a court may withhold certain offender information from law enforcement to protect a victim's identity, particularly if the injured party is the offender's spouse or relative. Nevertheless, the plain meaning evident in his concurring brief revealed judicial temperament to clarify the fact that "the Court's rejection of respondents' procedural due process claim does not immunize publication schemes like Connecticut's from an equal protection challenge" (p. 10).

In the landmark decision, *Kansas v. Hendricks,* the Court articulated one of the most widely cited opinions on civil commitment and sexually violent predators. Data collected from the opinion offered insight into the Court's underlying jurisprudential intent. The rhetoric employed in the decision conveyed the perception that although the right to be free from physical restraint is fundamental, the necessity of civil commitment as a means for confining sexually violent predators who cannot control their behavior because of a "mental abnormality" (p. 356) can supersede protected liberty interests. Indeed, the majority agreed that the "Court has recognized that an individual's constitutionally protected interest in avoiding physical restraint may be overridden even in the civil context" (pp. 356–357). Moreover, the Court opined that "involuntary civil confinement of a limited subclass of dangerous persons" is well within the bounds of "ordered liberty" (p. 357). Thus, the language relied on in the *Hendricks* decision expressed the view that because it is "difficult, if not impossible, for [sexually violent predators] to control [their] dangerous behavior" (p. 358), "incapacitation may be a legitimate end of the civil law" (p. 366) that seeks to protect society from certain troubled offender groups.

The *Hendricks* ruling clearly voiced the Court's attitude toward the pre-commitment requirements that were central to the legal challenges raised in the case. The Court noted that risk of future dangerousness alone "is ordinarily not a sufficient ground" (p. 358) for civil commitment. The majority opined, "We have sustained civil commitment statutes when they have coupled proof of dangerousness with the proof of some additional factor, such as a 'mental illness' or 'mental abnormality.' These added statutory requirements serve to limit involuntary civil confinement to those who suffer from a volitional impairment rendering them dangerous beyond their control" (p. 358). However, the majority expressed a desire to defer to Kansas lawmakers on this matter. The Court acknowledged that "we have traditionally left to legislators the task of defining terms of a medical nature that have legal significance" (p. 420). The Court articulated the position that Kansas' SVPA is consistent with similar statutes and asserted that based on the pre-commitment requirements delineated by the Act, "Hendricks' condition . . . satisfies those criteria" (p. 360).

The rationale supporting the *Hendricks* decision included a detailed assessment of the conditions under which sexually violent predators are held in civil confinement. In determining that Kansas' SVPA constituted a "legitimate nonpunitive governmental objective" (p. 363), the Justices considered the intended purpose and milieu of correctional institutions and of civil commitment facilities. As the Court explained:

> The State has represented that an individual confined under the Act is not subject to the more restrictive conditions placed on state prisoners, but instead experiences essentially the same conditions as any involuntarily committed patient in the state mental institution. App. 50–56, 59–60. Because none of the parties argues that people institutionalized under the Kansas general civil commitment statute are subject to punitive conditions, even though they may be involuntarily confined, it is difficult to conclude that persons confined under this Act are being 'punished.' (p. 363)

Further, the majority reasoned that the "[civil] confinement's duration is instead linked to the stated purposes of the commitment, namely, to hold the person until his mental abnormality no longer causes him to be a threat to others" (p. 363). Thus, in distinguishing and weighing the differences between these two means of incapacitation, the Court made clear that Kansas' SVPA was not designed to exact punishment.

The Court expressed some obligation to consider whether Hendricks had received appropriate treatment consistent with the stated aim of the SVPA. The opinion delineated an important duty of care for civilly committed sexually violent predators. As the Court noted, "[C]ritical language in the Act itself demonstrates that the Secretary of Social and Rehabilitation Services, under whose custody sexually violent predators are committed, has an obligation to provide treatment to individuals like Hendricks" (p. 367). Despite this requirement, the majority ultimately concluded that "[a]lthough the treatment program initially offered [to] Hendricks may have seemed somewhat meager, it must be remembered that he was the first person committed under the Act. That the State did not have all of its treatment procedures in place is thus not surprising" (pp. 367–368). This admission notwithstanding, the Court clearly posited a felt obligation to ensure that those responsible for the care of SVPs confined to civil commitment facilities uphold their duty to provide treatment.

Although mindful of the expressed need for Hendricks to receive treatment that was consistent with the distinct therapeutic purpose of civil commitment, the plain meaning discernable in the case communicated the Court's deeper concern to "protect the public from harm" (p. 361). Indeed, the language employed made explicit the Justices' collective unease regarding sexually violent predators and the threat that such offenders pose to the public. As the Court reasoned:

> Hendricks even conceded that, when he becomes "stressed out," he cannot "control the urge" to molest children. This admitted lack of volitional control, coupled with a prediction of future dangerousness, adequately distinguishes Hendricks from other

dangerous persons who are perhaps more properly dealt with
exclusively through criminal proceedings. (p. 360)

Thus, the majority asserted that when "States have in certain narrow
circumstances provided for the forcible civil detainment of people who are
unable to control their behavior and who thereby pose a danger to the public
health and safety . . . [w]e have consistently upheld such involuntary commitment statutes" (p. 357). Further, the Court stipulated, "If detention for the
purpose of protecting the community from harm necessarily constituted
punishment, then all involuntary civil commitments would have to be
considered punishment. But we have never so held" (p. 363).

Justice Kennedy offered a concurring opinion in *Hendricks*. He filed the
statement to "caution against dangers inherent when a civil confinement law
is used in conjunction with the criminal process, whether or not the law is
given retroactive application" (p. 372). Justice Kennedy expressed the view
that "while incapacitation is a goal common to both the criminal and civil
systems of confinement, retribution and general deterrence are reserved for
the criminal system alone" (p. 373). Aside from noting this concern, he
nevertheless agreed with the prevailing opinion. The rhetoric employed by
Justice Kennedy suggested that he, too, shared in the majority's desire to
ensure that legitimate means existed to confine sexually violent predators who
threaten the public's safety. As he noted, "With his (Hendricks) criminal
record, after all, a life term may well have been the only sentence appropriate
to protect society and vindicate the wrong" (p. 373).

Justice Breyer, joined by Justices Scalia and Souter and Justice Ginsburg
in Parts II and III, filed a dissenting opinion. He indicated that the Court
historically relies on the lower courts to determine whether a statute created
by state legislators is consistent with a non-punitive regulatory scheme. Along
these lines, Justice Breyer explained, "We have generally given considerable
weight to the findings of state and lower federal courts regarding the intent or
purpose underlying state officials' actions" (p. 383).

This observation notwithstanding, when the plain meaning is made more
explicit in this dissenting opinion, it offers insight into an alternative perspective on the provocative issues raised in *Hendricks*. Specifically, Justice Breyer
agreed that "because many mental health professionals consider pedophilia a
serious mental disorder" and "[Hendricks] is so afflicted . . . that he cannot
'control the urge' to most children," he has been appropriately designated as
"mentally ill" and "dangerous" (pp. 376–377). Thus, Justice Breyer asserted
that the "law traditionally has considered this kind of abnormality [pedophilia]
akin to insanity for purposes of confinement" (p. 375).

Although the Court was not persuaded by the argument that Hendricks
had not received timely or adequate treatment, Justice Breyer regarded this
contention as critical when evaluating the intent underlying Kansas' SVPA.
Citing case testimony, he stated that "Dr. Befort's last words made clear that
Hendricks has 'wasted ten months . . . in terms of treatment effects' and that,

as far as treatment goes, 'today, it's still not available'" (p. 392). Consequently, Justice Breyer maintained, "When a State decides offenders can be treated and confines an offender to provide that treatment, but then refuses to provide it, the refusal to treat while a person is fully incapacitated begins to look punitive" (p. 390).

Thus, at the core of this dissenting opinion was the matter of protected liberty interests. Justice Breyer articulated the perspective that "where so significant a restriction of an individual's basic freedoms is at issue, a State cannot cut corners. Rather, the legislature must hew to the Constitution's liberty-protecting line" (p. 396). In making his position clear, Justice Breyer concluded, "Legislation that seeks to help the individual offender as well as to protect the public would avoid significantly greater restriction" (p. 388) and would "prevent judgmental mistakes that would wrongly deprive a person of important liberty" (p. 381).

Consistent with previous cases involving various control and confinement measures designed for SVPs and sex offenders, an assessment of the plain meaning of the legal rhetoric employed in *Crane* revealed its underlying jurisprudential intent. Relying on its evaluation of Kansas' SVPA in *Hendricks*, the *Crane* Court primarily focused on the issue of volitional impairment. As delineated in *Hendricks*, a diagnosis of a mental abnormality that hinders an offender's ability to control his behavior is essential when making civil commitment determinations. Crane was diagnosed with a personality disorder, but was not conclusively found to lack volitional control.

Despite the distinction in his diagnosis, the *Crane* Court articulated the perspective that reaching a judgment of absolute volitional impairment was not required. Reflecting on the reasoning it adopted in *Hendricks*, the *Crane* Court explained:

> We did not give to the phrase "lack of control" a particularly narrow or technical meaning. And we recognize that in cases where lack of control is at issue, 'inability to control behavior' will not be demonstrable with mathematical precision. It is enough to say that there must be proof of serious difficulty in controlling behavior. And this, when viewed in light of such features of the case as the nature of the psychiatric diagnosis, and the severity of the mental abnormality itself, must be sufficient to distinguish the dangerous sexual offender whose serious mental illness, abnormality, or disorder subjects him to civil commitment from the dangerous but typical recidivist convicted in an ordinary criminal case.
> (p. 413)

The Justices elucidated the fact that, in the past, they had not "ordinarily distinguished for constitutional purposes among volitional, emotional, and cognitive impairments" (p. 415). However, the Court perceived its rightful role as one in which it "provide[s] constitutional guidance in this area by . . . elaborating generally stated constitutional standards and objectives" (pp. 413–414).

Indeed, the language appropriated in the opinion revealed the Court's underlying intent to defer to the states when determining what constitutes a psychiatric condition. The Justices acknowledged that "the Constitution's safeguards of human liberty in the area of mental illness and the law are not always best enforced through precise bright-line rules" because states "retain considerable leeway in defining the mental abnormalities and personality disorders that make an individual eligible for commitment" (pp. 413–414).

The plain meaning elicited from the *Crane* opinion further disclosed the perception that the "science of psychiatry" (p. 413) does not provide the Court with a comprehensible understanding of volition, and furthermore, it does not supplant the Court's judicial decision-making. The Court opined that "as in other areas of psychiatry, there may be 'considerable overlap between a . . . defective understanding or appreciation and . . . [an] ability to control . . . behavior'" (p. 415). Nevertheless, the Justices made clear that psychiatry, which "informs, but does not control ultimate legal determinations, is an ever-advancing science, whose distinctions do not seek precisely to mirror those of the law" (p. 413).

Given these collective views and assertions, the Court ruled that the Kansas Supreme Court interpreted *Hendricks* too rigidly in its application to Crane's case. The majority concluded, "Insistence upon [a finding of] absolute lack of control would risk barring the civil commitment of highly dangerous persons suffering severe mental abnormalities" (p. 412). Thus, the Court vacated the Kansas Supreme Court's ruling and concluded that Kansas' SVPA was inconsistent with substantive due process.

Justice Scalia, joined by Justice Thomas, proffered the dissenting opinion. Scalia argued that the Kansas Supreme Court's ruling should have been reversed rather than vacated. Poignantly expressing his perspective regarding the Court's decision, Justice Scalia stated, "[S]natching back from the State of Kansas a victory so recently awarded-cheapens the currency of our judgments" (p. 416). The plain meaning elicited from Justice Scalia's dissenting opinion principally conveyed a profound disagreement with what he saw as the Court's failure to adequately grapple with and resolve the issue of volition. As Justice Scalia explained:

> I suspect that the reason the Court avoids any elaboration
> [on volition] is that elaboration which passes the laugh test is
> impossible. How is one to frame for a jury the degree of 'inability to
> control' which, in the particular case, 'the nature of the psychiatric
> diagnosis, and the severity of the mental abnormality' require? Will
> it be a percentage ('Ladies and gentlemen of the jury, you may
> commit Mr. Crane under the SVPA only if you find, beyond a
> reasonable doubt, that he is 42% unable to control his penchant
> for sexual violence')? Or a frequency ratio ('Ladies and gentlemen
> of the jury, you may commit Mr. Crane under the SVPA only if
> you find, beyond a reasonable doubt, that he is unable to control
> his penchant for sexual violence 3 times out of 10')? Or merely

> an adverb ('Ladies and gentlemen of the jury, you may commit
> Mr. Crane under the SVPA only if you find, beyond a reasonable
> doubt, that he is appreciably – or moderately, or substantially,
> or almost totally – unable to control his penchant for sexual
> violence')? None of these seems to me satisfactory. (pp. 423–424)

Mindful of the implications of the *Crane* decision, Justice Scalia indicated that "the Court has an obligation to [elaborate on] the 'specific circumstances' of the present case, so that the trial court will know what is expected of it on remand" (p. 424).

The plain meaning evident in the dissenting opinion further conveyed Justice Scalia's judicial temperament and rationale. Consistent with the concern raised in *Smith, Connecticut, Hendricks,* and the *Crane* majority, he made clear that regardless of the degree to which a SVP can control his or her behavior, such offenders remain a serious threat to the public. To illustrate, Justice Scalia noted, "It is obvious that a person may be able to exercise volition and yet be unfit to turn loose upon society. The man who has a will of steel, but who delusionally believes that every woman he meets is inviting crude sexual advances, is surely a dangerous sexual predator" (p. 422). Thus, the rhetoric employed in the dissenting opinion exposed a prevailing desire to ultimately protect the public from sexually violent predators like Crane.

In *Seling v. Young,* the Court communicated its perspective regarding the civil commitment of an offender also deemed a SVP. Although *Young* involved an "as-applied" challenge on double jeopardy and *ex post facto* claims, the Court noted that the Washington statute at issue in the case was "strikingly similar" (p. 261) to the Kansas SVPA in question in the *Hendricks* case.[33] Further, Hendricks' initial challenge squarely centered on the conditions of confinement at the treatment facility in which he resided. Young presented a similar argument before the Court. In reviewing the decision-making employed in the *Hendricks* case, the Court reasoned:

> The [Kansas] Act called for confinement in a secure facility
> because the persons confined were dangerous to the community.
> We noted, however, that conditions within the unit were essentially
> the same as conditions for other involuntarily committed persons
> in mental hospitals. Moreover, confinement under the Act was
> not necessarily indefinite in duration. Finally, we observed that in
> addition to protecting the public, the Act also provided treatment
> for sexually violent predators. (p. 262)

Thus, consistent with their decision in *Crane,* the Justices expressed the clear intention to rely on their earlier landmark ruling to assess the arguments under consideration in *Young.*

Accordingly, the *Young* Court noted, "Since deciding *Hendricks,* [it] reaffirmed the principle that determining the civil or punitive nature of an Act must begin with reference to its text and legislative history" (p. 262). Indeed, the *Hendricks* decision conveyed the Court's intention to defer to the capability of the legislature that creates SVP statutes, as well as to defer to the wisdom of lower courts that decide matters involving such laws. Articulating a sense of confidence in other judicial decision-making bodies, the *Young* Court asserted, "State courts, in addition to federal courts, remain competent to adjudicate and remedy challenges to civil confinement schemes" (p. 265). Recognizing that the civilly confined "have the right to adequate care and individualized treatment," (p. 265), the Justices maintained that it was up to the Washington courts to "provide a remedy" if they determined that the treatment facility failed to operate "in accordance with the law" (p. 265).

Similar to the previous cases reviewed in this data set, the *Young* opinion considered the interests of those designated SVPs as well as the public. Once again, specifically relying on the rhetoric employed in *Hendricks*, the Justices further affirmed their position that confinement measures such as civil commitment are essential when containing those citizens deemed "dangerous to the community" (p. 261). As the Court opined, "[In *Hendricks*] we explained that there was no federal constitutional bar to their civil confinement, because the State had an interest in protecting the public from dangerous individuals with treatable as well as untreatable conditions" (p. 262). Consistent with the Court's previous decisions on matters regarding sex offender registration and notification as well as civil commitment, the majority weighed the interests of society against and above the rights of offenders designated as SVPs.

Justice Scalia, joined by Justice Souter, filed a concurring opinion. He wrote separately to address a specific statement included in the opinion. Scalia noted that the Court expressed the view that it never had an "occasion to consider the . . . conditions of confinement and implementation of [a] statute to determine [if it was] civil in nature" (p. 267). Citing a previous decision, Justice Scalia asserted that, indeed, the Court previously had the opportunity to judge a "first instance" case (p. 267). This point notwithstanding, in agreeing with the Court's explicit intent to defer to the state courts, Scalia reasoned:

> When, as here, a state statute is at issue, the remedy for
> implementation that does not comport with the civil nature of the
> statute is resort to the traditional state proceedings that challenge
> unlawful executive action . . . . Only this approach, it seems to me,
> is in accord with our sound and traditional reluctance to be the
> initial interpreter of state law. (pp. 269–270)

Thus, Justice Scalia articulated the importance of affirming the role and purpose of other judicial decision-making bodies.

Justice Thomas offered a separate concurring opinion. He made clear his perspective on the *Young* decision when noting:

> I write separately to express my view, first, that a statute which
> is civil on its face cannot be divested of its civil nature simply
> because of the manner in which it is implemented, and second,

that the distinction between a challenge in the "first instance" and a subsequent challenge is one without a difference. (pp. 270–271)

As such, Justice Thomas concluded that a "suit based on [improper implementation] conditions cannot prevail" (pp. 273–274).

In filing the sole dissenting opinion, Justice Stevens communicated his perspective on the specific confinement conditions issue raised in *Young*. The core of his argument is contained in the following passage:

> In essence, the majority argues that because the constitutional query must be answered definitively and because confinement is not a "fixed event," conditions of confinement should not be considered at all, except in the first challenge to a statute, when, as a practical matter, the evidence of such conditions is most likely not to constitute the requisite "clearest proof." This seems to me quite wrong. (pp. 276–277)

Indeed, Justice Stevens expressed a genuine concern that, if proven, would show that the conditions under which Young was civilly confined were similar to those found in Washington's correctional institutions more generally. In other words, the mental health care provided for civilly confined offenders was indistinguishable from the treatment (or lack thereof) that convicts received. Still further, he alleged that if Young's claims were well-founded, then "they (those civilly confined) receive significantly worse treatment" (p. 277). As such, Justice Stevens disagreed with the majority. He concluded that, as the Court of Appeal's ruled, Young should have been granted the opportunity to "come forward with the 'clearest proof' that his allegations [were] true" (p. 277).

Level 2 Analysis

The second level of qualitative analysis reconsidered each instance of jurisprudential intent as derived from plain meaning and subjected it to an additional level of textual scrutiny.[34] The aim of this endeavor was to interpret what this legal language (i.e., manifest content) communicated ethically (i.e., deeper meaning embedded in the words/phrases themselves). Put another way, the goal of this particular inquiry was to determine what moral philosophy was conveyed through judicial temperament, mindful of the three normative approaches under consideration, including their respective variants and corresponding principles. Table 4.2 identifies the specific phrases under review for each legal case that forms the data set.

The manifest content discernable in the *Smith* opinion revealed the Court's reliance on consequentialism and its variant utilitarianism. At the core of utilitarianism is the notion of basing moral decision making on that which promotes the most interests for the greatest number of individuals (Bank, 2008; Cahn, 2009; Mill, 1957). By employing reasoning consistent with

Table 4.2 Underlying Ethical Reasoning Conveying Jurisprudential Intent

	Consequentialism (Utilitarianism)	Formalism (Kantian Ethics)	Virtue Ethics
Smith v. Doe	"notice of a criminal conviction subjects the offender to public shame, the humiliation increasing in proportion to the extent of the publicity" "Although the public availability of the information may have a lasting and painful impact on the convicted sex offender, these consequences flow not from the Act's registration and dissemination provisions, but from the fact of conviction" "To hold that the mere presence of a deterrent purpose renders such sanctions 'criminal' . . . would severely undermine the Government's ability to engage in effective regulation" "Widespread public access is necessary for the efficacy of the scheme, and the attendant humiliation is but a collateral consequence of a valid regulation"	"the legislature has power . . . to make a rule of universal application" "These precedents instruct us" "conviction of specified crimes should entail particular regulatory consequences" "The obligations the statute imposes are the responsibility of registration, a duty not predicated upon some present or repeated violation" "our criminal law tradition insists on . . ." "Transparency is essential to maintaining public respect for the criminal justice system, ensuring its integrity, and protecting the rights of the accused"	
Smith v. Doe Concur by Souter	"While the Court accepts the State's explanation that the Act simply makes public information available in a new way, the scheme does much more . . . [s]election makes a statement, one that affects common reputation and sometimes carries harsher consequences" "Ensuring public safety is, of course, a fundamental regulatory goal . . . and this objective should be given serious weight in the analyses. But, at the same time, it would be naive to look no further, given pervasive attitudes toward sex offenders"		

(Continued)

Table 4.2 Continued

	Consequentialism (Utilitarianism)	Formalism (Kantian Ethics)	Virtue Ethics
CT Dept. of Public Safety v. Doe	"While the Court accepts the State's explanation that the Act simply makes public information available in a new way, the scheme does much more . . . [s]election makes a statement, one that affects common reputation and sometimes carries harsher consequences" "Ensuring public safety is, of course, a fundamental regulatory goal . . . and this objective should be given serious weight in the analyses. But, at the same time, it would be naive to look no further, given pervasive attitudes toward sex offenders"		
CT Dept. of Public Safety v. Doe Concur by Scalia		" . . . a convicted sex offender has no more right to additional "process . . ." "	

Kansas v. Hendricks

"The Court has recognized that an individual's constitutionally protected interest in avoiding physical restraint may be overridden even in the civil context" "We have sustained civil commitment statutes when they have coupled proof of dangerousness with the proof of some additional factor, such as a 'mental illness' or 'mental abnormality'. These added statutory requirements serve to limit involuntary civil confinement to those who suffer from a volitional impairment rendering them dangerous beyond their control" "The State has represented that an individual confined under the Act is not subject to the more restrictive conditions placed on state prisoners, but instead experiences essentially the same conditions as any involuntarily committed patient in the state mental institution. [E]ven though they may be involuntarily confined, it is difficult to conclude that persons confined under this Act are being 'punished' 'States have in certain narrow circumstances provided for the forcible civil detainment of people who are unable to control their behavior and who thereby pose a danger to the public health and safety . . . [w]e have consistently upheld such involuntary commitment statutes"

"The State may take measures to restrict the freedom of the dangerously mentally ill. This is a legitimate nonpunitive governmental objective and has been historically so regarded" "It thus cannot be said that the involuntary civil confinement of a limited subclass of dangerous persons is contrary to our understanding of ordered liberty" "We have already observed that, under the appropriate circumstances and when accompanied by proper procedures, incapacitation may be a legitimate end of the civil law" " . . . we have traditionally left to legislators the task of defining terms of a medical nature that have legal significance" "the Secretary of Social and Rehabilitation Services . . . has an obligation to provide treatment to individuals like Hendricks"

(Continued)

Table 4.2 Continued

	Consequentialism (Utilitarianism)	Formalism (Kantian Ethics)	Virtue Ethics
Kansas v. Hendricks Concur by Kennedy	"The point, however, is not how long Hendricks and others like him should serve a criminal sentence. With his criminal record, after all, a life term may well have been the only sentence appropriate to protect society and vindicate the wrong"	"We should bear in mind that while incapacitation is a goal common to both the criminal and civil systems of confinement, retribution and general deterrence are reserved for the criminal system alone"	
Kansas v. Hendricks Concur by Breyer with whom Stevens & Souter join & Ginsburg in Parts II & III		"We have generally given considerable weight to the findings of state and lower federal courts regarding the intent or purpose underlying state officials' actions" "where so significant a restriction of an individual's basic freedoms is at issue, a State cannot cut corners. Rather, the legislature must hew to the Constitution's liberty-protecting line" "The law traditionally has considered this kind of abnormality akin to insanity for purposes of confinement" "... wrongly deprive a person of important liberty ..."	
Kansas v. Crane	"Legislation that seeks to help the individual offender as well as to protect the public would avoid significantly greater restriction." "... would risk barring the civil commitment of highly dangerous persons suffering severe mental abnormalities"	"... provide constitutional guidance..." "... safeguards of human liberty ..." "States retain considerable leeway in defining the mental abnormalities and personality disorders that make an individual eligible for commitment"	

Kansas v. Crane *Dissent by Scalia joined by Thomas*	"It is obvious that a person may be able to exercise volition and yet be unfit to turn loose upon society."	"... the Court has an obligation to do so ..."
Seling v. Young	"... in addition to protecting the public, the Act also provided treatment for sexually violent predators." "the State had an interest in protecting the public from dangerous individuals with treatable as well as untreatable conditions."	"those confined under its [the Act's] authority have the right to adequate care and individualized treatment" "It is for the Washington courts to determine ..." "Since deciding Hendricks, this Court has reaffirmed the principle that determining the civil or punitive nature of an Act must begin with reference to its text and legislative history" "State courts, in addition to federal courts, remain competent to adjudicate and remedy challenges to civil confinement schemes"
Seling v. Young *Concur by Scalia joined by Souter*		"Only this approach ... is in accord with our sound and traditional reluctance to be the initial interpreter of state law"

this principle, the *Smith* majority agreed that Alaska's version of Megan's Law exacted sanctions (i.e., registration and public notification) that were necessary to advance the most good for the State's citizenry. To illustrate, the Court opined, "Although the public availability of the information may have a lasting and painful impact on the convicted sex offender, these consequences flow not from the Act's registration and dissemination provisions, but from the fact of conviction" (p. 101). The majority perceived the shame and humiliation stemming from sex offender registration and notification provisions as being "a collateral consequence of a valid regulation" (p. 99). Thus, the Court concluded by finding that the "mere presence of a deterrent purpose" was not a sufficient reason to "undermine the Government's ability to engage in effective regulation" (p. 102). The Court's decision to ultimately disregard the factor of psychological harm suffered by offenders in favor of pursuing alternative objectives intended to protect society made evident the notion that utilitarian objectives informed *Smith's* underlying jurisprudential intent.

The manifest content determined in the *Smith* Court's language was consistent with a second normative theory—namely, formalism and its Kantian variant. As delineated in Chapter 2, ethical formalism asserts that one's moral decision making should firmly be based on resolute obligation. Moreover, Kantian philosophy dictates that these duties, as universal, demand absolute adherence. For example, the opinion intimated that "[t]he obligations the statute imposes are the responsibility of registration, a duty not predicated upon some present or repeated violation" (p. 105). Further, the Court's invocation of numerous phrases such as, "the legislature has power;" "rule of universal application;" "precedents instruct us;" "should entail particular consequences;" "criminal law tradition insists on;" and "maintaining public respect for the criminal justice system, ensuring its integrity, and protecting the rights of the accused," all reveal a felt responsibility to uphold both legal and moral obligations. As such, the *Smith* opinion's rhetoric also disclosed an unstated and underlying reliance on Kantian ethics.

In the concurring opinion offered by Justice Souter, the manifest content discernable in the language employed aligned most fully with utilitarian principles. Consistent with this moral philosophical approach, Justice Souter engaged in a weighing of interests between those of the public against those of convicted sex offenders. Noting that "[w]hile the Court accepts the State's explanation that the Act simply makes public information available in a new way," the "common reputation" of those required to comply with this sanction may be harmed (p. 109). Indeed, registration and notification provisions "sometimes [carry] harsher consequences" (p. 109). Demonstrating a clear preference to advance the greatest good, Justice Souter stated that "[e]nsuring public safety is, of course, a fundamental regulatory goal . . . and this objective should be given serious weight in the analyses. But, at the same time, it would be naïve to look no further, given pervasive attitudes toward sex offenders'" (pp. 108–109).

The manifest content discernable in the *Connecticut* decision was also reviewed to determine the ethical import informing the case's jurisprudential intent.

After subjecting this content to additional textual exegesis, the findings revealed that the Court's intent lined up with the logic of utilitarianism. Communicating the perspective that SVPs and sex offenders pose a significant threat to the safety of the public, the Court expressed a clear desire to seek the greater good and protect the public, particularly those members perceived as most vulnerable ("juveniles"). Indeed, as the majority reasoned, "[W]hen convicted sex offenders reenter society, they are much more likely than any other type of offender to be re-arrested for a new rape or sexual assault" (p. 4). Asserting that convicted sex offenders "had no more right to additional 'due process'" (p. 9), the normative approach discernable in Justice Scalia's concurring opinion was consistent with Kantian ethics.

Similar to the *Smith* and *Connecticut* decisions, the underlying ethical rationale advanced in the *Hendricks* case was utilitarian in its composition. The Court attempted to strike a balance between the Kansas' ability to civilly commit involuntarily those designated as SVPs versus the liberty interests at stake for those subjected to this confinement practice. As the majority noted, "[A]n individual's constitutionally protected interest in avoiding physical restraint may be overridden even in the civil context" (pp. 356–357), and "[w]e have sustained civil commitment statutes when they have coupled proof of dangerousness with the proof of some additional factor, such as a 'mental illness' or 'mental abnormality.' These added statutory requirements serve to limit involuntary civil confinement to those who suffer from a volitional impairment rendering them dangerous beyond their control" (p. 358). The Court further revealed its interest-balancing stance when stating that the conditions under which an SVP is civilly committed are not "more restrictive" than those "placed on state prisoners" (p. 363). Rather, they are more consistent with the conditions experienced by "any involuntarily committed patient in the state mental institution" (p. 363). In seeking to establish the greatest good, the Court further affirmed its previous findings in similar challenges. The opinion, guided by utilitarian principles, indicated that a state may expose its citizens to involuntary civil commitment if they are "unable to control their behavior" and "pose a danger to the public health and safety" (p. 357).

Words and phrases employed in the *Hendricks* decision were also consistent with the logic of formalism—particularly Kantian ethics. Mindful of their "understanding of ordered liberty" (p. 357), the Justices were firm in their assertion that the State reserved the right to "restrict the freedom of the dangerously mentally ill" (p. 363). Indeed, rhetoric utilized by the *Hendricks* Court revealed a clear sense of responsibility to ensure that state legislatures benefit from deference when committing individuals based on a "legitimate nonpunitive governmental objective [that] has been historically so regarded" (p. 363).

The manifest content discernable in the concurring opinion by Justice Kennedy was consistent with both utilitarian philosophy and Kantian ethical formalism. Drawing upon the consequentialist principle of establishing the greatest good as best interest, Justice Kennedy asserted that civilly confining Hendricks forcibly was imperative to "protect society and vindicate the wrong" (p. 373). Moreover, mindful of the Kantian-endorsed duty to defer to the government's right to confine those who pose a threat to society, his concurring opinion intimated that "while incapacitation is a goal common to both the criminal and civil systems of confinement, retribution and general deterrence are reserved for the criminal system alone" (p. 373).

As noted previously, Justice Breyer also offered a concurring opinion. He was joined in this view by Justices Stevens and Souter and in parts II and III by Justice Ginsburg. A textual evaluation of the opinion indicated that his judicial temperament was guided by the formalism of Kantian ethics. Statements and phrases such as "the legislature must hew to the Constitution's liberty-protected line" (p. 396), "[t]he law traditionally has considered," and "wrongly deprive a person of important liberty" all express the Kantian philosophical principle of absolute moral obligations. Indeed, the opinion revealed the Justices' desire to defer categorically to the "state and lower federal courts regarding the intent and purpose underlying state officials' actions" (p. 383). Once again, this intention to honor absolutely governmental authorities (i.e., state and lower federal courts) is consistent with Kantian moral reasoning.

Similar to the rulings tendered in *Smith*, *Connecticut*, and *Hendricks*, the manifest content distinguishable in *Crane* was characterized by an underlying utilitarian ethic. Specifically, the *Crane* Court engaged in an interest-balancing deliberation when reaching its decision. The majority opined that although access to sex offender information might harm an ex-incarcerate, any consequences suffered (e.g., shame) stemmed solely from the "fact of conviction" (p. 101). Thus, in communicating the Court's desire to ensure that sexually violent predators did not pose a threat to the public, the Justices reasoned that failing to uphold such a practice "would severely undermine the Government's ability to engage in effective regulation" (p. 102). This logic is consistent with the utilitarian-derived notion of advancing the most good for the greatest number of citizens.

The *Crane* Court also conveyed a perspective that clearly resonates with Kantian moral philosophy. Mindful of establishing and upholding categorical imperatives (i.e., absolute moral rules), the Justices' rhetoric disclosed an obligation to adhere to certain individual rights. The Court opined that ". . . the Constitution's safeguards of human liberty in the area of mental illness and the law are not always best enforced through precise bright-line rules" (p. 413). The underlying ethical reasoning lodged within this statement is consistent with Kantian formalism. Further, as the Justices noted, "the States retain considerable leeway" in discerning these matters (p. 413). In this instance, the Court's language mirrors an obligation to exhibit the deference that is due to the states, given their right to establish statutes that permit the involuntary civil confinement of sex offenders they deem psychiatrically disordered and incapable of controlling their behavior. After acknowledging their unwavering fidelity to and respect for state power, the Court made clear its role in adjudicating legal matters regarding civil commitment and sex offenders. As the majority observed, "we have sought to provide constitutional guidance in this area by . . . elaborating generally stated constitutional standards and objectives" (pp. 413–414). When filtered through the prism of normative theory, the underlying meaning situated within this collective legal language is consistent with the formalism of Kantian ethics.

Justice Scalia, joined by Justice Thomas, offered a dissenting opinion. The judicial temperament of his dissent was informed by a utilitarian-inspired ethic in which Scalia sought to promote what he deemed was in the best interest of society. His expressed concern was for those offenders considered to be "unfit to turn loose upon society" and "dangerous sexual predator[s]" (p. 422). When subjected to further textual exegesis, the language that informed the dissent also revealed a commitment to Kantian ethical reasoning. Justice Scalia asserted that "the Court has an obligation" to make clear the "specific circumstances" such that the "trial court will know what is expected of it on remand" (p. 424). By invoking this discourse, Justice Scalia communicated a formalistic duty to provide the necessary clarification regarding all the circumstances surrounding the *Crane* case.

Finally, the *Young* case relied on legal rhetoric that, when evaluated ethically, indicated that utilitarian principles grounded the decision's jurisprudential intent. Consistent with the *Smith, Connecticut, Hendricks*, and *Crane* opinions, the Court in *Young* articulated a fundamental concern regarding the public's safety. Indeed, the Justices maintained that "the State had an interest in protecting the public from dangerous individuals with treatable as well as untreatable conditions" (p. 262). The Court also noted, "[I]n addition to protecting the public, the Act also provided treatment for sexually violent predators" (p. 261). In weighing the competing interests of citizen safety/welfare against the rights of sexually violent predators, the majority concluded that civil commitment provided a logical balance.

Further, as disclosed within each case constituting the data set with the exception of the ruling in *Connecticut*, the *Young* Court appropriated the language and logic of ethical formalism. Consistent with Kantian moral maxims, the Justices spoke to the matter of ensuring that involuntarily hospitalized sexually violent predators be treated with decency. As the Court asserted, civilly confined offenders have the "right to adequate care and individualized treatment" (p. 265). However, beyond this right, the Justices refused to deliberate on what they perceived to be within the scope of the Washington courts' decision making. For example, the *Young* Court made apparent that the state courts must "determine whether the Center is operating in accordance with state law and [if not to] provide a remedy" (p. 265). The Justices agreed that "[s]tate courts, in addition to federal courts, remain competent to adjudicate and remedy challenges to civil confinement schemes" (p. 265). Thus, the contention in *Young* that the state and federal courts maintain responsibility for such legal determinations is consistent with the notion of duty as delineated through the philosophy of ethical formalism.

Justice Scalia, joined by Justice Souter, offered a concurring opinion. Consistent with Kantian deontology, the language employed in his judicial statement revealed a strong preference to defer matters regarding statutes to the state courts, including the civil commitment law at issue in *Young*. As noted previously, Justice Scalia explained, "When, as here, a state statute is at issue, the remedy for implementation that does not comport with the civil nature of the statute is resort to the traditional state proceedings that challenge unlawful executive action . . . Only this approach, it seems to me, is in accord with our sound and traditional reluctance to be the initial interpreter of state law" (p. 270).

To complete the second phase of qualitative legal inquiry for the data set, both intra- and inter-textual analysis must occur. These methodological steps emphasize thematic scrutiny. Accordingly, the underlying ethic informing the jurisprudential intent discernable in the five Supreme Court decisions (including their accompanying concurring and dissenting opinions), consisted of consequentialist reasoning (especially utilitarianism principles) and formalist logic (notably Kantian deontology). Intra-textually, consequentialism and its utilitarian variant were most prominently featured in *Connecticut* and *Crane*. The underlying ethical reasoning conveying jurisprudential intent within the *Seling* opinion principally featured Kantian formalism. The decisions in *Smith* and *Hendricks* revealed that the Justices were primarily guided by ethical rationales emanating from both consequentialism (including utilitarianism) and formalism (especially Kantian moral reasoning).

Interestingly, all of the opinions normatively endorsed one very clear and underlying perspective as conveyed through judicial temperament—to consider the welfare of society. In each of the five cases, the presiding Justices engaged in interest-balancing deliberations wherein they weighed the demands of the public against the needs of SVPs and sex offenders subjected to various control and confinement measures. When made manifest through careful textual exegeses, citizen safety was deemed to be of the utmost ethical importance. Thus, underscoring and informing the jurisprudential intent lodged within and located across each Court decision was the utilitarian objective of achieving the greatest good for the greatest number of individuals. This is an inter-textual finding for the data set.

Some thematic commentary also is warranted regarding the concurring and dissenting opinions. Among the concurring opinions, only the jurisprudential intent discernable in Justice Souter's concurrence with the decision in *Smith* communicated a reliance on consequentialism. Further, the concurring opinions offered in *Connecticut* and *Seling* revealed moral principles consistent with formalism. Still further, when the judicial temperament of Justice Scalia's assessment of *Seling* was made ethically explicit, the language employed specifically conveyed a felt obligation to avail due deference to the proper interpreter of state law (i.e., the lower courts). Finally, principles reflecting a consequentialist and formalist perspective were present in the *Hendricks* concurring opinion filed by Justice Kennedy.

The jurisprudential intent in the *Hendricks* dissenting opinion proffered by Justice Breyer was informed by a clear reliance on Kantian deontological ethics. For example, consistent with the categorical imperative, Justice Breyer's rhetoric communicated a resolute concern obligating the Court to uphold an individual's (i.e., a sex offender's) right to liberty. Further, the dissenting opinion filed by Justice Scalia in *Crane* conveyed, through its jurisprudential intent, consequentialist and formalist moral principles. Indeed, in crafting his judicial view, Justice Scalia employed language that placed the protection of the public from dangerous sexual predators above the rights of those within this troubled collective (i.e., utilitarianism). Additionally, the judicial sentiment of his opinion was ethically informed by a Court duty to establish a precedent by which the lower court could properly assess the *Crane* case on remand.

To summarize, then, the thematic textual exegeses undertaken in this Level-2 analysis portion of the discussion section heuristically indicate that the data set on control and confinement measures exacted on SVPs and sex offenders was ethically informed and guided by utilitarian principles and Kantian formalism. This conclusion obtains for both the intra- and inter-textual domains of inquiry. Accordingly, these two moral philosophical perspectives underscored the jurisprudential intent of this law–psychology–crime matter.

Implications: the Dynamics of Madness, Citizenship, and Social Justice

This chapter qualitatively explored the precedent-setting decisions rendered by the United States Supreme Court on containment measures imposed on those deemed sexually violent. These control measures ranged from criminal confinement to civil commitment, from sex offender registration to community notification. The preceding inquiry involved two levels of analyses. Guided by a series of seven queries, the first level of analysis located the plain meaning (i.e., key terms and phrases) that revealed the Court's underlying jurisprudential intent. To determine the moral reasoning communicated by the Justices, the second level of analysis entailed an evaluation of these words and expressions as filtered through prevailing ethical philosophy.

Consistent with the findings delineated in the previous two chapters, the results indicated that the Court's decision making was primarily informed by the utilitarian principle of seeking the greatest good for the greatest number of people. In this instance, the Court weighed the interests of the public against the rights of sex offenders and SVPs. In reviewing the majority opinions, the citizenry's overall safety was consistently thought to be more valuable than the ex-incarcerate's human welfare and re-communalization needs. Further, the Court acknowledged that the sanctions in question—particularly the registration and notification requirements—could create societal reintegration difficulties, including protracted shame and humiliation. Still further, although psychiatric care was acknowledged as the expressed aim of this confinement remedy (and a critical component in rehabilitation), some former convicts objected to their civil commitment, alleging that they received little to no treatment. However, the Court regarded these consequences as minor when compared to the threat adjudicated sex offenders posed to others.

Additionally, the findings stemming from this qualitative endeavor also documented that the Court principally endorsed a decision-making approach sympathetic to the perceived needs of an organized society. Although protecting the public is a fair-minded and commonsense objective, the Justices largely failed to consider the relevant social and behavioral science literature delineating the psychosocial adjustment issues that sex offenders and SVPs problematically confront. When these individuals are denied opportunities for effective rehabilitative treatment and meaningful societal reintegration, the possibility for engaging community members in a healthy and pro-social manner is severely hampered. Consistent with this assessment, the heuristic analysis revealed that the underlying ethical reasoning that informs the precedent-setting case law on the criminal/civil detention, inspection, and surveillance of adjudicated SVPs is inadequate. This insufficiency is linked to the absence of virtue-based normative theory underscoring the Court's jurisprudential intent.

Accordingly, we contend that the total confinement practice operating in this instance wrongly demonizes far too many citizens who are already susceptible to the experiences of distress and vulnerability that follow in the wake of their criminal transgressions. Moreover, the judicial affirmation that sustains involuntary civil commitment and the subsequent forms of scrupulously structured community supervision—as sourced through the ethics-based evaluation of the case law on the matter—is indicative of juridical *madness*. Indeed, as previously identified in the discussion portion of Chapters 2 and 3, this madness is lodged in the moral panic that is fear of crime and fear of potential offenders. To prevent a crisis in governmental legitimacy (Habermas, 1975), institutional responses to such imagined terror necessitate excessive investments in order maintenance that effectively reifies (would-be) crime and criminals. These extreme investments include hypervigilant and panoptic policing exercised through institutional techniques and technologies of discipline, normalization, and control. The grounding of such reactive (and harmful) regulation can be sourced in the underexamined symbolic, linguistic, material, and cultural conditions of control that instantiate captivity for all. This prescient theme is revisited in the concluding portion of the book.

Although a series of potential limitations could be leveled against the research findings of this chapter, these shortcomings are consistent with those identified elsewhere (*see* Chapters 2 and 3 respectively). Concerns for the generalizability of the results, their explanatory and predictive properties, and the relevance of ethical inquiry overall are questions that suggest the need for further investigation. We agreed with this recommendation before and we certainly agree with it now. However, to be clear, our qualitative textual analysis concerning the precedent-setting case law on the matter of SVPs, criminal and civil confinement, and community re-entry produced a compelling and provocative finding. In brief, the manifest content of the U. S. Supreme Court decisions themselves on which judicial intent was derived from plain meaning fundamentally was not based on an ethic of virtue. No observations on Aristotelian habits of character (e.g., gentleness, humility, compassion, courage) operated as guiding moral principles by which judicial temperament was communicated in any case or across the entire data set. Citizenship standards (i.e., dignity, the therapeutic, and critique) and excellence habits (practiced virtues) for victims, offenders, and the communities that bind them together were conspicuously absent. This deficiency forestalls, if not undoes, the cultivation of *transformative habits of character.* It is this very possibility that mobilizes prospects for citizenship and activates the evolution in social justice for a people yet to come (Deleuze & Guattari, 1984, 1987).

We also note that the qualitative findings drew attention to a number of significant concerns regarding legal challenges to the total confinement measures employed as a basis to control and contain sex offenders and SVPs. Simply stated, the Court mostly failed to consider the relevant literature that empirically questioned the soundness of involuntary civil commitment, offender registration, and community notification for those convicted of sexually violent crimes. First, despite ample evidence documenting that these total confinement measures exact harm on offenders, the Court repeatedly expressed a steadfast commitment to protecting the public from individuals thought to be so dangerous that only their removal from society or their monitored control in the community would be acceptable. Second, the Court noted that any psychological trauma or social harm experienced by sex offenders and SVPs as a result of the identified containment measures was of little to no concern, especially given their conviction statuses. Indeed, the Court's majority opinions consistently made clear that although detention, inspection, and surveillance sanctions might cause ex-incarcerates to confront troubling feelings of humiliation or significantly prevent them from securing a permanent residence stemming from communal stigma, these outcomes were of little consequence. Third, the Court relied on prescribed psychiatric treatment standards of care to render its decisions. Admittedly, the U. S. Supreme Court's avowed purpose is to evaluate cases brought before it through the framework of the Constitution. However, under circumstances wherein an SVP did not receive anticipated remedial treatment, the majority refused to consider whether the confinement on which said treatment was predicated was reasonable, given the intended rehabilitative aims of involuntary civil commitment.

As this and the previous two application chapters repeatedly demonstrated, an ethic of total confinement engulfs the lives of troubled, vulnerable, and distressed citizens as sourced through our proposed qualitative and textual examination of prevailing and/or precedent-setting case law. More problematic than this, however, was the suggestion that this ethic fosters harm for the kept and their keepers, for their managers and their watchers. A comprehensive review of the three data sets indicates that dignified, healing, and restorative citizenship for one and all was not advanced. Further, habits of character that could potentially transform victims, offenders, and their communities by way of practiced excellence and human flourishing were not simply deferred, they were altogether denied. We submit that sustaining this quality of captivity is dangerous; it is the very essence of madness currently operating within and throughout the twin dynamics of individual accountability and societal responsibility. It is this circumstance that precludes the pursuit of justice.

What remains to be delineated, however, is whether specific proposals for reform could overcome the limit-setting at the core of total confinement rule-making and its debilitating (and incomplete) logic of judicial ethics. This is a reference to translating the theory of psychological jurisprudence into meaningful social and public policy. Along these lines, Chapter 5 considers how recommendations from commonsense justice, therapeutic jurisprudence, restorative justice, and their intersectionalities foreshadow progressive change among legal actors and in courtroom decision making. These proposed changes, both speculative and provisional in their content, feature reforms relating to developmentally immature juveniles waived to the adult system found competent to stand trial; inmates with pre-existing psychiatric conditions placed in long-term disciplinary isolation; and SVPs subjected to criminal and civil confinement, community notification, and public surveillance. To be sure, articulating these reforms begins the necessary process of rethinking the critique of madness, citizenship, and social justice.

5

Rethinking Total Confinement:
Translating Social Theory Into Justice Policy

Introduction

The three previous application chapters revealed a number of disturbing findings regarding the total confinement practices that impact the lives of juveniles transferred to the adult system, psychiatrically disordered incarcerates placed in long-term disciplinary isolation, and formerly adjudicated sexually violent predators subjected to civil detention, community inspection, and re-entry monitoring. Perhaps most significantly, the results repeatedly confirmed the view that seeking the greatest good for the greatest number of individuals constituted an appropriate moral principle by which to evaluate prevailing and/or precedent-setting case law and render judicial opinions pertaining to the same. We agree. However, as a practical matter, for the courts this meant that the unmet and complex needs of offenders were understood to be less valuable than the demands of a fearfully hypervigilant and dangerously panoptic citizenry. We questioned the ethical viability of this decision making by way of psychological jurisprudence and the virtue philosophy that informs it, especially when noting the compelling empirical evidence that documents the harmful health, mental health, and resocialization effects that follow when total confinement practices are sustained. We argued that the legal endorsement of such practices problematically erodes a quality of humanity in that one is reduced to (i.e., limits to being) and repressed by (i.e., denials of becoming) the crime and injury that one most assuredly commits and/or causes. Thus, abiding by this logic is not consistent with human flourishing. The greatest good is not advanced for one and all (i.e., the greatest number).

As an alternative point of departure, a framework for evaluating total confinement was proposed in Chapter 1 in which individual responsibility and institutional accountability (the twin dynamics) were said to represent a critical source of inquiry. When fitted to the data-based analysis pursued in the application chapters, we found that total confinement furthers a quality of justice that (unreflectively) nurtures harm. The court opinions dramatically substantiate this conclusion. When a troubled adolescent's wayward actions belie collective notions of youthful innocence, then criminal processing and likely culpability as an adult follows. When an irascibly prone prisoner with diagnosable mental health issues threatens correctional and societal order and is perceived as lacking the capacity to conform, then programmed isolation attaches. When a convicted sexually violent predator with unresolved predilections toward perversion is released, then the label of "incurable monster" is affixed and multiple and continuous forms of surveillance ensue.

Our objection here is not about the exercise of responsibility; in fact, it is a construct whose role in growing practiced excellence is integral to that evolving enterprise. But responsibility is shared; it is cohabited by the human agency—social structure mutuality. This cohabitation forges the contract of which Rousseau and Mill wrote (*see* the Introduction). When more completely exercised as a habit of character, responsibility is not filled with burden but with the promise that sharing in the duty that it obliges is an *unconditional* affirmation of humanity, for everyone. Indeed, responsibility as described here is one of our categorical imperatives. Regrettably, however, in each of the judicially sanctioned total confinement instances cited above, individual well-being, collective good, and social change (i.e., humanity's justice) is eclipsed; the ethical grounding of the self/society binary is rendered a shadow of what this mutuality could be.

Admittedly, the three criminal transgressor groups studied throughout this volume are typically designated as the *worst of the worst* because their thoughts, impulses, and/or actions are considered by many to be well outside the realm of acceptable *normal* comportment. Here, too, we agree. Thus, it is unsurprising that they are defined by some as less than or other than fully human. The inevitable byproduct of such labeling is criminalization, pathologization, and demonization. However, this objectification is disconcerting because the harm manufactured extends not only to the kept but to their keepers, managers, and watchers. Stated differently, these stigmatizing outcomes, at best, dubiously protect the safety and well-being of society. Maintaining this uncertainty is nothing short of madness. One way out of the madness is to translate the nascent theory of psychological jurisprudence into relevant justice policy. This translation begins by recalling the comprehensive ethical footing of the examined court cases.

Although utilitarian principles and, to some lesser extent, Kantian deontology informed and underscored judicial temperament in the overall data set, the legal opinions were devoid of Aristotelian virtues such as empathy, courage, and compassion. This deficiency guaranteed a quality of juridical decision making that foreclosed prospects for individual, collective, and societal excellence. As we asserted, it is only by working habits of character that the probability of realizing such citizenship can be furthered and fostered for those who offend, those offended, and the communities to which both are inexorably bound. Indeed, in the midst of splintering madness, the efficacy of these principles is in their transformative potential to authentically restore and effectively reconnect all human beings in meaningful relationships that are essential to leading flourishing lives. Thus, in the interest of reform, one question is begged: What can and should be done to advance this moral imperative of practiced goodness and to overcome the captivity secured by its absence?

Mindful of the considerable ethical problems that plague total confinement sanctions, this chapter delineates several proposals that represent an emergent response. These proposals explore a number of key concerns. Can a collectivist dignity be incorporated into judicial decision making? Can the law be fashioned as a therapeutic instrument of well-being, restoration, and change? Can a quality of social justice be established consisting of life-affirming properties that extend to all parties affected by violence and victimization? To address these matters, the practices of psychological jurisprudence sourced in Aristotelian virtue philosophy are provisionally applied to the three total confinement issues investigated throughout this volume. These practices include commonsense justice, therapeutic jurisprudence, and restorative justice. The intention with this exercise is to demonstrate how the proposed legal reforms possess the capacity to grow dignity, advance healing, and specify critique in ways that begin to reconceive madness, citizenship, and social justice. Moreover, consistent with the transformative thesis developed in this book, several thorny challenges are tentatively reviewed that impede prospects for successfully implementing such policy changes.

The Law–Psychology–Justice Perspective: Three Provisional Applications

Adolescent Transfer

As the findings in Chapter 2 indicated, the current legal theory informing automatic juvenile transfer cases is dominated by the philosophy of consequentialism, and less significantly, deontology. These forms of jurisprudential ethics perceive the function of law as a guarantor of personal safety and property, as well as a securer against the invasion of or harm to the moral rights of others (Farrelly & Solum, 2008, p. 2). However, consequentialist and formalist approaches do not recognize that the "proper end of law is the promotion of human flourishing," (Farrelly & Solum, 2008, p. 2). This philosophy constitutes the foundation of Aristotelian virtue ethics.[1] As such, if judicial decision making is to resemble this brand of moral philosophy, then outcomes must be sought that enable *all* people to excel (Farrelly & Solum, 2008, p. 16). In support of this view, we recall that the prevailing science repeatedly indicates that transferred juveniles who receive adult sanctions undergo grave harm throughout the course of their incarceration and recidivate more violently upon release. Hence, current judicial actions taken against youthful offenders do little (if anything) to encourage them to lead integrity-based lives. Moreover, and consistent with virtue jurisprudence, a judge who acts as a "fully virtuous agent" "is not disposed [or required] to act in accord with social norms that would undermine human flourishing" (Solum, 2008, p. 190). Regrettably, the punitive path endorsed by the courts fails to nurture or grow such potential excellence. Accordingly, an alternative jurisprudence is sorely needed—one that is consistent with a virtue-based philosophy and one that moves past the harm and ineffectiveness perpetuated by consequentialist and formalist thinking.

Ethical inquiry is an undertaking that is prescriptive more so than descriptive (Williams & Arrigo, 2008, p. 5). What this means is that the study of ethics does not merely cease when the moral beliefs, principles, and goals of the subject (e.g., adolescent waiver, developmental maturity, and trial fitness) are evaluated. Instead, it endeavors to establish what ought to be in light of what is (Williams & Arrigo, 2008). Therapeutic jurisprudence, restorative justice, and commonsense justice are three distinct practices that advance the law–psychology–justice agenda, consistently with the aims of psychological jurisprudence and the moral philosophy of virtue-based reasoning. In what follows, their respective key principles are speculatively applied to the problem of juvenile-mandated transfer. The goal here is to outline a direction that court decision making could pursue and adopt for offending youths, their victims, and the communities to which both are intimately connected, to grow human excellence for all.

Winick and Wexler (2006) maintained that if lawyers and judges are to practice therapeutic jurisprudence wherein less harmful outcomes for crime are sought, then they must employ an ethic of care. Care ethics utilizes virtues such as compassion, tolerance, relationships, and benevolence when assessing the contextual and situational factors of conflict (Bernstein & Gilligan, 1990, p. 155; Gilligan, Lyons, & Hanmer, 1990). In this approach, what is promoted is effective resolution rather than the scrutiny of essential legal facts (Williams & Arrigo; 2008, pp. 263–265). Thus, the role of the legal professional entails "sensitive counseling" (Winick & Wexler, 2006, pp. 605–606). This is a jurisprudence in which the client's psychological well-being is valued by the judge-as-counselor (Winick & Wexler, 2003). This judge/counselor is a decision maker whose honed interpersonal skills follow from a revamped approach to clinical legal education.

In the instance of juvenile transfer where the adolescent possesses psycholegal deficits resulting from developmental immaturity, embracing a therapeutic ethic of care could be quite beneficial, especially if the courtroom workgroup was sensitive to the youth's limited trial fitness. However, to retool

how practicing lawyers and judges approach juvenile transgressors, a "recon-
ceptualization" of skills training for these professionals must occur (Winick &
Wexler, 2003, p. 606). In other words, and especially in the case of youthful
offenders, additional consideration would need to be given to the defendant's
cognitive deficits and emotional well-being rather than merely attending to
their legal rights (Winick & Wexler, 2003, p. 607). Thus, education is pivotal
to the application of therapeutic jurisprudence and to the anti-therapeutic
response the criminal justice system engenders toward waived adolescents.
Indeed, re-educating legal professionals (including judges) in the principles
of therapeutic jurisprudence helps make the case that decision brokers can
identify alternatives to harsh punishments (including transfer) for juvenile
offenders, particularly because this punitive response often leads to recidivism in most cases (McGuire, 2000). Consequently, the lawyer and judge
would need to learn the importance of seeking resolutions that attempted to
heal the character flaws of the wayward youth. This strategy would entail a
commitment "to keep the client out of trouble, to reduce conflict, and to
increase the client's life opportunities" (Winick & Wexler, 2006, p. 609), built
on an ethic of care. If successfully undertaken, such an approach could foster
a reduction in recidivism benefiting both potential victims and society more
generally.

Rather than focus on punishing the offender, restorative justice emphasizes repairing the relationship between the victim and transgressor while
seeking to "maintain order and social and moral balance in the community"
(Braswell, Fuller, & Lozoff, 2001, p. 141; *see also* Sullivan & Tifft, 2005; Van
Ness & Heetdirks Strong, 2007). This is because the "nature of crime" is not
perceived "as an offense against the state [or] as deviant behavior that needs
to be suppressed, punished, or treated" through the formal court system
(McCold, 2004 p. 14). Rather, and especially in the instance of youth justice
reform, decision making is best addressed vis-à-vis a "community conference
model" (Dignan & Marsh, 2001, p. 99).

Restorative justice recognizes that when a harm or injury occurs, the
manner by which the criminal justice system responds can potentially cause
the community, the victim, and/or the offender to feel "alienated, more damaged, disrespected, disempowered, less safe and less cooperative with society"
(Braswell et al., 2001, p. 142). In the context of youthful transgressors, this
outcome can and does lead to recidivism (Abrams, Umbreit, & Gordon,
2006). The restorative justice approach seeks to prevent this potential outcome through discussion, dialogue, and negotiation among those involved
in and affected by a crime (Karp, Sweet, Kirshenbaum, & Bazemore, 2004,
p. 199). The ensuing conversation among offender, victim, mediator, and the
broader community strives to construct an effective and pro-social course of
reparative action for the juvenile (Dignan & Marsh, 2001). Additionally, the
objective is to heal the harm done to the victim and to society (Karp et al.,
2004, pp. 199–200). Along these lines, the community might undertake action
to correct the underlying causes of the criminality (e.g., Van Ness & Heetdirks

Strong, 2007). These reparative efforts could be social, economic, or environmental in nature (Tifft & Sullivan, 2005).

Interestingly, a courtroom workgroup, educated in the principles of therapeutic jurisprudence, might perceive the benefits of a restorative justice program and seek it out as a venue better suited to address the needs of youthful offenders, as well as those injured and the community in which such transgressors and victims reside (Braithwaite, 2002). As an integrative expression of psychological jurisprudence, such a course of action would specify where and how community justice might be embodied for all parties in dispute (McCold, 2004). In this proposed conceptual synthesis, "improving the quality of community life and the capacity of local communities to prevent [adolescent] crime and to effectively respond to criminal incidents when they occur" would be strategically promoted (Karp & Clear, 2002, p. xiii). As a tangible expression of virtue ethics, the integration of therapeutic jurisprudence and restorative justice would acknowledge that juvenile transgression is caused by "young people growing up in . . . dysfunctional areas with high neighborhood disorder, poor public services, high fear of crime, and poor quality of life . . . ." (McCold, 2004, p. 16). Moreover, as a practical basis to advance policy and to honor and affirm the dignity and needs of offenders, victims, and the neighborhoods in which both live, an ethic of care would underscore the jurisprudential decision-making analysis.

Finkel's (1995) approach to commonsense justice is not limited to promoting a more informed opinion of practical judgment from the jury box alone; rather, re-engaging the conscience of the community in justice matters also is pursued. An important aspect of restorative justice is to bring the neighborhood back into the conflict resolution process (Sullivan & Tifft, 2005). Thus, restorative justice is a practice that engages the public so that citizens can take a more active role in a process that seeks a remedial response to juvenile offending while also being cognizant of those concerns emanating from the community at large. Indeed, the mediation process is the setting in which all citizens in disagreement (e.g., victim, offender, family members, and civic leaders) work to establish a fair and just resolution guided by the logic of determining the best solutions with minimal harm. Here, too, commonsense justice is consistent with virtue ethics in that ordinary people are encouraged to articulate their felt regard for such notions as fairness, equity, and honor— in short, *morality*. (Finkel, Harre, & Rodriguez-Lopez, 2001).

In this respect, then, a very important dimension of restoring justice is to engage the adolescent offender and the victim in a form of "empathetic association" (Corriero, 2006, pp. 87–88). Although forms of restorative justice mediation assume several approaches (e.g., victim–offender reconciliation programs, family group conferencing, victim–offender panels) (Sullivan & Tifft, 2005; Van Ness & Heetderks Strong, 2007), they all place the transgressor and the injured party (as well as other concerned citizens) in a setting where varying points of view are voiced regarding pain and harm, remorse and repentance, healing and forgiveness (e.g., Abrams et al., 2006; Arrigo &

Schehr, 1998; McGarrell & Hipple, 2007). Following the logic of psychological jurisprudence in which the moral philosophy of virtue ethics underscores the judicial analysis, legal tribunals would do well to assess whether and to what extent reliance on such restorative programming, as a dimension of their courtroom decision making, would yield reparative outcomes beneficial to all parties in dispute.

When judicial decision making on the issue of youthful offending is guided by an ethic of care and sensitive counseling (therapeutic jurisprudence), relationship building in which injury is owned and healing promoted (restorative justice), and community conscience in which everyday citizens discuss fairness and morality (commonsense justice), then the resolutions sought entail integrity-based dialogical exchange. Most specifically, these are exchanges in which the wayward youth and the aggrieved party convene in a non-adversarial setting whereby a mediator facilitates the conversation so that "resolving" the pain caused by the conflict can commence (Arrigo & Schehr, 1998, p. 649). Moreover, when judges face decision making in which juvenile crime is at issue, empathic insight underscoring the jurisprudential reasoning necessitates that considerations of character also inform the mediated discussion. These are discussions among those in dispute where the adolescent is encouraged to assess how his or her criminal actions were morally flawed and why adopting pro-social behavior would advantage the individual and society. Along these lines, Braithwaite (1989) explained the powerful impact that "shaming," rather than punishment, can have on an offender's character. As he observed:

> Shaming is more pregnant with symbolic content than punishment. Punishment is a denial of confidence in the morality of the offender by reducing norm compliance to a crude cost-benefit calculation; shaming can be a reaffirmation of the morality of the offender by expressing personal disappointment that the offender should do something so out of character, and, if shaming is reintegrative, by expressing personal satisfaction in seeing the character of the offender restored. Punishment erects barriers between the offender and punisher through transforming the relationship into one of power assertion and injury; shaming produces a greater interconnectedness between the parties, albeit a painful one, and interconnectedness which can produce the repulsion of stigmatization or the establishment of a potentially more positive relationship following reintegration. Punishment is often shameful and shaming usually punishes. But whereas punishment gets its symbolic content only from its denunciatory association with shaming, shaming is pure symbolic content. (Braithwaite, 1989, pp. 72–73)

The theory and practice of re-integrative shaming fosters "earned redemption" for the offender, and it has shown success in empirical research

(McGarrell & Hipple, 2007, p. 241). When fitted to the mediation process, the dialogical exchange becomes more therapeutic in design in that it enhances a sense of community, promotes participation, and aims to empower all parties involved in healing the injury caused by (adolescent) crime (Levine, 2000). Additionally, psychosocial factors such as peer pressure, risk taking, and blunted autonomy—so prominent among developmentally immature youths—can be explored while seeking a reparative outcome. Thus, when recognized as a dimension of virtue ethics, as well as an expression of how psychological jurisprudence translates evolving theory into worthwhile public policy, the judge's decision making in support of mediation becomes as fully informed as it does potentially enlightened. Arguably, the gains from endorsing such an approach benefit the adolescent offender, the aggrieved victim, and the community that purposefully binds both together.

As a matter of establishing cogent law and policy, the reality of automatic adolescent transfer in which cognitive and emotional deficits are featured raises significant questions about the youth's trial fitness, as well as the adolescent's amenability to processing, treatment, and successful community re-entry. These empirical concerns notwithstanding, the prevailing case law on the subject as articulated in state supreme court and appellate court decisions repeatedly overlooks or ignores this scientific evidence when rendering judicial opinions.

As Chapter 2 documented, the jurisprudential intent that forms the basis for the court's decision making ethically conveys its meaning in the form of utilitarian reasoning wherein the "greater good" amounts to protecting the public against persistent wayward adolescents. However, as tentatively reviewed in this subsection, more can be—and thus should be—done to address the interests of society (including the victim) and, correspondingly, the needs of delinquent or troubled youth. A law–psychology–justice approach, steeped in the logic of psychological jurisprudence, suggests that this direction already exists in practice in several very noteworthy respects. Therapeutic jurisprudence, commonsense justice, and restorative justice are three distinct, although related, strategies whose conceptual underpinnings advance the moral philosophy of virtue ethics. This moral philosophy endeavors to grow, deepen, and transform the character of all people. Accordingly, legal tribunals are encouraged to appropriate the principles of each when rendering their judicial opinions. This undertaking may very well represent a necessary basis by which the flourishing of developmentally immature juveniles, injured victims, and their respective communities is more fully and responsively achieved. Indeed, from our perspective, this recommended direction helps to make healing, reintegration, and prospects for social justice that much more achievable.

Inmate Mental Health and Solitary Confinement

As the results indicated in Chapter 3, the moral philosophy of utilitarianism and Kantian formalism inform the prevailing Eighth Amendment cases involving mentally ill prisoners placed in protracted disciplinary isolation. Reflecting the legal system's long-held perception that its role is to safeguard citizens and to promote their moral rights, these ethical stances disregard the notion that "the proper end of the law is [the] promotion of human flourishing" (Farrelly & Solum, 2008, p. 2). Rather than enabling offenders to pursue lives of excellence, the prescribed response of confining them in segregated units—where social interaction and mental stimulation are minimal—all but eliminates the possibility that they will learn how to engage others in a constructive manner that is consistent with a correctional institution's rules and with society's expectations.

Indeed, as noted in Chapter 1, a moral logic steeped in utilitarian principles is problematic in that the needs of some individuals are subjectively perceived as more worthy than those of others. This ethic endorses, if not requires, that the interests of some be wholly neglected and/or disregarded. Determining the value of an individual according to their ability to contribute to the satisfaction of the majority is inherently troubling. Moreover, relying upon deontological principles is equally distressing. Although treating others with unqualified dignity is fundamental, decisions made about the welfare of citizens based on prescribed duties primarily fails to acknowledge, let alone account for, the complexity of being human. As Mossman (2006) explained, Kant "informs us about what sorts of interactions we may have with others in an ideal realm where everyone acts justly. But to figure out how to act in the real world, we must contend with the fact that not everyone will comply with rules" (p. 600). Thus, judicial decision making that relies chiefly on utilitarian and deontological reasoning both legitimizes and ensures that the distinct needs of vulnerable populations—particularly mentally ill offenders—will not be met.

Although not without its own shortcomings (especially *see* Chapter 1), virtue ethics warrants that *all* individuals have value and as such can thrive. As Aristotle (1998) asserted, people are social beings. Long-term disciplinary solitary confinement denies prisoners that which is within their nature: the fundamental need to connect with other humans. Thus, although courts may reason that an isolated and mentally disordered inmate's "basic life necessities" are met while in isolative care, their longing for affirmative interaction is not met. Indeed, as Haney (2009) explained:

> Because so much of our individual identity is socially constructed
> and maintained, the virtually complete loss of genuine forms of
> social contact and the absence of routine and recurring
> opportunities to ground thoughts and feelings in recognizable
> human contexts is not only painful but also personally destabilizing.
> This is precisely why long-term isolated prisoners are literally at risk
> of losing their grasp on who they are, of how and why they are
> connected to a larger social world. (p. 16)

Although this perilous prospect unquestionably threatens the well-being of inmates without pre-existing mental health conditions, it profoundly endangers those with psychiatric disorders who consistently struggle to maintain a sense of self and of place in society. Furthermore, it makes the promise of being able to do so for these individuals all but unattainable. Unsurprisingly, therefore, significant confinement and recidivism problems persist for this constituency group (Briggs, Sundt, & Castellano, 2003; Elsner, 2004; Gagliardi, Lovell, Peterson, & Jemelka, 2004; Lovell, Johnson, & Cain, 2007; Pizarro & Stenius, 2004; Rhodes, 2005). As a result, the security of society and the well-being of its citizenry, at best, remain suspect.

If virtue-based ethics are to underscore the decision making of legal tribunals, it follows, then, that proposed resolutions must enable all individuals involved to flourish (Farrelly & Solum, 2008, p. 16). Further, as Solum (2008) noted, judges must become "fully virtuous agent[s]" (p. 190)—that is, they must promote an excellence in being for offenders rather than strictly adhering to prescribed legal protocols or acting in deference to social norms (*see also* Chappell, 2006). To move beyond the utilitarian and deontological reasoning that engulfs judicial decision making, an alternative jurisprudence is recommended.

Mindful of the principles espoused by virtue-based reasoning, psychological jurisprudence considers "whether something more, or something better can (and should) be done for all parties" (Sellers & Arrigo, 2009, p. 478). Along these lines, the practices of therapeutic jurisprudence, restorative justice, and commonsense justice all promote the law–psychology–justice agenda and, as such, support an integrity-oriented morality. In what follows, key principles stemming from these practices are applied to the dilemma of psychiatrically disordered prisoners and solitary confinement. The aim of this exposition is to outline how an alternative jurisprudential ethic could begin to meaningfully reconnect offenders, their victims, and the communities that bind them in ways that enable excellence in character for all.

As noted previously, therapeutic jurisprudence draws "attention [to] the emotional well-being of those who come into contact with law and the legal system" (Winick, 1997, p. 1; *see also* Winick & Wexler, 2003, 2006). Thus, as practice, it relies on the role that the participants within the system (e.g., judges, attorneys) can assume so that they can act therapeutically. As Winick (1997) suggested, "[W]hen consistent with other justice values, the law's potential for increasing emotional well-being of the individual and society as a whole will be increased" (p. 1). Moreover, as he and his colleague, David Wexler, asserted, the current criminal justice system is anti-therapeutic in nature in that it engenders harm (2006, pp. 605–606).

To maximize the potential for salubrious results, an ethic of care must be adopted (Winick & Wexler, 2006). Care ethics emphasizes "relationships, situational and contextual factors, and the unique needs and interests of affected parties as key considerations in the face of conflicts and dilemmas" (Williams & Arrigo, 2008, p. 262). This approach requires jurists to embody a "judge-as-counselor" role and to "know the defendant, consider her or his life circumstances and motives, and take these into consideration when making a ruling" (Williams & Arrigo, 2008, p. 265; *see also* Strang & Braithwaite, 2001; Winick & Wexler, 2006). By doing so, virtues such as empathy, benevolence, and tolerance supersede the need to weigh competing interests or rigidly uphold duties that could subsequently result in greater injury (Bernstein & Gilligan, 1990; Noddings, 2003). Thus, this care ethic "is a form of substantive justice" in which legal decision brokers "cultivate a sense of otherness" (Arrigo & Milovanovic, 2009, p. 69).

When practiced as described above, therapeutic jurisprudence makes salutary outcomes possible for psychiatrically disordered offenders (Wexler, 2008b). To ensure that judges and attorneys have the skills necessary to respond appropriately to mentally ill prisoners, psychologists of law must provide counseling advice and clinical training to justice professionals (Winick & Wexler, 2003). Under these conditions, an approach based on the insights of therapeutic jurisprudence yields a response to harm absent the prescribed punitive confinement resolution. Instead, its care ethic stresses a "readiness for rehabilitation" (Wexler, 2008b, p. 169) as a more effective way to address the emotional needs of the mentally ill incarcerate. In this way, the offender is afforded an increased opportunity to develop moral character so vital to curbing persistent criminal behavior that often leads to prison management concerns, at times resulting in protracted placement in a solitary confinement unit.

As Hancock and Sharp (2004) noted, "It is important to bear in mind that penal sanctions, like crimes, are intended harms" (p. 398). Thus, as opposed to a strictly retributive response to crime, restorative justice seeks to acknowledge the injury resulting from an offense and, essentially, to repair those individuals affected by it. Its practice is to challenge the "character of justice" as delineated by the State (Bayley, 2001, p. 211). In other words, a restorative strategy contests the legal system's prescription of how and for whom justice is served. Moreover, as Bayley asserted, the perception of justice advanced by an organized society's legal edifice is one in which attorneys stand guard, codified rules instruct judges and juries on determining a defendant's guilt or innocence, and an appeal is a reasonable avenue through which those alleging a wrongful conviction have recourse (2001, p. 211). However, whereas the system is consumed with preserving a "just order," restorative justice enables a community to nurture a "just peace" (Strang & Braithwaite, 2001, p. 14; cf., Arrigo & Milovanovic, 2009, pp. 42–44). In other words, as practice, restorative justice endeavors to heal the relationship between the offender and victim and to reinstate the moral equilibrium of a community (Braswell et al., 2001, p. 141; *see also* Sullivan & Tifft, 2005; Van Ness & Heetdirks Strong, 2007). As Quinney (1991) noted:

> Crime is suffering and . . . the ending of crime is possible only with
> the ending of suffering. And the ending both of suffering and of
> crime, which is the establishing of justice, can come only out of
> peace, out of a peace that is spiritually grounded in our very being.
> To eliminate crime – to end the construction and perpetuation of

an existence that makes crime possible – requires a transformation
of our human being. (pp. 11–12)

In contrast to restoration, the current response to crime leaves psychiatrically disordered inmates feeling "alienated, more damaged, disrespected, disempowered, less safe and less cooperative with [and toward] society" (Braswell
et al., 2001, p. 142; *see also* Christie, 1981). This is particularly problematic for
these offenders. Not only are they isolated socially (and, at times, physically)
from others, they effectively feel detached from the dynamics of their own
being as their mental states fluctuate or progressively deteriorate beyond their
control (Arrigo, 2002b; Haney, 2003; Rhodes, 2004). Thus, rather than further disaffecting and stigmatizing incarcerates with (pre-existing) mental
health issues, restorative justice offers a pro-social alternative. Further, as Van
Ness and Heetdirks Strong (2007) noted, engaging offenders in healing efforts
may also encourage the community to become more active in determining
and abating some of the social and economic barriers that contribute to
(neighborhood) criminality. In this respect, then, the needs of psychologically
disordered individuals, those they injure, and the milieus they all inhabit are
more completely addressed.

Commenting on the relationship between restorative and community
justice, Presser (2004, p. 105) remarked: "Crime fundamentally silences, justice gives voice." Thus, commonsense justice, as described and advocated by
Finkel (1995), seeks to inject public sentiment into the juridical decision-
making process. Offenders with psychological health conditions are often
presented in court as dangerous and irascible, warranting confinement and
sometimes placement in an isolation unit or a Supermax facility. Without
question, untreated mental disorders can facilitate risk-taking and violent
behavior, deeply affecting the ability of those afflicted to conform to societal
and institutional rules. However, the logic of psychological jurisprudence
informed by the practice of commonsense justice offers a considerable remedy. Where restorative justice attempts to dialogically connect the offender,
the offended, and their community, commonsense justice encourages all parties in dispute to adopt a resolution that they deem fair, equitable, and just
(Finkel, 1997, 2000).

Indeed, through interventions such as victim–offender mediation, restorative justice provides a critical opportunity for all aggrieved citizens to heal
vis-à-vis an interactive and reparative exchange where felt harm is voiced can-
didly, where lived injury is acknowledged remorsefully, and where this mutuality is embraced respectfully, mercifully, and forgivingly (Arrigo & Schehr,
1998; Braithwaite, 2002; Presser, 2004). This healing dialogue, when guided
by public sentiment that re-engages the community's conscience, challenges
the necessity for retributive responses such as solitary confinement. Instead,
as an integrative and applied expression of psychological jurisprudence
steeped in the moral philosophy of virtue, commonsense justice as proposed

here enables legal tribunals to render decisions that are as salubrious as they are reparative, that are as fair-minded as they are empathic.

Efforts to translate theory into meaningful policy undoubtedly are challenging. Although retributive responses remain the prescribed recourse, the question lingers whether something more salutary in nature can be done for offenders with mental health conditions serving time in long-term disciplinary solitary confinement. Along these lines, the preamble to the nineteenth century Philadelphia Society for Alleviating the Miseries of Public Prisons suggested the following:

> When we reflect upon the miseries [seen in prisons] . . . it becomes us to extend our compassion to that part of mankind, who are the subjects of these miseries. By the aids of humanity, their undue and illegal sufferings may be prevented . . . and such degrees and modes of punishment may be discovered and suggested, as may, instead of continuing habits of vice, become the means of restoring our fellow creatures to virtue and happiness. (Vaux, 1826, p. 9)

When reviewing law–psychology–crime matters such as inmate mental health and solitary confinement, the legal reasoning employed by the courts demands critical re-examination. As Chapter 3 demonstrated, the jurisprudential intent discernable through the courts' decision-making conveyed an unmistakable reliance on the philosophy of utilitarianism and Kantian formalism. The prevailing case law aspired to achieve a greater good in which the interests of society (and its correctional apparatus) superseded the mental health concerns of prisoners in prolonged punitive isolation. Moreover, the bench perceived an unwavering obligation to uphold a particular duty (e.g., deference to prison officials) rather than to thoughtfully consider those circumstances that led incarcerates to raise Eighth Amendment challenges regarding their confinement. However, as previously delineated, something beyond this can and ought to be done to effectively manage the distinct concerns of society and the unmet needs of psychiatrically disordered offenders.

Developed within the law, psychology, and justice tradition, as well as the theorizing of psychological jurisprudence, this subsection proposed an alternative policy-based agenda. Collectively, the practices of therapeutic jurisprudence, restorative justice, and commonsense justice (including their assorted principles) are consistent with Aristotelian ethics. This moral philosophy seeks to grow character so that citizens, including those with mental health conditions, can lead lives of excellence. Accordingly, legal tribunals are encouraged to incorporate virtue-based reasoning into their judicial rulings. Moreover, courts are reminded that when they promote such flourishing, all parties affected by harm benefit: the possibility of recovery and transformation thrives. This is how healing is promoted and justice is achieved for individuals and within institutions by a society that affirms—indeed celebrates—the unrealized potential of both.

Total Confinement Measures and Sexually Violent Predators

The qualitative inquiry pursued in Chapter 4 indicated that the underlying moral philosophies informing judicial decision making for cases involving control and confinement measures of sexually violent predators included formalism (and its utilitarian variant) and consequentialism (especially Kantian deontology). The U.S. Supreme Court's ethical stance upheld a perceived obligation to protect citizens and to advance the interests of some over those of others. This moral posture is inconsistent with the view that "the proper end of the law is [the] promotion of human flourishing" (Farrelly & Solum, 2008, p. 2). Indeed, as the data set demonstrated, the jurists consistently relied on prescribed (and harmful) remedies when responding to legal challenges raised by sex offenders and sexually violent predators (SVPs). Moreover, when ex-incarcerates undergo civil detention, community inspection, and re-entry monitoring, they are denied the opportunity to engage in positive character-enhancing social interactions that are crucial for their capacity to become constructive (and productive) societal members. Stated differently, they are less able to develop a fuller sense of moral character and to lead lives of more complete excellence. Growing this quality of ethical engagement is consistent with Aristotle's virtue philosophy.

Virtue ethics seeks to ensure that *all* individuals are equally valued and equipped to flourish. Sanctions, such as community notification and indefinite civil confinement, prevent sex offenders and SVPs from meaningfully reconnecting with others. Furthering such expressive interaction is an intrinsic need possessed by all human beings. Although judicial decision makers might reason that total confinement measures are necessary to protect the public from criminal transgressors, requiring that this objective be met at the expense of the ex-convict does not logically follow. To be clear, the existing research overwhelming indicates that as a group, convicted SVPs struggle to re-integrate into communities that largely regard them as dangerous monsters incapable of controlling their distorted sexual proclivities. As such, they continue to be defined as societal threats who are at risk for recidivating (Janus, 2006; Olver & Wong, 2006; Tewksbury, 2005; Tewksbury & Lee, 2006; Wright, 2008). However, as we documented in Chapter 4, the empirical findings do not fully substantiate this conclusion.

To transform the character of the kept and the keepers in a way that *all* can flourish an alternative jurisprudence must be considered steeped in Aristotelian virtue philosophy. As described previously, the practices of psychological jurisprudence create this very possibility. Accordingly, therapeutic jurisprudence, restorative justice, and commonsense justice are fitted to the problem of SVPs and those measures designed to control and confine them. Noting that the aim of virtue ethics is to promote excellence for all citizens, the ensuing commentary elucidates how psychological jurisprudence, as policy reform, can meaningfully reunite offenders, victims, and their respective communities.

Based on Winick and Wexler's (2006) notion that the justice system's current retributive approach engenders harm, therapeutic jurisprudence endeavors to reframe injury for all parties involved in a legal matter. To do so, it determines and facilitates opportunities in which the law can act as a healing agent (Wexler & Winick, 1996; Winick & Wexler, 2003, 2006). In contrast to the traditional adversarial model, therapeutic jurisprudence recognizes the debilitating emotional and physical impact this process has on attorneys and clients, and it seeks solutions that better meet the felt needs of both parties (Arrigo, 2004a). As noted earlier, therapeutic jurisprudence emphasizes the "emotional well-being of those who come into contact with the law and the legal system" (Winick, 1997, p. 1; see also Winick & Wexler, 2006). With respect to judicial decision making, values such as mutual respect, dignity, autonomy, non-invasiveness, and community form the core of this practice (Wexler, 2008a). By combining these principles with "other justice values, the law's potential for increasing [the] emotional well-being of the individual and society as a whole is increased" (Winick, 1997, p. 1).

According to Winick and Wexler (2006), the implementation of thera-peutic jurisprudence necessitates adopting an ethic of care. Grounded in hab-its of character such as compassion and tolerance, this moral regard promotes an understanding of the contextual and situational factors that engulf a con-flict, as well as the needs and interests of each party involved in the dispute (Bernstein & Gilligan, 1990; Gilligan, Lyons, & Hanmer, 1990; see also Williams & Arrigo, 2008). As noted in Chapter 1 and as provisionally described in the previous two subsection applications, care ethics advocates that jurists endorse a judge-as-counselor role. Fully embracing such a role enables these decision brokers to "know the defendant, consider her or his life circumstances and motives, and take these into consideration when making a ruling" (Williams & Arrigo, 2008, p. 265; see also Strang & Braithwaite, 2001; Winick & Wexler, 2006). Moreover, to ensure that justice professionals are sufficiently and sen-sitively equipped to meet the mental health needs of sex offenders and SVPs, psychologists of the law must provide instruction on counseling and clinical treatment to agents within the legal system (Winick & Wexler, 2003; see also Birgden, 2004). Thus, in contrast to current judicial decision making wherein competing interests are delicately balanced and duties steadfastly evaluated, legal tribunals are encouraged to skillfully incorporate virtuous reasoning into their judicial opinions as a basis to further critical healing for one and all (Bernstein & Gilligan, 1990; Noddings, 2003).

As described previously, restorative justice challenges the system's goal of preserving a "just order" by offering the means to cultivate a "just peace" (Strang & Braithwaite, 2001, p. 14; see also Arrigo & Milovanovic, 2009, pp. 42–44). Confirming this practice is consistent with transforming how and for whom justice is served by way of the legal edifice. To accomplish this objective, restorative justice displaces the harm stemming from and promulgated by existing strategies with healing interventions that contest the State's "character of justice" (Bayley, 2001, p. 211). The prevailing character of justice advances retribution and incapacitation; however, it is important to acknowledge that "penal sanctions, like crimes, are intended harms" (Hancock & Sharp, 2004, p. 398). As such, restorative justice endorses an approach in which injury resulting from an offense is addressed and the individuals impacted by this transgression are repaired. Additionally, the moral equilibrium of the community that unites the offender and the victim is similarly reinstated (Braswell et al., 2001, p. 141; *see also* Sullivan & Tifft, 2005; Van Ness & Heetdirks Strong, 2007). Indeed, "[r]estorative justice is about flipping vicious circles of hurt begetting hurt into virtuous circles of healing begetting healing" (Braithwaite, 2006, p. 403).

Although the psychological and social damage resulting from current SVP sanctions may be justified according to public sentiment, these retributive approaches create a "major deficit of well-being" for the offender (Clear, 1994, p. 24). The controls that sexually violent ex-convicts are subjected to regulate nearly every aspect of their lives. They are removed both physically and interpersonally from others by way of civil commitment, offender registration, and community notification, and they are deemed incapable of managing their own behavior. Such programming and sentiment fuels the common perception that SVPs "often seem to lack the essential empathy and conscience that mark human beings" (Janus, 2006 p. 2). It is not surprising, therefore, that the empirical research documents how such sanctions foster deep-seated feelings of self-loathing in the ex-incarcerate, undermining prospects for effective cognitive-behavioral change.

In response to the stigmatizing, isolative, and destructive effects of total confinement tactics, restorative justice seeks a more reparative solution. As practice, it encourages the community of which the offender is a part to recognize and address the social and economic challenges that resocializing sex offenders and SVPs confront (Van Ness & Heetdirks Strong, 2007). By taking stock of these hurdles, one's critical needs for pro-social engagement, a place of residence, and gainful employment can more effectively be met. Moreover, by eliminating these social and economic barriers, the possibility of successful community reintegration is increased and the well-being of the offender, the victim, and the community is more fully re-established.

As delineated by Finkel (1995), commonsense justice considers public sentiment in the judicial decision-making process. As we have documented, the extant social and behavioral science literature indicates that SVPs are largely demonized as societal "outcasts," "monsters," or "degraded others" (Janus, 2006) warranting containment and control. However, as psychological jurisprudential practice, commonsense justice solicits and advances public sentiment that is fair-minded and just. This is achieved through the connectedness that a restorative dialogue affirms. This connectedness acknowledges that harm stemming from violence is real and that pain sourced in victimization is deep.

But it also encourages all parties in dispute to consider how such injury could be healed. Overcoming such harm—especially for an aggrieved community conscience—begins as a conversation about the widely held misconceptions regarding those who commit sexually violent acts. It is in this reparative respect, then, that commonsense justice makes the pursuit of a dignified resolution possible for all parties embroiled in a conflict (Finkel, 1997, 2000).

Given the profound misconceptions surrounding sex offenders and SVPs, restorative interventions such as victim–offender mediation are critical. Undertaking reconciliation of this sort helps to make possible the understanding of felt harm, the articulation and acceptance of remorse, and the achievement of genuine forgiveness (Arrigo & Schehr, 1998; Braithwaite, 2002; Presser, 2004). Although total confinement practices engender humiliation for all offenders, shame is perhaps most deeply experienced by SVP designees. As described in Chapter 4, the stigmatizing shame promulgated by sex offender registration and community notification requirements often inflicts severe psychological trauma and social seclusion on these former felons.[2] However, as practice, restorative justice provides an opportunity for re-integrative shaming that allows offenders to evaluate their criminal actions and to determine how they might pursue more pro-social interactions with others (Braithwaite, 1989, 2006). This is because shame is a "vulnerable emotion" (Braithwaite, 2006, p. 403). As Lynd (1958) noted, "the very fact that shame is an isolating experience means that if one can find ways of sharing and communicating it, this communication can bring about particular closeness with others" (p. 66).

By instantiating opportunities that further this vulnerability, this openness, the reparative process can unfold. Indeed, "when we see others express painful as opposed to aggressive emotions, we see them as human beings" (Braithwaite, 2006, p. 404). By removing the threat of stigmatizing shame through reparative dialogue that engages the community's conscience, the rationale for imposing excessive control and confinement measures on offenders is supplanted by a genuine desire for healing. As demonstrated in the two previous application subsections, commonsense justice—as an integrative expression of psychological jurisprudence and as consistent with virtue ethics—facilitates a judicial decision-making process in which salubrious, restorative, and just resolutions can be reached.

Without question, creating public policies based on nascent theory presents a number of challenges. However, the empirical evidence suggests that something beyond restraint and incapacitation can be implemented for sex offenders and SVPs. As Nancy Sabin, the executive director of the Jacob Wetterling Foundation explained:

> We keep getting sidetracked on issues like castration and pink license plates for sex offenders . . . . But these people are coming from us – society – and we have to stop the hemorrhage. We have

to stop pretending that these people are coming from other planets. (Janus, 2006, p. 1)

The notion that SVPs are incurable monsters, societal outcasts, deranged others, or otherwise less than fully human establishes the flawed foundation for detainment, inspection, and monitoring interventions that further isolate and fracture the offender, their victim(s), and the community to which both are intimately connected. Regrettably, this is the sentiment that perpetually holds captive the kept and their keepers, their managers and their watchers.

The qualitative findings from Chapter 4 revealed that the Supreme Court affirmed ethically derived conclusions that were consistent with meeting the needs of an organized society. However, the results also pointed out the ways in which the majority failed to consider the extensive empirical evidence delineating the problematic efficacy of sustaining civil commitment, sex offender registration, and community notification for ex-incarcerates. As conditionally proposed in this portion of Chapter 5, an alternative judicial decision-making strategy can more adequately attend to the critical needs of both constituencies. Along these lines, the practices of psychological jurisprudence suggest a worthwhile basis for reform. When grounded by way of Aristotelian virtue philosophy, therapeutic jurisprudence, commonsense justice, and restorative justice each advances a quality of justice that acknowledges the importance of individual responsibility and institutional accountability. Collectively, they grow dignity, advance healing, and specify critique. These efforts represent an emergent direction for cultivating individual well-being, collective good, and societal change. When applied to judicial decision making in the instance of sexually violent offenders, the practices of psychological jurisprudence seed and nurture a potential transformation in moral character for *all* citizens. Indeed, under these conditions, those who injure violently, those who experience victimization profoundly, and the communities that join them together uniquely have a heightened opportunity to overcome and flourish.

Psychological Jurisprudence, Habits of Character, and Social Justice

This chapter suggested, by way of several provisional and speculative reformist strategies, that the relevance of psychological jurisprudence extends beyond theory and method to the province of policy. This is policy whose assessment of total confinement practices recognizes that legal actors and judicial decision makers have an important role to play in furthering individual well-being, collective good, and societal accord. This role is about changing the conversation and landscape for developmentally immature and troubled juveniles transferred to the adult system and found fit for trial; psychiatrically disordered and vulnerable offenders placed in protracted disciplinary isolation; and formerly adjudicated and distressed sex offenders subjected to civil commitment, community inspection, and re-entry monitoring. This conversation begins by honoring a quality of justice (individual responsibility and institutional accountability) that makes systematic ethical engagement that much more fully realizable. The dignity, healing, and critique endorsed by our proposals pragmatically initiates a move in this necessary and timely direction.

Still, our reformist recommendations, although well-intended in design and thought-provoking in implementation, fail to consider the depth of the contemporary problem that is madness, citizenship, and social justice. Our proposed solutions only superficially outline how human flourishing and progressive change can take place. However, as we have argued, *transformative* habits of character are needed to transcend the limits set and the denials imposed by the conditions of control (*see* the application chapters and their respective "implications" subsections for more about this notion). This is a reference to the fearful hypervigilance and dangerous panopticism that presently sustains the ethic of harm circulating in and throughout total confinement practices. Thus, the question is begged: What are these forces of captivity, how do they operate, and how can we overcome them? This query deliberately draws attention to the symbolic, linguistic, material, and cultural realms that influence and are shaped by the self/society duality (the twin dynamics). These are images, narratives, inscriptions, and replications that deny being and thwart becoming. Stated differently, to displace the conditions of madness and to change the landscape that total confinement currently guarantees for one and about all, a deeper quality of citizenship must be advanced and a richer expression of social justice must be pursued.

As a practical matter, then, this means that several complex and mostly underexamined issues will continue to impede prospects for successfully establishing the very reforms proposed in this chapter. These issues, both existential and material in character, reduce and repress how the human agency–social structure mutuality settles on choice and action. This cohabitation includes those contentious matters situated at the law–psychology–crime divide. As a basis to explore these impediments, the heuristics of psychological jurisprudence warrant an additional level of reconsideration, especially if such barriers are to be removed or, better still, eliminated. To be clear, this re-engagement extends the analysis undertaken throughout this volume. Such an endeavor acknowledges that more can and should be done to more fully experience the transformative potential that grows dignity, advances healing, and specifies critique.

Accordingly, the concluding chapter locates and examines the pressing challenges that must be addressed to destabilize the harmful ethic manufactured by the forces of captivity for the kept and their keepers, for their managers and their watchers. What is documented by way of this exercise is a further departure—a movement away from what ought to be and beyond what could become. Thus, the concluding chapter represents a glimpse into the next generation (the awaiting revolution) of psychological jurisprudence as theory, method, and praxis.

Conclusion

Total Confinement, Psychological Jurisprudence, and Transformative Habits of Character: "Almost a Revolution"

Introduction

Thus far, the thesis entertained throughout this book has examined judicial decision-making in three law-psychology-crime areas. These areas include: *(1)* juveniles transferred to the adult system, despite developmental maturity concerns, where they subsequently are found competent to stand trial; *(2)* psychiatrically disordered offenders placed in long-term disciplinary segregation where said isolation is not always deemed to be cruel and unusual punishment; and *(3)* sexually violent predators (SVPs) subjected to criminal/civil confinement, followed by offender registration and community notification. In each instance, prevailing or precedent-setting case law endorses the practice (when challenged in courts), despite the social/behavioral science evidence significantly demonstrating the debilitating or harmful health, mental health, and/or resocialization effects that follow from their continuance. As such, we argued that these practices amount to total confinement. Total confinement's teleology is to criminalize, pathologize, and demonize. We asserted that this "madness" is legitimized when sustained by judicial decision-making. We questioned the character of these court rulings by way of novel theory and method sourced in psychological jurisprudence (PJ).

As theory, it was conjectured that by considering individual and institutional responsibility for wrongdoing, a type of justice could be advanced that made more attainable the development of a systematic ethical critique. This normative undertaking pondered the needs of the public (especially those victimized), the rights of offenders (often, vulnerable, troubled, and distressed populations), and the demands of an ordered society (fearfully hypervigilant and dangerously panoptic in its insistence). Further, as theory, it was postulated that the integration and intersection of commonsense justice, therapeutic jurisprudence, and restorative justice promotes a type of dignity, healing, and critique that is remarkably consistent with Aristotelian virtue ethics. Indeed, their assorted principles suggest an approach to addressing harm or injury that is quite sensitive to human flourishing or excellence, for one and all. This excellence encompasses victims, offenders, and the communities that tether them. Thus, we wondered how, if at all, judicial decision making on matters of total confinement embraced or employed this brand of PJ reasoning.

As method, a two-phase framework for qualitative textual analysis was devised. This approach was guided by the identification of precedent-setting and/or prevailing case law, and the LexisNexis criterion-based sampling design that located the decisions led to the construction of three separate data sets. Under investigation were the ways in which courts talked about and ruled on the three law–psychology–crime total confinement practices that formed the research subject matter for this book.

The first level of qualitative scrutiny situated the case's jurisprudential intent as derived from the decision's plain meaning. Stated differently, this level of review delineated instances of judicial temperament (attitudes, perceptions, and concerns) as guided by several questions specifically designed to extract these findings. The second stage of textual inquiry, more probing and interpretive in nature, identified the underlying normative theory that framed and communicated each instance of judicial temperament. This critical examination phase consisted of both intra- and inter-textual inspection.

The comprehensive results showed that the case law "total confinement" data sets did not advance virtue ethics at all. Instead, the juridical language was freighted with a concern for duties, obligations, interest-balancing, equivalences, and so forth. The language of citizenship was altogether absent. In other words, a quality of excellence that was fair-minded and dignified (commonsense justice), therapeutic and healing (therapeutic jurisprudence), and reparative and communal (restorative justice) was conspicuously missing. However, as we previously mentioned, the assimilation of this kind of citizenship is akin to Aristotle's virtue philosophy. And this jurisprudence was wanting in the cases themselves. Stated more plainly, the precedent-setting and/or prevailing case law on the three total confinement practices under review said nothing about how waiving troubled juveniles to the adult system, subjecting vulnerable mentally ill citizens to disciplinary solitary confinement, or thoroughly controlling the already distressed lives of formerly incarcerated SVPs was courageous, generous, or compassionate. This meant that the possibility for maximizing individual flourishing (for those who injure and are harmed), collective well-being (for the communities to which they are bound), and societal accord (for a nation held captive by its fear) was mostly deferred, if not disturbingly denied. Several reformist-based suggestions were sketched explaining how such human/social excellence could (and should) be advanced practically in these law–psychology–crime areas by diverse members of the legal profession. From our perspective, these proposals began to reflect the role that PJ theory (and method) could assume at the level of relevant policy-making.

However, as we indicated in the implications portion of each application chapter, our interests extend to *transformative habits of character*. Cultivating such citizenship requires a different and deeper level of theoretical, method-ological, and analytical engagement with this book's central thesis than supplied thus far. To date, this level of PJ engagement remains mostly under-developed (cf. Arrigo, 2010a, in press; Arrigo & Milovanovic, 2009, 2010; Bersot & Arrigo, 2011). Pursuing such a project would entail a reassessment of total confinement, of captivity, whose harm co-productively and interde-pendently implicates the kept and their keepers, their managers and their watchers. The balance of this conclusion provisionally investigates these very prescient issues.

To be clear, the subtitle of this concluding chapter intends to communicate its meaning at the level of meditation and metaphor. As meditation, "almost a revolution" is a response to what Appelbaum (1994) called for: A quality of change and well-being for troubled, vulnerable, and distressed groups guided by insight in psychiatry and law that was to happen and, regrettably, remains largely unfulfilled. The ethical grounding of this book begins to seed how that potential could be reconceived for victims, offenders, and their communities. As we just indicated, the reformist intention here extends to the work of lawyers, judges, and others who advocate or adjudicate by way of the legal apparatus. A number of these proposals were enumerated in Chapter 5, mindful of our Aristotelian-derived model of psychological jurisprudence.

As metaphor, however, the nearness of revolution is a call for change not simply in who we are (or could be) but in what we do (or could do). This is the realm in which the diagnosis of madness must be de/reconstructed, the pursuit of citizenship must be dis/re-assembled, and the search for social justice must be dis/re-engaged. Each of these activities draws attention to the total confinement forces, or the conditions of captivity that engulf the kept, their keepers, their managers, and their watchers. Collectively, this immersion is a kind of madness in which current notions of citizenship and social justice victimize and/or devalue far too many individuals and/or groups, in far too many human/social contexts. Efforts to overcome such injury warrant some review, even if mostly tentative and speculative in essential composition.

Accordingly, this concluding chapter addresses the meditative and metaphorical dimensions of its subtitle. To accomplish this endeavor, several matters are investigated. The first three of these considers revolution in terms of theory, method, and praxis. Respectively, this is a reference to reconceiving the diagnosis of madness, undertaking a fuller exploration of citizenship, and experiencing (thinking about and acting on) an alternative kind of social justice. These observations, incomplete and in need of additional and prospective elaboration, suggest still another journey—an "awaiting" revolution. This is a quality of change or transformation for a people yet to come (Deleuze & Guattari, 1984, 1987). Along these lines, and fourth, we propose reforms in legal education, clinical/mental health training and practice, and future research, as well as human/social welfare programming and policy. As we argue, working the habits of character at the core of these suggested activities further grounds the book's commitment to growing a transformational ethic steeped in the philosophy of PJ and its corresponding methodological approach as situated in normative theory.

Re-Diagnosing Madness

Total confinement practices can be sourced in the conditions of control or captivity. These conditions include four spheres of interdependent and overlapping influence consisting of the symbolic, linguistic, material, and cultural realms, as well as the co-productive effects of the self/society duality (the twin dynamics). Figure 6.1 describes the operation of these interactive forces, locates their meaning within the theory of PJ, and examines their relevance for re-diagnosing madness.

The Conditions of Control, Psychological Jurisprudence, and the Revolution in Theory

The four mutually supporting spheres of influence include circumscribed images (Symbolic realm), privileged texts (Linguistic realm), embodied inscriptions (Material realm), and replicated imitations about them all (Cultural realm). The self–society duality consists of the human agent and the structural forces and/or organizational intensities to and from which the person is subjected. Examples of the former encompass the kept, their keepers, their managers, and their watchers. Each individual is implicated in the process of captivity. Instances of the latter involve waiving developmentally immature juveniles to the adult system subsequently declared fit for trial; isolating in long-term disciplinary confinement offenders with pre-existing psychiatric disorders; detaining, inspecting, and monitoring previously adjudicated SVPs. Each institutional response imposes material and/or existential restrictions on all human subjects whose constraints are maintained, much like a feedback loop, by way of the figure's constituent interconnectivity. The four spheres of influence and the twin dynamics are fluid constructions. Each is informed by and contributes to the composition of the others. The arrows located within the diagram convey this porous movement. What this means, then, is that the possibility for de/reconstructing the conditions of control awaits more detailed elaboration and clarification. In what follows, some of these protean directions are briefly enumerated.

The Symbolic sphere is the realm of consumerism. What are consumed are prevailing, although limited, mental representations (or pictures in our

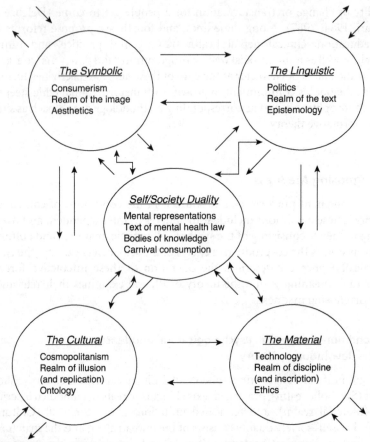

Figure 6.1 Deconstructing Psychological Jurisprudence
Adapted from Arrigo and Milovanovic (2010, p. xiv) and Arrigo (2010b, p. 365).

minds) about juvenile delinquency, psychiatric disorder, predatory and sexualized violence; those harmed or otherwise victimized; and the institutional responses that attach to them all. Stated differently, the Symbolic sphere is about the consumption of a particular and dominant aesthetic regarding vulnerable, troubled, and distressed individuals; those professionals whose expertise includes treatment, corrections, and societal re-entry; and the interventions exercised to ameliorate offenders and the offended.[1]

The Linguistic sphere is the realm of politics. Because current image-making is inadequate (incomplete, circumscribed, less), the story that is told about delinquent youth (as deviant), the psychiatrically disordered (as diseased), and the formerly incarcerated (as dangerous), communicates only summary representations (Cicourel, 1981; Knorr-Cetina, 1981) for and about the same. These summary representations form a text (the text of mental health law) that confirms the images on which the text itself is based. In other words, the Linguistic sphere is about the politics of a preferred knowledge (an epistemology) for and about vulnerable, troubled, and distressed individuals; those specialists whose proficiencies include treatment, corrections, and recommunalization; and the interventions deployed to assist victims and curtail assailants.[2]

The Material sphere is the realm of technology. The favored text of mental health law endorses systems of (bodies of) knowledge in psychiatry, penology, social work, education, and the like. These bodies of knowledge are expressions of power that legitimize a corresponding ethic about the self, the social, and their mutuality. Presently, this ethic reifies techniques of control, containment, and normalization whose purpose is to discipline (restore) the subject. This ethical restoration extends from the kept to their keepers, from their managers to their watchers. In this way, the narrative of power as knowledge instantiated by disciplinary systems establishes regimes of truth and regimens of human/social existence. These truths and regimens inscribe the twin dynamics and problematically tend toward closure; that is, to render docile and silent manifestations of dissent. In short, difference is vanquished, knowledge is territorialized, identity is homogenized, and community is sanitized. Put another way, the notion of "disciplining" the subject begs the question: Restore the person to what and on whose terms (e.g., Acorn, 2005, Pavlich, 2006)? This matter will be further reviewed in a subsequent section of this chapter (see Re-visiting Social Justice).[3]

The cultural sphere is the realm of cosmopolitanism.[4] Its ethos includes the replication and dissemination of established images, texts, and technologies about the self–society mutuality that effectively support the status quo. This is the realm of simulated reproduction and carnival consumption that celebrates the virtual over the visceral, the sensational over the sensual. This is the manufactured *industry* of fictionalized or representational reality in which print and electronic media continuously and repetitively circulate, imitations of "serial sexual offenders," "mind hunters," "crazed psychotic killers," "clinical forensic specialists," "crime scene experts," and the like, *ad infinitum.* This illusory and derivative state of affairs functions as both the source and product of the fragmented depiction and counterfactual consumption that nurtures and maintains the forces of captivity. As such, the nature of being is immersed in reduction; its counterpart, becoming, is ensconced in repression. Both circumstances reflect no more than the *shadow* of our potential human flourishing.[5] This disturbing ontology helps to recursively sustain total confinement and its ethic of harm for one and about all.[6]

To transcend the conditions of control in PJ, it is necessary to initiate some efforts that destabilize their grounding. This destabilization recognizes that total confinement is a cyclical and debilitating process of madness that presently endures unabated. Regrettably, in countless instances of human/social struggle, this madness overwhelms *all* of our lives. As such, what must be pursued are challenges to the constructed images, texts, embodiments, and replications (i.e., summary representations) that mirror prevailing and incomplete sentiment about offenders, victims, and the communities to which both are bound. Along these lines, one strategy that has the potential to foster a way out of this captivity is to revisit the question of citizenship as entertained throughout this volume. At issue, then, are the contexts in which transformative habits of character—from the symbolic to the linguistic, from the material to the cultural—could be more fully realizable. This query invites some reconsideration of psychological jurisprudence and its novel and emergent methodology.

Re-Advancing Citizenship

As hypothesis, the proposed re-diagnosis of madness suggests the need for theory testing. To put the issue in the form of a question: How can the conditions of control, understood as total confinement, be researched more micrologically? By way of a provisional response, we return to our Aristotelian-derived ethical inquiry for amplification and guidance. Specifically, the forces of captivity are probed for their underexamined normative import, this assessment is positioned in case law textual inquiry, and the relevance of this commentary is linked to growing and deepening citizenship understood as evolving human flourishing.

The Conditions of Control, Psychological Jurisprudence, and the Revolution in Method

As the qualitative research at the core of this book has demonstrated, habits of character fail to find expression in the constructed opinions of judicial decision makers, especially when sourced by way of (and through) jurisprudential intent. Concomitantly, the investigatory focus that was pursued emphasized a normative evaluation only of manifest content. In other words, once instances of judicial temperament were discerned (Level-1 analysis), they were resituated within their plain meaning contexts and then filtered through prevailing ethical theory (Level-2 analysis). This produced a series of heuristic findings that clearly warranted more detailed examination to substantiate (or not) their ostensible evidentiary soundness. In particular, these data did not comment on the consumerism, politics, technology, and cosmopolitanism advanced in the three data sets or throughout the collective legal cases themselves. This is the next (and deeper) level of signification that awaits careful textual scrutiny.

Accordingly, the methodology of this subsequent research enterprise would include two stages. The first of these would return to the underlying ethical reasoning that conveyed jurisprudential intent for each of the three data sets. This phase of inquiry would be guided by several questions about the forces and intensities of captivity embedded within the existing findings. First, what dominant and partial images were consumed about psychiatric disorder, violence and victimization, and treatment and recovery through the selection of juridical language? Second, what preferred mental health law text was constructed regarding each of these matters such that the politics of this narrative, once identified, could be made apparent? Third, how did this text, as an expression of material power, inscribe bodies of knowledge onto subjects technologically (i.e., by way of disciplinary systems), and what were the features of this disciplining? Fourth, what incomplete, fictionalized, and counterfactual reality (if any) concerning troubled juveniles, vulnerable offenders, distressed ex-incarcerates, violence, victimization, treatment, and recovery, was reproduced and circulated through a court's choice of legal images, discourse, and/or types of disciplinary technologies? Having retrieved these data, the question, then, could be stated thusly: What transformative habits of character emerged from these responses? Consistent with our earlier analyses concerning the three total confinement practice issues under review, this more novel stage of citizenship inquiry would include both an intra- and inter-textual thematic assessment. In other words, thematic commentary on transformative habits of character would be retrieved within each case, for all cases constituting a particular data set, and across all three data sets. And, if examples of human flourishing or excellence for one and all could not be specified through this more deliberately systematic qualitative undertaking, then the veracity of the previously recounted heuristic findings would receive enhanced confirmation.

The second stage of our proposed two-phase follow-up methodology would be more global in composition. It would source its investigation within multiple facets of each case rather than simply within the normative reasoning that communicated juridical temperament for the same. For example, the elements of a legal opinion include such components as procedural history, legal issue in dispute, facts of the case, statement of rule, policy, dicta, reasoning, and the holding. Once having divided each case in a data set into these discrete areas, it would then be possible to subject these elements to the same kind of citizenship-based textual examination as identified beforehand. Indeed, this comprehensive analysis would yield an additional level of evidence about the quality of dignity (for one and all?), the type of healing (individual, collective, and social?), and the nature of critique (Aristotelian-derived?) lodged within and communicated through the respective legal decisions. Here, too, both intra- and inter-textual thematic analysis would be featured. This degree of methodical inquiry awaits more thorough elaboration and in-depth clarification.

In both stages of this more nascent methodology, the research focus disassembles the consumerism, politics, technologies, and cosmopolitanism situated within a judicial opinion and across a data set. Additionally, however, as a basis to specify transformative habits of character and to translate worthwhile theory into meaningful policy, recommendations beyond this level of analysis would be needed. These proposals would re-assemble the case by way of images, narratives, inscriptions, and replications that more completely communicate the prospect of excellence for the kept and their keepers, for their managers and their watchers. Among other things, this would require an evaluation of how virtues such as courage, compassion, generosity, mercifulness, gentleness, liberality, tolerance, honesty, kindness, benevolence, wisdom, justice and the like could produce a different, more fully affirming, quality of excellence for one and about all when guiding and underscoring juridical reasoning. When routinely exercised through judicial decision making, these practices possess the capacity to renovate—indeed, innovate— the aesthetical, epistemological, ethical, and ontological footing of the law– psychology–crime issue under consideration. This suggestion does not dismiss juridical commitments to weighing and balancing competing interests; assessing rights, duties, and responsibilities; or furthering the logic of equivalence. Rather, the metamorphosis intended by our recommendation seeks to instantiate a quality of citizenship that could, and from our perspective should, inform how flourishing for one and all occurs.[7]

Clearly, what we have outlined is a strategy for advancing habits of character as originating in the construction of case law that extends the qualitative approach of PJ examined in previous chapters of this book. Although this endeavor is relevant to developing an empirically derived reconsideration of the conditions of control that sustain total confinement practices, it nonetheless remains insufficient. This is because our inquiry also must entail a re-engagement with the notion of social justice. Thus, several remarks are warranted—even if provisional—that indicate how a transformational citizenship could be made more feasible by way of everyday human/social praxis.

Revisiting Social Justice

Our interest in praxis intends to communicate a two-fold meaning: *(1)* the integration of theory and method that establishes evolving action and *(2)* the reliance on action to further fuel the development of theory and method (e.g., Adorno, 1973; Freire, 1970; Habermas, 1984). In this way, praxis seeks change in thinking about and undertaking social justice. Thus, the question to ponder can be articulated as such: How do the extant practices of commonsense justice, therapeutic jurisprudence, and restorative justice (especially at their intersections) make the search for growing individual well-being, collective good, and societal accord an emergent reality? These are the essential principles through which PJ furthers its reformist agenda. Accordingly, to address our concern for praxis, we revisit these constructs, assess their relationship with respect to the forces and intensities of captivity, and suggest the cultivation of replacement meanings for each whose untapped potential could very well signal the experiential nearing of unimagined reform.

The Conditions of Control, Psychological Jurisprudence, and the Revolution in Praxis

At the core of our critique concerning madness and citizenship is an effort to overcome the excess borne of fearful hypervigilance and dangerous panopticism. In an era of total confinement, ideas like "dignity," "the therapeutic," "restorative," "fair-mindedness," "injury," "community," "health," "self," "society," and the like are all filtered through the intemperance that this captivity most assuredly guarantees. This condition erodes, and in our estimation undoes, the evolution in social justice. In other words, even the well-intentioned reformist strategies proposed in Chapter 5 must be disengaged, to some extent, to evaluate the quality of action they seek to promote. It is not enough to lobby for individual well-being, collective good, and societal change. What must be studied are the symbolic, linguistic, material, and cultural meanings that are legitimized and thus advanced by way of social justice's unexamined footing. Thus, to speak of growing dignity, healing, care, restoration, and community as artifacts of praxis made more realizable by way of PJ is to question the very basis on which these constructs are given preferred aesthetical, epistemological, ethical, and ontological grounding.[8] This perspective leads to several complexities about furthering the case for social justice. What images are consumed when we picture it in our minds? What politics are lodged in this text as we write or narrate this story? What technologies discipline and inscribe the subject when we heal, correct, and re-commune by way of its disciplinary systems of knowledge (e.g., in psychiatry, penology, social work)? Given our praxis efforts, what cosmopolitanism is counterfactually replicated and disseminated, if any, in the digital age that rapaciously manufactures their illusions and derivatives?

This disengagement with the practices of PJ acknowledges that social justice is fluid. As such, the meanings that attach to the principles that grow it must themselves be provisional, positional, and relational (Arrigo & Milovanovic, 2009). Otherwise, totalities are established whose tendencies are to set limits to one's being (the recovering subject) and to impose denials to one's becoming (the transforming subject). Indeed, this concern for totalities extends to the kept and their keepers, to their mangers and their watchers. Thus, when praxis is pursued by way of PJ, what mutating summary representations of principles are deployed, if any: *(1)* by, for, and about vulnerable, troubled, and distressed individuals (the kept); *(2)* by those professionals who educate, litigate, and legislate about such collectives (their keepers); *(3)* by those specialists whose programming expertise includes treatment, corrections, and societal re-entry for offenders and those victimized (their managers); and *(4)* by those who question, critique, or otherwise observe the unfolding of it all (their watchers). In short, on what conditions of control and on whose terms for the same does the praxis of social justice take place?[9]

Additionally, however, this proposed evaluative and disassembling exercise occurs with respect to the meanings that attach to the constructs of responsibility, rights, duties; interesting balancing and the logic of equivalence; and the Aristotelian virtues previously enumerated throughout this volume. In other words, the praxis that enables social justice to foster an evolution in human flourishing by way of PJ's core practices seeks to instantiate a transformative ethic that is itself conditional, especially in the interconnections and interstices of its consumerism, politics, technologies, and cosmopolitanism. The contingent universalities (Butler, 1992) that emerge from such dynamic configurations celebrate a people yet to come and the nomadic journey that makes their potentialities that much more fully attainable (Deleuze & Guattari, 1984, 1987).

The policy-making that follows from this revisitation of praxis foreshadows unimagined possibilities. Disengaging and re-engaging the principles and practices of PJ, the summary representations that hold one and all captive, and the moral philosophy that underscores and informs both is an exercise in renovation (restoring the subject) and innovation (transforming the subject). It is an exercise in overcoming the shadow in and of us all. The experimentation implied by these action-based efforts intends to feed the development of theory and method, and the assimilation of theory and method that naturally emerges aims to fuel the evolution in social justice. From our perspective, this is how transformative habits of character are embodied as praxis. When this praxis is personified, greater expressions of spontaneous compassion and mutual regard for others can materialize.[10]

Journeying as a People Yet to Come

The nearness and urgency of revolution also is a recognition that something must be done right now to forestall the ethic of total confinement. This is reference not only to the three law–psychology–crime matters investigated in this volume but to all expressions of captivity reified by the self–society duality. Thus, in this final subsection, several tangible reforms are put forth consistent with this chapter's re-assessment of madness, citizenship, and social justice. These proposals include a number of changes in legal education, clinical/mental health training and practice, and future research, as well as human/social welfare programming and policy. As we argue, embracing the flourishing and excellence seeded by these activities deepens the book's commitment to nurturing a transformational ethic situated within the novel philosophy of PJ and its nascent methodology as derived from normative theory.

Psychological Jurisprudence, Habits of Character, and the Awaiting Revolution

Lawyers, judges, and other legal actors would do well to take a required course (or even sequence of courses) in humanitarian ethics. This course (or these courses) would emphasize PJ analysis based on the theoretical and methodological model-making as outlined in our re-diagnosis of madness, re-advancement of citizenship, and revisitation of social justice. Applications of this framing to specific other required or elective course offerings warrant attention as well. Instructional cognate areas such as Medicine and the Law; Bioethics; Law and Psychology; Law and Social/Public Policy; Criminal Law; Law and Philosophy; and Juvenile and Family Law would be outlets for potential course development and/or reconfiguration. Continuing legal education is yet another venue for exploration, especially in relation to the PJ practices of commonsense justice, therapeutic jurisprudence, restorative justice; their intersections, and the integration of their principles. Here, too, the critique of madness and citizenship would inform the observations concerning praxis.

Moreover, psychiatrists, psychologists, mental health therapists, and other treatment specialists in the human/social services all would need exposure to similar forms of PJ training (including the pre-doctoral and post-doctoral stages, as well as continuing education). This training would be especially useful with respect to assessment, diagnosis, and intervention. On this matter, the particular instructional focus would test for and examine the presence of total confinement practices and their debilitating impact for the kept and their keepers, for their managers and their watchers. This harm and the disturbing ethic that it sustains is the presence of self–society systemic pathology. Its symptoms (the conditions of control) must be identified, treated, and prevented. Offender groups (troubled, vulnerable, and distressed populations); persons and collectives injured by way of violence and victimization; those experts who educate, litigate, and legislate; and the specialists who treat, correct, and restore are all held captive by this material and existential disease.[11] This proposed recommendation is a call for a *clinical sociology*. Its efficacy is anchored in the realization that overcoming the images, narratives, inscriptions, and replications that reduce/repress flourishing is an ongoing and mutating journey whose purpose is human agency—social structure insight and change.

Still further, graduate students and academic researchers would benefit from coursework in the philosophy of PJ and the logic of its normatively derived methodology as developed throughout this book. Interdisciplinary instruction and pedagogical border-crossing is envisioned here. To illustrate, aspects of this education would investigate the construct of "captivity" sourced similarly, yet distinctly, in the experiences of the kept, their keepers, their managers, and their watchers. Additional curricular offerings or training components would subject the synthetic practices of commonsense justice, therapeutic jurisprudence, and restorative justice (and their corresponding principles) to further theoretical exploration, conceptual fusions, and sensible applications. As this volume has suggested, total confinement practices abound at the law–psychology–crime nexus; we examined but three of them, and clearly, many others await careful scrutiny.

Field placements (research-based, programming-focused, or policy-relevant) as well as practice work in human and social services also would be pursued based on the critique of madness, citizenship, and social justice. As praxis, the reformist agenda of PJ seeks to grow individual well-being, collective good, and societal change. As such, its search for a transforming social justice can (and must) be fitted to a range of human/social struggles. Responding to these struggles relates to a shift in the kind of assistance made available to various individuals, couples, families, social groups, communities, and even societies. Moreover, the forces of captivity are of particular concern within such probed categories and among such contentious divides as race, gender, and/or class. As such, and by way of example, interventions targeted on behalf of minorities, women, and the poor would undergo de/reconstruction consistent with an assessment of the interdependent symbolic, linguistic, material, and cultural spheres of influence that shape and are informed by the extant self–society intensities these categories and divides simultaneously experience and nurture. This endeavor would identify and ameliorate the forces of reduction and/or repression that impede the prospect of citizenship and compromise the evolution in social justice.

Still, perhaps unremarkably, some might question why these reforms would matter for any of the constituencies mentioned, for those to whom the proposals are directed, or for society more generally. Indeed, why should courts be guided by concerns for training in humanitarian ethics (not just legal ethics), clinicians drawn to social dysfunction (not just individual pathology), investigators schooled in novel theory/methods (not just prevailing instructional paradigms) in their respective occupational routines or workplace endeavors? To be sure, the question itself anticipates the problem we have repeatedly identified and explained. Regrettably, attorneys, judges, clinicians, mental health specialists, and educators are (and will continue to be) held captive if unexamined limit-setting (gate-keeping) informs the quality of citizenship to which they (we) claim allegiance. The images, stories, inscriptions, and replications manufactured by way of this ethic are less, far less, than what they could be or could become. Moreover, if an Aristotelian-derived morality that seeds and cultivates transformative habits of character is to be remotely possible, then relevant professionals must be exposed to a different type of training so that they can properly adjudicate captivity's absence, appropriately diagnose and treat its presence, or instructively educate and research either or both.

The preceding observations are also a kind of reform committed to the tri-fold conceptual pillars of PJ. These are the pillars of dignity, the therapeutic, and critique. And, as we have reasoned throughout this volume—theoretically, methodologically, and analytically—to do anything other than further their cause is to sustain the contemporary crisis in madness, citizenship, and social justice. This is an ethical crisis that presently forestalls a people yet to come. However, the path to its overcoming, as an evolving journey, is one in which excellence is celebrated in the nearing of its long-awaited revolution.

This moment, energized by cascading instances of will mobilized to power, is the locus of transformation. Seizing this moment, then, is our collective challenge. The emergents that most assuredly will follow signal an untapped direction for cultivating unimagined and ever-evolving self/society flourishing.

APPENDIX A

Plain Meaning Results

Tate v. State

Data from Question 1:

"The court had an obligation to ensure that the juvenile defendant, who was less than the age of fourteen, with known disabilities raised in his defense and who faced mandatory life imprisonment, was competent to understand the plea offer and the ramifications thereof, and understand the defense being raised and the state's evidence to refute the defense position, so as to ensure that Tate could effectively assist in his defense" (p. 51).

> *"We also recognize that competency hearings are not, per se, mandated simply because a child is tried as an adult"* (p. 50).
>
> *". . . there is no absolute right requiring children to be treated in a special system for juvenile offenders"* (p. 52).
>
> *". . . the common law presumption of incapacity of a minor between the ages of seven and fourteen years to commit a crime no longer applies"* (p. 53).
>
> *"It is not unreasonable for the legislature to treat children who commit serious crimes as adults in order to protect societal goals"* (p. 54).

Data from Question 2:

> *". . . there is nothing in the law or constitution requiring children be afforded a special system for juveniles who commit crime"* (p. 54).

"*The legislature, however, has supplanted the common law defense of 'infancy' with a statutory scheme . . .*" (p. 53).

Data from Question 3:

". . . *the trial court's reasoning in rejecting the post-trial motion overlooks the argument that the proper inquiry was whether the defendant may be incompetent, not whether he is incompetent*" (p. 51).

". . . *Tate was only twelve . . . this was Tate's first arrest*" (p. 51).

". . . *sentences imposed on juveniles [as adults] of life imprisonment are not uncommon in Florida Courts*" (p. 54).

". . . *there was no violation of proportionality . . .*" (p. 54).

". . . *substantial evidence of intent in this case . . .*" (p. 53).

Data from Question 4:

". . . *Tate was entitled to a complete evaluation and hearing . . .*" (p. 50).

". . . *if a pre-trial or post-trial competency hearing had been ordered, the court would have been able to properly assess Tate's appreciation of the charges, the range and nature of the possible penalties, determine whether he understood the adversary nature of the legal process, his capacity to disclose to his attorney pertinent facts surrounding the alleged offense, his ability to relate to his attorney, his ability to assist his attorney in planning his defense, his capacity to realistically challenge prosecution witnesses, his ability to manifest appropriate courtroom behavior, his capacity to testify relevantly, and his motivation to help himself in the legal process, as well as his ability to evaluate and make a decision concerning the plea offer*" (p. 51).

Data from Question 5:

". . . *we reject the argument that a life sentence without the possibility of parole is cruel or unusual punishment on a twelve-year-old child . . .*" (p. 54).

". . . *sentences imposed on juveniles [as adults] of life imprisonment are not uncommon in Florida Courts*" (p. 54).

". . . *the Florida Legislature has fixed the second most severe penalty to the most severe crime recognized by our law*" (p. 54).

Data from Question 6:

". . . *treat children who commit serious crimes as adults in order to protect society goals*" (p. 54).

Data from Question 7:

". . . *treat children who commit serious crimes as adults in order to protect society goals*" (p. 54).

Otis v. State

Data from Question 1:

". . . *it can be inferred from the serious and violent nature of the offense that the protection of society demands that Otis be tried as an adult*" (p. 607).

". . . *while Otis's lack of sophistication and maturity may be mitigating factors, they are not of such a nature to warrant a transfer to juvenile court*" (p. 609).

Data from Question 2:

". . . the trial court is not required to give equal weight to each of the statutory factors" (p. 608).

"*The State was not required to put on proof of each statutory factor*" (p. 609).

". . . *each factor need not be supported by clear and convincing evidence*" (p. 610).

". . . *the second factor does not require proof of premeditation; rather, the second factor pertains to whether the alleged offense was committed in an aggressive, violent, premeditated, or willful manner*" (p. 608).

Data from Question 3:

". . . *the weight to be afforded to each statutory factor is within the discretion of the trial court*" (p. 608).

Data from Question 4:

No data could be ascertained.

Data from Question 5:

> ". . . *the programs and facilities available to Otis were not likely to rehabilitate him*" (p. 609).

Data from Question 6:

> ". . . *the decision to treat 'serious' offenders different from 'non-serious' offenders is neither arbitrary nor irrational*" (p. 613).

> ". . . *greater protection from serious offenders* . . ." (p. 613).

Data from Question 7:

> "*Society demands greater protection from serious offenders, such as those who commit capital murder* . . ." (p. 613).

State v. McCracken

Data from Question 1:

> "*It is a balancing test by which public protection and societal security are* . . . *weighed against the practical and nonproblematical rehabilitation of the juvenile*" (p. 247).

> ". . . *it is not appropriate that Mr. McCracken be treated as a juvenile because of the extreme risk of danger that he presents to himself and society*" (p. 248).

> "*In spite of McCracken's youthful age at the time of the crime, the extreme violence perpetrated upon the victim and the protection of the public in light of McCracken's poor psychiatric prognosis lead us to conclude that the district court did not abuse its discretion when it denied McCracken's motion to transfer to the juvenile court*" (p. 249).

Data from Question 2:

> "*There are no weighted factors and no prescribed method by which more or less weight is assigned to each specific factor*" (p. 247).

> ". . . *the offense for which McCracken was brought to trial was of a particularly violent and aggressive nature*" (p. 248).

Data from Question 3:

> ". . . *the crime involved extreme violence, which favored retaining jurisdiction* . . ." (p. 247).

"The record therefore reveals that the district court's decision to retain jurisdiction rested, to a great extent, upon the nature of the offense with which McCracken was charged" (p. 249).

Data from Question 4:

"... the type of treatment that McCracken would be most amenable to is a at a youth facility, which favored transferring jurisdiction to the juvenile court ..." (p. 247).

"... McCracken's age of 13 years favored transferring jurisdiction ..." (p. 247).

"... McCracken had no prior criminal history, which also favored transferring the case to juvenile court ..." (p. 247).

"McCracken's sophistication and maturity was unclear ..." (p. 247).

Data from Question 5:

"... without question the best interests of the juvenile and the security of the public require that the district court retain jurisdiction, especially since the crime was so violent and McCracken's psychiatric prognosis was so poor" (p. 248).

Data from Question 6:

"... the best interests of the juvenile and security of the public [(factor 8)] without question [weigh] in favor of the Court continuing the court here in the District Court, because of the extremely violent nature of the actions that occurred" (p. 248).

"... McCracken should 'be held accountable through proceedings in the adult criminal justice system for effective deterrence of future antisocial misconduct ...'" (p. 249).

Data from Question 7:

"... security of the public ..." (p. 248).

"... deterrence of future antisocial misconduct ..." (p. 249).

Williams v. State

Data from Question 1:

"... Williams's offenses were serious; that they were committed in an aggressive, violent, and premeditated manner ..." (p. 161).

"... the protection of society required prosecution in the criminal division of circuit court" (p. 162).

Data from Question 2:

"... evidence showing that Williams had great culpability in a serious crime..." (pp. 164–165).

Data from Question 3:

"Dr. Deyoub concluded that Williams had no mental disease or defect, was competent to proceed to trial, had no problems understanding the criminality of his actions, and had the ability to conform his conduct to the law" (p. 161).

Data from Question 4:

"... Williams claims that because of his age, I.Q., immaturity and lack of sophistication, mental retardation, and ability to be rehabilitated, the circuit court's decision to refuse transfer was clearly erroneous" (p. 164).

"... Dr. Deyoub did testify that Williams's I.Q. was 'borderline,' meaning that Williams was functioning intellectually at a lower-than-average range" (p. 161).

Data from Question 5:

"The trial court failed to make a written finding on factor seven, which requires the court to consider 'whether there are facilities or programs available to the judge of the juvenile division of circuit court that are likely to rehabilitate the juvenile ..." (p. 163).

Data from Question 6:

"... protection of society ..." (p. 162).

Data from Question 7:

"... protection of society ..." (p. 162).

State v. Nevels

Date from Question 1:

". . . *in addition to considering the defendant's age, we 'are obliged to consider protection for the public and deterrence'*" (p. 53).

". . . *dealing with Nevels in the juvenile court system might diminish the seriousness of the offense*" (p. 48).

". . . *if Nevels' case were to have been transferred to the juvenile court, he might have viewed the transfer as his manipulation of the system and not take responsibility for the crime*" (p. 52).

"*Rehabilitation has traditionally played a key role in the treatment of young offenders . . . Nevertheless, the concept of deterrence and the need to balance individual justice with the needs of society . . . also have a place in the juvenile justice system*" (pp. 50–51).

Data from Question 2:

"*There is no arithmetical computation or formula required in a court's consideration of the statutory criteria of factors*" (p. 50).

". . . *the court need not resolve every factor against the juvenile*" (p. 50).

"*The statutory criteria or factors of . . . disclose a balancing test by which public protection and societal security are weighed against practical and not problematic rehabilitation of the juvenile*" (p. 50).

Data from Question 3:

"*Nevels has repeatedly violated the law and performed other antisocial acts, culminating in the very violent and cruel beating . . .*" (p. 51).

Data from Question 4:

"*Cole stated that Nevels' personality problems revolved around Nevels' lack of identity in that Nevels engages in negative behavior which makes him feel more secure about his black, male identity and which secures acceptance in his peer groups*" (p. 46).

". . . *Nevels is insecure and 'less mature than a 15 year old'*" (p. 46).

"*Cole was of the opinion that Nevels is treatable because he does not yet have a fixed personality . . . has a strong need for acceptance and to feel worthwhile . . .*" (p. 46).

"*According to Cole, the failure to treat Nevels would result in his 'becoming much more of a hardened, antisocial type'*" (p. 46).

"... *Nevels suffers from several disorders and disabilities, including a mixed development disorder involving several speech-and language-base learning disabilities ... a 'conduct disorder socialized aggressive,' which means Nevels is aggressive during periods of anxiety and has difficulty in conforming his behavior to the norms of society; a major depressive disorder ... and an adolescent identity disorder which means Nevels is 'still ... in the process of forming his own identity, [is] very immature ....'"* (p. 44).

"*Palombi warned that mainstreaming Nevels into an adult prison population 'would probably be [devastating]'"* (p. 45).

"*Palombi opined that Nevels' disorders are treatable as evidenced by his favorable response to treatment ..."* (p. 45).

Date from Question 5:

"*The district court was apparently not convinced that Nevels could be rehabilitated within the time the juvenile court would retain jurisdiction over him"* (p. 51).

"*As the trier of fact, the district court was not required to take the opinions of experts as binding upon it"* (p. 51).

"*... if Nevels' case were to have been transferred to the juvenile court, he might have viewed the transfer as his manipulation of the system and not take responsibility for the crime"* (p. 52).

"*... Palombi also acknowledged that neither he nor any other mental health professional could predict an individual's future dangerousness"* (p. 45).

Data from Question 6:

"*... the concept of deterrence and the need to balance individual justice with the needs of society"* (p. 51).

"*... effective deterrence of future antisocial misconduct"* (p. 51).

"*... protection for the public and deterrence"* (p. 53).

Data from Question 7:

"*... the concept of deterrence and the need to balance individual justice with the needs of society"* (p. 51).

"*... effective deterrence of future antisocial misconduct"* (p. 51).

"*... protection for the public and deterrence"* (p. 53).

"*... the facilities available to the juvenile court would not provide enough protection to the public"* (p. 52).

Bravil v. State

Data from Question 1:

". . . there is no absolute right conferred by common law, constitution, or otherwise, requiring children to be treated in a special system for juvenile offenders" (p. 287).

"It is not unreasonable for the legislature to treat children who commit serious crimes as adults in order to protect societal goals" (p. 288).

"The legislature could reasonably have determined that for some crimes the rehabilitative aspect of juvenile court must give way to punishment" (p. 288).

"The legislature was entitled to conclude that the parens patriae function of the juvenile system would not work for certain juveniles, or that society demanded greater protection from these offenders than that provided by that system" (p. 288).

Data from Question 2:

"The legislature has the power to determine who, if anyone, is entitled to treatment as a juvenile" (p. 287).

". . . the discretion of a prosecutor in deciding whether and how to prosecute is absolute in our system of criminal justice" (p. 289).

Data from Question 3:

"Doubtless the Florida legislature considered carefully the rise in the number of crimes committed by juveniles as well as the growing recidivist rate among this group" (p. 288).

Data from Question 4:

". . . it allows the state to bypass a hearing on the suitability of adult sanctions by securing an indictment" (p. 288).

"Section 985.225 does not require a court to hold a hearing to decide whether adult sanctions are appropriate" (p. 288).

"Section 985.225 applies to '[a] child of any age who is charged with a violation of state law punishable by death or life imprisonment . . . It does not differentiate between age groups'" (p. 289).

Data from Question 5:

No data could be ascertained.

Data from Question 6:

> "*. . . interest in crime deterrence and public safety*" (p. 288).

> "*. . . protect societal goals*" (p. 288).

Data from Question 7:

> "*. . . interest in crime deterrence and public safety*" (p. 288).

> "*. . . protect societal goals . . . society demanded greater protection from these offenders than that provided by that system*" (p. 288).

APPENDIX B

Plain Meaning Results

Madrid v. Gomez

Data from Question 1:

"By virtue of their conviction, inmates forfeit many of their constitutional liberties and rights . . ." (p. 1244).

"all humans are composed of more than flesh and bone—even those who, because of unlawful and deviant behavior, must be locked away not only from their fellow citizens, but from other inmates as well" (p. 1261).

". . . it is beyond any serious dispute that mental health is a need as essential to a meaningful human existence as other basic physical demands our bodies may make for shelter, warmth or sanitation" (p. 1261)

". . . the general concept of segregating inmates for disciplinary or security reasons is a well established and penologically justified practice" (p. 1261).

"it is not the Court's function to pass judgment on the policy choices of prison officials" (p. 1262).

"On the one hand, a condition that is sufficiently harmful to inmates or otherwise reprehensible to civilized society will at some point yield to constitutional constraints, even if the condition has some penological justification. Thus, defendants' insistence that the SHU is "working"

as a secure environment for disruptive prisoners does not and cannot determine whether the SHU passes constitutional muster. No prison, for example, can deprive inmates of a basic human need, even though the underlying conditions might otherwise arguably promote some penological objective. On the other hand, a condition or other prison measure that has little or no penological value may offend constitutional values upon a lower showing of injury or harm" (pp. 1262–1263).

Data from Question 2:

"As the Supreme Court has made quite clear, we can not, consistent with contemporary notions of humanity and decency, forcibly incarcerate prisoners under conditions that will, or very likely will, make them seriously physically ill. Helling, 125 L. Ed. 2d 22, 113 S. Ct. 2475. Surely, these same standards will not tolerate conditions that are likely to make inmates seriously mentally ill" (p. 1261).

"The decision to segregate inmates who threaten the security of the general population falls well within defendants' far ranging discretion to manage California's prison population" (p. 1261).

"Defendants are thus entitled to design and operate the SHU consistent with the penal philosophy of their choosing, absent constitutional violations. Peterkin v. Jeffes, 855 F.2d 1021, 1033 (3rd Cir. 1988). They may impose conditions that are 'restrictive and even harsh' Farmer, 114 S. Ct. at 1977 (quoting Rhodes, 452 U.S. at 347, 101 S. Ct. at 2399); they may emphasize idleness, deterrence, and deprivation over rehabilitation. This is not a matter for judicial review or concern unless the evidence demonstrates that conditions are so extreme as to violate basic concepts of humanity and deprive inmates of a minimal level of life's basic necessities" (p. 1262).

". . . the very nature of prison confinement may have a deleterious impact on the mental state of prisoners, for reasons that are self-evident" (p. 1262).

". . . if the particular conditions of segregation being challenged are such that they inflict a serious mental illness, greatly exacerbate mental illness, or deprive inmates of their sanity, then defendants have deprived inmates of a basic necessity of human existence—indeed, they have crossed into the realm of psychological torture" (p. 1263).

". . . the conditions of extreme social isolation and reduced environmental stimulation found in the Pelican Bay SHU will likely inflict some degree of psychological trauma upon most inmates confined there for more than brief periods" (p. 1265).

Data from Question 3:

". . . our jurisprudence is clear: while incarceration may extinguish or curtail many rights, the Eighth Amendment's protection against cruel and unusual punishment still retains its 'full force' behind prison doors" (pp. 1244–1245).

". . . the Constitution imposes 'a corresponding duty to assume some responsibility for his safety and general well being'" (p. 1245).

". . . government officials must ensure that prisons . . . do not degenerate into places that violate basic standards of decency and humanity" (p. 1245).

". . . there is nothing per se improper about segregating inmates, even for lengthy or indefinite terms" (p. 1261).

". . . absent a showing of constitutional infringement, courts may not substitute their judgment or otherwise interfere with decisions made by prison officials" (p. 1262).

". . . the 'psychological pain' that results from idleness in segregation is not sufficient to implicate the Eighth Amendment" (p. 1262).

". . . giving defendants the wide-ranging deference they are owed in these matters, we can not say that the conditions overall lack any penological justification" (p. 1263).

"The Eighth Amendment simply does not guarantee that inmates will not suffer some psychological effects from incarceration or segregation" (p. 1263).

". . . the totality of the SHU conditions may be harsher than necessary to accommodate the needs of the institution with respect to these populations. However, giving defendants the wide-ranging deference they are owed in these matters, we can not say that the conditions overall lack any penological justification" (p. 1263).

". . . while the conditions in the SHU may press the outer bounds of what most humans can psychologically tolerate, the record does not satisfactorily demonstrate that there is a sufficiently high risk to all inmates of incurring a serious mental illness from exposure to conditions in the SHU to find that the conditions constitute a per se deprivation of a basic necessity of life" (p. 1267).

". . . continued confinement in the SHU, under present conditions, constitutes cruel and unusual punishment in violation of the Eighth Amendment for two categories of inmates: those who are already mentally ill and those who, as identified above, are at an unreasonably high risk of suffering serious mental illness as a result of present conditions" (p. 1267).

Data from Question 4:

"*A significant number of inmates at Pelican Bay, in both the SHU and the general population section of the prison, suffer from serious mental health problems*" (p. 1215).

"*Defendants were also aware that such conditions could pose a significant risk to the mental health of inmates, particularly for those who are mentally ill or otherwise at a high risk for suffering substantial mental deterioration in the SHU*" (p. 1236).

Data from Question 5:

"*Treatment for seriously ill inmates is primarily limited to medication management through use of antipsychotic or psychotropic drugs and intensive outpatient treatment is not available. The lack of staffing is particularly problematic in the SHU. As Dr. Dvoskin testified, current staffing levels are not sufficient to enable the mental health staff to quickly and effectively respond when inmates exhibit serious mental health problems in the SHU*" (p. 1218).

Data from Question 6:

". . . *those who have transgressed the law are still fellow human beings—most of whom will one day return to society. Even those prisoners at the 'bottom of the social heap . . . have, nonetheless, a human dignity'*" (p. 1244).

". . . *our jurisprudence is clear: while incarceration may extinguish or curtail many rights, the Eighth Amendment's protection against cruel and unusual punishment still retains its 'full force' behind prison doors*" (pp. 1244–1245).

". . . *the mental impact of a challenged condition should be considered in conjunction with penological considerations*" (p. 1262).

"*A risk this grave—this shocking and indecent—simply has no place in civilized society. It is surely not one "today's society [would] choose to tolerate*" (p. 1266).

"*Conditions in the SHU may well hover on the edge of what is humanly tolerable for those with normal resilience, particularly when endured for extended periods of time. They do not, however, violate exacting Eighth Amendment standards, except for the specific population subgroups identified in this opinion*" (p. 1280).

Data from Question 7:

"... those who have transgressed the law are still fellow human beings—most of whom will one day return to society. Even those prisoners at the 'bottom of the social heap . . . . have, nonetheless, a human dignity' " (p. 1244).

"... in a country such as ours, which aspires to the highest standards of civilization, there is simply no place for abuse and mistreatment, even in the darkest of jailhouse cells" (p. 1245).

Scarver v. Litscher

Data from Question 1:

"It is a fair inference that conditions at Supermax aggravated the symptoms of Scarver's mental illness and by doing so inflicted severe physical and especially mental suffering" (p. 975).

"... inmates . . . like Scarver are . . . undeterrable" (p. 976).

"There is no evidence . . . that defendants knew . . . that he would be at risk of severe distress. Probably they should have known, but that would make them guilty merely of negligence and not of deliberate indifference" (p. 975).

"Prison authorities must be given considerable latitude in the design of measures for controlling homicidal maniacs without exacerbating their manias beyond what is necessary for security. It is a delicate balance" (p. 976).

"Federal judges must always be circumspect in imposing their ideas about civilized and effective prison administration on state prison officials . . ." (p. 976).

"... federal judges know little about the management of prisons . . ." (p. 977).

Data from Question 2:

"Scarver is schizophrenic and delusional, and, unlike most schizophrenics, extremely dangerous. He has murdered three people, two of them in prison . . ." (p. 973).

"The murderous ingenuity of murderous inmates, especially in states such as Wisconsin that do not have capital punishment, so that inmates who like Scarver are already serving life terms are undeterrable, cannot be overestimated" (p. 976).

"The Constitution does not speak with precision to the issue of prison conditions . . ." (p. 976).

Data from Question 3:

"Measures reasonably taken to protect inmates and staff from him may unavoidably aggravate his psychosis . . . the measures would not violate the Constitution" (p. 976).

". . . managerial judgments generally are the province of other branches of government than the judicial . . ." (p. 977).

". . . it is unseemly for federal courts to tell a state . . . how to run its prison system" (p. 977).

Data from Question 4:

". . . the treatment of a mentally ill prisoner who also happens to have murdered two other inmates is much more complicated than the treatment of a harmless lunatic . . ." (p. 976).

"The constant illumination of the cells disturbs psychotics. And without audiotapes or a radio or any other source of sound Scarver could not still the voices in his head" (pp. 974–975).

"The Constitution does not speak with precision to the issue of prison conditions . . ." (p. 976).

Data from Question 5:

"Maybe there is some well-known protocol for dealing with the Scarvers of this world, though probably there is not (we have found none, and his lawyer has pointed us to none) . . ." (p. 976).

Data from Question 6:

". . . inmates . . . like Scarver are . . . undeterrable" (p. 976).

". . . it is unseemly for federal courts to tell a state . . . how to run its prison system" (p. 977).

". . . protect other inmates or guards from Scarver or Scarver from himself . . ." (p. 977).

Data from Question 7:

No data could be ascertained.

Jones 'El v. Berge

Data from Question 1:

"Confinement in a supermaximum security prison such as Supermax is known to cause severe psychiatric morbidity, disability, suffering and mortality" (p. 1101).

"Although these inmates may be manipulating staff, this does not mean that they are not also seriously mentally ill" (p. 1118).

Data from Question 2:

"Seriously mentally ill inmates have difficulty following the rules necessary to advance up the level system and, as a result, find themselves "stuck" in Levels One, sometimes Two and only rarely Three" (p. 1101).

"Supermax was built to respond to a perceived need by wardens for an increased number of segregation cells for dangerous and recalcitrant inmates" (p. 1103).

Data from Question 3:

". . . conditions at Supermax can lead to the gradual deterioration of inmates prone to mental illness, I trust that defendants . . . will conduct their own monitoring with increased awareness of the adverse effects of the restrictive conditions at Supermax on those who are ill-equipped to adapt to them" (p. 1125).

"The Prison Litigation Reform Act limits the scope of preliminary injunctive relief available in challenges to prison conditions" (p. 1116).

"Several features of Supermax are particularly damaging to inmates with serious mental illnesses. The almost total sensory deprivation in Levels One and Two is relentless: inmates are kept confined alone in their cells for all but four hours a week. The exercise cell is devoid of equipment. The constant illumination is disorienting, as is the difficulty in knowing the time of day. The vestibule architecture and solid boxcar doors prevent any incidental interaction between inmates and guards. No programming is offered in Level One; the limited programming in Level Two takes place on a solitary basis at the door of each prisoner's cell rather than in a different setting or with other prisoners" (p. 1118).

"If the purpose of monitoring is not to identify seriously mentally ill inmates and transfer them from Supermax, all the monitoring in the world would not protect these inmates from the harshly isolating conditions of confinement" (p. 1122).

Data from Question 4:

"Many of the severe conditions serve no legitimate penological interest; they can only be considered punishment for punishment's sake" (p. 1117).

"Defendants initially had a policy that no mentally ill prisoners would be housed at Supermax but abandoned that policy in the year 2000" (p. 1115).

". . . it is well settled that the Eighth Amendment protects the mental health of prisoners no less than their physical health" (p. 1117).

". . . the screening process is not a reasonable step taken to prevent the risk of harm in sending seriously mentally ill inmates to Supermax" (p. 1122).

Data from Question 5:

"Supermax was designed to house especially disruptive and recalcitrant prisoners but not mentally ill ones" (p. 1118).

"They are given no programming unless they progress out of the lower levels of the incentive program and they receive limited psychiatric support" (p. 1117).

"Kupers and Nathan are both of the opinion that no amount of staffing would counteract the isolating effect of the physical layout at Supermax" (p. 1118).

". . . seriously mentally ill inmates do not have access to the programming because they are not able to control their behavior to reach higher levels" (p. 1120).

Data from Question 6:

". . . I decline to order the monitoring of Supermax inmates on a monthly basis. This requirement would interfere much more significantly with defendants' management of the institution than a one-time assessment of all inmates" (p. 1125).

"By ordering the evaluation of these segments of the population only, the court interferes in the management of Supermax to a minimal degree yet casts the net wide enough to catch any seriously mentally ill inmates who are stuck at Supermax because of their disability" (p. 1125).

"Balancing of harms" (p. 1123).

"Transferring five prisoners would not burden the department logistically or financially" (p. 1123).

"Defendants assert that an order from this court requiring the transfer of seriously mentally ill inmates is not the least intrusive means of alleviating the problems the inmates are experiencing. Instead, defendants suggest, increasing the mental health staff would be a way to lessen the court's interference with prison management. I disagree. I am convinced that the staffing ratio is not the sole factor making up the potentially damaging conditions for mentally ill inmates; the physical architecture of Supermax and the customs and policies also contribute to the conditions" (pp. 1123–1124).

"Although I recognize that defendants should be afforded due deference, I conclude that it does not overstep these bounds to order that Prisoners 1 through 5 not be housed at Supermax" (p. 1124).

"Defendants object to this form of relief for the same reason they object to the request to transfer seriously mentally ill inmates: the court should refrain from interfering in prison management. However, the potential harm to yet unidentified seriously mentally ill inmates is just as detrimental as to those who have already been identified" (p. 1124).

Data from Question 7:

". . . the public interest is not served by housing seriously mentally ill inmates at Supermax under conditions in which they risk irreparable emotional damage and, in some cases, a risk of death by suicide" (p. 1125).

". . . the public interest will be served by protecting the Eighth Amendment rights of inmates housed at Supermax" (p. 1125).

Goff v. Harper

Data from Question 1:

"the Court notes initially, Justice Douglas's pronouncement that, 'The Eighth Amendment expresses the revulsion of civilized man against barbarous acts—the 'cry of horror' against man's inhumanity to his fellow man.' Along these same lines, Justice Brennan described a court's duty in Eighth Amendment cases as the need to determine 'whether a challenged punishment comports with human dignity' (pp. 111–112).

". . . deliberate indifference to serious medical needs of prisoners constitutes the unnecessary and wonton infliction of pain proscribed by the Eighth Amendment" (pp. 113–114).

". . . mentally ill or mentally disordered inmates meet the objective component of an Eighth Amendment claim because the courts have *found that mental problems are included in the category of 'serious medical needs'"* (p. 117).

"The Court is persuaded that the above analysis is sufficient to show that Dr. Loeffelholz and those prison officials he described as his bosses, had knowledge that mental health needs of inmates with mental health disorders at ISP were not being met and were deliberately indifferent to the situation" (p. 120).

"This Court, as is the Eighth Circuit, is 'keenly aware . . . that federal courts owe great deference to the expertise of the officials who perform the always difficult and often thankless task of running a prison'" (p. 153).

"The Court does not pretend that it knows more than the men and women who run the Penitentiary about how best to eliminate the constitutional violations described" (p. 153).

"The Court's job is only to identify constitutional violations if any exist; it is in the province of the Penitentiary's officials to attend to those violations" (p. 153).

"The Court is not attempting to run or micromanage the prisons" (p. 157).

"Iowa should be ashamed that such conditions have not been improved upon or terminated. This Court has the choice of ignoring the situation or directing the State to submit an 'improvement plan' on its own. This is really the only course this Court believes it can take" (p. 157).

Data from Question 2:

"The Court could have easily taken the position that a hands-off position as to these violations is the only way to go based on today's law-and-order mentality" (p. 156).

"This Court has the choice of ignoring the situation or directing the State to submit an 'improvement plan' on its own" (p. 157).

Data from Question 3:

"[T]he defendants have and are violating the Eighth Amendment rights of those inmates who are mentally ill or mentally disordered because they have acted with deliberate indifference to the serious medical need these inmates have for the treatment they would receive in a special needs unit" (p. 129).

"[T]he court is not persuaded that the extraordinarily long lockup sentences the Penitentiary assigns by themselves violate the cruel and unusual punishment clause of the Eighth Amendment" (p. 153).

"*[T]he Court is unpersuaded that the small size of the cells in which lockup inmates serve twenty-three or twenty-four hours a day are small enough to violate the Eighth Amendment's cruel and unusual punishment clause*" (p. 153).

"*pursuant to the recently enacted Prison Litigation Reform Act, Prospective relief in any civil action with respect to prison conditions shall extend no further than necessary to correct the violation of the Federal right of a particular plaintiff or plaintiffs. The court shall not grant or approve any prospective relief unless the court finds that such relief is narrowly drawn, extends no further than necessary to correct the violation of the Federal right, and is the least intrusive means necessary to correct the violation of the Federal right. The court shall give substantial weight to any adverse impact on public safety or the operation of a criminal justice system caused by relief.*

18 U.S.C. § 3626(a)(1)(A) (1994). Asking the Penitentiary officials to bear this in mind, the Court will order Penitentiary officials to prepare a plan to alleviate the enumerated constitutional violations. This approach will serve justice with a minimum of judicial intervention and provide prison officials with the maximum possible discretion to manage their own institution" (pp. 155–156).

Data from Question 4:

"*Dr. Loeffelholz testified there is a great demand for a special needs program at the Penitentiary which can handle maximum security inmates*" (p. 118).

"*[T]hose inmates with mental health disorders at ISP who are not receiving treatment for their needs, are being held under conditions which violate the Eighth Amendment*" (p. 120).

"*The State has had opportunities to rectify or partially rectify the situation and has done nothing*" (p. 156).

Data from Question 5:

"*[T]here is a great demand for a special needs program at the Penitentiary which can handle maximum security inmates. The Court also found Dr. Loeffelholz has expressed this professional opinion to his bosses (presumably the director of the Iowa Department of Corrections) but no action has been taken. Then-Warden Acevedo, testified that the Illinois Department of Corrections, his immediate past employer, had special needs programs such as separate wings of prisons devoted to taking care of inmates with mental problems, that were far superior to those established by the Iowa Department of Corrections. He said, when a facility devotes itself exclusively to taking care of mentally ill patients, it can provide much better psychiatric care"* (p. 118).

"The director of the special needs program at Oakdale, Lowell Brandt, testified his program is designed to help inmates who are unable to reside in the general population of their prison. He said many of these inmates have mental problems and the special needs program is run similarly to a mental health hospital. Brandt testified it is difficult for inmates at the Iowa State Penitentiary to be placed in Oakdale's special needs program for two reasons. First, Brandt said the special needs unit is not equipped to handle violent, aggressive or high risk inmates that are commonly housed at the Penitentiary. Second, Brandt testified the waiting list for spaces in the special needs unit is often more than a year long. Moreover, some Penitentiary mental health professionals such as Hassan and Brown testified they rarely, if ever, recommend any inmates for placement in the Oakdale special needs program. Counselor Martin Rung testified he has only recommended two inmates for the special needs unit in the years he has worked at the Penitentiary. Clearly, most inmates in lockup at ISP will never be admitted to the special needs unit at Oakdale and will never be able to take advantage of its services" (pp. 119–120).

Data from Question 6:

"There is no doubt that those inmates at the Iowa State Penitentiary whom the Department of Corrections medical staff has found to be mentally ill or mentally disordered have objectively serious health needs" (p. 116).

"Based on the present aura that everybody must take a tough-on-crime position, it is unlikely that these constitutional violations would be corrected by Iowa officials in the foreseeable future" (pp. 156–157).

Data from Question 7:

No data could be ascertained.

Vasquez v. Frank

Data from Question 1:

"Vasquez suffers from emotional distress, depression, anxiety, and 'other psychological problems'" (p. 540).

". . . his cell in segregation was illuminated 24 hours a day. Although
he was able to lower the lighting, he could not turn it off completely.
He alleges that the constant illumination aggravated his mental
illness and caused him to suffer from insomnia, migraines, eye pain,
and blurry vision. Even though he received medications to fight the
headaches and psychological effects, prison officials would not allow
him to extinguish the light" (p. 540).

"The excessive heat also 'increase[d] the interaction, adverse reactions,
and side effects' of his psychotropic medications" (p. 540).

"Vasquez's allegations about the lighting and air quality in his cell
are not so fantastical that the district court could dismiss them out
of hand" (p. 540).

". . . constant cell illumination may inflict severe suffering on mentally
ill inmates" (p. 541).

Data from Question 2:

"The district court dismissed these claims along with the rest of
Vasquez's complaint. The court reasoned that Vasquez's constitutional
claim about the illumination in his cell cannot succeed because in
another lawsuit involving a different plaintiff the court found that the
lighting in the Health and Segregation Complex at Waupun does not
violate the Eighth Amendment" (p. 540).

"Prison officials violate the Eighth Amendment when they deliberately
ignore a serious medical condition . . . or create 'an unreasonable risk
of serious damage' to an inmate's future health" (p. 540).

"his claim is not barred merely because the district court decided the
same issue in an unrelated case in which Vasquez was not a party"
(p. 541).

Data from Question 3:

"Although injunctive relief is no longer necessary or appropriate
because documents submitted by Vasquez with his supplemental brief
to this court indicate that he has been released from segregation, he
may still be entitled to damages" (p. 541).

Data from Question 4:

"He filed grievances and told medical personnel about these
conditions, but prison officials did not rectify the problem for
over three years" (p. 540).

"*A district court may strongly suspect that an inmate's claims lack merit, but that is not a legitimate ground for dismissal*" (p. 540).

"*Vasquez alleged that he is mentally ill and that the constant illumination in his cell aggravated his mental illness, caused him headaches, and prevented him from sleeping*" (p. 541).

"*Prison officials were aware of these adverse reactions but refused to extinguish the light*" (p. 541).

Data from Question 5:

No data could be ascertained.

Data from Question 6:

"*There will come a time in this litigation when Vasquez will be required to set forth specific facts, but dismissal under 28 U.S.C. § 1915A was premature. Accordingly, we VACATE the judgment as to Vasquez's Eighth Amendment claims concerning the cell lighting and ventilation and REMAND for further proceedings on those claims*" (p. 541).

Data from Question 7:

No data could be ascertained.

Torres Et Al. v. Commissioner of Correction Et Al

Data from Question 1:

"*. . . whether prison conditions are sufficiently harmful to establish an Eighth Amendment violation, is a purely legal determination for the court to make . . . expert opinion regarding what constitutes cruel and unusual punishment is entitled to little weight*" (p. 614).

"*there is no factual dispute over the conditions endured by DDU inmates . . . the only arguable dispute concerned the extent to which these conditions generally caused inmates' psychological problems. In these circumstances the judge properly concluded that no genuine issue of material fact existed*" (p. 614).

"*the judge acted properly in allowing the defendants' motion for summary judgment*" (p. 615).

"*The judge's findings and the parties' stipulation demonstrate that DDU confinement, while uncomfortable, is a far cry from the 'barbaric' conditions*" (p. 617).

Data from Question 2:

"*To succeed on an Eighth Amendment claim, a plaintiff-inmate must demonstrate that (1) a prison's conditions of confinement present 'a substantial risk of serious harm'; and (2) prison officials acted with 'deliberate indifference' to inmate health or safety*" (pp. 613–614). "*If conditions of confinement harsher than those posed by DDU did not offend the Eighth Amendment, it follows that DDU's confinement is likewise constitutional*" (p. 615).

Data from Question 3:

"*As the United States Court of Appeals for the First Circuit has observed, 'federal appellate decisions during the past decade which have focused on the factor of segregated confinement and lack of inmate contact reveals to us a widely shared disinclination to declare even very lengthy periods of segregated confinement beyond the pale of minimally civilized conduct on the part of prison authorities. Similarly, in Libby v. Commissioner of Correction, 385 Mass. 421, 431, 432 N.E.2d 486 (1982), we held that a prison isolation unit whose conditions were more restrictive than those in DDU did not offend the Eighth Amendment because its inmates were provided adequate food, clothing, sanitation, medical care, and communication with others.' Libby, 385 Mass. at 431-432. 'The 'isolation' and 'loneliness' of which the plaintiffs complain,' we concluded, 'is not in and of itself unconstitutional'*" (p. 615).

Data from Question 4:

"*In support of their claim that a factual dispute exists the plaintiffs cite the affidavit of Dr. Stuart Grassian, who opined that DDU's conditions of confinement can cause severe psychiatric harm. The plaintiffs therefore contend that a genuine issue exists as to whether DDU's conditions pose 'a substantial risk of serious harm'* (p. 614).

Data from Question 5:

No data could be ascertained.

Data from Question 6:

No data could be ascertained.

Data from Question 7:

No data could be ascertained.

APPENDIX C

Plain Meaning Results

Doe v. Smith

Data from Question 1:

"We conclude, as did the District Court and the Court of Appeals, that the intent of the Alaska Legislature was to create a civil, nonpunitive regime" (p. 96).

"The fact that Alaska posts the information on the Internet does not alter our conclusion. It must be acknowledged that notice of a criminal conviction subjects the offender to public shame, the humiliation increasing in proportion to the extent of the publicity. And the geographic reach of the Internet is greater than anything which could have been designed in colonial times. These facts do not render Internet notification punitive" (p. 99).

"The State's Web site does not provide the public with means to shame the offender by, say, posting comments underneath his record" (p. 99).

"The Act imposes no physical restraint, and so does not resemble the punishment of imprisonment, which is the paradigmatic affirmative disability or restraint" (p. 100).

"As stated in Hawker: 'Doubtless, one who has violated the criminal law may thereafter reform and become in fact possessed of a good moral character. But the legislature has power in cases of this kind to make a rule of universal application . . . .'" (p. 103).

"A statute is not deemed punitive simply because it lacks a close or perfect fit with the nonpunitive aims it seeks to advance" (p. 103).

Data from Question 2:

". . . the stigma of Alaska's Megan's Law results not from public display for ridicule and shaming but from the dissemination of accurate information about a criminal record, most of which is already public" (p. 98).

"The Act does not restrain activities sex offenders may pursue but leaves them free to change jobs or residences" (p. 100).

"Although the public availability of the information may have a lasting and painful impact on the convicted sex offender, these consequences flow not from the Act's registration and dissemination provisions, but from the fact of conviction, already a matter of public record" (p. 101).

". . . offenders subject to the Alaska statute are free to move where they wish and to live and work as other citizens, with no supervision. Although registrants must inform the authorities after they change their facial features (such as growing a beard), borrow a car, or seek psychiatric treatment, they are not required to seek permission to do so" (p. 101).

"The Act's rational connection to a nonpunitive purpose is a 'most significant' factor in our determination that the statute's effects are not punitive" (p. 102).

"The duration of the reporting requirements is not excessive. Empirical research on child molesters, for instance, has shown that, 'contrary to conventional wisdom, most reoffenses do not occur within the first several years after release,' but may occur 'as late as 20 years following release'" (p. 104).

Data from Question 3:

"These precedents instruct us that even if the objective of the Act is consistent with the purposes of the Alaska criminal justice system, the State's pursuit of it in a regulatory scheme does not make the objective punitive" (p. 94).

"An individual seeking the information must take the initial step of going to the Department of Public Safety's Web site, proceed to the sex offender registry, and then look up the desired information. The process is more analogous to a visit to an official archive of criminal records than it is to a scheme forcing an offender to appear in public with some visible badge of past criminality. The Internet makes the

document search more efficient, cost effective, and convenient for Alaska's citizenry" (p. 99).

"Landlords and employers could conduct background checks on the criminal records of prospective employees or tenants even with the Act not in force. The record in this case contains no evidence that the Act has led to substantial occupational or housing disadvantages for former sex offenders that would not have otherwise occurred through the use of routine background checks by employers and landlords. The Court of Appeals identified only one incident from the 7-year history of Alaska's law where a sex offender suffered community hostility and damage to his business after the information he submitted to the registry became public. Id., at 987–988. This could have occurred in any event, because the information about the individual's conviction was already in the public domain" (p. 100).

"Any number of governmental programs might deter crime without imposing punishment. To hold that the mere presence of a deterrent purpose renders such sanctions 'criminal' . . . would severely undermine the Government's ability to engage in effective regulation" (p. 102).

"The Ex Post Facto Clause does not preclude a State from making reasonable categorical judgments that conviction of specified crimes should entail particular regulatory consequences" (p. 103).

"The Court of Appeals' reliance on the wide dissemination of the information is also unavailing. The Ninth Circuit highlighted that the information was available 'world-wide' and 'broadcas[t]' in an indiscriminate manner. 259 F.3d at 992. As we have explained, however, the notification system is a passive one: An individual must seek access to the information" (pp. 104–105).

"The excessiveness inquiry of our ex post facto jurisprudence is not an exercise in determining whether the legislature has made the best choice possible to address the problem it seeks to remedy. The question is whether the regulatory means chosen are reasonable in light of the nonpunitive objective. The Act meets this standard" (p. 105).

"The regulatory scheme applies only to past conduct, which was, and is, a crime. This is a necessary beginning point, for recidivism is the statutory concern. The obligations the statute imposes are the responsibility of registration, a duty not predicated upon some present or repeated violation" (p. 105).

Data from Question 4:

"The purpose and the principal effect of notification are to inform the public for its own safety, not to humiliate the offender. Widespread

public access is necessary for the efficacy of the scheme, and the attendant humiliation is but a collateral consequence of a valid regulation" (p. 99).

"The risk of recidivism posed by sex offenders is 'frightening and high'" (p. 103).

Data from Question 5:

No data could be ascertained.

Data from Question 6:

"This is the first time we have considered a claim that a sex offender registration and notification law constitutes retroactive punishment forbidden by the Ex Post Facto Clause. The framework for our inquiry, however, is well established. We must 'ascertain whether the legislature meant the statute to establish 'civil' proceedings.' Kansas v. Hendricks, 521 U.S. 346, 361, 138 L. Ed. 2d 501, 117 S. Ct. 2072 (1997). If the intention of the legislature was to impose punishment, that ends the inquiry. If, however, the intention was to enact a regulatory scheme that is civil and nonpunitive, we must further examine whether the statutory scheme is 'so punitive either in purpose or effect as to negate [the State's] intention' to deem it 'civil." Ibid. (quoting United States v. Ward, 448 U.S. 242, 248-249, 65 L. Ed. 2d 742, 100 S. Ct. 2636 (1980)). Because we 'ordinarily defer to the legislature's stated intent,' Hendricks, supra, at 361, 'only the clearest proof ' will suffice to override legislative intent and transform what has been denominated a civil remedy into a criminal penalty" (p. 92).

"Our system does not treat dissemination of truthful information in furtherance of a legitimate governmental objective as punishment. On the contrary, our criminal law tradition insists on public indictment, public trial, and public imposition of sentence. Transparency is essential to maintaining public respect for the criminal justice system, ensuring its integrity, and protecting the rights of the accused. The publicity may cause adverse consequences for the convicted defendant, running from mild personal embarrassment to social ostracism. In contrast to the colonial shaming punishments, however, the State does not make the publicity and the resulting stigma an integral part of the objective of the regulatory scheme" (pp. 98–99).

"Some colonial punishments indeed were meant to inflict public disgrace . . . [a]ny initial resemblance to early punishments is, however, misleading. Punishments such as whipping, pillory, and branding inflicted physical pain and staged a direct confrontation between the offender and the public. Even punishments that lacked the corporal

component, such as public shaming, humiliation, and banishment, involved more than the dissemination of information. They either held the person up before his fellow citizens for face-to-face shaming or expelled him from the community" (pp. 97–98).

"Although the public availability of the information may have a lasting and painful impact on the convicted sex offender, these consequences flow not from the Act's registration and dissemination provisions, but from the fact of conviction, already a matter of public record" (p. 101).

"The risk of recidivism posed by sex offenders is 'frightening and high'" (p. 103).

Data from Question 7:

"As we observed in Hendricks, where we examined an ex post facto challenge to a post-incarceration confinement of sex offenders, an imposition of restrictive measures on sex offenders adjudged to be dangerous is 'a legitimate nonpunitive governmental objective and has been historically so regarded.' 521 U.S., at 363. In this case, as in Hendricks, "nothing on the face of the statute suggests that the legislature sought to create anything other than a civil . . . scheme designed to protect the public from harm" (p. 93).

"The purpose and the principal effect of notification are to inform the public for its own safety, not to humiliate the offender. Widespread public access is necessary for the efficacy of the scheme, and the attendant humiliation is but a collateral consequence of a valid regulation" (p. 99).

"The State makes the facts underlying the offenses and the resulting convictions accessible so members of the public can take the precautions they deem necessary before dealing with the registrant" (p. 101).

"As the Court of Appeals acknowledged, the Act has a legitimate nonpunitive purpose of 'public safety, which is advanced by alerting the public to the risk of sex offenders in their community'" (pp. 102–103).

"The legislature's findings are consistent with grave concerns over the high rate of recidivism among convicted sex offenders and their dangerousness as a class. The risk of recidivism posed by sex offenders is 'frightening and high.' McKune v. Lile, 536 U.S. 24, 34, 153 L. Ed. 2d 47, 122 S. Ct. 2017 (2002); see also id., at 33 ('When convicted sex offenders reenter society, they are much more likely than any other type of offender to be rearrested for a new rape or sexual assault')" (p. 103).

Concur by Justice Thomas
Justice Thomas Concurring

Data from Question 1:

> *"As we have stated, the categorization of a proceeding as civil or criminal is accomplished by examining 'the statute on its face'"* (p. 106).

Data from Question 2:

> *". . . the determination whether a scheme is criminal or civil must be limited to the analysis of the obligations actually created by statute. See id., at 273–274 ('To the extent that the conditions result from the fact that the statute is not being applied according to its terms, the conditions are not the effect of the statute, but rather the effect of its improper implementation')"* (p. 106).

Data from Question 3:

> *No data could be ascertained.*

Data from Question 4:

> *No data could be ascertained.*

Data from Question 5:

> *No data could be ascertained.*

Data from Question 6:

> *No data could be ascertained.*

Data from Question 7:

> *No data could be ascertained.*

Concur by Justice Souter
Justice Souter Concurring

Data from Question 1:

> *"Widespread dissemination of offenders' names, photographs, addresses, and criminal history serves not only to inform the public but also to humiliate and ostracize the convicts"* (p. 109).

Data from Question 2:

No data could be ascertained.

Data from Question 3:

No data could be ascertained.

Data from Question 4:

No data could be ascertained.

Data from Question 5:

No data could be ascertained.

Data from Question 6:

"Widespread dissemination of offenders' names, photographs, addresses, and criminal history serves not only to inform the public but also to humiliate and ostracize the convicts. It thus bears some resemblance to shaming punishments that were used earlier in our history to disable offenders from living normally in the community. See, e.g., Massaro, Shame, Culture, and American Criminal Law, 89 Mich. L. Rev. 1880, 1913 (1991). While the Court accepts the State's explanation that the Act simply makes public information available in a new way, ante, at 11, the scheme does much more. Its point, after all, is to send a message that probably would not otherwise be heard, by selecting some conviction information out of its corpus of penal records and broadcasting it with a warning. Selection makes a statement, one that affects common reputation and sometimes carries harsher consequences, such as exclusion from jobs or housing, harassment, and physical harm" (p. 109).

Data from Question 7:

"Ensuring public safety is, of course, a fundamental regulatory goal, see, e.g., United States v. Salerno, 481 U.S. 739, 747, 95 L. Ed. 2d 697, 107 S. Ct. 2095 (1987), and this objective should be given serious weight in the analyses. But, at the same time, it would be naive to look no further, given pervasive attitudes toward sex offenders, see infra, at 4, n. See Weaver v. Graham, 450 U.S. 24, 29, 67 L. Ed. 2d 17, 101 S. Ct. 960 (1981) (Ex Post Facto Clause was meant to prevent 'arbitrary and potentially vindictive legislation'). The fact that the Act uses past crime as the touchstone, probably sweeping in a significant number of people

who pose no real threat to the community, serves to feed suspicion that something more than regulation of safety is going on; when a legislature uses prior convictions to impose burdens that outpace the law's stated civil aims, there is room for serious argument that the ulterior purpose is to revisit past crimes, not prevent future ones" (pp. 108–109).

Connecticut Dept. of Public Safety v. Doe

Data from Question 1:

"Sex offenders are a serious threat in this Nation." McKune v. Lile, 536 U.S. 24, 32, 153 L. Ed. 2d 47, 122 S. Ct. 2017 (2002) (plurality opinion)" (p. 4).

Data from Question 2:

"The victims of sex assault are most often juveniles," and *"when convicted sex offenders reenter society, they are much more likely than any other type of offender to be re-arrested for a new rape or sex assault."* (p. 4).

"Because the question is not properly before us, we express no opinion as to whether Connecticut's Megan's Law violates principles of substantive due process" (p. 7).

Data from Question 3:

". . . the fact that respondent seeks to prove—that he is not currently dangerous—is of no consequence under Connecticut's Megan's Law. As the DPS Website explains, the law's requirements turn on an offender's conviction alone—a fact that a convicted offender has already had a procedurally safeguarded opportunity to contest. 271 F.3d at 44 ('Individuals included within the registry are included solely by virtue of their conviction record and state law' (emphasis added)). No other fact is relevant to the disclosure of registrants' information. Conn. Gen. Stat. §§ 54–257, 54–258 (2001). Indeed, the disclaimer on the Website explicitly states that respondent's alleged nondangerousness simply does not matter. 271 F.3d at 44 ('[DPS] has made no determination that any individual included in the registry is currently dangerous')" (p. 7).

". . . even if respondent could prove that he is not likely to be currently dangerous, Connecticut has decided that the registry information of all sex offenders—currently dangerous or not—must be publicly disclosed" (p. 7).

Data from Question 4:

No data could be ascertained.

Data from Question 5:

No data could be ascertained.

Data from Question 6:

"Sex offenders are a serious threat in this Nation." McKune v. Lile, 536 U.S. 24, 32, 153 L. Ed. 2d 47, 122 S. Ct. 2017 (2002) (plurality opinion)" (p. 4).

Data from Question 7:

"Sex offenders are a serious threat in this Nation." McKune v. Lile, 536 U.S. 24, 32, 153 L. Ed. 2d 47, 122 S. Ct. 2017 (2002) (plurality opinion). "The victims of sex assault are most often juveniles," and "when convicted sex offenders reenter society, they are much more likely than any other type of offender to be re-arrested for a new rape or sex assault" (p. 4).

Concur by Scalia; Souter
Justice Scalia Concurring

Data from Question 1:

"I join the Court's opinion, and add that even if the requirements of Connecticut's sex offender registration law implicate a liberty interest of respondent, the categorical abrogation of that liberty interest by a validly enacted statute suffices to provide all the process that is 'due'—just as a state law providing that no one under the age of 16 may operate a motor vehicle suffices to abrogate that liberty interest" (p. 8).

". . . as the Court's opinion demonstrates, a convicted sex offender has no more right to additional 'process' enabling him to establish that he is not dangerous than (in the analogous case just suggested) a 15-year-old has a right to "process" enabling him to establish that he is a safe driver" (p. 9).

Data from Question 2:

No data could be ascertained.

Data from Question 3:

No data could be ascertained.

Data from Question 4:

No data could be ascertained.

Data from Question 5:

No data could be ascertained.

Data from Question 6:

No data could be ascertained.

Data from Question 7:

No data could be ascertained.

Justice Souter, With Whom Justice Ginsburg Joins, Concurring

Data from Question 1:

"I write separately only to note that a substantive due process claim may not be the only one still open to a test by those in the respondents' situation" (p. 9).

Data from Question 2:

"Connecticut allows certain sex offenders the possibility of avoiding the registration and reporting obligations of the statute. A court may exempt a convict from registration altogether if his offense was unconsented sexual contact, Conn. Gen. Stat. § 54–251(c) (2001), or sexual intercourse with a minor aged between 13 and 16 while the offender was more than two years older than the minor, provided the offender was under age 19 at the time of the offense, § 54–251(b). A court also has discretion to limit dissemination of an offender's registration information to law enforcement purposes if necessary to protect the identity of a victim who is related to the offender or, in the case of a sexual assault, who is the offender's spouse or cohabitor" (p. 9).

Data from Question 3:

No data could be ascertained.

Data from Question 4:

No data could be ascertained.

Data from Question 5:

No data could be ascertained.

Data from Question 6:

"The refusal to allow even the possibility of relief to, say, a 19-year-old who has consensual intercourse with a minor aged 16 is therefore a reviewable legislative determination. Today's case is no occasion to speak either to the possible merits of such a challenge or the standard of scrutiny that might be in order when considering it. I merely note that the Court's rejection of respondents' procedural due process claim does not immunize publication schemes like Connecticut's from an equal protection challenge" (p. 10).

Data from Question 7:

No data could be ascertained.

Kansas v. Hendricks

Data from Question 1:

"Kansas argues that [HN8] the Act's definition of 'mental abnormality' satisfies 'substantive' due process requirements. We agree. Although freedom from physical restraint 'has always been at the core of the liberty protected by the Due Process Clause from arbitrary governmental action,' Foucha v. Louisiana, 504 U.S. 71, 80, 118 L. Ed. 2d 437, 112 S. Ct. 1780 (1992), that liberty interest is not absolute. The Court has recognized that an individual's constitutionally protected interest in avoiding physical restraint may be overridden even in the civil context:

'[T]he liberty secured by the Constitution of the United States to every person within its jurisdiction does not import an absolute right in each person to be, at all times and in all circumstances, wholly free from restraint. There are manifold restraints to which every person is necessarily subject for the common good. On any other basis

organized society could not exist with safety to its members.' Jacobson v. Massachusetts, 197 U.S. 11, 26, 49 L. Ed. 643, 25 S. Ct. 358 (1905)" (pp. 356–357).

"It thus cannot be said that the involuntary civil confinement of a limited subclass of dangerous persons is contrary to our understanding of ordered liberty" (p. 357).

"As we have recognized, 'previous instances of violent behavior are an important indicator of future violent tendencies.' Heller v. Doe, 509 U.S. 312, 323, 125 L. Ed. 2d 257, 113 S. Ct. 2637 (1993); see also Schall v. Martin, 467 U.S. 253, 278, 81 L. Ed. 2d 207, 104 S. Ct. 2403 (1984) (explaining that 'from a legal point of view there is nothing inherently unattainable about a prediction of future criminal conduct')" (p. 358).

"The Kansas Act is plainly of a kind with these other civil commitment statutes: It requires a finding of future dangerousness, and then links that finding to the existence of a 'mental abnormality' or 'personality disorder' that makes it difficult, if not impossible, for the person to control his dangerous behavior" (p. 358).

"Contrary to Hendricks' assertion, the term 'mental illness' is devoid of any talismanic significance" (p. 359).

"To the extent that the civil commitment statutes we have considered set forth criteria relating to an individual's inability to control his dangerousness, the Kansas Act sets forth comparable criteria and Hendricks' condition doubtless satisfies those criteria" (p. 360).

"We are unpersuaded by Hendricks' argument that Kansas has established criminal proceedings" (p. 360).

"The Act's purpose is not retributive because it does not affix culpability for prior criminal conduct. Instead, such conduct is used solely for evidentiary purposes, either to demonstrate that a 'mental abnormality' exists or to support a finding of future dangerousness" (p. 362).

". . . the Kansas Act does not make a criminal conviction a prerequisite for commitment—persons absolved of criminal responsibility may nonetheless be subject to confinement under the Act" (p. 362).

"Absent a treatable mental illness, the Kansas court concluded, Hendricks could not be detained against his will. Accepting the Kansas court's apparent determination that treatment is not possible for this category of individuals does not obligate us to adopt its legal conclusions. We have already observed that, under the appropriate circumstances and when accompanied by proper procedures, incapacitation may be a legitimate end of the civil law" (pp. 365–366).

"*We hold that the Kansas Sexually Violent Predator Act comports with due process requirements and neither runs afoul of double jeopardy principles nor constitutes an exercise in impermissible ex post facto lawmaking*" (p. 371).

Data from Question 2:

"*In 1994, Kansas enacted the Sexually Violent Predator Act, which establishes procedures for the civil commitment of persons who, due to a 'mental abnormality' or a 'personality disorder,' are likely to engage in 'predatory acts of sexual violence.' Kan. Stat. Ann. § 59-29a01 et seq. (1994). The State invoked the Act for the first time to commit Leroy Hendricks, an inmate who had a long history of sexually molesting children, and who was scheduled for release from prison shortly after the Act became law*" (p. 350).

"*The Kansas Legislature enacted the Sexually Violent Predator Act (Act) in 1994 to grapple with the problem of managing repeat sexual offenders.[1] Although Kansas already had a statute addressing the involuntary commitment of those defined as 'mentally ill,' the legislature determined that existing civil commitment procedures were inadequate to confront the risks presented by 'sexually violent predators'*" (pp. 350–351).

"*The precommitment requirement of a 'mental abnormality' or 'personality disorder' is consistent with the requirements of these other statutes that we have upheld in that it narrows the class of persons eligible for confinement to those who are unable to control their dangerousness*" (p. 358).

"*Not only do 'psychiatrists disagree widely and frequently on what constitutes mental illness,' Ake v. Oklahoma, 470 U.S. 68, 81, 84 L. Ed. 2d 53, 105 S. Ct. 1087 (1985), but the Court itself has used a variety of expressions to describe the mental condition of those properly subject to civil confinement*" (p. 359).

Data from Question 3:

"*A finding of dangerousness, standing alone, is ordinarily not a sufficient ground upon which to justify indefinite involuntary commitment. We have sustained civil commitment statutes when they have coupled proof of dangerousness with the proof of some additional factor, such as a 'mental illness' or 'mental abnormality.' These added statutory requirements serve to limit involuntary civil confinement to those who suffer from a volitional impairment rendering them dangerous beyond their control*" (p. 358).

"The Kansas Act is plainly of a kind with these other civil commitment statutes: It requires a finding of future dangerousness, and then links that finding to the existence of a 'mental abnormality' or 'personality disorder' that makes it difficult, if not impossible, for the person to control his dangerous behavior" (p. 358).

". . . we have never required State legislatures to adopt any particular nomenclature in drafting civil commitment statutes. Rather, we have traditionally left to legislators the task of defining terms of a medical nature that have legal significance" (p. 359).

". . . the States have, over the years, developed numerous specialized terms to define mental health concepts. Often, those definitions do not fit precisely with the definitions employed by the medical community. The legal definitions of 'insanity' and 'competency,' for example, vary substantially from their psychiatric counterparts. See, e.g., Gerard, The Usefulness of the Medical Model to the Legal System, 39 Rutgers L. Rev. 377, 391-394 (1987) (discussing differing purposes of legal system and the medical profession in recognizing mental illness). Legal definitions, however, which must 'take into account such issues as individual responsibility . . . and competency,' need not mirror those advanced by the medical profession" (p. 359).

"Hendricks' diagnosis as a pedophile, which qualifies as a 'mental abnormality' under the Act, thus plainly suffices for due process purposes" (p. 360).

"Nothing on the face of the statute suggests that the legislature sought to create anything other than a civil commitment scheme designed to protect the public from harm" (p. 361).

"Although we recognize that a 'civil label is not always dispositive,' Allen, supra, at 369, we will reject the legislature's manifest intent only where a party challenging the statute provides 'the clearest proof' that 'the statutory scheme [is] so punitive either in purpose or effect as to negate [the State's] intention' to deem it 'civil.' United States v. Ward, 448 U.S. 242, 248-249, 65 L. Ed. 2d 742, 100 S. Ct. 2636 (1980). In those limited circumstances, we will consider the statute to have established criminal proceedings for constitutional purposes. Hendricks, however, has failed to satisfy this heavy burden" (p. 361).

"An absence of the necessary criminal responsibility suggests that the State is not seeking retribution for a past misdeed. Thus, the fact that the Act may be 'tied to criminal activity' is 'insufficient to render the statute punitive.' United States v. Ursery, 518 U.S. __ (1996) (slip op., at 24)" (p. 362).

". . . unlike a criminal statute, no finding of scienter is required to commit an individual who is found to be a sexually violent predator; instead, the commitment determination is made based on a 'mental

*abnormality' or 'personality disorder' rather than on one's criminal
intent. The existence of a scienter requirement is customarily an
important element in distinguishing criminal from civil statutes. See
Kennedy v. Mendoza-Martinez, 372 U.S. 144, 168, 9 L. Ed. 2d 644, 83
S. Ct. 554 (1963). The absence of such a requirement here is evidence
that confinement under the statute is not intended to be retributive"*
(p. 362).

*"The State has represented that an individual confined under
the Act is not subject to the more restrictive conditions placed on
state prisoners, but instead experiences essentially the same conditions
as any involuntarily committed patient in the state mental institution.
App. 50–56, 59–60. Because none of the parties argues that people
institutionalized under the Kansas general civil commitment statute
are subject to punitive conditions, even though they may be
involuntarily confined, it is difficult to conclude that persons
confined under this Act are being 'punished'"* (p. 363).

*"The State may take measures to restrict the freedom of the
dangerously mentally ill. This is a legitimate nonpunitive
governmental objective and has been historically so regarded"* (p. 363).

*"Far from any punitive objective, the confinement's duration is instead
linked to the stated purposes of the commitment, namely, to hold the
person until his mental abnormality no longer causes him to be a
threat to others"* (p. 363).

*". . . commitment under the Act is only potentially
indefinite . . . pursuant to the Act [an offender cannot] remain
confined any longer than he suffers from a mental abnormality
rendering him unable to control his dangerousness"* (p. 364).

*"The numerous procedural and evidentiary protections afforded here
demonstrate that the Kansas Legislature has taken great care to confine
only a narrow class of particularly dangerous individuals, and then
only after meeting the strictest procedural standards"* (p. 364).

*"We therefore hold that the Act does not establish criminal proceedings
and that involuntary confinement pursuant to the Act is not punitive.
Our conclusion that the Act is nonpunitive thus removes an essential
prerequisite for both Hendricks' double jeopardy and ex post facto
claims"* (p. 369).

*"Hendricks' involuntary detention does not violate the Double
Jeopardy Clause, even though that confinement may follow a prison
term. Indeed, in Baxstrom v. Herold, 383 U.S. 107, 15 L. Ed. 2d 620,
86 S. Ct. 760 (1966), we expressly recognized that civil commitment
could follow the expiration of a prison term without offending double
jeopardy principles. We reasoned that 'there is no conceivable basis for
distinguishing the commitment of a person who is nearing the end of a*

penal term from all other civil commitments.' Id., at 111–112. If an individual otherwise meets the requirements for involuntary civil commitment, the State is under no obligation to release that individual simply because the detention would follow a period of incarceration" (pp. 369–370).

"Under Blockburger, 'where the same act or transaction constitutes a violation of two distinct statutory provisions, the test to be applied to determine whether there are two offenses or only one, is whether each provision requires proof of a fact which the other does not.' Id., at 304. The Blockburger test, however, simply does not apply outside of the successive prosecution context. A proceeding under the Act does not define an 'offense,' the elements of which can be compared to the elements of an offense for which the person may previously have been convicted. Nor does the Act make the commission of a specified 'offense' the basis for invoking the commitment proceedings. Instead, it uses a prior conviction (or previously charged conduct) for evidentiary purposes to determine whether a person suffers from a 'mental abnormality' or 'personality disorder' and also poses a threat to the public. Accordingly, we are unpersuaded by Hendricks' novel application of the Blockburger test and conclude that the Act does not violate the Double Jeopardy Clause" (p. 370).

"Because the Act does not criminalize conduct legal before its enactment, nor deprive Hendricks of any defense that was available to him at the time of his crimes, the Act does not violate the Ex Post Facto Clause" (p. 371).

Data from Question 4:

"The statute thus requires proof of more than a mere predisposition to violence; rather, it requires evidence of past sexually violent behavior and a present mental condition that creates a likelihood of such conduct in the future if the person is not incapacitated" (p. 358).

Data from Question 5:

"Although the treatment program initially offered Hendricks may have seemed somewhat meager, it must be remembered that he was the first person committed under the Act. That the State did not have all of its treatment procedures in place is thus not surprising" (pp. 367–368).

Data from Question 6:

"Hendricks even conceded that, when he becomes 'stressed out,' he cannot 'control the urge' to molest children. App. 172. This admitted

lack of volitional control, coupled with a prediction of future dangerousness, adequately distinguishes Hendricks from other dangerous persons who are perhaps more properly dealt with exclusively through criminal proceedings" (p. 360).

"Those persons committed under the Act are, by definition, suffering from a 'mental abnormality' or a 'personality disorder' that prevents them from exercising adequate control over their behavior. Such persons are therefore unlikely to be deterred by the threat of confinement" (pp. 362–363).

"A State could hardly be seen as furthering a 'punitive' purpose by involuntarily confining persons afflicted with an untreatable, highly contagious disease. Accord Compagnie Francaise de Navigation a Vapeur v. Louisiana Bd. of Health, 186 U.S. 380, 46 L. Ed. 1209, 22 S. Ct. 811 (1902) (permitting involuntary quarantine of persons suffering from communicable diseases). Similarly, it would be of little value to require treatment as a precondition for civil confinement of the dangerously insane when no acceptable treatment existed. To conclude otherwise would obligate a State to release certain confined individuals who were both mentally ill and dangerous simply because they could not be successfully treated for their afflictions" (p. 366).

". . . critical language in the Act itself demonstrates that the Secretary of Social and Rehabilitation Services, under whose custody sexually violent predators are committed, has an obligation to provide treatment to individuals like Hendricks. § 59-29a07(a) ('If the court or jury determines that the person is a sexually violent predator, the person shall be committed to the custody of the secretary of social and rehabilitation services for control, care and treatment until such time as the person's mental abnormality or personality disorder has so changed that the person is safe to be at large' (emphasis added)). Other of the Act's sections echo this obligation to provide treatment for committed persons. See, e.g., § 59-29a01 (establishing civil commitment procedure 'for the long-term care and treatment of the sexually violent predator'); § 59-29a09 (requiring the confinement to 'conform to constitutional requirements for care and treatment'). Thus, as in Allen, 'the State has a statutory obligation to provide 'care and treatment for [persons adjudged sexually dangerous] designed to effect recovery," 478 U.S. at 369 (quoting Ill. Rev. Stat., ch. 38, P 105-8 (1985)), and we may therefore conclude that 'the State has . . . provided for the treatment of those it commits'"* (p. 367).

Data from Question 7:

"States have in certain narrow circumstances provided for the forcible civil detainment of people who are unable to control their behavior and

who thereby pose a danger to the public health and safety. See, e.g., 1788 N. Y. Laws, ch. 31 (Feb. 9, 1788) (permitting confinement of the 'furiously mad'); see also A. Deutsch, The Mentally Ill in America (1949) (tracing history of civil commitment in the 18th and 19th centuries); G. Grob, Mental Institutions in America: Social Policy to 1875 (1973) (discussing colonial and early American civil commitment statutes). We have consistently upheld such involuntary commitment statutes provided the confinement takes place pursuant to proper procedures and evidentiary standards" (p. 357).

"The Court has, in fact, cited the confinement of 'mentally unstable individuals who present a danger to the public' as one classic example of nonpunitive detention. Id., at 748–749. If detention for the purpose of protecting the community from harm necessarily constituted punishment, then all involuntary civil commitments would have to be considered punishment. But we have never so held" (p. 363).

Concur by Kennedy
Justice Kennedy Concurring

Data from Question 1:

"Confinement of such individuals is permitted even if it is pursuant to a statute enacted after the crime has been committed and the offender has begun serving, or has all but completed serving, a penal sentence, provided there is no object or purpose to punish. See Baxstrom v. Herold, 383 U.S. 107, 111–112, 15 L. Ed. 2d 620, 86 S. Ct. 760 (1966). The Kansas law, with its attendant protections, including yearly review and review at any time at the instance of the person confined, is within this pattern and tradition of civil confinement. In this case, the mental abnormality—pedophilia—is at least described in the DSM-IV" (p. 372).

"On the record before us, the Kansas civil statute conforms to our precedents. If, however, civil confinement were to become a mechanism for retribution or general deterrence, or if it were shown that mental abnormality is too imprecise a category to offer a solid basis for concluding that civil detention is justified, our precedents would not suffice to validate it" (p. 373).

Data from Question 2:

No data could be ascertained.

Data from Question 3:

No data could be ascertained.

Data from Question 4:

"At this stage of medical knowledge, although future treatments cannot be predicted, psychiatrists or other professionals engaged in treating pedophilia may be reluctant to find measurable success in treatment even after a long period and may be unable to predict that no serious danger will come from release of the detainee" (p. 372).

Data from Question 5:

No data could be ascertained.

Data from Question 6:

"My brief, further comment is to caution against dangers inherent when a civil confinement law is used in conjunction with the criminal process, whether or not the law is given retroactive application" (p. 372).

"The concern instead is whether it is the criminal system or the civil system which should make the decision in the first place. If the civil system is used simply to impose punishment after the State makes an improvident plea bargain on the criminal side, then it is not performing its proper function. These concerns persist whether the civil confinement statute is put on the books before or after the offense. We should bear in mind that while incapacitation is a goal common to both the criminal and civil systems of confinement, retribution and general deterrence are reserved for the criminal system alone" (p. 373).

Data from Question 7:

"The point, however, is not how long Hendricks and others like him should serve a criminal sentence. With his criminal record, after all, a life term may well have been the only sentence appropriate to protect society and vindicate the wrong" (p. 373).

Dissent by Breyer
Justice Breyer, With Whom Justices Stevens and
Souter Join, and With Whom Justice Ginsburg Joins
as to Parts II and III, Dissenting

Data from Question 1:

"The psychiatric debate, therefore, helps to inform the law by setting the bounds of what is reasonable, but it cannot here decide just how States must write their laws within those bounds" (p. 375).

"Kansas' 1994 Act violates the Federal Constitution's prohibition of 'any . . . ex post facto Law' if it 'inflicts' upon Hendricks 'a greater punishment' than did the law 'annexed to' his 'crimes' when he 'committed' those crimes in 1984. Calder v. Bull, 3 U.S. 386, 3 Dall. 386, 390, 1 L. Ed. 648 (1798) (opinion of Chase, J.); U.S. Const., Art. I, § 10. The majority agrees that the Clause 'forbids the application of any new punitive measure to a crime already consummated.' California Dept. of Corrections v. Morales, 514 U.S. 499, 131 L. Ed. 2d 588, 115 S. Ct. 1597 (1995) (slip op., at 5) (citation omitted; emphasis added). Ante, at 23-24. But it finds the Act is not 'punitive.' With respect to that basic question, I disagree with the majority" (p. 379).

"Civil commitment of dangerous, mentally ill individuals by its very nature involves confinement and incapacitation. Yet 'civil commitment,' from a constitutional perspective, nonetheless remains civil" (p. 380).

"If these obvious similarities cannot by themselves prove that Kansas' 'civil commitment' statute is criminal, neither can the word 'civil' written into the statute, § 59-29a01, by itself prove the contrary. This Court has said that only the 'clearest proof' could establish that a law the legislature called 'civil,' was, in reality a 'punitive' measure. United States v. Ward, 448 U.S. 242, 248–249, 65 L. Ed. 2d 742, 100 S. Ct. 2636 (1980). But the Court has also reiterated that a 'civil label is not always dispositive,' Allen v. Illinois, supra, at 369; it has said that in close cases the label is 'not of paramount importance,' Kurth Ranch, supra, at 777 (citation omitted); and it has looked behind a 'civil' label fairly often. E.g., United States v. Halper, 490 U.S. 435, 447, 104 L. Ed. 2d 487, 109 S. Ct. 1892 (1989)" (p. 381).

"We have generally given considerable weight to the findings of state and lower federal courts regarding the intent or purpose underlying state officials' actions" (p. 383).

". . . the Kansas statute insofar as it applies to previously convicted offenders, such as Hendricks, commits, confines, and treats those offenders after they have served virtually their entire criminal sentence. That time-related circumstance seems deliberate. The Act explicitly defers diagnosis, evaluation, and commitment proceedings until a few

weeks prior to the 'anticipated release' of a previously convicted offender from prison. Kan. Stat. Ann. § 59-29a03(a)(1) (1994). But why, one might ask, does the Act not commit and require treatment of sex offenders sooner, say soon after they begin to serve their sentences? An Act that simply seeks confinement, of course, would not need to begin civil commitment proceedings sooner" (p. 385).

"I recognize one possible counter-argument. A State, wanting both to punish Hendricks (say, for deterrence purposes) and also to treat him, might argue that it should be permitted to postpone treatment until after punishment in order to make certain that the punishment in fact occurs. But any such reasoning is out of place here. Much of the treatment that Kansas offered here (called 'ward milieu' and 'group therapy') can be given at the same time as, and in the same place where, Hendricks serves his punishment" (p. 386).

". . . the practical experience of other States, as revealed by their statutes, confirms what the Kansas Supreme Court's finding, the timing of the civil commitment proceeding, and the failure to consider less restrictive alternatives, themselves suggest, namely, that for Ex Post Facto Clause purposes, the purpose of the Kansas Act (as applied to previously convicted offenders) has a punitive, rather than a purely civil, purpose" (p. 389).

". . . when a State decides offenders can be treated and confines an offender to provide that treatment, but then refuses to provide it, the refusal to treat while a person is fully incapacitated begins to look punitive" (p. 390).

"I have pointed to those features of the Act itself, in the context of this litigation, that lead me to conclude, in light of our precedent, that the added confinement the Act imposes upon Hendricks is basically punitive" (p. 395).

"To find that the confinement the Act imposes upon Hendricks is 'punishment' is to find a violation of the Ex Post Facto Clause" (p. 395).

Data from Question 2:

"Because (1) many mental health professionals consider pedophilia a serious mental disorder; and (2) Hendricks suffers from a classic case of irresistible impulse, namely he is so afflicted with pedophilia that he cannot 'control the urge' to molest children; and (3) his pedophilia presents a serious danger to those children; I believe that Kansas can classify Hendricks as 'mentally ill' and 'dangerous' as this Court used those terms in Foucha" (pp. 367–377).

"... one would expect a nonpunitively motivated legislature that confines because of a dangerous mental abnormality to seek to help the individual himself overcome that abnormality (at least insofar as professional treatment for the abnormality exists and is potentially helpful, as Kansas, supported by some groups of mental health professionals, argues is the case here, see supra, at 6). Conversely, a statutory scheme that provides confinement that does not reasonably fit a practically available, medically oriented treatment objective, more likely reflects a primarily punitive legislative purpose" (pp. 382–383).

"I have found 17 States with laws that seek to protect the public from mentally abnormal, sexually dangerous individuals through civil commitment or other mandatory treatment programs. Ten of those statutes, unlike the Kansas statute, begin treatment of an offender soon after he has been apprehended and charged with a serious sex offense. Only seven, like Kansas, delay 'civil' commitment (and treatment) until the offender has served his criminal sentence (and this figure includes the Acts of Minnesota and New Jersey, both of which generally do not delay treatment). Of these seven, however, six (unlike Kansas) require consideration of less restrictive alternatives" (pp. 388–389).

"This Court, in Foucha, emphasized the fact that the confinement at issue in Salerno was 'strictly limited in duration.' 504 U.S. at 82. It described that 'pretrial detention of arrestees' as 'one of those carefully limited exceptions permitted by the Due Process Clause.' Id., at 83. And it held that Salerno did not authorize the indefinite detention, on grounds of dangerousness, of 'insanity acquittees who are not mentally ill but who do not prove they would not be dangerous to others.' 504 U.S. at 83. Whatever Salerno's 'due process' implications may be, it does not focus upon, nor control, the question at issue here, the question of 'punishment' for purposes of the Ex Post Facto Clause" (pp. 393–394).

"The statutory provisions before us do amount to punishment primarily because, as I have said, the legislature did not tailor the statute to fit the nonpunitive civil aim of treatment, which it concedes exists in Hendricks' case. The Clause in these circumstances does not stand as an obstacle to achieving important protections for the public's safety; rather it provides an assurance that, where so significant a restriction of an individual's basic freedoms is at issue, a State cannot cut corners. Rather, the legislature must hew to the Constitution's liberty-protecting line" (p. 396).

Data from Question 3:

No data could be ascertained.

Data from Question 4:

"Hendricks' mental abnormality also makes him dangerous. Hendricks 'has been convicted of . . . a sexually violent offense,' and a jury found that he 'suffers from a mental abnormality . . . which makes' him 'likely to engage' in similar 'acts of sexual violence' in the future. Kan. Stat. Ann. §§ 59-29a02, 59-29a03 (1994). The evidence at trial favored the State. Dr. Befort, for example, explained why Hendricks was likely to commit further acts of sexual violence if released. See, e.g., App. 248-254. And Hendricks' own testimony about what happens when he gets 'stressed out' confirmed Dr. Befort's diagnosis" (p. 376).

". . . as of the time of Hendricks' commitment, the State had not funded treatment, it had not entered into treatment contracts, and it had little, if any, qualified treatment staff" (p. 384).

"Dr. Befort's last words made clear that Hendricks has 'wasted ten months . . . in terms of treatment effects' and that, as far as treatment goes, 'today, it's still not available.' Id., at 420–421. Nor does the assertion made by the Kansas Attorney General at oral argument help the majority. She never stated that Hendricks, as opposed to other SVPs, was receiving this treatment. And we can find no support for her statement in the record" (pp. 392–393).

Data from Question 5:

"The record provides support for the Kansas court's conclusion. The court found that, as of the time of Hendricks' commitment, the State had not funded treatment, it had not entered into treatment contracts, and it had little, if any, qualified treatment staff. See Hendricks, 912 P.2d at 131, 136; Testimony of Dr. Charles Befort, App. 255 (acknowledging that he has no specialized training); Testimony of John House, SRS Attorney, id., at 367 (no contract has been signed by bidders); Testimony of John House, SRS Attorney, id., at 369 (no one hired to operate SVP program or to serve as clinical director, psychiatrist, or psychologist). Indeed, were we to follow the majority's invitation to look beyond the record in this case, an invitation with which we disagree, see infra, at 20-21, it would reveal that Hendricks, according to the commitment program's own director, was receiving 'essentially no treatment.' Dr. Charles Befort in State Habeas Corpus Proceeding, App. 393; 259 Kan. at 249, 258, 912 P.2d at 131, 136. See also App. 421 ('the treatment that is prescribed by statute' is 'still not available'); id., at 420–421 (the 'needed treatment' 'hasn't been delivered yet' and 'Hendricks has wasted ten months' in 'terms of treatment effects'); id., at 391–392 (Dr. Befort admitting that he is not qualified to be SVP program director)" (p. 384).

"... the statute, at least as of the time Kansas applied it to Hendricks, did not require the committing authority to consider the possibility of using less restrictive alternatives, such as postrelease supervision, halfway houses, or other methods that amici supporting Kansas here have mentioned. Brief for the Menninger Foundation et al. as Amici Curiae 28; Brief for the Association for the Treatment of Sexual Abusers as Amicus Curiae 11–12. The laws of many other States require such consideration. See Appendix, infra. This Court has said that a failure to consider, or to use, 'alternative and less harsh methods' to achieve a nonpunitive objective can help to show that legislature's 'purpose... was to punish.' Bell v. Wolfish, 441 U.S. 520, 539, n. 20, 60 L. Ed. 2d 447, 99 S. Ct. 1861 (1979). And one can draw a similar conclusion here" (pp. 387–388).

Data from Question 6:

"... the psychiatric profession itself classifies the kind of problem from which Hendricks suffers as a serious mental disorder. E.g., American Psychiatric Assn., Diagnostic and Statistical Manual of Mental Disorders 524–525, 527–528 (4th ed. 1994) (describing range of paraphilias and discussing how stress aggravates pedophilic behavior); Abel & Rouleau, Male Sex Offenders, in Handbook of Outpatient Treatment of Adults 271 (M. Thase, B. Edelstein, & M. Hersen eds. 1990). I concede that professionals also debate whether or not this disorder should be called a mental 'illness'" (p. 375).

"Hendricks' abnormality does not consist simply of a long course of antisocial behavior, but rather it includes a specific, serious, and highly unusual inability to control his actions. (For example, Hendricks testified that, when he gets "stressed out," he cannot 'control the urge' to molest children, see ante, at 7.) The law traditionally has considered this kind of abnormality akin to insanity for purposes of confinement" (p. 375).

"... the legal question before us is whether the Clause forbids Hendricks' confinement unless Kansas provides him with treatment that it concedes is available" (p. 378).

"The Act's insistence upon a prior crime, by screening out those whose past behavior does not concretely demonstrate the existence of a mental problem or potential future danger, may serve an important noncriminal evidentiary purpose. Neither is the presence of criminal law-type procedures determinative. Those procedures can serve an important purpose that in this context one might consider noncriminal, namely helping to prevent judgmental mistakes that would wrongly deprive a person of important liberty" (pp. 380–381).

"... it is difficult to see why rational legislators who seek treatment
would write the Act in this way–providing treatment years after
the criminal act that indicated its necessity. See, e.g., Wettstein,
A Psychiatric Perspective on Washington's Sexually Violent Predators
Statute, 15 U. Puget Sound L. Rev. 597, 617 (1992) (stating that
treatment delay leads to 'loss of memory' and makes it 'more difficult
for the offender' to 'accept responsibility,' and that time in prison leads
to attitude hardening that 'engenders a distorted view of the
precipitating offense'). And it is particularly difficult to see why
legislators who specifically wrote into the statute a finding that
'prognosis for rehabilitating . . . in a prison setting is poor' would leave
an offender in that setting for months or years before beginning
treatment" (p. 386).

Data from Question 7:

"Because (1) many mental health professionals consider pedophilia a
serious mental disorder; and (2) Hendricks suffers from a classic case of
irresistible impulse, namely he is so afflicted with pedophilia that he
cannot 'control the urge' to molest children; and (3) his pedophilia
presents a serious danger to those children; I believe that Kansas can
classify Hendricks as 'mentally ill' and 'dangerous' as this Court used
those terms in Foucha" (pp. 376–377).

"Legislation that seeks to help the individual offender as well as to
protect the public would avoid significantly greater restriction of an
individual's liberty than public safety requires" (p. 388).

Kansas v. Crane

Data from Question 1:

"We agree with Kansas insofar as it argues that Hendricks set forth no
requirement of total or complete lack of control. Hendricks referred to
the Kansas Act as requiring a 'mental abnormality' or 'personality
disorder' that makes it 'difficult, if not impossible, for the [dangerous]
person to control his dangerous behavior' (p. 411).

"[M]ost severely ill people—even those commonly termed
'psychopaths'—retain some ability to control their behavior" (p. 412).

"We do not agree with the State, however, insofar as it seeks to claim
that the Constitution permits commitment of the type of dangerous
sexual offender considered in Hendricks without any lack-of-control
determination" (p. 412).

"... the Constitution's safeguards of human liberty [are] in the area of mental illness and the law are not always best enforced through precise bright-line rules" (p. 413).

"... it is often appropriate to say of such individuals, in ordinary English, that they are "unable to control their dangerousness" (p. 415).

"Hendricks must be read in context. The Court did not draw a clear distinction between the purely 'emotional' sexually related mental abnormality and the 'volitional' (p. 415).

Data from Question 2:

"After a jury trial, the Kansas District Court ordered Crane's civil commitment. 269 Kan. at 579–584, 7 P.3d at 286–288. But the Kansas Supreme Court reversed. Id., at 586, 7 P.3d at 290. In that court's view, the Federal Constitution as interpreted in Hendricks insists upon 'a finding that the defendant cannot control his dangerous behavior'—even if (as provided by Kansas law) problems of 'emotional capacity' and not 'volitional capacity' prove the 'source of bad behavior' warranting commitment. Ibid., see also Kan. Stat. Ann. § 59-29a02(b) (2000 Cum. Supp.) (defining 'mental abnormality' as a condition that affects an individual's emotional or volitional capacity). And the trial court had made no such finding" (pp. 410–411).

"Kansas now argues that the Kansas Supreme Court wrongly read Hendricks as requiring the State always to prove that a dangerous individual is completely unable to control his behavior. That reading, says Kansas, is far too rigid" (p. 411).

"Hendricks underscored the constitutional importance of distinguishing a dangerous sexual offender subject to civil commitment 'from other dangerous persons who are perhaps more properly dealt with exclusively through criminal proceedings.' 521 U.S. at 360. That distinction is necessary lest 'civil commitment' become a 'mechanism for retribution or general deterrence'—functions properly those of criminal law, not civil commitment" (p. 412).

"... a critical distinguishing feature of that 'serious ... disorder' there [Hendricks] consisted of a special and serious lack of ability to control behavior" (p. 413).

"... States retain considerable leeway in defining the mental abnormalities and personality disorders that make an individual eligible for commitment" (p. 413).

"... the science of psychiatry, which informs but does not control ultimate legal determinations, is an ever-advancing science, whose distinctions do not seek precisely to mirror those of the law" (p. 413).

"We agree that Hendricks limited its discussion to volitional disabilities. And that fact is not surprising. The case involved an individual suffering from pedophilia—a mental abnormality that critically involves what a lay person might describe as a lack of control. DSM-IV 571–572 (listing as a diagnostic criterion for pedophilia that an individual have acted on, or been affected by, 'sexual urges' toward children). Hendricks himself stated that he could not 'control the urge' to molest children" (p. 414).

". . . as in other areas of psychiatry, there may be 'considerable overlap between a . . . defective understanding or appreciation and . . . [an] ability to control . . . behavior'" (p. 415).

Data from Question 3:

"Nor, when considering civil commitment, have we ordinarily distinguished for constitutional purposes among volitional, emotional, and cognitive impairments" (p. 415).

"The Court in Hendricks had no occasion to consider whether confinement based solely on 'emotional' abnormality would be constitutional, and we likewise have no occasion to do so in the present case" (p. 415).

Data from Question 4:

"In recognizing that fact, we did not give to the phrase 'lack of control' a particularly narrow or technical meaning. And we recognize that in cases where lack of control is at issue, 'inability to control behavior' will not be demonstrable with mathematical precision. It is enough to say that there must be proof of serious difficulty in controlling behavior. And this, when viewed in light of such features of the case as the nature of the psychiatric diagnosis, and the severity of the mental abnormality itself, must be sufficient to distinguish the dangerous sexual offender whose serious mental illness, abnormality, or disorder subjects him to civil commitment from the dangerous but typical recidivist convicted in an ordinary criminal case" (p. 413).

". . . our cases suggest that civil commitment of dangerous sexual offenders will normally involve individuals who find it particularly difficult to control their behavior—in the general sense described above. Cf. Seling v. Young, 531 U.S. 250, 256, 148 L. Ed. 2d 734, 121 S. Ct. 727 (2001); cf. also Abel & Rouleau, Male Sex Offenders, in Handbook of Outpatient Treatment of Adults: Nonpsychotic Mental Disorders 271 (M. Thase, B. Edelstein, & M. Hersen, eds. 1990) (sex offenders' 'compulsive, repetitive, driven behavior . . . appears to fit *the criteria of an emotional or psychiatric illness'). And it is often appropriate to say of such individuals, in ordinary English, that they are 'unable to control their dangerousness'"* (pp. 414–415).

Data from Question 5:

No data could be ascertained.

Data from Question 6:

". . . Insistence upon absolute lack of control would risk barring the civil commitment of highly dangerous persons suffering severe mental abnormalities" (p. 412).

". . . the Constitution's safeguards of human liberty in the area of mental illness and the law are not always best enforced through precise bright-line rules. For one thing, the States retain considerable leeway in defining the mental abnormalities and personality disorders that make an individual eligible for commitment. Hendricks, 521 U.S. at 359; id., at 374–375 (BREYER, J., dissenting). For another, the science of psychiatry, which informs but does not control ultimate legal determinations, is an ever-advancing science, whose distinctions do not seek precisely to mirror those of the law. See id., at 359. See also, e.g., Ake v. Oklahoma, 470 U.S. 68, 81, 84 L. Ed. 2d 53, 105 S. Ct. 1087 (1985) (psychiatry not 'an exact science'); DSM-IV xxx ('concept of mental disorder . . . lacks a consistent operational definition'); id., at xxxii-xxxiii (noting the 'imperfect fit between the questions of ultimate concern to the law and the information contained in [the DSM's] clinical diagnosis'). Consequently, we have sought to provide constitutional guidance in this area by proceeding deliberately and contextually, elaborating generally stated constitutional standards and objectives as specific circumstances require. Hendricks embodied that approach" (pp. 413–414).

Data from Question 7:

". . . it is often appropriate to say of such individuals, in ordinary English, that they are "unable to control their dangerousness" (p. 415).

Dissent Justice Scalia, With Whom Justice Thomas Joins, Dissenting

Data from Question 1:

> "Not only is the new law that the Court announces today wrong, but the Court's manner of promulgating it—snatching back from the State of Kansas a victory so recently awarded—cheapens the currency of our judgments. I would reverse, rather than vacate, the judgment of the Kansas Supreme Court" (p. 416).

> "The first words of our opinion dealing with the merits of the case were as follows: "Kansas argues that the Act's definition of 'mental abnormality' satisfies 'substantive' due process requirements. We agree." Hendricks, 521 U.S. at 356. And the reason it found substantive due process satisfied was clearly stated:

> "The Kansas Act is plainly of a kind with these other civil commitment statutes [that we have approved]: It requires a finding of future dangerousness [viz., that the person committed is 'likely to engage in repeat acts of sexual violence'], and then links that finding to the existence of a 'mental abnormality' or 'personality disorder' that makes it difficult, if not impossible, for the person to control his dangerous behavior. Kan. Stat. Ann. § 59-29a02(b) (1994)." 521 U.S. at 358 (emphasis added) (pp. 418–419).

> "What the opinion was obviously saying was that the SVPA's required finding of a causal connection between the likelihood of repeat acts of sexual violence and the existence of a 'mental abnormality' or 'personality disorder' necessarily establishes 'difficulty if not impossibility' in controlling behavior. This is clearly confirmed by the very next sentence of the opinion, which reads as follows:

> * As quoted earlier in the Hendricks opinion, see 521 U.S. at 352, § 59-29a02(b) defines 'mental abnormality' as a "congenital or acquired condition affecting the emotional or volitional capacity which predisposes the person to commit sexually violent offenses in a degree constituting such person a menace to the health and safety of others." (p. 419).

> "The precommitment requirement of a 'mental abnormality' or 'personality disorder' is consistent with the requirements of . . . other statutes that we have upheld in that it narrows the class of persons eligible for confinement to those who are unable to control their dangerousness" (p. 419).

> "It could not be clearer that, in the Court's estimation, the very existence of a mental abnormality or personality disorder that causes a likelihood of repeat sexual violence in itself establishes the requisite 'difficulty if not impossibility' of control. Moreover, the passage in

question cannot possibly be read as today's majority would read it because nowhere did the jury verdict of commitment that we reinstated in Hendricks contain a separate finding of 'difficulty, if not impossibility, to control behavior'" (pp. 419–420).

"The Court appears to argue that, because Hendricks involved a defendant who indeed had a volitional impairment (even though we made nothing of that fact), its narrowest holding covers only that application of the SVPA, and our statement that the SVPA in its entirety was constitutional can be ignored. See ante, at 7–8. This cannot be correct. The narrowest holding of Hendricks affirmed the constitutionality of commitment on the basis of the jury charge given in that case (to wit, the language of the SVPA); and since that charge did not require a finding of volitional impairment, neither does the Constitution" (p. 422).

"It is obvious that a person may be able to exercise volition and yet be unfit to turn loose upon society. The man who has a will of steel, but who delusionally believes that every woman he meets is inviting crude sexual advances, is surely a dangerous sexual predator" (p. 422).

"I not only disagree with the Court's gutting of our holding in Hendricks; I also doubt the desirability, and indeed even the coherence, of the new constitutional test which (on the basis of no analysis except a misreading of Hendricks) it substitutes" (p. 422).

"I suspect that the reason the Court avoids any elaboration is that elaboration which passes the laugh test is impossible. How is one to frame for a jury the degree of 'inability to control' which, in the particular case, 'the nature of the psychiatric diagnosis, and the severity of the mental abnormality' require? Will it be a percentage ('Ladies and gentlemen of the jury, you may commit Mr. Crane under the SVPA only if you find, beyond a reasonable doubt, that he is 42% unable to control his penchant for sexual violence')? Or a frequency ratio ('Ladies and gentlemen of the jury, you may commit Mr. Crane under the SVPA only if you find, beyond a reasonable doubt, that he is unable to control his penchant for sexual violence 3 times out of 10')? Or merely an adverb ('Ladies and gentlemen of the jury, you may commit Mr. Crane under the SVPA only if you find, beyond a reasonable doubt, that he is appreciably—or moderately, or substantially, or almost totally—unable to control his penchant for sexual violence')? None of these seems to me satisfactory" (pp. 423–424).

Data from Question 2:

"Today the Court holds that the Kansas Sexually Violent Predator Act (SVPA) cannot, consistent with so-called substantive due process, be

applied as written. It does so even though, less than five years ago, we upheld the very same statute against the very same contention in an appeal by the very same petitioner (the State of Kansas) from the judgment of the very same court" (pp. 415–416).

"Several psychologists examined respondent and determined he suffers from exhibitionism and antisocial personality disorder" (p. 416).

". . . the notion that the Constitution requires in every case a finding of 'difficulty if not impossibility' of control does not fit comfortably with the broader holding of Hendricks, which was that 'we have never required state legislatures to adopt any particular nomenclature in drafting civil commitment statutes. Rather, we have traditionally left to legislators the task of defining terms of a medical nature that have legal significance'" (p. 420).

"The Court relies upon the fact that 'Hendricks underscored the constitutional importance of distinguishing a dangerous sexual offender subject to civil commitment 'from other dangerous persons who are perhaps more properly dealt with exclusively through criminal proceedings.' Ante, at 4–5 (quoting 521 U.S. at 360). But the SVPA as written—without benefit of a supplemental control finding—already achieves that objective. It conditions civil commitment not upon a mere finding that the sex offender is likely to reoffend, but only upon the additional finding (beyond a reasonable doubt) that the cause of the likelihood of recidivism is a 'mental abnormality or personality disorder'" (p. 420).

Data from Question 3:

"The Court relies upon the fact that 'Hendricks underscored the constitutional importance of distinguishing a dangerous sexual offender subject to civil commitment 'from other dangerous persons who are perhaps more properly dealt with exclusively through criminal proceedings'" (p. 420).

"I cannot resist observing that the distinctive status of volitional impairment which the Court mangles Hendricks to preserve would not even be worth preserving by more legitimate means. There is good reason why, as the Court accurately says, 'when considering civil commitment . . . we [have not] ordinarily distinguished for constitutional purposes between volitional, emotional, and cognitive impairments,' ante, at 7. We have not done so because it makes no sense" (p. 422).

Data from Question 4:

"That Act permits the civil detention of a person convicted of any of several enumerated sexual offenses, if it is proven beyond a

reasonable doubt that he suffers from a 'mental abnormality'—a disorder affecting his 'emotional or volitional capacity which predisposes the person to commit sexually violent offenses'—or a 'personality disorder,' either of 'which makes the person likely to engage in repeat acts of sexual violence'" (p. 416).

"Several psychologists examined respondent and determined he suffers from exhibitionism and antisocial personality disorder. Though exhibitionism alone would not support classification as a sexual predator, a psychologist concluded that the two in combination did place respondent's condition within the range of disorders covered by the SVPA, 'citing the increasing frequency of incidents involving [respondent], increasing intensity of the incidents, [respondent's] increasing disregard for the rights of others, and his increasing daring and aggressiveness.' In re Crane, 269 Kan. 578, 579, 7 P.3d 285, 287 (2000). Another psychologist testified that respondent's behavior was marked by 'impulsivity or failure to plan ahead,' indicating his unlawfulness 'was a combination of willful and uncontrollable behavior,' id., at 584–585, 7 P.3d at 290. The State's experts agreed, however, that 'respondent's mental disorder does not impair his volitional control to the degree he cannot control his dangerous behavior'" (pp. 416–417).

"Ordinary recidivists choose to reoffend and are therefore amenable to deterrence through the criminal law; those subject to civil commitment under the SVPA, because their mental illness is an affliction and not a choice, are unlikely to be deterred. We specifically pointed this out in Hendricks. 'Those persons committed under the Act,' we said, 'are, by definition, suffering from a 'mental abnormality' or a 'personality disorder' that prevents them from exercising adequate control over their behavior. Such persons are therefore unlikely to be deterred by the threat of confinement.'" (pp. 420–421).

"Under our holding in Hendricks, a jury in an SVPA commitment case would be required to find, beyond a reasonable doubt, (1) that the person previously convicted of one of the enumerated sexual offenses is suffering from a mental abnormality or personality disorder, and (2) that this condition renders him likely to commit future acts of sexual violence. Both of these findings are coherent, and (with the assistance of expert testimony) well within the capacity of a normal jury. Today's opinion says that the Constitution requires the addition of a third finding: (3) that the subject suffers from an inability to control behavior—not utter inability, ante, at 4, and not even inability in a particular constant degree, but rather inability in a degree that will vary 'in light of such features of the case as the nature of the psychiatric diagnosis, and the severity of the mental abnormality itself,'" (pp. 422–423).

*"This formulation of the new requirement certainly displays an
elegant subtlety of mind. Unfortunately, it gives trial courts, in future
cases under the many commitment statutes similar to Kansas's SVPA,
not a clue as to how they are supposed to charge the jury! Indeed,
it does not even provide a clue to the trial court, on remand, in this
very case. What is the judge to ask the jury to find? It is fine and good
to talk about the desirability of our 'proceeding deliberately and
contextually, elaborating generally stated constitutional standards and
objectives as specific circumstances require,' ante, at 6, but one would
think that this plan would at least produce the 'elaboration' of what
the jury charge should be in the 'specific circumstances' of the present
case. 'Proceeding deliberately' is not synonymous with not proceeding
at all"* (p. 423).

Data from Question 5:

No data could be ascertained.

Data from Question 6:

*". . . the Court also reopens a question closed by Hendricks: whether
the SVPA also cannot be applied as written because it allows for the
commitment of people who have mental illnesses other than volitional
impairments. "Hendricks," the Court says, "had no occasion to
consider" this question.*

*But how could the Court possibly have avoided it? The jury whose
commitment we affirmed in Hendricks had not been asked to find a
volitional impairment, but had been charged in the language of the
statute, which quite clearly covers nonvolitional impairments. And the
fact that it did so had not escaped our attention. To the contrary, our
Hendricks opinion explicitly and repeatedly recognized that the SVPA
reaches individuals with personality disorders, 521 U.S. at 352, 353,
357, 358, and quoted the Act's definition of mental abnormality
(§ 59-29a02(b)), which makes plain that it embraces both emotional
and volitional impairments, id., at 352. It is true that we repeatedly
referred to Hendricks's "volitional" problems—because that was
evidently the sort of mental abnormality that he had. But we nowhere
accorded any legal significance to that fact—as we could not have
done, since it was not a fact that the jury had been asked to determine.
We held, without any qualification, "that the Kansas Sexually Violent
Predator Act comports with [substantive] due process requirements,"
id., at 371, because its "precommitment requirement of a 'mental
abnormality' or 'personality disorder' is consistent with the
requirements of . . . other statutes that we have upheld in that it*

narrows the class of persons eligible for confinement to those who are unable to control their dangerousness . . ." (pp. 421–422).

". . . if it is indeed possible to 'elaborate' upon the Court's novel test, surely the Court has an obligation to do so in the 'specific circumstances' of the present case, so that the trial court will know what is expected of it on remand. It is irresponsible to leave the law in such a state of utter indeterminacy . . ." (p. 424).

Data from Question 7:

"It is obvious that a person may be able to exercise volition and yet be unfit to turn loose upon society. The man who has a will of steel, but who delusionally believes that every woman he meets is inviting crude sexual advances, is surely a dangerous sexual predator" (p. 422).

Seling v. Young

Data from Question 1:

"As the Washington Supreme Court held and the Ninth Circuit acknowledged, we proceed on the understanding that the Washington Act is civil in nature. The Washington Act is strikingly similar to a commitment scheme we reviewed four Terms ago in Kansas v. Hendricks, 521 U. S. 346, 138 L. Ed. 2d 501, 117 S. Ct. 2072 (1997)" (p. 261).

"We explained that the Act called for confinement in a secure facility because the persons confined were dangerous to the community. Id. at 363. We noted, however, that conditions within the unit were essentially the same as conditions for other involuntarily committed persons in mental hospitals. Ibid. Moreover, confinement under the Act was not necessarily indefinite in duration. Id. at 364. Finally, we observed that in addition to protecting the public, the Act also provided treatment for sexually violent predators" (p. 261).

". . . we do not deny that some of respondent's allegations are serious. Nor do we express any view as to how his allegations would bear on a court determining in the first instance whether Washington's confinement scheme is civil. Here, we evaluate respondent's allegations as presented in a double jeopardy and ex post facto challenge under the assumption that the Act is civil" (p. 263).

"We hold that respondent cannot obtain release through an 'as-applied' challenge to the Washington Act on double jeopardy and ex post facto grounds" (p. 263).

"*Our decision today does not mean that respondent and others committed as sexually violent predators have no remedy for the alleged conditions and treatment regime at the Center. The text of the Washington Act states that those confined under its authority have the right to adequate care and individualized treatment*" (p. 265).

"*We reject the Ninth Circuit's 'as-applied' analysis for double jeopardy and ex post facto claims as fundamentally flawed*" (p. 265).

"*As petitioner acknowledges, if the Center fails to fulfill its statutory duty, those confined may have a state law cause of action*" (p. 265).

"*It is for the Washington courts to determine whether the Center is operating in accordance with state law and provide a remedy*" (p. 265).

Data from Question 2:

"*Washington State's Community Protection Act of 1990 authorizes the civil commitment of 'sexually violent predators,' persons who suffer from a mental abnormality or personality disorder that makes them likely to engage in predatory acts of sexual violence*" (p. 253).

"*The State's expert concluded that Young's condition, in combination with the personality disorder, the span of time during which Young committed his crimes, his recidivism, his persistent denial, and his lack of empathy or remorse, made it more likely than not that he would commit further sexually violent acts. The victims of Young's rapes also testified. The jury unanimously concluded that Young was a sexually violent predator*" (pp. 255–256).

"*. . . Kansas patterned its Act after Washington's. See In re Hendricks, 259 Kan. 246, 249, 912 P.2d 129, 131 (1996). In Hendricks, we explained that the question whether an Act is civil or punitive in nature is initially one of statutory construction. 521 U.S. at 361 (citing Allen v. Illinois, 478 U.S. 364, 368, 92 L. Ed. 2d 296, 106 S. Ct. 2988 (1986)). A court must ascertain whether the legislature intended the statute to establish civil proceedings. A court will reject the legislature's manifest intent only where a party challenging the Act provides the clearest proof that the statutory scheme is so punitive in either purpose or effect as to negate the State's intention. 521 U.S. at 361 (citing United States v. Ward, 448 U.S. 242, 248–249, 65 L. Ed. 2d 742, 100 S. Ct. 2636 (1980)). We concluded that the confined individual in that case had failed to satisfy his burden with respect to the Kansas Act. We noted several factors: The Act did not implicate retribution or deterrence; prior criminal convictions were used as evidence in the commitment proceedings, but were not a prerequisite to confinement; the Act required no finding of scienter to commit a person; the Act was not intended to function as a deterrent; and although the procedural*" *safeguards were similar to those in the criminal context, they did not alter the character of the scheme"* (p. 261).

"The Court was aware that sexually violent predators in Kansas were to be held in a segregated unit within the prison system" (p. 261).

"Our conclusion that the Kansas Act was 'nonpunitive thus removed an essential prerequisite for both Hendricks' double jeopardy and ex post facto claims' " (p. 262).

"Since deciding Hendricks, this Court has reaffirmed the principle that determining the civil or punitive nature of an Act must begin with reference to its text and legislative history. Hudson v. United States, 522 U.S. 93, 139 L. Ed. 2d 450, 118 S. Ct. 488 (1997). In Hudson, which involved a double jeopardy challenge to monetary penalties and occupational debarment, this Court expressly disapproved of evaluating the civil nature of an Act by reference to the effect that Act has on a single individual. Instead, courts must evaluate the question by reference to a variety of factors 'considered in relation to the statute on its face'; the clearest proof is required to override legislative intent and conclude that an Act denominated civil is punitive in purpose or effect" (p. 262).

"Respondent essentially claims that the conditions of his confinement at the Center are too restrictive, that the conditions are incompatible with treatment, and that the system is designed to result in indefinite confinement. Respondent's claims are in many respects like the claims presented to the Court in Hendricks, where we concluded that the conditions of confinement were largely explained by the State's goal to incapacitate, not to punish" (p. 262).

Data from Question 3:

"Unlike a fine, confinement is not a fixed event. As petitioner notes, it extends over time under conditions that are subject to change. The particular features of confinement may affect how a confinement scheme is evaluated to determine whether it is civil rather than punitive, but it remains no less true that the query must be answered definitively" (p. 263).

"The Act requires 'adequate care and individualized treatment,' Wash. Rev. Code § 71.09.080(2) (Supp. 2000), but the Act is silent with respect to the confinement conditions required at the Center, and that is the source of many of respondent's complaints . . ." (p. 264).

"State courts, in addition to federal courts, remain competent to adjudicate and remedy challenges to civil confinement schemes arising under the Federal Constitution. As noted above, the Washington

Supreme Court has already held that the Washington Act is civil in nature, designed to incapacitate and to treat" (p. 265).

"We have not squarely addressed the relevance of conditions of confinement to a first instance determination, and that question need not be resolved here. An Act, found to be civil, cannot be deemed punitive 'as applied' to a single individual in violation of the Double Jeopardy and Ex Post Facto Clauses and provide cause for release" (p. 268).

Data from Question 4:

"The Act requires 'adequate care and individualized treatment,' Wash. Rev. Code § 71.09.080(2) (Supp. 2000), but the Act is silent with respect to the confinement conditions required at the Center, and that is the source of many of respondent's complaints . . ." (p. 264).

Data from Question 5:

No data could be ascertained.

Data from Question 6:

"The civil nature of a confinement scheme cannot be altered based merely on vagaries in the implementation of the authorizing statute" (p. 263).

". . . our analysis in this case turns on the prior finding by the Washington Supreme Court that the Act is civil, and this Court's decision in Hendricks that a nearly identical Act was civil. Petitioner could not have claimed that the Washington Act is 'otherwise' or 'facially' civil without relying on those prior decisions" (p. 264).

"Our decision today does not mean that respondent and others committed as sexually violent predators have no remedy for the alleged conditions and treatment regime at the Center. The text of the Washington Act states that those confined under its authority have the right to adequate care and individualized treatment" (p. 265).

Data from Question 7:

"We also examined the conditions of confinement provided by the Act. Id. at 363–364. The Court was aware that sexually violent predators in Kansas were to be held in a segregated unit within the prison system. Id. at 368. We explained that the Act called for confinement in a secure facility because the persons confined were dangerous to the community" (p. 261).

". . . .*we explained that there was no federal constitutional bar to their civil confinement, because the State had an interest in protecting the public from dangerous individuals with treatable as well as untreatable conditions*" (p. 262).

Concur by Scalia; Thomas
Justice Scalia, With Whom Justice
Souter Joins, Concurring

Data from Question 1:

"*I agree with the Court's holding that a statute, 'found to be civil in nature, cannot be deemed punitive' or criminal 'as applied' for purposes of the Ex Post Facto and Double Jeopardy Clauses. Ante, at 15. The Court accurately observes that this holding gives us "no occasion to consider the extent to which a court may look to actual conditions of confinement and implementation of the statute to determine in the first instance whether a confinement scheme is civil in nature." Ante, at 14. I write separately to dissociate myself from any implication that this reserved point may be an open question*" (p. 267).

Data from Question 2:

"*I do not regard it as such since, three years ago, we rejected a similar double jeopardy challenge (based upon the statute's implementation "as applied" to the petitioner), where the statute had not yet been determined to be civil in nature, and where we were making that determination 'in the first instance'*" (pp. 267–268).

Data from Question 3:

"*When, as here, a state statute is at issue, the remedy for implementation that does not comport with the civil nature of the statute is resort to the traditional state proceedings that challenge unlawful executive action; if those proceedings fail, and the state courts authoritatively interpret the state statute as permitting impositions that are indeed punitive, then and only then can federal courts pronounce a statute that on its face is civil to be criminal. Such an approach protects federal courts from becoming enmeshed in the sort of intrusive inquiry into local conditions at state institutions that are best left to the State's own judiciary, at least in the first instance. And it avoids federal invalidation of state statutes on the basis of executive implementation that the state courts themselves, given the opportunity, would find to be ultra vires. Only this approach, it seems to me, is in accord with our sound and traditional reluctance to be the initial interpreter of state law*" (pp. 269–270).

Data from Question 4:

No data could be ascertained.

Data from Question 5:

No data could be ascertained.

Data from Question 6:

No data could be ascertained.

Data from Question 7:

No data could be ascertained.

Justice Thomas, Concurring in the Judgment

Data from Question 1:

"I write separately to express my view, first, that a statute which is civil on its face cannot be divested of its civil nature simply because of the manner in which it is implemented, and second, that the distinction between a challenge in the 'first instance' and a subsequent challenge is one without a difference" (pp. 270–271).

Data from Question 2:

". . . as we explained in Hudson, a court may not elevate to dispositive status any of the factors that it may consider in determining whether a sanction is criminal" (p. 272).

Data from Question 3:

"To the extent that the conditions are actually provided for on the face of the statute, I of course agree. Cf. Hudson, supra, at 101 (directing courts to look at 'the statute on its face'). However, to the extent that the conditions result from the fact that the statute is not being applied according to its terms, the conditions are not the effect of the statute, ante, at 13, but rather the effect of its improper implementation. A suit based on these conditions cannot prevail" (pp. 273–274).

Data from Question 4:

No data could be ascertained.

Data from Question 5:

No data could be ascertained.

Data from Question 6:

No data could be ascertained.

Data from Question 7:

No data could be ascertained.

Dissent
Justice Stevens Dissenting

Data from Question 1:

*"In essence, the majority argues that because the constitutional query
must be answered definitively and because confinement is not a 'fixed
event,' conditions of confinement should not be considered at all,
except in the first challenge to a statute, when, as a practical matter,
the evidence of such conditions is most likely not to constitute the
requisite 'clearest proof.' This seems to me quite wrong"*
(pp. 276–277).

Data from Question 2:

*"A sexual predator may be imprisoned for violating the law,
and, if he is mentally ill, he may be committed to an institution until
he is cured. Whether a specific statute authorizing the detention of such
a person is properly viewed as 'criminal' or 'civil' in the context of
federal constitutional issues is often a question of considerable
difficulty"* (p. 274).

*"In this case, Young has made detailed allegations concerning both
the absence of treatment for his alleged mental illness and the starkly
punitive character of the conditions of his confinement. If proved, those
allegations establish not just that those detained pursuant to the statute
are treated like those imprisoned for violations of Washington's
criminal laws, but that, in many respects, they receive significantly
worse treatment. If those allegations are correct, the statute in question
should be characterized as a criminal law for federal constitutional*

purposes. I therefore agree with the Court of Appeals' conclusion that respondent should be given the opportunity to come forward with the 'clearest proof' that his allegations are true" (p. 277).

Data from Question 3:

"It is settled, however, that the question whether a state statute is civil or criminal in nature for purposes of complying with the demands of the Federal Constitution is a question of federal law" (p. 275).

Data from Question 4:

No data could be ascertained.

Data from Question 5:

No data could be ascertained.

Data from Question 6:

No data could be ascertained.

Data from Question 7:

No data could be ascertained.

Endnotes

Introduction: On Madness, Citizenship, and Social Justice

1 To be clear, the ensuing textual analysis does not imply that jurists who engage in judicial decision making are legally mandated to deliberate mindful of a particular ethic. Rather, the question under consideration is one of decoding the moral philosophy, if any, that is lodged within and communicated through the relevant court rulings of a particular law–psychology–crime domain of inquiry. Deciphering the underlying ethic that informs jurisprudential intent and reasoning then makes it possible to assess whether something more or other could and should be done to promote human flourishing for all parties concerned (i.e., the kept, their keepers, their managers, and their watchers).

2 Aristotle identified several virtues or traits of character that predisposed a person to act morally (e.g., courage, temperance, wisdom, truthfulness, justice, modesty, compassion, liberality). Additionally, he specified several vices or traits of deficient and excess character that inclined a person to act immorally or harmfully (e.g., cowardice/foolhardiness, inhibition/overindulgence, and miserliness/extravagance). For a more thorough cataloguing of these virtue/vice habits, along with corresponding discussion, *see* Barcalow (1998, pp. 107–108); Williams & Arrigo (2008; pp. 248–251, 260–262).

Chapter 1: The Ethics of Psychological Jurisprudence

1 The ethical framework identified and developed in this volume explores this very issue by relying on the theory and method of psychological jurisprudence. This chapter, then, represents a preliminary step that seeks to consider how

the self/society twin dynamics or the mutuality of individual responsibility and institutional accountability could be more fully examined ethically. The law–psychology–crime nexus is the access point for such an inquiry. For some initial work on moral philosophy and psychological jurisprudence in the realm of penology and psychology, *see* Bersot and Arrigo (2011), and in psychiatric justice more generally, *see* Arrigo (in press).

2 We do not intend to critique this phenomenon as much as to point out how epidemiological criminology links the criminal justice and public health systems together without fundamentally questioning the ethical grounding (and corresponding legitimacy) that sustains the institutional policies and practices emanating from either, both, or their interstices. As Lanier (2010, p. 72) explained it, "Epidemiological Criminology is the explicit merging of epidemiological and criminal justice theory, methods and practice. Consequently, it draws from criminology and public health for its epistemological foundation. As such, EpiCrim involves the study of anything that affects the health of a society" (cf. Polizzi & Lanier, 2010).

3 Many majority views at the law–psychology–crime nexus are particularly whimsical, especially when individual liberty deprivations (e.g., solitary confinement, capital punishment, civil commitment) support politically entrenched and scientifically suspect collectivist interests and ends (e.g., sustaining the death penalty, tightening restrictions on the insanity defense, enforcing involuntary psychiatric treatments) (Arrigo, 2002a, 2010b). Some have even suggested that these interests and ends promote certain hidden mental disability law prejudices (Perlin, 2000).

4 In further support of this notion, Rawls postulated the "difference principle." As he explained, "social and economic inequalities are to be arranged so that they are . . . to the greatest benefit of the least advantaged" (Rawls, 1971, p. 302). What this means as a practical matter, then, is that "whatever distributive scheme a society has in place, particularly where it allows inequalities, it should work in such a way that the worst-off benefit maximally" (Capeheart & Milovanovic, 2007, p. 19). However, Marxist and postmodern critics of the Rawlsian position argue that his theory emphasizes the distribution and circulation of justice absent a consideration of the *sources* for its production (Hardt & Negri, 1994). In other words, institutional definitions of justice remain unexamined, intact, and, consequently, altogether "mystified" (Capeheart & Milovanovic, 2007, p. 138). Such a critical examination is provisionally undertaken in the concluding chapter.

5 We note that jury nullification is not without its criticisms (e.g., Conrad, 1998). Whereas the practice of commonsense justice represents the *humanizing* influence of the community conscience in opposition to an oppressive government, it has the potential to legitimize bigotry and bias depending on the particular case at hand (Siegel, 1991). For example, in 1979 a group of Klansmen and American Nazis in Greensboro, North Carolina, were acquitted of the charge of murder in the killing of five Civil Rights protesters (Siegel, 1991). In fact, jury nullification was used in the racially divided South for many years as a form of prejudicial defiance to the Civil Rights Movement (Conrad, 1998). Although it is possible for jury nullification to be utilized similarly in current cases dealing with discrimination and hate crimes against groups such as Muslim Americans, the principal goal of commonsense justice

is to operate as a safe practice that allows the community's conscience to overcome repressive laws (Finkel, 1995).

6 Therapeutic jurisprudence has been the source of some criticisms. For example, Carson (2003) questioned whether the social and behavioral science footing of the presumably beneficial outcomes that follow in the wake of so-called healing legal interventions fail to consider the structural dynamics that sustain marginalizing status quo dynamics. Moreover, Arrigo (2004b) explored the ethical underpinnings of therapeutic jurisprudence and considered whether its logic and language reproduced extant relations of power that limited its potential to advance a more complete vision of justice and well-being for all. However, we note that therapeutic jurisprudence proposes to *humanize* the law and, in this endeavor, it seeks to grow a sense of personal well-being and character for legal actors and participants exposed to its debilitating or corrosive effects.

7 Crime victim participation is crucial for the following reasons: *(1)* the victim population is large (e.g., more than 23 million in U.S. in 2005) and requires recognition; *(2)* victimization has a negative impact on victim perception of the government and the community; *(3)* the criminal justice system depends on the cooperation and participation of victims in the clearance of cases; *(4)* criminal victimization has potentially harmful psychological impacts; and *(5)* victim participation reveals promising results for the reduction of recidivism rates for particular offenders under certain conditions (Hurley, 2009, p. 16).

8 Ideally, when all stakeholders are actively engaged in the healing process, victims, offenders, and the community that binds both are sufficiently empowered to capitalize on the humanizing benefits of restorative justice such that re-offending and re-victimization are abated (O'Hara & Robbins, 2009). This logic is designed to build character for one and all. However, restorative justice has not been without its detractors. Similar to the charges leveled against commonsense justice and therapeutic jurisprudence, critics draw attention to the reparative dialogue itself, questioning how it fundamentally changes existing relationships, and whether this very shortcoming limits greater prospects for recovery and healing (e.g., Arrigo, 2010a; Schehr & Milovanovic, 1999). In short, the question is: "restore to what and on whose terms?" (Polizzi, 2008).

9 To be clear, with respect to each application chapter, concurring/dissenting opinions will be a part of the data set. This will occur only when legal cases identified through the LexisNexis search process yield court decisions that include additional opinions warranting textual scrutiny.

10 For example, reliance on *stare decisis* (i.e., precedent), fact-based reasoning, and rule-bound decision-making all condition the meaning and intention of a court case. Conversely, interpreting legislative history as a basis to ascertain statutory meaning and intent is a more ambiguous process and ambitious enterprise (e.g., Brown & Brown, 2003).

11 These are "essential legal assumptions" about values such as duty, intention, and obligations; self/other interests, agreements, and consequences; integrity, happiness, and community. These values are often communicated in encoded ways when derived from case law canons. However, these essential assumptions can be sourced in meta-ethical and normative theory. Thus, the pivot from jurisprudential intent (judicial temperament) to underlying ethics (judicial morality) is one of kind and not degree.

12 A more critically animated methodology would go beyond the narrative's manifest content. This radical methodology, developed most recently in the ultramodern assessment of criminology proper (Arrigo & Milovanovic, 2010) and the law–psychiatry interface (Arrigo, 2010b; in press), extends to the symbolic, material, and cultural spheres of influence as well. Then, too, the mutuality of latent and manifest content would be the source of data retrieval by way of the linguistic sphere. These matters will receive some attention in the concluding chapter. However, as a point of methodological departure, unearthing ethical regard by way of manifest content is strategically important to Level-2 textual legal exegeses.

Chapter 2: Juvenile Transfer, Developmental Maturity, and Competency to Stand Trial

1 There is reason for concern among state legislatures if juvenile offenders are found incompetent because of immaturity alone. Maturity can only be restored through age and experience; therefore, the courts could not hold such juvenile offenders indefinitely because it is unconstitutional. See *Jackson v. Indiana*, 406 U.S. 715 (U.S. 1972), which states that the state must release an incompetent defendant if competence cannot be restored within a reasonable amount of time (as cited in Grisso et al., 2003, p. 361).
2 Initially, the search for relevant cases to evaluate focused on decisions rendered by the United States Supreme Court. However, the specific parameters informing the identification of such cases (i.e., juvenile [automatic] transfer, developmental maturity, and trial fitness) did not yield any results. Consequently, attention was subsequently directed toward state supreme court and appellate court cases that met the criteria.
3 The criteria for case selection specifically required that the decision: *(1)* involve automatic or direct-file juvenile transfer; *(2)* discuss developmental maturity; and *(3)* review the competency to stand trial doctrine. *Roper v. Simmons* (2005) is an automatic transfer case in which the defendant, Simmons, was described as "very immature," "very impulsive," "and very susceptible to being manipulated or influenced" (p. 559). However, the trial fitness of Simmons is not raised by the court, despite these deficits. Instead, the defendant's age is mentioned as a factor that limits the immature youth from reaching the threshold requirements to be *sentenced to death*. As such, *Roper* fundamentally represents a death penalty case, in which the court's concern for age and developmental immaturity are used to explain why such juveniles cannot be deemed as the most deserving for execution. Given the absence of a discussion on the important issue of defendant Roper's competency, the case was excluded.
4 Darren McCracken went to the bedroom of his mother, Vicky Bray, to retrieve a handgun, which he proceeded to load and then shot Bray twice in her head as she slept on the sofa in the downstairs family room [*See State v. McCracken*, 260 Neb. 234, 615 N.W.2d 902, (Neb. 2000)].
5 Robert Lee Williams, Jr. and an accomplice, Kevin Barton, entered the home of Alena Tate, who was a 74-year-old woman with Alzheimer's disease. They intended to steal her car. During the robbery, Tate was struck in the head and then shot in the neck area, killing her [*See Williams v. State*, 96 Ark. App. 160, 239 S.W.3d 44 (Ark. App. 2006)].

6 Eugene Nnakwe made sexual overtures toward the defendant, Nevels. A struggle ensued between the two. Nnakwe was taken to the ground, where Nevels proceeded to stomp, kick, and strike him. Nnakwe was then dragged by Nevels, with the help of Jason Daniels, 40 feet away, where Nevels began to strike Nnakwe in the chest and head with a metal tire iron. Later, Nevels pulled a pine branch from a tree and began striking Nnakwe with it and then stole his car keys and left the area [*See State v. Nevels*, 235 Neb. 39, 453 N.W.2d 579, (Neb. 1990)].

Chapter 3: Inmate Mental Health, Solitary Confinement, and Cruel and Unusual Punishment

1 Additionally, the logic of psychological jurisprudence and the philosophy of ethics conveyed through the judicial opinions on disciplinary solitary confinement and incarcerates *without* pre-existing psychiatric disorders has yet to be explored. The prevailing research suggests that the risks of placing these inmates in isolation are, most assuredly, serious. However, the existing literature overwhelmingly demonstrates that confining mentally ill prisoners in punitive segregation is acutely devastating. Nevertheless, future research regarding the former offender group (those without preexisting mental health conditions) is both undeniably worthwhile and altogether necessary.

2 A literature base exists that explores the ethics of solitary confinement from the academic (Kleinig & Smith, 2001; Lippke, 2004; Schwartz, 2003), the programmatic (Shalev, 2008), and the correctional practice (American Psychological Association, 2003; Bonner & Vandecreek, 2006) perspectives. However, the purpose of this chapter is to examine the moral reasoning that informs the courts' decisions on long-term disciplinary isolation. As such, dialogue involving the ethical practice of solitary confinement is not germane to the ensuing inquiry.

3 Early empirical research is also useful to the ensuing analysis. For example, a study by Toch (2003) examined data from the mid-nineteenth century identifying the effects of solitary confinement on prisoners. Among the accounts he assessed was a report prepared in 1845 by Dr. Thomas Cleveland who indicated that 25% of inmates kept in solitary confinement "manifested decided symptoms of derangement" (p. 223). In addition to his empirical findings, Dr. Cleveland included written observations of prisoners who were placed in solitary confinement:

> Now, suddenly abstract from a man these senses, to which he has been so long accustomed; shut him up . . . in a solitary cell, where he must pass the same unvarying round, from week to week, with hope depressed, with no subjects for reflection but those which give him pain to review, in the scenes of his former life; after a few days, with no new impressions made upon his senses . . . one unvarying sameness relaxes the attention and concentration of his mind, and it will not be thought strange, that, through the consequent dibility and irritability of its organ, the mind should wander and become impaired (Gray, 1847/1973 as cited in Toch, 2003, p. 223).

4 It is important to note that, like the general prison population, those placed in long-term solitary confinement disproportionately represent economically disadvantaged individuals. Further, research indicates that the deleterious effects of extended isolation are perhaps uniquely harmful to women (Arrigo & Bullock, 2008). For example, Shaylor's (1998) study at the SHU at Valley State Prison for Women in Chowchilla, California, described how female incarcerates are more vulnerable to sexual harassment and abuse by male prison guards. Cell extractions performed with force, common in long-term solitary confinement, may also trigger post-traumatic episodes in women who have experienced violent sexual assaults in their past. For an overview of the mental health issues women confront, especially while confined, *see* Gido and Dalley (2009).

5 In *Ruiz v. Johnson,* the court considered the extant research on the adverse psychological consequences of placing prisoners with pre-existing mental health conditions in long-term administrative segregation. Acknowledging the deleterious effects of such confinement, the court ruled that exposing mentally ill inmates to extended isolation violated the Eighth Amendment's prohibition against cruel and unusual punishment. *See Ruiz v. Johnson, 37 F. Supp. 855 (1999).*

6 Citing the existing literature, two landmark cases established an Eighth Amendment violation regarding prisoners with pre-existing mental health conditions in long-term disciplinary segregation. In *Madrid v. Gomez* and *Jones 'El v. Berge,* the court determined that placing inmates with such disorders in isolation constituted cruel and unusual punishment. *See Madrid v. Gomez, 889 F. Supp. 1280 (N.D. Cal. 1995) and Jones 'El v. Berge, 164 F.Supp.2d 1096 (2001).*

7 In the past, prisoners in the United States were considered "slaves of the State" and, as such, had no constitutional rights. Beginning with the prison reform movement in the 1960s, the courts began to acknowledge that these protections extended to inmates. Even with this recognition, the courts largely maintain a "hands-off" approach to cases involving incarcerated offenders. As Weidman noted, "Concerns about separation of powers, federalism, and courts' lack of expertise in prison management [are] sometimes cited in support of this position" (2004, p. 3).

8 The methodology focuses on ascertaining prevailing case law and analyzing the extant legal history. The methodology describes how the prevailing case law was determined. The extant legal history refers to the most fully developed statements on disciplinary long-term solitary confinement for prisoners with preexisting psychiatric disorders as rendered by the courts. This latter strategy entails selecting those judicial opinions, guided by the identified qualitative methodology, that advance jurisprudential knowledge of the psycho-legal problem under consideration. Thus, the stipulated methodology (i.e., Lexis Nexis search followed by two levels of textual analysis) is complemented by evaluating the evolution of the correctional law in this area. Presenting the most fully developed statements concerning protracted and punitive solitary confinement for mentally ill inmates is not governed by appellate court decision making wherein a contraction or diminution of the law is subsequently delineated. All cases chosen for review were guided by the logic of both research strategies. For more on this complementary strategy of capturing the most advanced legal history in relation to the present inquiry, compare, for example,

Goff v. Harper (1997) and *Goff v. Harper* (1999). In 1997, the trial court determined four constitutional violations and, in rendering its decision, ordered a remedial plan. The subsequent review in 1999 involved an evaluation of the Iowa State Penitentiary's efforts to correct the violations. Thus, *Goff v. Harper* (1997) more fully captures the court's statement on long-term disciplinary solitary confinement and the Eighth Amendment. For more on qualitatively analyzing the evolution of a cognate area of mental health law, *see* Arrigo (1993, 2002b).

9 The Supreme Court has delineated a two-prong test by which the courts must evaluate violations of Eighth Amendment claims. To satisfy the objective requirement of the test, courts must "assess whether society considers the risk that the prisoner complains of to be so grave that it violates contemporary standards of decency to expose anyone unwillingly to such a risk. In other words, the prisoner must show that the risk of which he complains is not one that today's society chooses to tolerate" *(Helling v. McKinney,* 509 U.S. 25 [1993]). To meet the subjective requirement, the prisoner must prove that an individual acted with "deliberate indifference" to an inmate's health or safety when aware that the prisoner would face a risk of serious harm and failed to acknowledge or avert it. Interestingly, although the Court established this standard, it neglected to explain what "contemporary standards of decency" are or to provide specific insight into how the analysis should be conducted (Fellner, 2006).

10 In *Farmer v. Brennan* (1994), the Supreme Court employed the two-prong test for determining if a pre-operative transsexual inmate's Eighth Amendment protection against cruel and unusual punishment had been violated when the prisoner was placed in segregation. Farmer raised the challenge based on the confinement conditions being so volatile that they placed him (as Farmer is referred to in the Court's language) at risk of being sexually assaulted. In *Rhodes v. Chapman* (1981), the Court heard arguments relating to double celling inmates in segregation. In delivering their opinion, the Court noted that the Constitution does not guarantee a comfortable prison environment. The Court gave deference to the legislature and prison administrators in their responsibility to implement and oversee correctional institution policies and procedures. See *Farmer v. Brennan 511 U.S. 825 (1994)* and *Rhodes v. Chapman, 452 U.S. 337 (1981).*

11 The existing social science and law review literature offers insight into why prisoners in solitary confinement—including those with and without pre-existing mental health conditions—fail to succeed on Eighth Amendment violation claims. A significant number of cases are either dismissed or proceed on another claim, such as due process (Fellner, 2006; Haney, 2003; Haney & Lynch, 1997; Perlin & Dlugacz, 2008; Weidman, 2004). Some researchers point to the difficulty of overcoming the two-prong test, in which the harm to be considered is traditionally interpreted by the courts to mean one that is corporeal in nature (Haney & Lynch, 1997; Perlin & Dlugacz, 2008; Romano, 1996; Weidman, 2004). As such, many inmates are unable to successfully associate their psychological harm to that of physical injury. Others assert that the Prison Litigation Reform Act (PLRA), passed by Congress in 1996, has hindered cases in which prisoners seek relief. Under the PLRA, correctional administrators are exempt from judicial supervision in most cases and when relief is granted, it

becomes ineffective after 2 years (Lobel, 2008; Perlin & Dlugacz, 2008; Rebman, 1999; Weidman, 2004). Further, inmates incarcerated at supermax facilities face a particularly difficult hurdle to overcome. As the *Madrid* court poignantly noted, "A challenge to supermax incarceration is not a case about inadequate or deteriorating physical conditions. There are no rat-infested cells, antiquated buildings, or unsanitary supplies . . . it is a case about 'a prison of the future'" (Weidman, 2004, p. 7; *see also* Lobel, 2008).

12 Interestingly, the social science and law review research indicates that the conditions at issue in *Ruiz v. Johnson* (1999) were similar in nature to those found within punitive solitary confinement (Haney, 2003; Harvard Law Review, 2008; Perlin & Dlugacz, 2008; Weidman, 2004). However, the present study examines only those cases involving confinement conditions formally classified as disciplinary segregation. Clearly, a subsequent study exploring administrative solitary confinement case law would be worthwhile.

13 The *Vasquez* case differs slightly from the other cases comprising the data set. In this instance, a psychiatrically disordered inmate raised an Eighth Amendment violation claim asserting that specific conditions, including constant illumination and poor ventilation, in long-term disciplinary isolation exacerbated his mental illness. Although the *Vasquez* court did not consider the *totality* of the conditions of isolation, the case was deemed appropriate for inclusion based on a twofold rationale. First, the conditions, continuous illumination and insufficient ventilation (e.g., heating, cooling, and lack of access to fresh air), are featured prominently in solitary confinement facilities. Second, the deleterious effects of these environmental factors, among others, on the mental well-being of inmates are noted in the relevant research (Cohen, 2008; Haney, 2003; McConville & Kelly, 2007; Rebman, 1999; Toch, 2003).

14 Admittedly, some of the cases comprising the data set have lengthy procedural histories and differing statuses. However, for the purpose of this qualitative endeavor, only those judicial decisions that most thoroughly captured the courts' statements on psychiatrically disordered inmates, prolonged disciplinary segregation, and the Eighth Amendment were included. Additionally, it is imperative to acknowledge the distinction between the type of review that occurs in a trial court versus an appellate court. Trial courts hear evidence and determine findings of fact. In contrast, appellate courts assess substantive or procedural errors occurring in the trial court's judicial decision-making. Although mindful that the method of review employed by the respective courts differs, this is not the source of analysis for the ensuing inquiry. Rather, the focus of this study is to examine the meaning conveyed by the courts' rhetoric (i.e., the jurisprudential intent and the moral reasoning that informs it) in the precedent-setting or prevailing cases on these matters.

15 The six judicial decisions selected for critical examination did not include any dissenting opinions. Consequently, the majority opinions were analyzed to obtain data appropriate for the two levels of analysis employed in the ensuing inquiry.

16 To be clear, discerning the underlying moral philosophy of a legal case by examining its jurisprudential intent, understood as manifest content, represents an exercise in interpretive reasoning. In other words, this is not a precise process of data finding; rather, it is a more heuristic, although cleary systematic, meaning-making endeavor. The method's conviction is that "it is possible to go beyond the surface meaning of legal texts [manifest content] to explore the

structure and the ideological content . . . [and in doing so] to search for the values expressed by the law" (Mercuro & Medema, 1998, p. 169).

17 The application of Level-2 analysis did not yield textual exegeses regarding the moral philosophy in the *Vasquez v. Frank* (2006) decision. Accordingly, the following discussion focuses on the results from the remaining five cases.

18 For example, we recommended developing a judicial survey instrument. But two limitations must be acknowledged when utilizing a self-report survey tool to gather data. An instrument designed to elicit the ethical reasoning employed by judges is particularly problematic in that moral attitudes are often complex and, as such, are not easily interpreted. Moreover, given their obligation to remain neutral arbiters of the law, judges may not be forthcoming in their responses.

19 Given the harsh conditions of long-term disciplinary solitary confinement, a number of leading domestic and international researchers as well as human rights activists advocate the abolition of its use within American correctional institutions. Abolitionist proponents assert that isolative confinement, of any type or duration, is psychologically devastating to both inmates with and without pre-existing mental health conditions (Fellner, 2006; Lobel, 2008; Rhodes, 2005). Indeed, according to the Inter-American Court of Human Rights, "prolonged isolation and coercive solitary confinement are, in themselves, cruel and inhuman treatments, damaging to the person's psychic and moral integrity" (Lobel, 2008, p. 123).

Chapter 4: Sexually Violent Predators, Criminal and Civil Confinement, and Community Re-Entry

1 Perhaps surprisingly, a study of official crime report records revealed that juveniles commit 17% to 20% of all sex crimes, with the exception of prostitution (Pastore & Maguire, 2007). According to victim reports and youth self-reports, the actual rate of youthful sex offending may be even higher (Finkelhor & Dziuba-Leatherman, 1994). Well over half of the states in the nation require those convicted of such offenses to register (Frierson et al., 2008). Among those states mandating juvenile sex offender registration, the specific conditions under which these offenders must register vary. For example, Alaska and Florida mandate registration only if the juvenile was tried as an adult. Other states require juveniles to register according to the age at which they committed the sexual offense (e.g., Indiana registries include those 14 years and older; South Dakota registers those 15 years and older). Juveniles in Mississippi must register once they are convicted of two sexual offenses (Frierson et al., 2008; KlaasKids Foundation, 2004). For an illuminating exploration of the history of registration and notification requirements (i.e., Megan's Law) for juvenile sex offenders, *see* Trivits and Repucci (2002). Furthermore, a number of SVP statutes include juveniles in mandating civil commitment (Frierson et al., 2008). Unquestionably, classifying juveniles as SVPs is a complex and controversial matter meriting considerable future research attention. For a thorough review of juvenile sex offending and the distinct challenges surrounding their treatment and confinement, *see* Barbaree and Marshall (2006) and Letourneau and Borduin (2008).

2 In some states, sexually violent predators are known as sexually *deviant* predators, sexually *dangerous persons*, or sexually dangerous *individuals*.

In Minnesota, an offender may be classified under two designations: sexually dangerous person and sexual psychopathic personality (Deming, 2006). However, the phrase *sexually violent predator* is more commonly used to refer to this particular subgroup of sex offender. Thus, for the purpose of the ensuing inquiry, the term *sexually violent predator* will be utilized except where a more specific distinction is required.

3 According to the American Psychiatric Association's Diagnostic and Statistical Manual of Mental Disorders, individuals exhibiting signs of antisocial personality disorder demonstrate "a pervasive pattern of disregard for, and violation of, the rights of others" (DSM-IV-TR, 2000, p. 701).

4 The influence of politics and the media on policymaking that lacks empirical support has been noted in the extant social science literature (LaCombe, 2008; Walker, 2007). Research suggests that this is particularly true for SVPs, wherein political interests and the media have shaped the public's perception of these "moral monsters" (Douard, 2007, p. 45) lurking in the shadows eager to attack unsuspecting victims (LaCombe, 2008; Wright, 2008). Indeed, according to Deming (2008), even the SVP designation "is an emotionally charged term that conjures up a number of associations in the public eye regarding the SVP that are sometimes misleading or inaccurate" (p.443). Some contend that it is fear of and a risk-avoidance approach to SVPs that fuel policymaking (Douard, 2007; LaCombe, 2008; Wright, 2008). The cycle begins with the brutal sexual assault and murder of a child whose plight is poignantly and extensively covered by the media. In this phase, video montages of the victim and his or her family are juxtaposed against images of a predator along with an account of the lurid details of the assailant's heinous crime. Emotional outrage and moral panic rise among the public. In response, political leaders seeking to satisfy their constituents hastily attach victims' names to legislation (e.g., Megan's Law, Jessica's Law) delineating increasingly restrictive measures designed to confine violent sexual offenders well beyond a prison's walls (Veysey et al., 2008; Ward, 2007; Wright, 2008).

To illustrate, Rayburn Yung (2007) points to Alabama's 2005 decision to reassess its extant sex offender laws after an episode of the *O'Reilly Factor*. During the program, host Bill O'Reilly "named Alabama as a state that does not care about sex offenders" (Rayburn Yung, 2007, p. 122). Following the episode, Alabama Governor Bob Riley ordered a special session of the legislature to review the state's current laws on sex offenders and consider whether any of them should be amended. As a result, the legislature widened the scope of the sex-offender-free zones to include those convicted of sex crimes against both adults and children and created a requirement that prohibits offenders from loitering within 500 feet of any facility with the "principal purpose of caring for, educating, or entertaining minors" (Rayburn Yung, 2007, p. 123). For more on the public's perception of sex offenders and its influence on policy, *see* Fortney, Levenson, Brannon, and Baker (2007).

5 It is imperative to note that psychopathy is a diagnostic construct rather than a DSM-IV-TR recognized psychiatric diagnosis (Prentky et al., 2006; Vess et al., 2004). Despite this distinction, psychopathy is commonly used to explain violent (or sexually violent) behavior. Thus, when making SVP commitment determinations, a "reliable diagnosis of psychopathy . . . may constitute a defensible mental abnormality" (Prentky et al., 2006, p. 369). For more

information on the history of psychopathy, *see* Arrigo and Shipley (2001) and for the practical implications of this construct on forensic assessment and offender treatment, *see* Shipley and Arrigo (2001).

6 Although states reserve the right to enact civil commitment laws and place those convicted of sexually violent acts in such confinement, there are limits to this power. As deliberated in the landmark Supreme Court case of *Kansas v. Hendricks* (1997), the Court upheld a constitutional challenge to Kansas' 1994 Sexually Violent Predator Act. The Court's decision (and later in the case of *Kansas v. Crane* [2002]) established that civil commitment of SVPs is a matter of offender rehabilitation rather than punishment (Janus & Bolin, 2008; Levenson, 2004; Petrila, 2008).

7 Recently, the Supreme Court heard arguments regarding whether Congress has the constitutional authority to enact a portion of the Adam Walsh Act that authorizes the federal government to civilly commit offenders classified as "sexually dangerous" persons. The Court ruled that Congress did indeed hold the power to pass the Act under the Necessary and Proper Clause. Justice Breyer, joined by Chief Justice Roberts and Justices Stevens, Ginsburg, and Sotomayor, delivered the majority opinion. Justices Kennedy and Alito filed separate concurring opinions. Justice Thomas, joined in part by Justice Scalia, filed a dissenting opinion (*U.S. v. Comstock* [2010]).

8 The extant literature notes that SVPs are often described as "monsters" in contemporary society (Douard, 2007; Janus, 2006). Foucault offered poignant commentary on those perceived as monsters. He wrote, "When the monster violates the law by its very existence, it triggers the response of something quite different from the law itself. It provokes either violence, the will for pure and simple suppression, or medical care or pity" (Foucault, 2004, p. 56).

9 Some early findings suggest that actuarial risk assessments and paraphilia diagnoses were capable of properly identifying SVPs suited for civil commitment (Levenson & Morin, 2004; Levenson, 2003). However, as researchers have noted, these findings are preliminary in nature and are limited in their ability to be generalized to civil commitment practices outside the state in which they were conducted (i.e., Florida) (Levenson, 2003; 2008; Levenson & Morin, 2004). Thus, future investigations concerning the processes and practices of civilly committing SVPs, including the robustness of actuarial risk assessment instruments, is essential.

10 While on their way home from a trip to a local convenience store, Jacob, his brother, and a friend were stopped by a masked man with a gun. While Jacob's brother and the brother's friend were ordered to leave, the man grabbed Jacob's arm and took him into the woods. In the years that have followed Jacob's disappearance, his mother, Patty, has become an advocate for tougher sex offender legislation (e.g., The Jacob Wetterling Act) and has established an organization to promote public awareness about child abduction and exploitation (Jacob Wetterling Resource Center, 2010).

11 The principal federal decision on the constitutionality of residency restrictions for convicted sex offenders is *Doe v.Miller* (2005). In 2002, the Iowa state legislature enacted a statute (Iowa Code § 692A.2A) that established an exclusionary zone in which certain types of convicted sex offenders were prohibited from living within 2000 feet of a school or registered child care facility. A group of sex offenders targeted by the new statute filed a lawsuit

alleging that the law was unconstitutional and the punishment was *ex post facto*. Among their claims, the plaintiffs argued that the residency restrictions made it impossible for them to find available housing and infringed on their fundamental rights. The district court determined that the statute was unconstitutional and, in delivering its opinion, ordered a permanent injunction against its enforcement. Upon review at the Eighth Circuit Court of Appeals, the court reversed the district court's decision. The appellate court ruled that the law did not violate any of the plaintiffs' constitutional rights nor did it represent retroactive punishment (*Doe v. Miller*, 405 F.3d 700 [8th Cir. 2005]; *see also* Logan, 2006; Noroian & Saleh, 2006). In delivering the majority opinion, the court gave deference to the state legislature and its ability to enact such a statute to ensure the safety of Iowa citizens, particularly "where precise statistical data are unavailable" to determine other means of protecting society (*Doe v. Miller*, 2005, p. 714).

12 In addition to formal sanctions exacting control over convicted sex offenders and SVPs, numerous informal sanctions exist to which these individuals are subjected. In recent years, law enforcement agencies across the nation have implemented "Trick No Treat" programs designed to prevent sex offenders from having access to children on Halloween (Robbers, 2009). For example, those convicted of sexually violent offenses in Virginia must report to their local sheriff's department during the hours in which children are trick-or-treating. At that time, they are required to confirm or update their registry information and undergo drug testing (Robbers, 2009; Virginia Department of Corrections, 2002). This informal sanction, in addition to a number of others, draws on little to no empirical evidence to support its purpose and/or effectiveness. Furthermore, as Robbers (2009) noted while conducting her research, "I did not come across a single violent sex offense that took place during Halloween (p. 8).

13 Because of the public scorn associated with being a sex offender and the stringent laws dictating nearly every aspect of SVPs' lives, some researchers suggest that surgical castration may be a viable option for those seeking to liberate themselves from the burdens of their paraphiliac proclivities and the legal and societal label of sexual predator (Weinberger, Sreenivasan, Garrick, & Osran, 2005; *see also* Edwards, 2009). Surgical castration, also called an *orchiectomy*, "has been used as a means for social control for centuries" (Scott & Holmberg, 2003, p. 502). In the past, the "mentally infirmed" as well as those convicted of a plethora of crimes were subjected to this procedure (Scott & Holmberg, 2003). Treatment involving surgical castration for sex offenders has re-emerged in recent years. Indeed, some states, including California and Georgia, have made it mandatory for offenders classified as SVPs or repeat sex offenders (Edwards, 2009; Norman-Eady, 2006; Scott & Holmberg, 2003). The surgical procedure involves the bilateral removal of a male's testes. In doing so, androgen production is reduced, lowering testosterone levels. By decreasing a male's testosterone, his sexual drive and performance is inhibited (Seto, 2008; Weinberger et al., 2005). Because of the nature of the procedure, there is no empirical evidence on the frequency with which it is performed as a therapeutic alternative for SVPs as compared to other treatment options. Notwithstanding this fact, it is prudent to assume that surgical castration is an extreme measure in rehabilitating sex offenders and not yet widely performed on SVPs (Edwards, 2009).

14 Similar to surgical castration, chemical castration has been utilized as an option in treating sex offenders and reducing recidivism. All states, with the exception of Texas, that either allow or require SVPs to be surgically castrated also permit them to be chemically castrated (Scott & Holmberg, 2003; Edwards, 2009). This procedure involves routinely injecting an adult male with anti-androgenic hormones to lower his testosterone level (Miller, 2003). Research suggests that chemical castration is perhaps more effective than surgical castration (Weinberger et al., 2005); however, it requires recurrent hormone treatments (Edwards, 2009).

15 Given the sentiment of disgust and the corresponding trend toward incapacitating and isolating sex offenders, perhaps it is unsurprising that both policymakers and citizens have suggested capital punishment for those deemed SVPs. A growing number of states have expanded their death penalty statutes to allow the execution of non-homicide offenders, particularly repeat sex offenders (Wright, 2008). Florida, Oklahoma, Texas, and South Carolina are among the states sanctioning the death penalty for those convicted of committing sexually violent acts. Interestingly, the Supreme Court has found that imposing capital punishment on those convicted of rape is an Eighth Amendment violation (*Coker v. Georgia, 433 U.S. 584* [1977]). The impact of this landmark ruling in the wake of recent legislative changes permitting the death penalty for sex offenders remains to be seen.

16 The Alaska Sex Offender Registration Act was created based on two legislative findings. The Legislature noted that, "sex offenders pose a high risk of reoffending after release from custody" and supplying Alaska's citizens with information about sex offenders "will assist in protecting public safety" (1994 Alaska Sess. Laws 41, p. 1). Known as one of the most stringent sex offender laws in the nation, registration determinations are based on an offender's conviction rather than his or her perceived dangerousness. The statute requires lifetime registration for offenders convicted of one aggravated sex offense, two or more sex offenses, two or more child kidnappings, or one sex offense and one child kidnapping (KlaasKids Foundation, 2004). In 2009, Alaska increased the reporting requirements to include the offender's email address (es) and instant messaging address(es). All other Internet communication identifiers, such as chat room handles and names used on websites like Myspace and Facebook, must also be reported (Alaska Department of Public Safety, 2010).

17 Justice Thomas filed a concurring opinion. Justice Souter concurred in the judgment only. Justice Stevens and Justice Ginsburg, who was joined by Justice Breyer, offered dissenting opinions asserting that the Act was punitive in nature and imposed a severe deprivation of liberty (*Smith v. Doe* [2003]).

18 The Court also ruled that the statute was not so overly broad that it unduly burdened those subjected to its provisions. Some researchers assert that in rendering this opinion, the *Smith* Court established a precedent that permits states to create broad and punitive registration and notification laws that are, indeed, *ex post facto* violations (McDonald, 2004; Wilkins, 2003).

19 On remand from the U.S. Supreme Court, the appellate court considered whether Alaska's sex offender registration and notification statute violated the plaintiffs' due process rights. The Does argued that the Act impeded their protected liberty interests without notice of the right to be heard. The appellate

court cited and relied heavily on the Supreme Court's ruling in *Connecticut Department of Public Safety v. Doe* (2003). Thus, "bound by controlling Supreme Court law," the appellate court reasoned that, like the law at issue in *Connecticut*, the Alaska statute requires registration and notification based only on an individual's previous conviction(s) (*Doe v. Tandeske*, 2004, p. 596). As such, it does not violate the Does' procedural due process rights. On the matter of whether the provisions of the Act violated their right to substantive due process, the court held that those convicted of serious sex offenses were not entitled to the fundamental right to be protected from the registration and notification provisions. In addition, the court noted that the *Smith* decision established that sex offender registration is a regulatory scheme and "reasonably related" to the danger of a sex offender's likelihood of re-offending. As such, the appellate court affirmed the district court's entry of summary judgment for the State (*Doe v. Tandeske* [2004]).

20 Based on Megan's Law, Connecticut's sex offender registration and community notification statute requires offenders to provide a broad range of personal information to officials. In addition to his or her name and address, convicted sex offenders must provide a recent photograph, fingerprints, a list of any other distinguishing characteristics, a record of their criminal history, and a DNA sample. The information, which must be updated with any changes, is disseminated to the public (Baldwin, 2004).

21 Doe, who pursued his claims on behalf of himself and other similarly situated sex offenders, was convicted of a sex offense based on an incident that occurred before the sex offender registration and community notification law became effective (Baldwin, 2004).

22 Justices Scalia and Stevens concurred. Justice Souter also filed a separate concurring opinion, in which Justice Ginsburg joined.

23 Prior to being released from a halfway house and following a jury trial, Hendricks was classified as a SVP. A state physician determined that he suffered from pedophilia, a diagnosis with which Hendricks agreed. Hendricks conceded that he could not control the urge to sexually molest children; however, he was not amenable to treatment (Fabian, 2009). Diagnosed with a "mental abnormality" (i.e., pedophilia), he was ordered to be civilly committed. Bringing an appeal before the Kansas Supreme Court, Hendricks argued that the Act violated the due process, double jeopardy, and *ex post facto* clauses of the Constitution (*Kansas v. Hendricks* [1997]).

24 Statutes, including the Kansas SVPA in question in *Kansas v. Hendricks*, elicit double-jeopardy challenges based on the fact that the offense for which the offender was first convicted and sentenced in a criminal court is the source of consideration in civil commitment hearings. As such, those ordered to be civilly committed argue that they are subjected to criminal incarceration that is followed by extended periods of confinement. On a similar note, claims of *ex post facto* violations typically arise from those who have served a criminal sentence and oppose being subjected to additional involuntary commitment. Due process challenges are based on the evolving standard of proof that must be met to lawfully deprive an individual of liberty (Price, 2005).

At the core of SVP civil commitment statutes' constitutionality is their expressed intent and purpose. These laws must be non-punitive and consistent with a regulatory scheme (Janus & Bolin, 2008; Ristroph, 2008). As such, the "only legally permissible justification for the SVP laws is that sexually violent predators are so dangerous that they need to be incapacitated" (Lave & McCrary, 2009, p. 6). To determine whether a statute violates the Constitution's Double Jeopardy Clause, courts utilize an "intent–effects" test (Price, 2005, pp. 993–994). The first part of this two-prong analysis requires jurists to determine whether the legislature intended the statute to exact punishment. The second part, known as the effects prong, is based on seven factors established in the landmark citizenship divesting case *Kennedy v. Mendoza-Martinez* (1963). The Mendoza-Martinez factors include whether: *(1)* the sanction involves an affirmative disability or restraint; *(2)* it has historically been regarded as a punishment; *(3)* it comes into play only after a finding of scienter; *(4)* its operation will promote the traditional aims of punishment, retribution, and deterrence; *(5)* the behavior to which it applies is already a crime; *(6)* an alternative purpose to which it may rationally be connected is assignable to it; and *(7)* it appears excessive in relation to the alternative purpose assigned (Barvir, 2008; Petracca, 2006). Each of these factors facilitates the court in determining whether a statute that is not intended to punish is, nevertheless, punitive in effect (Petracca, 2006; Price, 2005).

25 The dissenting opinion was offered by Justices Breyer, Stevens, and Souter and with Justice Ginsburg joining in pertinent part (*Kansas v. Hendricks* (1997)).

26 The case established that "a sex offender has a diminished right to liberty if he is 'mentally abnormal,' even though not 'mentally ill'" (Douard, 2007, p. 37). Subsequent cases challenging the constitutionality of civil commitment for SVPs have largely followed this ruling. "These decisions, taken together with *Hendricks*, suggest that state legislatures enjoy more discretion in reshaping civil commitment laws than at any time in the last 30 years" (Petrila, 2008, p. 364).

27 In 1993, Michael Crane exposed himself at a tanning salon and a video store. During the video store incident, Crane threatened to rape the clerk if she did not perform oral sex on him. He pled guilty to aggravated sexual battery. As authorized by Kansas' SVPA, the state moved to have Crane evaluated and adjudicated a sexual predator. The Act requires that evidence of a "mental abnormality" or a "personality disorder" that impedes an individual's volition be proven beyond reasonable doubt. According to the statute, a mental abnormality includes a "congenital or acquired condition affecting the emotional or volitional capacity that predisposes the person to commit sexually violent offenses in a degree constituting such person a menace to the health and safety of others" (Fabian, 2009, pp. 46–47). Upon review at the Kansas Supreme Court, the jurists reversed the lower court's decision and held that the SPVA was unconstitutional based on the fact that Crane suffered from a personality disorder rather than a volitional impairment.

28 Justice Scalia, joined by Justice Thomas, dissented. Justice Scalia opined that the ruling should have been reversed. He noted that by vacating the decision, it "cheapens the currency of our judgments" (*Kansas v. Crane*, 2002, p. 416).

29 With six rape convictions dating back to 1962, Andre Brigham Young was civilly committed following a prison term and held at the Special Commitment Center on McNeil Island in Washington State. His indefinite commitment at the Center was the source of the "as-applied" challenge at issue before the U.S. Supreme Court (*Seling v. Young* [2001]).

30 Although SVPs have raised "as-applied" challenges to civil commitment in cases that have failed to reach the U.S. Supreme Court, none of the lower courts have invalidated these laws such that the statutes can no longer be applied to others (Janus & Bolin, 2008).

31 Justices Scalia and Thomas each filed a separate concurrence. Justice Stevens dissented, asserting that an Act's consequences can be taken into account when determining whether a statute's effect is punitive (*Seling v. Young* [2001]).

32 Indeed, the decision "left open the possibility that an SVP law might be invalidated based on evidence of improper purpose derived from implementation of the law, as opposed to 'facial' considerations" (Janus & Bolin, 2008, p. 26).

33 Much like Kansas' SVPA, Washington State's Community Protection Act permits the involuntary civil commitment of sexually violent offenders who suffer from a mental abnormality or a personality disorder and are likely to commit future predatory acts of sexual violence. When an offender who has committed such an offense is preparing for release, the prosecuting attorney may seek to have the individual designated as a SVP. Once at trial, the state must prove beyond a reasonable doubt that the offender meets the SVP criteria. If the offender is deemed a SVP, then they are civilly committed for the purposes of care, control, and treatment (*Seling v. Young* [2001]).

34 The application of Level-2 analysis yielded textual exegeses regarding the ethical philosophy in all five U.S. Supreme Court decisions and their corresponding concurring and dissenting opinions with the exception of the following concurring opinions: Justice Thomas in *Smith*, Justice Souter (joined by Justice Ginsburg) in *Connecticut*, and Justice Thomas in *Seling*.

Chapter 5: Rethinking Total Confinement: Translating Social Theory Into Justice Policy

1 Aristotle (2007) recognized the immature rationality of youths and regarded it as natural. He referred to adolescents as "prone to desires and inclined to do whatever they desired . . ., unable to resist their impulses" (p. 149). He noted that youths resort to impulses because they have not yet experienced much failure. Aristotle (2007) suggested that adolescents were "inexperienced with constraints" because they had only been "educated by conventions," lacking an understanding in the complexities of life (p. 150). He argued that youths act out of an excess of emotion because they are convinced that they know everything worth knowing and are passionate in their stubbornness. For this reason, Aristotle maintained that adolescents commit wrongs out of insolence rather than malice. Thus, he argued that youths who committed crimes warranted pity for their emotional immaturity; they still possessed innocence yet were often placed in the realm of adult matters (Aristotle, 2007, pp. 150–151).

2 Some researchers assert that shaming that is re-integrative and restorative is necessary because offenders undergo a "degradation ceremony" (Garfinkel, 1956) during their criminal trial (Bankowski & Mungham, 1976; Braithwaite, 1989). This is a "ceremony" in which the offender is stigmatized and reduced to

the label of criminal. Bankowski and Mungham (1976) described the process as follows:

> At the core of the "ceremony" is a precisely ordered exercise in role-stripping. By this we refer to a systematic undermining of the self-identity of the individual being "degraded" . . . a degradation ceremony [is] any communicative work between persons whereby the public identity of an actor is transformed into something looked on as lower in the local scheme of social types . . . [t]he purpose of this planned subversion is to weaken the individual's power to resist the demands of the organization or institution in which he is placed. The more thorough-going the "ceremony" the more precarious the individual's individuality becomes. He appears as a stranger to himself. (p. 331)

Conclusion: Total Confinement, Psychological Jurisprudence, and Transformative Habits of Character: "Almost a Revolution"

1 For more detailed elaboration on the operation of the symbolic sphere, *see* Lacan (1977, 1981, 1985).
2 For more detailed elaboration on the operation of the linguistic sphere, *see* Derrida (1973, 1977, 1978).
3 For more detailed elaboration on the operation of the material sphere, *see* Foucault (1965, 1972, 1977).
4 The cosmopolitanism at issue here extends Beck's (1992) insights to the realm of the *cosmopolitan imagination* (Delanty, 2009, 2006). This is the realm in which the concept's "empirical and normative" significance is made relevant for and by way of "critical social theory" (Delanty, 2009, p. ix). Beck's (1992) position argues for a culturally grounded approach wherein novel ways of interpreting and responding to the risk society thesis (e.g., with respect to individual identities, collective group behavior, institutional formations, and political/national movements), can constructively take place when diverse people experience a common social issue or problem. However, critical cosmopolitanism pivots, somewhat, from the cultural footing of these "common problems" to their "social and economic . . . and political implications which require[s] a new kind of imagination—[one that is] cosmopolitan as opposed to national or market based" (Delanty, 2009, p. ix). Thus, critical cosmopolitanism as social theory is sensitive to the manifold experiences of risk by way of globalization. The theory's imaginative capacities intend to avoid static normative conceptions of harm, hazard, and social structures of the same and, by way of its critical attitude, to elude simple diminutions of diversity described as observable and therefore quantifiable representations.
5 This is the province in which restrictions on being and denials of becoming are seeded as *harms* of reduction and *harms* of repression (Henry & Milovanovic 1996). For example, the former refers to reducing one's difference through forms of routine limit-setting (e.g., drug therapy, institutionalization/incarceration, mechanical restraints, solitary confinement, execution, protracted community surveillance), repeatedly legitimized because one's

difference is co-productively defined as deviant, diseased, and/or dangerous. The latter refers to repressing one's ability to make a difference because of some agent's renunciation of one's difference, one's humanity (e.g., denying the difference one can make *through* the difference that is mental illness; disavowing the difference one can make *through* the difference that is one's standing, one's possibilities, as an ex-incarcerate, recovering addict, incest or sexual assault survivor, and the like). But the harm of total confinement reduces and represses the keepers of the kept, as well as their managers and their watchers. They, too, are subjected to limits placed and denials imposed on their transforming human flourishing.

6 For more detailed elaboration on the operation of the cultural sphere, *see* Baudrillard (1972, 1976, 1983a, 1983b). For commentary on the individual and systemic pathology propagated by such "negative freedom" *see* Fromm (1994).

7 The observation here concerning the incorporation of habits of character into the construction of legal opinions endorses a descriptive rather than prescriptive accounting. The purpose of this accounting would be to dramatically reframe how the conditions of control could function such that prospects for dignity, healing, and critique for all parties in dispute could be brought to fruition more completely. For example, notions of juvenile delinquency, psychiatric illness, sexual predators, criminal offending, victimization, institutional treatment, community corrections, and societal re-entry would all undergo a kind of *experimental conversion*. This conversion could radically recast each of their meanings in symbolic, linguistic, material, and cultural contexts, especially when channeled through practices of excellence.

8 On this point we note that the radicality of our position is not wedded to liberal or conservative thought. Oppression, especially as hierarchy, when enacted and lived by way of the left is just as harmful and debilitating as when it is legislated and experienced by way of the right. Authoritarianism is to be avoided here. Indeed, as Dyer-Witherford (1999, p. 191) noted, "[T]he aim should be to create a space where a diversity of social, cultural, and economic ways of being can coexist" (*see also* Negri, 1984; Hardt & Negri, 2004).

9 Nietzsche's (1966, p. 146) pronouncement on this very matter is perhaps the most instructive and illuminating. "[One] who fights with monsters should look to it that [one] does not become a monster. And when you gaze long into an abyss the abyss also gazes into you."

10 One area in need of further elaboration includes the interventions that would energize the experimental conversion suggested by our praxis commentary. Some preliminary suggestions include: Lacan (1991) on the integration of the *discourse of the hysteric and analyst*; Freire (1970) on conscientization and dialogical pedagogy; Derrida (1977, 1978) on the temporary reversal of hierarchies demonstrating the mutuality of (rather than the privileging of) terms in binary opposition; Deleuze and Guattari (1984, 1987) on schizo-analytics, deterritorialization/reterritorialization, and rhizomatics; Foucault (1980) on bodies of resistance and in-process inscriptions; Levinas (1987, 2004) on care ethics as ethics of the other; Sen (2011) on capabilities theory, freedom, and democracy; and chaos theory's notion of dissipative structures, strange attractors, and far-from-equilibrium conditions (e.g., Williams & Arrigo, 2002a). For a more detailed description of these and related strategies whose

deployment seeks to overcome the forces of captivity and risk management in historically contingent though manifest form, *see* Arrigo and Milovanovic (2009).

11 For example, current conditions of control make victims into "offenders" (by way of fearful hypervigilance and dangerous panopticism) and offenders into "victims" (by way of limits to being and denials of becoming) when neither offending nor victimization has much to tell us about dignified, healing, restorative, and transformative habits embodied as practiced excellence. The images, narratives, inscriptions, and replications of this offender/victim binary are incomplete. As a source of psychological jurisprudential analysis, these "partialities" are the critique of praxis we seek to specify, overcome and transform.

References

Abrams, L. S., Umbreit, M., & Gordon, A. (2006). Young offenders speak about meeting their victims: Implications for future programs. *Contemporary Justice Review, 9*(3), 243–256.

Abramsky, S., & Fellner, J. (1999). *Ill-equipped: U.S. prisons and offenders with mental illness.* New York, NY: Human Rights Watch.

Ackers, T., & Lanier, M. M. (2009). Epidemiological criminology: Coming full circle. Journal of Public Health, 99(3), 397–402.

Acorn, A. E. (2005). *Compulsory compassion: A critique of restorative justice.* Vancouver, Canada: University of British Columbia.

Adorno, T. (1973). *Negative dialectics.* New York, NY: Continuum International Publishing Group.

Alaska Department of Public Safety. *Sex offender/Child kidnapper registration central registry.* Retrieved from http://www.dps.state.ak.us/Sorweb/sorweb.aspx.

Albanese, J. S. (2006). *Professional ethics in criminal justice: Being ethical when no one is looking.* Boston, MA: Pearson Education.

Alexander, M. A. (1999). Sexual offender treatment efficacy revisited. *Sexual Abuse: A Journal of Research and Treatment, 11,* 101–116.

Allard, P., & Young, M. C. (2002). Prosecuting juveniles in adult court: The practitioner's perspective. *Journal of Forensic Psychology Practice, 2*(2), 65–78.

American Psychological Association. (2003). *Ethical principles of psychologists and code of conduct.* Retrieved from http://www.apa.org/ethics/code2002.html.

Andreas, P. (2009). *Border games: Policing the U.S.–Mexico divide.* Ithaca, NY: Cornell University Press.

Appelbaum, P. S. (1994). *Almost a revolution: Mental health law and the limits of change.* New York, NY: Oxford University Press.

Appelbaum, P. S. (2008). Sex offenders in the community: Are current approaches counterproductive? *Psychiatric Services, 59,* 325–354.

Aristotle. (1976). *Ethics.* (J. A. K. Thomson, Trans.). New York, NY: Penguin.

Aristotle. (1998). *Nicomachean ethics.* London, UK: Dover.

Aristotle. (2000). *Nicomachean ethics.* (R. Crisp, Trans.). Cambridge, UK: Cambridge University Press (Original work composed 4th Century, B.C.E).

Aristotle. (2007). *On rhetoric: A theory of civic discourse* (G.A. Kennedy, Trans.). Oxford, UK: Oxford University Press (Original work composed 4th Century B.C.E).

Arrigo, B. A. (1993). *Madness, language, and law.* Albany, NY: Harrow and Heston.

Arrigo, B. A. (1999). Martial metaphors and medical justice: Implications for law, crime and deviance. *Journal of Political and Military Sociology, 27,* 307–322.

Arrigo, B. A. (2001). Reviewing graduate training models in forensic psychology: Implications for practice. *Journal of Forensic Psychology Practice, 1*(1), 9–31.

Arrigo, B. A. (2002a). *Punishing the mentally ill: A critical analysis of law and psychiatry.* Albany, NY: SUNY Press.

Arrigo, B. A. (2002b). The critical perspective in psychological jurisprudence: Theoretical advances and epistemological assumptions. *International Journal of Law and Psychiatry, 25*(1), 151–172.

Arrigo, B. A. (2003a). Psychology and the law: The critical agenda for citizen justice and radical social change. *Justice Quarterly, 20*(2), 399–444.

Arrigo, B. A. (2003b). Justice and the deconstruction of psychological jurisprudence: The case of competency to stand trial. *Theoretical Criminology, 7*(1), 55–88.

Arrigo, B. A. (Ed). (2004a). *Psychological jurisprudence: Critical explorations in law, crime, and society.* Albany, NY: SUNY Press.

Arrigo, B. A. (2004b). The ethics of therapeutic jurisprudence: A critical and theoretical inquiry of law, psychology, and crime. *Psychiatry, Psychology, and Law: An Interdisciplinary Journal, 11*(1), 23–43.

Arrigo, B. A. (2007). Punishment, freedom, and the culture of control: The case of brain imaging and the law. *American Journal of Law and Medicine, 33*(3), 457–482.

Arrigo, B. A. (2010a). Identity, international terrorism, and negotiating peace: Hamas and ethics-based considerations from critical restorative justice. *British Journal of Criminology, 50*(4), 772–790.

Arrigo, B. A. (2010b). De/reconstructing psychological jurisprudence: Strategies of resistance and struggles for justice. *International Journal of Law in Context, 6*(4): 363–396).

Arrigo, B. A. (in press). Madness, citizenship, and social justice: On the ethics of the shadow and the ultramodern. *Law and Literature, 23*(2).

Arrigo, B. A., & Bullock, J. L. (2008). The psychological effects of solitary confinement on prisoners in supermax units: Reviewing what we know and recommending what should change. *International Journal of Offender Therapy and Comparative Criminology, 52*(6), 622–640.

Arrigo, B. A., & Fox, D. (2009). Psychology and law: The crime of policy and the search for justice. In D. Fox, I. Prilleltensky, & S. Austin (Eds.), *Critical psychology: An introduction* (2nd ed.) (pp. 159–175). London, UK: Sage.

Arrigo, B. A., & Milovanovic, D. (2009). *Revolution in penology: Rethinking the society of captives.* Lanham, MD: Rowman & Littlefield.

Arrigo, B. A., & Milovanovic, D. (2010). Introduction: Postmodern and post-structural criminology. In B. A. Arrigo & D. Milovanovic (Eds.). *Postmodernist and post-structuralist theories of crime* (pp. xi–xxiv). Farnham, Surrey, UK: Ashgate Publishing.

Arrigo, B. A., & Schehr, R. C. (1998). Restoring justice for juveniles: A critical analysis of victim-offender mediation. *Justice Quarterly, 15*(4), 629–665.

Arrigo, B. A., & Shipley, S. (2001). The confusion over psychopathy (I): Historical considerations. *International Journal of Offender Therapy and Comparative Criminology, 45,* 325–343.

Arrigo, B. A., & Shipley, S. L. (2005). *Introduction to forensic psychology: Issues and controversies in law, law enforcement, and corrections* (2nd ed.). Burlington, MA: Elsevier Academic Press.

Baerger, D. R., Griffin, E. F., Lyons, J. S., & Simmons, R. (2003). Competency to stand trial in preadjudicated and petitioned juvenile defendants. *The Journal of the American Academy of Psychiatry and the Law, 31,* 314–320.

Baillargeon, J., Binswanger, I. A., Penn, J. V., Williams, B. A., & Murray, O. J. (2009). Psychiatric disorders and repeat incarcerations: The revolving prison door. *The American Journal of Psychiatry, 166,* 103–109.

Baldwin, G. (2004). CDPS v. Doe: The Supreme Court's clarification of whether sex offender registration and notification laws violate convicted sex offenders' right to procedural due process. *Journal of the National Association of Administrative Law Judiciary, 24,* 383–398.

Banks, C. (2008). *Criminal justice ethics: Theory and practice* (2nd ed.). Thousand Oaks, CA: Sage Publications.

Bankowski, Z., & Mungham, G. (1976). *Images of law.* London, UK: Routledge.

Barbaree, H. E., & Marshall, W. L. (Eds.) (2006). *The juvenile sex offender* (2nd ed.). New York, NY: The Guilford Press.

Barcalow, E. (1998). *Moral philosophy: Theories and issues.* Belmont, CA: Wadsworth.

Bardwell, M. C., & Arrigo, B. A. (2002a). Competency to stand trial: A law, psychology, and policy assessment. *The Journal of Psychiatry & Law, 30,* 147–269.

Bardwell, M. C., & Arrigo, B. A. (2002b). *Criminal competency on trial: The case of Colin Ferguson.* Durham, NC: Carolina Academic Press.

Barvir, A. (2008). When hysteria and good intentions collide: Constitutional considerations of California's Sexual Predator Punishment and Control Act. *Whittier Law Review, 29,* 679–706.

Baudrillard, J. (1972). *For a critique of the political economy of the sign.* St Louis, MO: Telos Press.

Baudrillard, J. (1976). *L'exchange symbolique et la mort.* Paris, France: Gallimard.

Baudrillard, J. (1983a). *Simulations.* New York, NY: Semiotext(e).

Baudrillard, J. (1983b). *In the shadow of the silent majorities.* New York, NY: Semiotext(e).

Bayley, D. H. (2001). Security and justice for all. In H. Strang, & J. Braithwaite, (Eds.) *Restorative justice and civil society* (pp. 211–221). Cambridge, UK: Cambridge University Press.

Bazemore, G., & Boba, R. (2007). Doing good to make good: Community theory for practice in a restorative justice civic engagement reentry model. *Journal of Offender Rehabilitation, 46*(1/2): 25–56.

Beck, U. (1992). *Risk society: Towards a new modernity.* London, UK: Sage.

Beck, U. (2009). *World at risk.* Cambridge, UK: Polity Press.

Bell, S. (2004). The aftermath of the Lionel Tate Case: Tate v. State: Highlighting the need for a mandatory competency hearing. *Nova Law Review.* 28 Nova L. Rev. 575.

Bentham, J., & Mill, J. S. (1973). *The utilitarians.* New York, NY: Anchor Press (Original work published 1789).

Bernstein, E., & Gilligan, C. (1990). Unfairness and not listening: Converging themes in Emma Willard girls' development. In C. Gilligan, N. P. Lyons, & T. J. Hanmer (Eds.), *Making connections: The relational worlds of adolescent girls at Emma Willard School* (pp. 147–161). Cambridge, MA and London, UK: Harvard University Press.

Bersot, H. Y., & Arrigo, B. A. (2010). Inmate mental health, solitary confinement, and cruel and unusual punishment: An ethical and justice policy inquiry. *Journal of Theoretical and Philosophical Criminology, 2*(3), 1–82.

Bersot, H. Y., & Arrigo, B. A. (2011). The ethics of mechanical restraints in prisons and jails: A preliminary inquiry from psychological jurisprudence. *Journal of Forensic Psychology Practice Special Double Issue, 11*(2–3), 232–265.

Bielefeldt, H. (2003). *Symbolic representation in Kant's practical philosophy.* Cambridge, UK: Cambridge University Press.

Birgden, A. (2004). Therapeutic jurisprudence and sex offenders: A psycho-legal approach to protection. *Sexual Abuse: A Journal of Research and Treatment, 16*(4), 351–364.

Birgden, A. (2007). Serious Sex Offenders Monitoring Act 2005 (Vic): A therapeutic jurisprudence analysis. *Psychiatry, Psychology and Law, 14*(1), 78–95.

Bishop, D., & Frazier, C. (2000). Consequences of transfer. In J. Fagan, & F. E. Zimring. (Eds.). *The changing borders of juvenile justice* (pp. 227–276). Chicago, IL: University of Chicago Press.

Bogard, W. (1996). *The simulation of surveillance: Hypercontrol in telematic society.* Cambridge, MA: Cambridge University Press.

Boldt, R., & Singer, J. (2006). Juristocracy in the trenches: Problem-solving judges and therapeutic jurisprudence in drug treatment courts and unified family courts. *Maryland Law Review, 65*(1), 82–99.

Bonner, R., & Vandecreek, L. D. (2006). Ethical decision making for correctional mental health providers. *Criminal Justice and Behavior, 33*(4), 542–564.

Bonnie, R. (1992). The competence of criminal defendants: A theoretical reformulation. *Behavioral Sciences and the Law, 10,* 291–316.

Bonnie, R., & Grisso, T. (2000). *Adjudicative competence and youthful offenders.* In T. Grisso & R. Swartz (Eds.), *Youth on Trial* (pp. 73–103). Chicago, IL: University of Chicago Press.

Bonta, J., & Gendreau, P. (1995). Reexamining the cruel and unusual punishment of prison life. *Law and Human Behavior, 14*(4), 347–372.

Braithwaite, J. (1989). *Crime, shame and reintegration.* Cambridge, UK: Cambridge University Press.

Braithwaite, J. (2002). Restorative justice and therapeutic jurisprudence. *Criminal Law Bulletin, 38*(2), 244–262.

Braithwaite, J. (2006). Doing justice intelligently in civil society. *Journal of Social Issues, 62*(2), 393–409.

Braswell, M., Fuller, J., & Lozoff, B. (2001). *Corrections, peacemaking, and restorative justice: Transforming individuals and institutions.* Cincinnati, OH: Anderson Publishing Co.

Briggs, C., Sundt, J., & Castellano, T. (2003). The effect of supermaximum security prisons on aggregate levels of institutional violence. *Criminology, 41*(4), 1341–1376.

Brink, D. O. (2004). Immaturity, normative competence, and juvenile transfer: How (not) to punish minors for major crimes. *Texas Law Review, 82*, 1555–1585.

Brown, R. B., & Brown, S. J. (2003). *Statutory interpretation: The search for legislative intent.* Washington, DC: National Institute for Trial Advocacy.

Bureau of Justice Statistics. (2000). *Sexual assault of young children as reported to law enforcement: Victim, incident, and offender characteristics.* No. NCJ 182990. Washington, DC: U.S. Department of Justice.

Bureau of Justice Statistics. (2005). *National crime victimization survey, 2004.* No. NCJ 210647. Washington, DC: U.S. Department of Justice.

Butler, J. (1992). Contingent foundations: Feminism and the question of postmodernism. In J. Butler & J. W. Scott (Eds.), *Feminists theorize the political* (pp. 3–21). London, UK: Routledge.

Cahn, S. M. (2009). *Exploring ethics: An introductory anthology.* New York, NY: Oxford University Press.

Capeheart, L., & Milovanovic, D. (2007). *Social justice: Theories, issues and movement.* New Brunswick, NJ: Rutgers University Press.

Carson, D. (2003). Therapeutic jurisprudence and adversarial injustice: Questioning limits. *Western Criminology Review, 4*(2), 124–133.

Catalano, S. (2005). *National Crime Victimization Survey: Criminal victimization, 2004.* Washington, DC: Bureau of Justice Statistics.

Chan, H. C., & Heide, K. M. (2009). Sexual homicide: A synthesis of literature. *Trauma, Violence, & Abuse, 10*(1), 31–54.

Chappell, T. (Ed.). (2006). *Values and virtues: Aristotelianism in contemporary ethics.* New York, NY: Oxford University Press.

Christie, N. (1981). *Limits to pain.* Oxford, UK: Martin Robertson & Co.

Cicourel, A. V. (1981). Notes on the integration of micro- and macro-levels of analysis. In K. D. Knorr-Cetina & A. V. Cicourel (Eds.), *Advances in social theory: Towards an integration of micro- and macro-Sociologies* (pp. 51–80). London: Routledge and Kegan Paul.

Cohen, F. (2008). Penal isolation: Beyond the seriously mentally ill. *Criminal Justice and Behavior, 53*(8), 1017–1047.

Coker, D. (2006). Restorative justice, Navajo peacemaking, and domestic violence." *Theoretical Criminology, 10*(1), 67–85.

Conrad, C. S. (1998). *Jury nullification: The evolution of a doctrine.* Durham, NC: Carolina Academic Press.

Corlett, J. A. (2008). *Responsibility and punishment* (3rd ed.). The Netherlands: Springer.

Corriero, M. A. (2006). *Judging children as children: A proposal for a juvenile justice system.* Philadelphia, PA: Temple University Press.

Darley, J., Fulero, S., Haney, C., & Tyler, T. (2002). Psychological jurisprudence: Taking psychology and law into the twenty-first century. In J. R. P. Ogloff (Ed.), *Taking psychology and law into the twenty-first century,* (pp. 35–59). New York, NY: Springer.

Dawson, R. O. (2000). Judicial waiver in theory and practice. In J. Fagan, & F. E. Zimring. (Eds.) *The changing borders of juvenile justice.* (pp. 45–81). Chicago, IL: University of Chicago Press.

Delanty, G. (2006). The cosmopolitan imagination: Critical cosmopolitanism and social theory. *British Journal of Sociology, 57*(1), 25–47.

Delanty, G. (2009). *The cosmopolitan imagination: The renewal of critical social theory.* New York, NY: Cambridge University Press.

Deleuze, G., & Guattari, F. (1984). *Anti-Oedipus: Capitalism and schizophrenia.* Minneapolis, MN: University of Minnesota Press.

Deleuze, G., & Guattari, F. (1987). *A thousand plateaus: Capitalism and schizophrenia.* Minneapolis, MN: University of Minnesota Press.

Deming, A. (2006). *Sex offender civil commitment program demographics and characteristics.* Paper presented at the Annual Meeting of the Association for the Treatment of Sexual Abusers, Chicago, IL.

Deming, A. (2008). Sex offender civil commitment programs: Current practices, characteristics, and resident demographics. *Journal of Psychiatry & Law, 36*(3), 439–461.

Derrida, J. (1973) *Speech and other phenomena.* Evanston, IL: Northwestern University Press.

Derrida, J. (1977). *Of grammatology.* Baltimore, MD: Johns Hopkins University Press.

Derrida, J. (1978). *Writing and difference.* Chicago, IL: University of Chicago Press.

Dignan, J., & Marsh, P. (2001). Restorative justice and family group conferences in England: Current state and future prospects. In G. Maxwell & A. Morris (Eds.), *Restorative justice for juveniles* (pp. 85–101). Oxford, UK: Hart Publishing.

Doren, D. M. (2002). Evaluating *sex offenders: A manual for civil commitments and beyond.* Thousand Oaks, CA: Sage Publications.

Douard, J. (2007). Loathing the sinner, medicalizing the sin: Why sexually violent predator statutes are unjust. *International Journal of Law and Psychiatry, 30,* 36–48.

Dreisbach, C. (2008). *Ethics in criminal justice.* New York, NY: McGraw-Hill Irwin.

Durose, M. R., Langan, P. A., & Schmitt, E. L. (2003). *Recidivism of sex offenders released from prison in 1994.* Washington, DC: Bureau of Justice Statistics.

Duwe, G., & Goldman, R. A. (2009). The impact of prison-based treatment on sex offender recidivism: Evidence from Minnesota. *Sexual Abuse: A Journal of Research and Treatment, 21*(3), 270–307.

Dyer-Witherford, N. (1999). *Cyber-Marx.* Chicago, IL: University of Illinois Press.

Easterbrook, F. H. (1994). Text, history, and structure in statutory interpretation. *Harvard Journal of Law & Public Policy, 17*(1), 61–70.

Ecclestone, C. E. J., Gendreau, P., & Knox, C. (1974). Solitary confinement of prisoners: An assessment of its effects on offenders' personal constructs and andrenocortical activity. *Canadian Journal of Behavioral Science, 6,* 178–191.

Edwards, R. G. (2009). Profiling the sexually violent predator: An examination of the current literature regarding candidacy for surgical castration. *Mind Matters: The Wesleyan Journal of Psychology, 4,* 17–26.

Edwards, W., & Hensley, C. (2001). Contextualizing sex offender management legislation and policy: Evaluating the problem of latent consequences in community notification laws. *International Journal of Offender Therapy and Comparative Criminology, 45*(1), 83–101.

Eldridge, K. (2009). Remembering "Little Tacoma Boy," 20 years later. Retrieved from www.komonews.com/news/45571582.

Elsner, A. (2004). *Gates of injustice: The crisis in America's prisons.* Upper Saddle River, NJ: Prentice Hall.

Fabian, J. M. (2003). Kansas v. Hendricks, Crane and beyond: "Mental abnormality," and "sexual dangerousness:" Volitional vs. emotional abnormality and the debate between community safety and civil liberties. *William Mitchell Law Review, 29,* 1367–1373.

Fabian, J. M. (2009). *To catch a predator, and then commit him for life: Analyzing the Adam Walsh Act's Civil Commitment Scheme under 18 U.S.C. § 4248.* Retrieved from http://www.criminaljustice.org/public.nsf/01c1e7698280d20385256d0b00 789923/7d37f12e9ce73ac1852575860069b99b?OpenDocument.

Fagan, J., & Zimring, F. E. (Eds.). (2000). *The changing borders of juvenile justice: Transfer of adolescents to the criminal court.* Chicago, IL: The University of Chicago Press.

Failer, J. L. (2002). *Who qualifies for rights: Homelessness, mental illness, and civil commitment.* Ithaca, NY: Cornell University Press.

Farrelly, C., & Solum, L. B. (Eds.). (2008). *Virtue jurisprudence.* New York, NY: Palgrave Macmillan.

Federal Bureau of Prisons Guidelines. (2008). Washington, DC: Federal Bureau of Prisons.

Feld, B. C. (2001). Race, youth violence, and the changing jurisprudence of waiver. *Behavioral Sciences and the Law, 19,* 3–22.

Feld, B. C. (2003). Competence, culpability, and punishment: Implications of Atkins for executing and sentencing adolescents. *Hofstra Law Review, 32*(1), 463–552.

Feld, B. C. (2004). Juvenile transfer. *Criminology & Public Policy, 3*(4), 599–603.

Fellner, J. (2006). A corrections quandary: Mental illness and prison rules. *Harvard Civil Rights & Civil Liberties Law Review, 41*(2), 391–415.

Finkel, N. J. (1995). *Commonsense justice: Jurors' notions of the law.* Cambridge, MA: Harvard University Press.

Finkel, N. (1996). Culpability and commonsense justice: Lessons learned betwixt murder and madness. *Notre Dame Journal of Law, Ethics & Public Policy, x*(1), 11–64.

Finkel, N. J. (1997). Commonsense justice, psychology, and the law: Prototypes that are common, sensible, and not. *Psychology, Public Policy, and Law, 3*(2/3), 461–489.

Finkel, N. (2000a). Commonsense justice and jury instructions: Instructive and reciprocating connections. *Psychology, Public Policy, and Law, 6*(3), 591–628.

Finkel, N. (2000b). Is justice just us? A symposium on the use of social science to inform the substantive criminal law: Commonsense justice, culpability, and punishment. *Hofstra Law Review, 28,* 669–705.

Finkel, N., Harre, R., & Lopez, J. R. (2001). Commonsense morality across cultures: Notions of fairness, justice, honor and equity. *Discourse Studies, 3*(1), 5–27.

Finkelhor, D., & Dziuba-Leatherman, J. (1994). Children as victims of violence: A national survey. *Pediatrics, 94*, 413–420.

Fortney, T., Levenson, J., Brannon, Y., & Baker, J. N. (2007). Myths and facts about sexual offenders: Implications for treatment and public policy. *Sex Offender Treatment, 2*(1), 1–17.

Foucault, M. (1965). *Madness and civilization: A history of insanity in the age of reason.* New York, NY: Vintage.

Foucault, M. (1972). *The archaeology of knowledge.* New York, NY: Pantheon.

Foucault, M. (1977). *Discipline and punish: The birth of a prison.* New York, NY: Pantheon.

Foucault, M. (1980). *Power/knowledge: Selected interviews and other writings, 1972–1977.* London, UK: Harvester.

Foucault, M. (2003). *Abnormal: Lectures at the College de France, 1974-1975.* (V. Marchetti, & A. Salomoni, Trans.). New York, NY: Picador.

Fox, D. R. (1993). Psychological jurisprudence and radical social change. *American Psychologist, 48*, 234–241.

Fox, D. R. (2001). A critical-psychology approach to law's legitimacy. *Legal Studies Forum, 25*, 519–538.

Freeman, N., & Sandler, J. (2009). The Adam Walsh Act: A false sense of security of an effective public policy initiative? *Criminal Justice Policy Review, 26*, 12–23.

Freire, P. (1970). *Pedagogy of the oppressed.* New York, NY: Continuum International Publishing Group.

Frierson, R. L., Dwyer, R. G., Bell, C. C., & Williamson, J. L. (2008). The mandatory registration of juvenile sex offenders and commitment of juveniles as sexually violent predators: Controversies and recommendations. In L. T. Flaherty (Ed.), *Adolescent psychiatry* (Vol. 30) (pp. 55–61). New York, NY: Taylor & Francis Group.

Fromm, E. (1994). *Escape from freedom.* New York, NY: Henry Holt & Company (originally published in 1941).

Gagliardi, G., Lovell, D., Peterson, P., & Jemelka, R. (2004). Forecasting recidivism in mentally ill offenders released from prison. *Law & Human Behavior, 28*(2), 133–155.

Gainey, R. R., Payne, B. K., & O'Toole, M. (2000). The relationship between time in jail, time on electronic monitoring, and recidivism: An event history analysis of a jail-based program. *Justice Quarterly, 17*, 733–752.

Gallagher, C. A., Wilson, D. B., Hirschfield, P., Coggeshall, M. B., & Mackenzie, D. L. (1999). A quantitative review of the effects of sex offender treatment on recidivism. *Corrections Management Quarterly, 3*, 19–29.

Garfinkel, H. (1956). Conditions of successful degradation ceremonies. *American Journal of Sociology, 61*, 420–424.

Gendreau, P., & Bonta, J. (1984). Solitary confinement is not cruel and unusual punishment: People sometimes are! *Canadian Journal of Criminology, 26*, 467–478.

Gendreau, P., Freedman, N. L., Wilde, J. S., & Scott, G. D. (1972). Changes in EEG alpha frequency and evoked response latency during solitary confinement. *Journal of Abnormal Psychology, 79*(1), 54–59.

Gido, R. L., & Dalley, L. (Eds.). (2009). *The mental health issue of women across the criminal justice system.* Upper Saddle River, NJ: Prentice Hall.

Gilligan, C. (1982). *In a different voice: Psychological theory and women's development.* Cambridge, MA: Harvard University Press.

Gilligan, C., Lyons, N. P., & Hanmer, T. J. (1990). *Making connections: The relational worlds of adolescent girls at Emma Willard School* (pp. 147–161). Cambridge, MA: Harvard University Press.

Gladwell, M. (2005). *Blink: The power of thinking without thinking.* New York, NY: Little, Brown and Company.

Glaser, B. (2003). Therapeutic jurisprudence: An ethical paradigm for therapists in sex offender treatment programs. *Western Criminology Review, 4*(2), 143–154.

Goffman, E. (1961). *Asylums: Essays on the social situation of mental patients and other inmates.* Garden City, NY: Anchor Books.

Gordon, B. (2005). *Neuroscience and the law: Brain, mind, and the scales of justice.* Chevy Chase, MD: The Dana Foundation.

Grady, M. D., & Brodersen, M. (2009). In their voices: Perspectives of incarcerated sex offenders on their treatment experiences. *Sexual Addiction & Compulsivity, 15*(4), 320–345.

Grassian, S. (1983). Psychopathological effects of solitary confinement. *American Journal of Psychiatry, 140*(11), 1450–1454.

Gray, F. C. (1973). *Prison discipline in America.* Montclair, NJ: Patterson Smith. (Original work published 1847).

Grisso, T. (2000). Forensic clinical evaluations related to waiver of jurisdiction. In J. Fagan & F. E. Zimring (Eds.), *The changing borders of juvenile justice* (pp. 321–352). Chicago, IL: University of Chicago Press.

Grisso, T. (2003). *Evaluating competencies: forensic assessments and instruments* (2nd ed). New York, NY: Plenum Publishers.

Grisso, T., Steinberg, L., Woolard, J., Cauffman, E., Scott, E., Graham, S., Lexcen, F., Ruppucci, N. D., & Schwartz, R. (2003). Juveniles' competence to stand trial: A comparison of adolescents' and adults' capacities as trial defendants. *Law and Human Behavior, 27*(4), 333–363.

Grisso, T., (2006). Adolescents' decision making: A developmental perspective on constitutional provisions in delinquency cases. *New England Journal on Criminal and Civil Confinement, 32,* 3–14.

Grisso, T., & Schwartz, R. G. (Eds.). (2000). *Youth on trial: A developmental perspective on juvenile justice.* Chicago, IL, and London, UK: University of Chicago Press.

Habermas, J. (1975). *Legitimation crises.* Boston, MA: Beacon Press.

Habermas, J. (1984). *The theory of communicative action. Vol. 1: Reason and the rationalization of society.* Boston, MA: Beacon Press.

Hall, M. A., & Wright, R. F. (2008). Systematic content analysis of judicial opinions. *California Law Review, 96,* 63–122.

Hampton, J. (2001). Mens Rea. In P. Leighton, & J. Reiman, (Eds.), *Criminal Justice Ethics* (pp. 50–72). Upper Saddle River, NJ: Prentice Hall.

Hancock, B. W., & Sharp, P. M. (2004). *Public policy, crime, and criminal justice.* Upper Saddle River, NJ: Prentice Hall.

Haney, C. (2003). Mental health issues in long-term solitary and "supermax" confinement. *Crime & Delinquency, 49*(1), 124–156.

Haney, C. (2009). The social psychology of isolation: Why solitary confinement is psychologically harmful. *Prison Service Journal, 181*(1), 12–20.

Haney, C., & Lynch, M. (1997). Regulating prisons of the future: A psychological analysis of supermax and solitary confinement. *New York University Review of Law and Social Change, 23,* 477–570.

Hanson, R. K., (2005). The validity of Static-99 with older sex offenders. Retrieved from www.sppc-psepc.gc.ca/publictions/Corrections/20050630.

Hanson, R. K., Gordon, A., Harris, A. J. R., Marques, J. K., Murphy, W. D., & Quinsey, V. L. (2002). First report on the collaborative outcome data project on the effectiveness of psychological treatment for sex offenders. *Sexual Abuse: A Journal of Research and Treatment, 14,* 169–194.

Hanson, R. K. & Morton-Bourgon, K. E. (2005). The characteristics of persistent sex offenders: A meta-analysis of recidivism studies. *Journal of Consulting and Clinical Psychology, 73*(6), 1154–1163.

Hardt, M., & Negri, A. (1994). *Labor of Dionysus.* Minneapolis, MN: University of Minnesota Press.

Hardt, M., & Negri, A. (2004). *Multitude: War and democracy in the age of empire.* New York, NY: Penguin Press.

Harris, A. J. R., & Hanson, R. K. (2004). *Sex offender recidivism: A simple question.* Ottawa, Canada: Public Safety and Emergency Preparedness (No. 2204–03).

Harvard Law Review. (2008). The impact of the prison litigation reform act on correctional mental health litigation. *Harvard Law Review, 121,* 1145–1155.

Henriques, Z. W. (2001). The path of least resistance: Sexual exploitation of female offenders as an unethical corollary to retributive ideology and correctional practice. In J. Kleinig & M. L. Smith, (Eds.), *Discretion, community, and correctional ethics* (pp. 193–201). Lanham, MD: Rowman & Littlefield.

Henry, S., & Milovanovic, D. (1996). *Constitutive criminology: Beyond postmodernism.* London, UK: Sage.

Hildebrand, M., de Ruiter, C., & de Voger, V. (2004). Psychopathy and sexual deviance in treated rapists: Association with sexual and nonsexual recidivism. *Sexual Abuse: A Journal of Research and Treatment, 16,* 1–24.

Hobbes, T. (1996). *Leviathan* (R. Tuck, Ed.). Cambridge, UK: Cambridge University Press (Original work published 1651).

Holsti, O. R. (1969). *Content analysis for the social sciences and humanities.* Reading, MA: Addison-Wesley Publishing Company.

Hudson, B. (2003). *Justice and the risk society: Challenging and reaffirming "justice" in late modernity.* London, UK: Sage.

Huigens, K. (1995). Virtue and inculpation. *Harvard Law Review, 108*(7), 1423–1480.

Hurley, M. H. (2009). Restorative practices in institutional settings and at release: Victim wrap around programs. *Federal Probation, 73*(1), 16–22.

Huss, M. T., Tomkins, A. J., Garbin, C. P., Schopp, R., & Killian, A. (2006). Battered women who kill their abusers: An evaluation of commonsense notions, cognitions, and judgments. *Journal of Interpersonal Violence, 21*(8), 1063–1080.

Jackson, R. L., & Hess, D. T. (2007). Evaluation of civil commitment of sex offenders: A survey of experts. *Sexual Abuse: A Journal of Research and Treatment, 19*(4), 425–448.

Jacob Wetterling Resource Center. (2010). Retrieved from www.jwrc.org.

James, D., & Glaze, L. (2006). *Mental health problems of prison and jail inmates.* Washington, DC: US Department of Justice, Bureau of Justice Statistics, NCJ-195670.

Janus, E. S. (2004). Closing Pandora's box: Sexual predators and the politics of sexual violence. *Seton Hall Law Review, 34*(4), 1233–1253.

Janus, E. S. (2006). *Failure to protect: America's sexual predator laws and the rise of the preventive state.* Ithaca, NY, and London, UK: Cornell University Press.

Janus, E. S., & Bolin, B. (2008). An end-game for sexually violent predator laws: As-applied invalidation. *Ohio State Journal of Criminal Law, 6*(25), 24–49.

Janus, E. S., & Logan, W. A. (2003). Substantive due process and the involuntary confinement of sexually violent predators. *Connecticut Law Review, 35*, 341–342.

Janus, E. S., & Prentky, R. (2003). Forensic use of actuarial risk assessment with sex offenders: Accuracy and accountability. *American Criminal Law Review, 40*, 1443–1499.

Johnson, R. (2002). *Hard time* (3rd ed.). Belmont, CA: Wadsworth.

Kant, I. (2002). *Groundwork for the metaphysics of morals.* In T. E. Hill, Jr. & A. Zweig, (Eds.). (A. Zweig, Trans.) Oxford, UK: Oxford University Press (Original work published 1785).

Karp, D. R., & Clear, T. (2002). The community justice frontier: An introduction. In D. Karp & T. Clear (Eds.), *What is community justice?* (pp. ix–xvi). Thousand Oaks, CA: Sage Publications.

Karp, D. R., Sweet, M., Kirshenbaum, A. & Bazemore, G. (2004). Reluctant participants in restorative justice? Youthful offenders and their parents. *Contemporary Justice Review, 7*(2), 199–216.

Katner, D. R. (2006). The mental health paradigm and the MacArthur study: Emerging issues challenging the competence of juveniles in delinquency systems. *American Journal of Law & Medicine. 32*(4), 503–583.

Kilty, J. M. (2006). Under the barred umbrella: Is there room for a women-centered self-injury policy in Canadian corrections? *Criminology & Public Policy, 5*(1), 161–182.

King, K., Steiner, B., & Breach, S. R. (2008). Violence in the supermax: A self-fulfilling prophecy. *The Prison Journal, 88*(1), 144–168.

KlaasKids Foundation. (2004). *Megan's Law by state.* Retrieved from www.klaaskids.org/pg-legmeg.htm.

Kleinig, J., & Smith, M. L. (2001). *Discretion, community, and correctional ethics.* New York, NY: Rowman & Littlefield.

Knorr-Cetina, K. D. (1981). Introduction: The micro-sociological challenge of macro-sociology: Towards a reconstruction of social and methodology. In K. D. Knorr-Cetina & A.V. Cicourel (Eds.), *Advances in social theory and methodology: Towards an integration of macro- and micro-sociologies* (pp. 1–47). London, UK: Routledge and Kegan Paul.

Kupchik, A. (2006). *Judging juveniles: Prosecuting adolescents in adult and juvenile courts.* New York, NY, and London, UK: New York University Press.

Kupers, T. (1999). *Prison madness: The mental health crisis behind bars and what we must do about it.* San Francisco, CA: Jossey-Bass.

Kupers, T. (2008). What to do with survivors? Coping with the long-term effects of isolated confinement. *Criminal Justice and Behavior, 35*(8), 1005–1016.

Kurki, L., & Morris, N. (2001). Supermax prisons. In M. H. Tonry (Ed.), *Crime and justice: A review of the research* (pp. 385–424). Chicago, IL: University of Chicago Press.

Kurlychek, M. C., & Johnson, B. D. (2004). The juvenile penalty: A comparison of juvenile and young adult sentencing outcomes in criminal court. *Criminology, 42*(2), 485–517.

Lacan, J. (1977). *Ecrits: A selection.* New York, NY: W. W. Norton.

Lacan, J. (1981). *The four fundamental concepts of psychoanalysis.* New York, NY: W. W. Norton.

Lacan, J. (1985). *Feminine sexuality.* New York, NY: W. W. Norton.

LaCombe, D. (2008). Consumed with sex: The treatment of sex offenders in risk society. *British Journal of Criminology, 48,* 55–74.

LaFond, J. Q. (2005). *Preventing sexual violence: How society should cope with sex offenders.* Washington, DC: American Psychological Association.

LaFond, J. Q. (2008). Sexually violent predator laws and the liberal state: An ominous threat to individual liberty. *International Journal of Law and Psychiatry, 31,* 158–171.

Lamb, H. R., & Weinberger, L. E. (1998). Persons with severe mental illness in jails and prisons: A review. *Psychiatric Services, 49*(4), 483–492.

Lanier, M. M. (2010). Epidemiological criminology (EpiCrim): Definition and application. *Journal of Theoretical and Philosophical Criminology, 2*(1), 63–103.

Lave, T., & McCrary, J. (2009). *Assessing the crime impact of sexually violent predator laws.* CELS 2009 4th Annual Conference on Empirical Legal Studies Paper. Retrieved from http://papers.ssrn.com/sol3/papers.cfm?abstract_id=1443718.

Leighton, P., & Reiman, J. (2001). *Criminal justice ethics.* Upper Saddle River, NJ: Prentice Hall.

Letourneau, E. J., & Borduin, C. M. (2008). The effective treatment of juveniles who sexually offend: An ethical imperative. *Ethics & Behavior, 18*(2–3), 286–306.

Levenson, J. S. (2004). Reliability of sexually violent predator civil commitment criteria in Florida. *Law and Human Behavior, 28*(4), 357–368.

Levenson, J. S. (2003). Factors predicting recommendations for civil commitment of sexually violent predators under Florida's Jimmy Ryce Act. *Dissertation Abstracts International, 64*(3). (UMI No. AAT3085817).

Levenson, J. S., & Cotter, L. P. (2005). The impact of sex offender residency restrictions: 1,000 feet from danger or one step from absurd? *International Journal of Offender Therapy and Comparative Criminology, 49,* 168–174.

Levenson, J. S., & Morin, J. W. (2004). Factors predicting selection of sexual offenders for civil commitment. *International Journal of Offender Therapy and Comparative Criminology, 50*(6), 609–629.

Levinas, E. (1987). *Time and the other.* Pittsburgh, PA: Duquesne University Press.

Levinas, E. (2004). *Otherwise than being.* Pittsburgh, PA: Duquesne University Press.

Levine, M. (2000). The family group conference in the New Zealand children, young persons, and their families act of 1989 (CYP&F): review and evaluation. *Behavioral Sciences and the Law, 18,* 517–556.

Lieb, R. (1996). Community notification laws: A step toward more effective solutions. *Journal of Interpersonal Violence, 11*(2), 298–300.

Lippke, R. L. (2004). Against supermax. *Journal of Applied Philosophy, 21*(2), 109–124.

Lobel, J. (2008). Prolonged solitary confinement and the Constitution. *Journal of Constitutional Law, 11*(1), 115–138.

Logan, W. A. (2006). Constitutional collectivism and ex-offender residence exclusion zones. *Iowa Law Review, 92,* 1–41.

Losel, F., & Schmucker, M. (2005). The effectiveness of treatment for sex offenders: A comprehensive meta-analysis. *Journal of Experimental Criminology, 1*, 117–146.

Lovell, D. (2008). Patterns of disturbed behavior in a supermax population. *Criminal Justice and Behavior, 35*(8), 985–1004.

Lovell, D., Cloyes, K., Allen, D., & Rhodes, L. (2000). Who lives in super-maximum custody? A Washington State study. *Federal Probation, 64*(2), 33–38.

Lovell, D., Johnson, L. C., & Cain, K. C. (2007). Recidivism of supermax prisoners in Washington State. *Crime & Delinquency, 53*(4), 633–656.

Louw, D., Strydom, C., & Esterhuyse, K. (2005). Prediction of violent behavior: Professionals' appraisals. *Criminal Justice, 5*(4), 379–406.

Lynd, H. M. (1958). *On shame and the search for identity.* London, UK: Routledge.

Lyon, D. (Ed.) (2006). *Theorizing surveillance: The panoptic and beyond.* Cullompton, Devon, UK: Willan Press.

MacIntyre, A. (2007). *After virtue: A study in moral theory* (3rd ed.). Notre Dame, IN: University of Notre Dame Press.

MacKenzie, D. L. (2006). *What works in corrections: Reducing the criminal activities of offenders and delinquents.* Cambridge, MA: Cambridge University Press.

McCold, P. (2004). Paradigm muddle: The threat to restorative justice posed by its merger with community justice." *Contemporary Justice Review, 7*(1), 13–35.

McConville, B., & Kelly, D. C. (2007). Cruel and unusual? Defining the conditions of confinement in the mentally ill. *The Journal of the American Academy of Psychiatry and the Law, 35*(4), 533–534.

McDonald, D. L. (2004). Smith v. Doe: Judicial deference towards the legislative intent behind a broad, punitive civil law betrays the core principles of the ex post facto clause. *Maryland Law Review, 63*, 369–400.

McGarrell, E. F. (2001). *Restorative justice conferences as an early response to young offenders.* Washington, DC: US Department of Justice, Office of Juvenile Justice and Delinquency Prevention.

McGarrell, E. F., & Hipple, N. K. (2007). Family group conferencing and re-offending among first-time juvenile offenders: The Indianapolis Experiment. *Justice Quarterly, 24*(2), 221–246.

McGarrell, E. F., Olivares, K., Crawford, K., & Kroovand, N. (2000). *Returning justice to the community: the Indianapolis juvenile restorative justice experiment.* Indianapolis, IN: Hudson Institute Crime Control Policy Center.

McGuire, J. (2000). Can the criminal law ever be therapeutic? *Behavioral Sciences and the Law, 18*, 413–426.

Mears, D. P. (2006). *Evaluating the effectiveness of supermax prisons.* Washington, DC: Urban Institute Justice Policy Center.

Mears, D. P., & Watson, J. (2006). Towards a fair and balanced assessment of supermax prisons. *Justice Quarterly, 23*(2), 232–270.

Melton, G. B. (1990). Law, science, and humanity: The normative foundation of social science in law. *Law and Human Behavior, 14*, 315–332.

Melton, G. B. (1992). The law is a good thing (psychology is, too). Human rights in psychological jurisprudence. *Law and Human Behavior, 16*, 381–398.

Melton, G. B., & Saks, M. J. (1986). The law as an instrument of socialization and social structure. In G. B. Melton (Ed.), *The law as a behavioral instrument* (pp. 235–277). Lincoln, NE: University of Nebraska.

Mercado, C. C., Schopp, R. F., & Bornstein, B. H. (2003). Evaluating sex offenders under sexually violent predator laws: How might mental health professionals conceptualize the notion of volitional impairment? *Aggression and Violent Behavior, 10*(1), 289–309.

Mercuro, N., & Medema, S. G. (1998). *Law and economics: From Posner to post-modernism.* Princeton, NJ: Princeton University Press.

Mill, J. S. (1989). *On liberty and other writings.* (S. Collini, Ed). Cambridge, UK: Cambridge University Press (Original work published 1859).

Mill, J. S. (1957). *Utilitarianism* (O. Piest, Ed.). Indianapolis, IN: Bobbs-Merrill Educational Publishing (Original work published 1861).

Miller, R. D. (2003). Chemical castration of sex offenders: Treatment or punishment? In B. J. Winick & J. Q. LaFond (Eds.), *Protecting society from sexually dangerous offenders: Law, justice, and therapy* (pp. 249–263). Washington, DC: American Psychological Association.

Mortensen, M. L. (2006). GPS monitoring: An ingenious solution to the threat pedophiles pose to California's children. *Journal of Juvenile Law, 27,* 17–32.

Mossman, D. (2006). Critique of pure risk assessment or, Kant meets Tarasoff. *University of Cincinnati Law Review, 75,* 523–609.

Mulligan, S. (2009). From retribution to repair: Juvenile justice and the history of restorative justice. *University of La Verne Law Review, 31,* 139–149.

Naday, A., Freilich, J. D., & Mellow, J. (2008). The elusive data on supermax confinement. *The Prison Journal, 88*(1), 69–93.

National Center for Missing and Exploited Children. (2007). *Registered sex offenders in the United States per 100,000 population.* Retrieved from www.missingkids.com/enUS/documents/sex-offender-map.pdf

Negri, A. (1984). *Marx beyond Marx.* New York, NY: Bergin and Garvey.

Nietzsche, F. W. (1966). *Beyond good and evil: Prelude to a philosophy of the future* (New Ed.) (Walter Kaufmann, Ed.). New York, NY: Vintage. (originally published in 1886).

Noddings, N. (2003). *Caring: A feminine approach to ethics and moral education* (2nd Ed.). Berkeley, CA: University of California Press.

Norman-Eady, S. (2006). *Castration of sex offenders.* Connecticut General Assembly. Retrieved from www.cga.ct.gov/2006/rpt/2006-R-0183.htm.

Noroian, P., & Saleh, F. M. (2006). Residency restrictions for convicted sex offenders: State law imposing residency restrictions for convicted sex offenders is not unconstitutional, given their presumed dangerousness. *Journal of the American Academy of Psychiatry and the Law, 34*(3), 422–425.

Oakes, L. (2008, June 9). Locked in limbo: Civil commitment for people convicted of sex offenses. *Minneapolis Star Tribune,* p. 1A.

Oberlander, L. B., Goldstein, N. E., & Ho, C. N. (2001). Preadolescent adjudicative competence: Methodological considerations and recommendations for practice standards. *Behavioral Sciences and the Law, 19,* 545–563.

Office of Program Policy Analysis & Government Accountability (OPPAGA). (2008). *The delays in screening sexually violent predators increase costs;*

Treatment facility security enhanced. Report No. 08–10. Retrieved January 18, 2010, from www.oppaga.state.fl.us/reports/pdf/0810rpt.pdf.

O'Hara, E. A., & Robbins, M. M. (2009). Using criminal punishment to serve both victim and social needs. *Law and Contemporary Problems, 72,* 199–217.

Ogloff, J. R. P. (2002). Two steps forward and one step backward: The law and psychology movement(s) in the 20th century. In J. R. P. Ogloff (Ed.), *Taking psychology and law into the twenty-first century,* (pp. 1–34). New York, NY: Springer.

O'Keefe, M. L. (2008). Administrative segregation from within: A corrections perspective. *The Prison Journal, 88*(1), 123–143.

Olver, M. E., & Wong, S. C. P. (2006). Psychopathy, sexual deviance, and recidivism among sex offenders. *Sexual Abuse: A Journal of Research and Treatment, 18*(1), 65–82.

Olver, M. E., Wong, S. C. P., & Nicholaichuck, T. P. (2009). Outcome evaluation of high-intensity inpatient sex offender treatment program. *Journal of Interpersonal Violence, 24*(3), 522–536.

O'Malley, P. (Ed.) (1998). *Crime and the risk society.* Surrey, UK: Ashgate Press.

O'Malley, P. (2004). *Risk, uncertainty, and government.* London, UK: The Glasshouse Press.

Padgett, K., Bales, W., & Blomberg, T. (2006). Under surveillance: An empirical test of the effectiveness and consequences of electronic monitoring. *Crime and Public Policy, 5*(1), 201–232.

Palermo, G. B. (2009). Sexual predator law or preventive detention? Call if for what it is. *International Journal of Offender Therapy and Comparative Criminology, 53*(4), 371–372.

Parker, L. (2005). RSVP: Restorative justice in a county jail. Retrieved from http://www.restorativejustice.org/editions/2005/december05/rsvp/.

Pastore, A. L., & Maguire, K. (Eds.). (2007). *Sourcebook of criminal justice statistics.* Albany, NY: Hindelang Criminal Justice Research Center.

Pavlich, G. (2006). *Paradoxes of restorative justice.* London, UK: Glasshouse Press.

Perlin, M., & Dlugacz, H. (2008). *Mental health issues in jails and prisons.* Durham, NC: Carolina Academic Press.

Perlin, M. L., Gould, K. K., & Dorfman, D. D. (1995). Therapeutic jurisprudence and the civil rights of institutionalized mentally disabled persons: Hopeless oxymoron or path to redemption. *Psychology, Public Policy, and Law, 1*(1), 80–119.

Perlin, M. L. (2000). *The hidden prejudice: Mental disability law on trial.* Washington, DC: APA Press.

Perlin, M. L. (2007). Recent criminal legal decisions: Implications for forensic mental health experts. In A. M. Goldberg (Ed.), *Forensic psychology: Emerging topics and expanding roles* (pp. 333–359). Hoboken, NJ: Wiley.

Petracca, M. R. (2006). Banished! New Jersey's municipalities' unconstitutional trend of banishing sex offenders. *Seton Hall Legislative Journal, 31,* 253–268.

Petrila, J. (2008). Because they do horrible things: Fear, science, and the erosion of civil liberties in sexually violent predator proceedings. *Journal of Psychiatry & Law, 36*(6), 359–363.

Phillips, S., & Grattet, R. (2000). Judicial rhetoric, meaning-making, and the institutionalization of hate crime law. *Law & Society Review, 34*(3), 567–606.

Pizarro, J., & Stenius, V. M. K. (2004). Supermax prisons: Their rise, current practices, and effect on inmates. *The Prison Journal, 84*(2), 248–264.

Pizarro, J. M., & Narag, R. E. (2008). Supermax prisons: What we know, what we do not know, and where we are going. *The Prison Journal, 88*(1), 23–42.

Polizzi, D. (2008). Restore to what?: Restorative justice and the social construction of the offender. *International Journal of Restorative Justice, 4*(2), 80–98.

Polizzi, D., & Lanier, M. M. (2010). The social construction of crime as dis-ease: Epidemiological criminology from a phenomenological perspective. American Society of Criminology Annual Conference (San Francisco, CA, November 17–20).

Pollock, J. M. (2007). *Ethical dilemmas and decisions in criminal justice*, (5th Ed.). Belmont, CA: Wadsworth, Cengage Learning.

Posner, R. (2008). *How judges think.* Cambridge, MA: Harvard University Press.

Poythress, N., Lexcen, F. J., Grisso, T., & Steinberg, L. (2006). The competence-related abilities of adolescent defendants in criminal court. *Law and Human Behavior, 30*(1), 75–92.

Prentky, R. A., Janus, E., Barbaree, H., Schwarts, B. K., & Kafka, M. P. (2006). Sexually violent predators in the courtroom: Science on trial. *Psychology, Public Policy, and Law, 12*(4), 357–393.

Presser, L. (2004). Justice here and now: A personal reflection on the restorative and community justice paradigms. *Contemporary Justice Review, 7*(1), 101–106.

Price, J. T. (2005). Reconciling morality and moral responsibility in the law: A due process challenge to the inconsistent mental responsibility standards at play in criminal insanity defenses and sexually violent predator civil commitment hearings. *Hastings Constitutional Law Quarterly, 32*, 987–1014.

Quinney, R. (1991). The way of peace: On crime, suffering, and service. In R. Quinney, & H. Pepinsky (Eds), *Criminology as peacemaking* (pp. 3–13). Bloomington, IN: Indiana University Press.

Rainville, G. A., & Smith, S. K. (2003). Juvenile felony defendants in criminal courts: Survey of 40 counties, 1998. U.S. Department of Justice. Bureau of Justice Statistics. United States.

Rand, A. (1964). *The virtue of selfishness.* West Bangal, India: Signet Press.

Randolph, A. R. (1994). Dictionaries, plain meaning, and context in statutory interpretation. *Harvard Journal of Law & Public Policy, 17*(1), 71–78.

Rawls, J. (1971). *A theory of justice.* Cambridge, MA: Harvard University Press.

Rayburn Yung, C. (2007). Banishment by a thousand laws: Residency restrictions of sex offenders. *Washington University Law Review, 85*, 101–160.

Rebman, C. (1999). The Eighth Amendment and solitary confinement: The gap in protection from psychology consequences. *DePaul Law Review, 49*(1), 567–586.

Redding, R. E., & Frost, L. E. (2001). Adjudicative competence in modern juvenile court. *The Virginia Journal of Social Policy and the Law, 9*, 353–409.

Reid, W. H., Wise, M., & Sutton, B. (1992). The use and reliability of psychiatric diagnosis in forensic settings. *Clinical Forensic Psychiatry, 15*(3), 529–537.

Reiman, J. (2007). *The rich get richer and the poor get prison* (8th ed.). Boston, MA: Allyn & Bacon.

Renzema, M. (2003). *Electronic monitoring's impact on reoffending.* Retrieved from www.campbellcollaboration.org/doc-pdf/elecmon.pdf.

Rhodes, L. (2004). *Total confinement: Madness and reason in the maximum security prison.* Berkeley and Los Angeles, CA: University of California Press.

Rhodes, L. (2005). Pathological effects of the supermaximum prison. *American Journal of Public Health, 95*(10), 1692–1695.

Ristroph, A. (2008). Criminal law: State intentions and the law of punishment. *Journal of Criminal Law & Criminology, 98,* 1353–1406.

Ritchie, J., & Spencer, L. (2002). Qualitative data analysis for applied policy research. In A. M. Huberman & M. B. Miles (Eds.), *The qualitative researcher's companion* (pp. 305, 307). Thousand Oaks, CA: Sage Publications.

Riveland, C. (1999). *Supermax prisons: Overview and general considerations.* Longmont, CO: U.S. Department of Justice, National Institute of Corrections.

Robbers, M. L. P. (2009). Lifers on the outside: Sex offenders and disintegrative shaming. *International Journal of Offender Therapy and Comparative Criminology, 53*(1), 5–28.

Roche, D. (2006). Dimensions of restorative justice. *Journal of Social Issues, 62*(2), 217–238.

Rodriguez, N. (2005). Restorative justice, communities, and delinquency: Whom do we reintegrate? *Criminology and Public Policy, 4,* 103–330.

Romano, S. M. (1996). If the SHU fits: Cruel and unusual punishment at California's Pelican Bay state prison. *Emory Law Journal, 45*(3), 1089–1138.

Ross, W. D. (1930). *The right and the good.* Oxford, UK: Clarendon Press.

Rossiter, M. J. (2006). Transferring children to adult criminal court: How to best protect our children and society. *La Verne Law Review,* Inc. 27 J. Juv. L. 123.

Rousseau, J. J. (1968). *The social contract.* Translated by M. Cranston. New York, NY: Penguin Classics (Original work published 1762).

Ryan, E. P., & Murrie, D. C. (2005). Competence to stand trial and young children is the presumption of competence valid? *Journal of Forensic Psychology Practice, 5*(1), 89–102.

Ryba, N. L., Cooper, V. G., & Zapf, P. A. (2003). Assessment of maturity in juvenile competency to stand trial evaluations: A survey of practitioners. *Journal of Forensic Psychology Practice, 3*(3), 23–45.

Saks, E. R. (2002). *Refusing care: Forced treatment and the rights of the mentally ill.* Chicago, IL: University of Chicago Press.

Schehr, R. C., & Milovanovic, D. (1999). Conflict mediation and the postmodern. *Social Justice, 25*(1), 208–232.

Schma, W., Kjervik, D., & Petrucci, C. (2005). Therapeutic jurisprudence: Using the law to improve the public's health. *Journal of Law, Medicine & Ethics, 33*(4), 59–63.

Schneider, J. E. (2008). A review of research findings related to the civil commitment of sex offenders. *Journal of Psychiatry & Law, 36*(3), 463–483.

Schopp, R. F., Scalora, M. J., & Pearce, M. (1999). Expert testimony and professional judgment: Psychological expertise and commitment as a sexual predator after *Hendricks. Psychology, Public Policy, and Law, 5,* 120–174.

Schwartz, B. K. (2003). *Correctional psychology: Practice, programming, and administration.* Kingston, NJ: Civic Research Institute.

Scott, C. (2004). Judging in a therapeutic key: Therapeutic jurisprudence and the courts. *The Journal of Legal Medicine, 25,* 377–388.

Scott, E. S. (2000). Criminal responsibility in adolescence: Lessons from developmental psychology. In T. Grisso & R. Swartz (Eds.), *Youth on trial* (pp. 291–324). Chicago, IL: University of Chicago Press.

Scott, C. L., & Gerbasi, J. B. (2003). Sex offender registration and community notification challenges: The Supreme Court continues its trend. *Journal of the Academy of Psychiatry and the law, 31*(4), 494–501.

Scott, E. S. & Grisso, T. (2005). Developmental incompetence, due process, and juvenile justice policy. *North Carolina Law Review.* 83 N.C.L. Rev. 793.

Scott, C. L. & Holmberg, T. (2003). Castration of sex offenders: Prisoners' rights versus public safety. *Journal of the American Academy of Psychiatry and Law, 31,* 502–509.

Scranton, P. (2007). *Power, conflict, and criminalization.* London, UK: Routledge.

Seto, M. C. (2008). *Pedophilia and sexual offending against children: Theory, assessment, and intervention.* Washington, DC: American Psychological Association.

Sellers, B. G., & Arrigo, B. A. (2009). Developmental maturity, adjudicative competence, and adolescent transfer: An ethical and justice policy inquiry. *The Journal of Criminal Law and Criminology, 99*(2), 435–488.

Sen, A. (2011). *The idea of justice.* Cambridge, MA: Belknap Press of Harvard University Press.

Shalev, S. (2008). *A sourcebook on solitary confinement.* London, UK: Manheim Centre for Criminology.

Shalev, S. (2009). Inside a supermax. *Prison Service Journal, 181*(1), 21–25.

Shaylor, C. (1998). "It's like living in a black hole": Women of color and solitary confinement in the prison industrial complex. *New England Journal of Criminal and Civil Confinement, 24*(2), 385–416.

Shichor, David. (2006). *The meaning and nature of punishment.* Long Grove, IL: Waveland Press.

Shipley, S., & Arrigo, B. A. (2001). The confusion of psychopathy (II): Implications for forensic (correctional) practice. *International Journal of Offender Therapy and Comparative Criminology, 45,* 407–419.

Siegel, D. Juror nullification. Whole Earth Review 72 (1991): 45. Expanded Academic ASAP. Retrieved from http://find.galegroup.com.ezproxy.lib.usf.edu/gtx/infomark.do?&contentSet=IACDocuments&type=retrieve&tabID=T002&prodId=EAIM&docId=A11255646&source=gale&srcprod=EAIM&userGroupName=tamp59176&version=1.0.

Simon, J. (2009). *Governing through crime: How the war on crime transformed American democracy and created a culture of fear.* New York, NY: Oxford University Press.

Slobogin, C. (1995). Therapeutic jurisprudence: Five dilemmas to ponder. *Psychology, Public Policy, and Law, 1,* 193–219.

Slobogin, C. (2006). *Minding justice: Laws that deprive people with mental disability of life and liberty.* Cambridge, MA: Harvard University Press.

Slote, M. (1985). *Common-sense morality and consequentialism.* London, UK: Routludge & Kegan Paul.

Small, M. (1993). Advancing psychological jurisprudence. *Behavioral Sciences and the Law, 11*(1), 3–16.

Smith, D. G. (2008). The constitutionality of civil commitment and the adequacy of treatment. *Boston College Law Review, 49*, 1383–1429.

Snyder, H. N., & Sickmund, M. (2006). Juvenile offenders and victims: 2006 national report. Washington, DC: U.S. Department of Justice, Office of Justice Programs, Office of Juvenile Justice and Delinquency.

Solum, L. B. (2008). Natural justice: An aretaic account of the virtue of lawfulness. In C. Farrelly & L. B. Solum (Eds.), *Virtue jurisprudence* (pp. 167–192). New York, NY: Palgrave Macmillan.

Sparks, R. (2008). Differences in legal and medical standards in determining sexually violent predator status. *Law and Psychology Review, 32*, 175–189.

Sreenivasan, S., Weinberger, L. E., & Garrick, T. (2003). Expert testimony in sexually violent predator commitments: Conceptualizing legal standards of "mental disorder" and "likely to reoffend." *Journal of the American Academy of Psychiatry and the Law, 31*(4), 471–485.

Steinberg, L., & Cauffman, E. (2000). A developmental perspective on jurisdictional boundary. In J. Fagan & F. E. Zimring (Eds.), *The changing borders of juvenile justice.* (pp. 379–404). Chicago, IL: University of Chicago Press.

Steinberg, L. (2003). Juveniles on trial: MacArthur Foundation study calls competency into question. *Criminal Justice, 18*(3), 20–25.

Steinberg, L., & Schwartz, R. G. (2000). Developmental psychology goes to court. In T. Grisso & R. Swartz (Eds.), *Youth on trial* (pp. 9–31). Chicago, IL: University of Chicago Press.

Steinbock, B. (1995). Megan's Law: A policy perspective. *Criminal Justice Ethics, 14*(2), 4–9.

Steiner, B. & Wright, E. (2006). Assessing the relative effects of state direct file waiver laws on violent juvenile crime: Deterrence or irrelevance? *The Journal of Criminal Law & Criminology, 96*(4), 1451–1477.

Steiner, B., Hemmens, C., & Valerie Bell, V. (2006). Legislative waiver reconsidered: General deterrent effects of statutory exclusion laws enacted post-1979. *Justice Quarterly, 23*(1), 34–59.

Sterba, J. P. (2003). *Social and political philosophy: Classical western texts in feminist and multicultural perspectives* (3rd ed.). Belmont, CA: Wadsworth/Thompson Learning.

Strang, H., & Braithwaite, J. (Eds.). (2001). *Restorative justice and civil society.* Cambridge: Cambridge University Press.

Sullivan, D., & Tifft, L. (2005). *Restorative justice: Healing the foundations of our everyday lives* (2nd Ed.). Monsey, NY: Criminal Justice Press.

Sykes, G. M. (1958). *Society of captives: A study of maximum security prison.* Princeton, NJ: Princeton University Press.

Tekle-Johnson, A. (2009). In the zone: Sex offenders and the ten-percent solution. *Iowa Law Review, 94*, 607–662.

Telsavaara, T. V. T., & Arrigo, B. A. (2006). DNA evidence in rape cases and the Debbie Smith Act: Forensic practice and criminal justice implications. *International Journal of Offender Therapy and Comparative Criminology, 50*(5), 487–505.

Tewksbury, R. (2005). Collateral consequences of sex offender registration. *Journal of Contemporary Justice, 21*(1), 67–81.

Tewksbury, R., & Lees, M. (2006). Consequences of sex offender registration: Collateral consequences and community experiences. *Sociological Spectrum, 26*(3), 309–334.

Tewksbury, R., & Lees, M. (2007). Perception of punishment: How registered sex offenders view registries. *Crime and Delinquency, 53*(3), 380–407.

Thomas, J., Leaf, M., Kazmierczak, S., & Stone, J. (2006). Self-injury in correctional settings: "Pathology" of prisons or of prisoners? *Criminology & Public Policy, 5*(1), 193–202.

Tifft, L.L., & Sullivan, D. (2005). Needs-based anarchist criminology. In S. Henry & M. Lanier (Eds.). *The essential criminology reader* (pp. 259–277). Boulder, CO: Westview.

Toch, H. (2001). The future of supermax confinement. *The Prison Journal, 81*(3), 376–388.

Toch, H. (2003). The contemporary relevance of early experiments with supermax reform. *The Prison Journal, 83*(2), 221–228.

Tonry, M. (2004). *Thinking about crime: Sense and sensibility in American penal culture.* New York, NY: Oxford University Press.

Toutant, C. (2005, November 21). Zoning out sex offenders. *New Jersey Law Journal,* p. 1A.

Trivits, L., & Reppucci, N.D. (2002). The application of Megan's Law to juveniles. *American Psychologist, 57,* 690–704.

Turner, E., & Rubin, S. (2002). Once a sex offender . . . always a sex offender. *Journal of Police and Criminal Psychology, 17*(2), 32–44.

Umbreit, M. S., Coates, R. B., & Armour, M. (2006). Victims of severe violence in mediated dialogue with offenders: The impact of the first multi-site study in the U. S. *International Review of Victimology, 13*(1), 27–48.

Van Ness, D., & Heetderks Strong, K. (2007). *Restorative justice: An introduction to restorative justice.* Cincinnati, OH: Lexis/Nexis Anderson.

Vaux, R. (1826). *Notices of the original and successive efforts to improve the discipline of the prison at Philadelphia, and to reform the criminal code of Pennsylvania: With a few observations on the penitentiary system.* Philadelphia, PA: Kimber and Sharpless.

Vess, J., Murphy, C., & Arkowitz, S. (2004). Clinical and demographic differences between sexually violent predators and other commitment types in a state forensic hospital. *Journal of Forensic Psychiatry and Psychology, 15,* 669–681.

Veysey, B. M., Zgoba, K., & Dellasandro, M. (2008). A preliminary step towards evaluating the impact of Megan's Law: A trend analysis of sexual offenses in New Jersey from 1985 to 2005. *Justice Research and Policy, 10*(2), 1–18.

Viljoen, J. L., & Grisso, T. (2007). Prospects for remediating juveniles' adjudicative incompetence. *Psychology, Public Policy and Law, 13*(2), 87–114.

Vollum, S., & Hale, C. (2002). Electronic monitoring: A research review. *Corrections Compendium, 27,* 1–26.

Wakefield, H. (2006). The vilification of sex offenders: Do laws targeting sex offenders increase recidivism and sexual violence? *Journal of Sexual Offender Civil Commitment: Science and the Law, 1,* 141–149.

Walker, S. (2007) *Sense and nonsense about crime and drugs: A policy guide* (6th Ed.). Belmont, CA: Brooks/Cole Publishing Co.

Ward, T. (2007). On a clear day you can see forever: Integrating values and skills in sex offender treatment. *Journal of Sexual Aggression, 13*(3), 187–201.

Way, B., Miraglia, R., Sawyer, D., Beer, R., & Eddy, J. (2005). Factors related to suicide in New York state prisons. *International Journal of Law and Psychiatry, 28*(3), 207–221.

Websdale, N. S. (1996). Predators: The social construction of "stranger-danger" in Washington State as a form of patriarchal ideology. *Women & Criminal Justice, 7*(2), 43–68.

Weidman, M. M. (2004). The culture of judicial deference and the problem of supermax prisons. *UCLA Law Review, 51*(5), 1505–1554.

Weinberger, L. E., Sreensivasan, S., Garrick, T., & Osran, H. (2005). The impact of surgical castration on sexual recidivism risk among sexually violent predatory offenders. *Journal of the American Academy of Psychiatry and Law, 33*, 16–36.

Wexler, D. B. (2008a). Two decades of therapeutic jurisprudence. *Tuoro Law, Review, 24*(1), 17–29.

Wexler, D. B. (Ed.). (2008b). *Rehabilitating layers: Principles of therapeutic jurisprudence for criminal law practice.* Durham, NC: Carolina Academic Press.

Wexler, D. B., and Winick, B. J. (Eds.). (1996). *Law in a therapeutic key: Developments in therapeutic jurisprudence.* Durham, NC: Carolina Academic Press.

Wilkins, K. B. (2003). Sex offender registration and community notification laws: Will these laws survive? *University of Richmond Law Review, 37*, 1245–1278.

Williams, C. R. (2008). Predictive efficacy and the preventive detention of dangerous sexual offenders: Contributions from nonlinear dynamic systems theory. *Critical Criminology, 16*, 185–196.

Williams, C. R., & Arrigo, B. A. (2002). Law, psychology, and the "new sciences": Rethinking mental illness and dangerousness. *International Journal of Offender Therapy and Comparative Criminology, 46*(1), 6–29.

Williams, C. R., & Arrigo, B. A. (2004). *Theory, justice, and social change: Theoretical integrations and critical applications.* New York, NY: Springer.

Williams, C. R. & Arrigo, B. A. (2008). *Ethics, crime, and criminal justice.* Upper Saddle River, NJ: Pearson Prentice Hall.

Winick, B. J. (1997). *Therapeutic jurisprudence applied: Essays on mental health law.* Durham, NC: Carolina Academic Press.

Winick, B. J., & Wexler, D. B. (Eds.). (2003). *Judging in a therapeutic key: therapeutic jurisprudence and the courts.* Durham, NC: Carolina Academic Press.

Winick, B. J., & Wexler, D. B. (2006). The use of therapeutic jurisprudence in law school clinical education: Transforming the criminal law clinic. *Clinical Law Review, 13*, 605–632.

Wright, R. G. (2008). Sex offender post-incarceration sanctions: Are there any limits? *New England Journal on Criminal and Civil Confinement, 34*, 17–50.

Wynn, J. R., & Szatrowski, A. (2004). Hidden prisons: Twenty-three-hour lockdown units in New York state correctional facilities. *Pace Law Review, 24*(2), 497–526.

Zehr, H., & Toews, B. (Eds.). (2004). *Critical issues in restorative justice.* Monsey, NY: Criminal Justice Press.

Zevitz, R. G., & Farkas, M. A. (2000). Sex offender community notification: Assessing the impact in Wisconsin. Washington, DC: Department of Justice. Retrieved from http://www.ncjrs.gov/pdffiles1/nij/179992.pdf.

Zimring, F. E. (2000). The punitive necessity of waiver. In J. Fagan & F. E. Zimring (Eds.), *The changing borders of juvenile justice*, (pp. 207–224). Chicago, IL: University of Chicago Press.

Zinger, I., & Wichmann, C. (1999). *The psychological effects of 60 days in administrative segregation.* (Research Report R85). Ottawa, ON: Correctional Services of Canada.

Zinger, I., Wichmann, C., & Andrews, D. A. (2001). The psychological effects of 60 days in administrative segregation. *Canadian Journal of Criminology*, 43(1), 47–83.

Zureik, E., & Salter, M. B. (Eds.). (2006). Global surveillance and policing: Borders, security, and identity. Cullompton, Devon, UK: Willan Press.

Statutes

Alaska Sess. Laws 41 § 1 (1994).
Iowa Code § 692A.2A.
N.M. Stat. Ann. § 32A.

Cases

Adnan v. *Santa Clara Co. Dept. of Corr.*, 2002 LEXIS 28368 (N.D. Cal. 2002).
Brazill v. *State*, 845 So.2d 282 (Fla. App. 2006).
Coker v. *Georgia*, 433 U.S. 584 (1977).
Coleman v. *Wilson*, 912 F.Supp. 1282 (E.D. Cal. 1995).
Comer v. *Stewart*, 230 F.Supp.2d 1016 (D. Ariz. 2002).
Connecticut Dept. of Public Safety v. *Doe*, 538 U.S. 1 (2003).
Dantzler v. *Beard*, 2007 LEXIS 21309 (W.D. Pa. 2007).
Davenport v. *DeRobertis*, 653 F.Supp. 649 (N.D. Ill. 1987).
Dawson v. *Kendrick*, 572 F.Supp. 1252 (S.D. W.Va. 1981).
Doe v. *Miller*, 405 F.3d 700 (8th Cir. 2005).
Doe v. *Tandeske*, 361 F.3d 594 (2004).
Dusky v. *United States*, 362 U.S. 402 (1960).
Farmer v. *Brennan*, 511 U.S. 825 (1994).
Giano v. *Kelly*, 2000 LEXIS 9138 (W.D.N.Y. 2000).
Goff v. *Harper*, 1997 LEXIS 24186 (S.D. Iowa 1997).
Goff v. *Harper*, 59 F.Supp.2d 910 (S.D. Iowa 1999).
Gonzales v. *Tafoya*, 2001 NMCA 25, 130 N.M. 341, 24 P.3d 776 (N.M. App. 2001).
Helling v. *McKinney*, 509 U.S. 25 (1993).
Jackson v. *Indiana*, 406 U.S. 715 (1972).
Jones 'El v. *Berge*, 164 F.Supp.2d 1096 (W.D. Wis. 2001).
In re Causey, 363 So.2d 472 (La. 1978).
Kane v. *Winn*, 319 F.Supp.2d 162 (D. Mass. 2004.
Kansas v. *Crane*, 534 U.S. 407 (2002).
Kansas v. *Hendricks*, 117 S. Ct. 2027 (1997).

Kennedy v. *Mendoza-Martinez*, 372 U.S. 144 (1963).

Laaman v. *Helgemoe*, 437 F.Supp. 269 (D. N.H. 1977).

Libby v. *Commissioner of Corr.*, 385 Mass. 421 (1982).

Madrid v. *Gomez*, 889 F.Supp. 1146 (N.D. Cal. 1995).

M.D. v. *State*, 701 So.2d 58 (Ala. Crim. App. 1997).

Otis v. *State*, 355 Ark. 590, 142 S.W.3d 615 (Ark. 2004).

Pearson v. *Fair*, 935 F.Supp.2d 401 (D. Mass. 1989).

People v. *Hana*, 443 Mich. 202,504 N.W.2d 166 (Mich. 1993).

Redden v. *Ricci*, 2008 LEXIS 95000 (D.N.J. 2008).

Rennie v. *Klein*, 653 F.2d 836 (3d Cir. 1981).

Rhodes v. *Chapman*, 452 U.S. 337 (1981).

Roper v. *Simmons*, 543 U.S. 551 (U.S. 2005).

Ruiz v. *Estelle*, 503 F.Supp. 1265 (S.D. Tex. 1980).

Ruiz v. *Johnson*, 37 F.Supp. 855 (S.D. Tex. 1999).

Scarver v. *Litscher*, 434 F.3d 972 (7th Cir. 2006).

Seling v. *Young*, 531 U.S. 250 (2001).

Smith v. *Doe*, 538 U.S. 84 (2003).

Stanford v. *Kentucky*, 492 U.S. 361 (1989).

State v. *McCracken*, 260 Neb. 234, 615 N.W.2d 902 (Neb. 2000).

State v. *Nevels*, 235 Neb. 39, 453 N.W.2d 579 (Neb. 1990).

Tillery v. *Owens*, 719 F.Supp. 1256 (W.D. Pa. 1989).

Torres et al. v. *Commissioner of Corr.* et al., 611 N.E.2d 200 (Mass. 1998).

Tate v. *State*, 864 So.2d 44 (Fla. App. 2003).

United States v. *Comstock*, 130 S. Ct. 1949(2010).

Vasquez v. *Frank*, 2006 LEXIS 30395 (7th Cir. 2006).

Williams v. *State*, 96 Ark. App. 160, 239 S.W.3d 44 (Ark. App. 2006).

Name Index

Subject Index

Cases & Statutes Index

About the Authors

Bruce A. Arrigo, Ph.D., is Professor of Criminology, Law, and Society in the Department of Criminal Justice and Criminology at the University of North Carolina – Charlotte. He holds additional faculty appointments in the Psychology Department, the Public Health Sciences Department, the Public Policy Program, and the Center for Professional and Applied Ethics. Dr. Arrigo is a highly prolific, internationally acclaimed, and award-winning author. He has published more than 150 peer-reviewed articles, law reviews, book chapters, and scholarly essays. In addition, he has (co)authored or (co)edited 28 volumes. Selected recent books include, *Psychological jurisprudence: Critical explorations in law, crime, and society* (SUNY Press, 2004), *Theory, justice, and social change* (Springer, 2005), *Philosophy, crime, and criminology* (University of Illinois Press, 2006), *Ethics, crime, and criminal justice* (Prentice Hall, 2008), *Revolution in penology* (Rowman & Littlefield, 2009), and *Postmodernist and post-structuralist theories of crime* (Ashgate, 2010). Professor Arrigo is a past recipient of the Criminologist of the Year Award (2000), sponsored by the Division on Critical Criminology of the American Society of Criminology. He also is an elected Fellow of the American Psychological Association (2002, Psychology-Law Division), as well as an elected Fellow of the Academy of Criminal Justice Sciences (2005). In 2007 he received the Bruce Smith Sr. Award (for distinguished research), sponsored by the Academy of Criminal Justice Sciences. In 2008 he was the recipient of the First Citizens Bank Scholars Medal, the most prestigious research honor bestowed upon a single UNC Charlotte faculty member annually. His book, *The French connection in criminology: Rediscovering crime, law, and social change*, received the 2005 Book-of-the-Year Award from the Crime and Juvenile Delinquency Section of the Society for the Study of Social Problems.

Heather Y. Bersot, M.S., earned a Bachelor of Arts degree in Political Science and Communication Arts from Georgetown College and a Master of Science degree in Criminal Justice from the University of North Carolina at Charlotte. Prior to pursuing graduate studies, she served as a Juvenile Justice Diversion Program Coordinator for the Administrative Office of the Courts. Her published work has appeared in the *Journal of Forensic Psychology Practice, Journal of Contemporary Drug Issues,* and the *Journal of Theoretical & Philosophical Criminology.*

Brian G. Sellers, M.S., is an instructor and doctoral student in the Department of Criminology at the University of South Florida. His current teaching areas are in Corrections, Critical Penology, and Ethics & Criminal Justice Dilemmas. He holds a M.S. from the University of North Carolina at Charlotte in Criminal Justice, and a B.A. from the University of North Carolina at Charlotte in History and Political Science. Recent publications have appeared in the *Journal of Criminal Law & Criminology, Journal of Forensic Psychology Practice,* and *Journal of Theoretical & Philosophical Criminology.*